GULF ISLANDS

A Boater's Guidebook

By

Shawn Breeding and Heather Bansmer

Gulf Islands: A Boater's Guidebook
First Edition

Shawn Breeding and Heather Bansmer

Published by Blue Latitude Press LLC
1213 18th Street
Anacortes, WA 98221
www.bluelatitudepress.com

ISBN: 978-0-9800901-6-1

Library of Congress Control Number: 2019937318

Printing History
1st edition - 2019

Printed in South Korea

Cover photo of Port Browning, North Pender Island. Back cover photos of Princess Cove, Wallace Island; Cabbage Island; and downtown Victoria harbor.

Table of Contents

 24
 56
 96
 118

About the Authors 6

About the Boat 7

How to Use the Book 8

Canada Information 10

Sample Itineraries 20

Chapter 1: Victoria Area 24
   Victoria 26
   Oak Bay 43
   Cadboro Bay 48
   Discovery and Chatham Islands 51
   Cordova Bay 53

Chapter 2: Sidney Area 56
   D'Arcy Island 58
   Saanichton Bay 60
   Sidney Spit, Sidney Island 63
   Sidney 67
   Roberts Bay 74
   Tsehum Harbour 76
   Canoe Cove 84
   Swartz Bay 88
   Rum Island (Isle-de-Lis) 88
   Portland Island 89
     Princess Bay 92
     Royal Cove 94

Chapter 3: Saanich Inlet 96
   Deep Cove 98
   Mill Bay 100
   Coles Bay 104
   Brentwood Bay 106
   Tod Inlet 114

Chapter 4: Pender Islands 118
   Pender Islands 120
     Camp Bay 121
     Bedwell Harbor 123
     Pender Canal 129
     Medicine Beach 130
     Port Browning 133
     Hope Bay 139
     Grimmer Bay 142
     Otter Bay 145

Table of Contents

150

183

199

216

Chapter 5: Saturna and Mayne Islands 150

  Saturna Island 152

    Winter Cove 153

    Lyall Harbour 157

    Boot Cove 161

    Narvaez Bay 162

  Tumbo and Cabbage Islands................ 164

  Irish Bay, Samuel Island 167

  Mayne Island 169

    Horton Bay 171

    Bennett Bay 173

    Campbell Bay 174

    Miners Bay 176

    Village and Dinner Bays 180

Chapter 6: Prevost Island 183

  Prevost Island 185

    James Bay 186

    Selby Cove 189

    Annette Inlet 191

    Glenthorne Passage 194

    Ellen Bay 196

    Diver Bay.. 198

Chapter 7: Galiano Island 199

  Galiano Island...................................... 201

    Montague Harbour........................... 202

    Active Pass 207

    Sturdies Bay 209

    Whaler Bay 210

    Porlier Pass 211

    Dionisio Point 213

    Retreat Cove 214

Chapter 8: Salt Spring Island 216

  Salt Spring Island 218

    Ganges Harbour 219

    Long Harbour 229

    Walker Hook 232

    Fernwood Point 234

    Southey Bay 234

    Vesuvius and Duck Bays..................... 236

    Burgoyne Bay 238

    Musgrave Landing 241

    Fulford Harbour 242

  Russell Island 246

Table of Contents

250

283

309

338

Chapter 9: Cowichan Bay to Ladysmith 250

Cowichan Bay 252

Genoa Bay 257

Maple Bay 262

Birds Eye Cove 264

Crofton 268

Chemainus 271

Ladysmith 275

Chapter 10: North Trincomali Channel Islands . 283

Wallace Island 285

   Conover Cove 287

   Princess Cove 291

Thetis, Penelakut, and Tent Islands 294

   Clam Bay 296

   Tent Island 299

   Telegraph Harbour 301

   Preedy Harbour 306

   North Cove 307

Chapter 11: Valdes and Gabriola Islands Area .. 309

Ruxton Island 311

Whaleboat Island 311

De Courcy Island 313

   Pirates Cove 315

Valdes Island 318

   Gabriola Passage 318

   Wakes Cove 320

   Dogfish Bay 320

Gabriola Island 321

   Degnen Bay 323

   Silva Bay 326

   Pilot and Taylor Bays 332

   Descanso Bay 334

Dodd Narrows 337

False Narrows 337

Chapter 12: Nanaimo 338

Nanaimo 340

Newcastle Island 348

GPS Waypoints Table 352

Suggested Reading & Bibliography 357

Index 358

About the Authors

Shawn Breeding and Heather Bansmer have transformed their passion for adventure and their love of sailing into informative, must-have boating guides. With decades of boating experience, the husband and wife team have created the works of *Sea of Cortez: A Cruiser's Guidebook,* *Pacific Mexico: A Cruiser's Guidebook,* and *San Juan Islands: A Boater's Guidebook.* From world renowned sailor and award winning author Beth Leonard, "...the authors have raised the standard for cruising guides in general and guides to Mexico in particular."

Combining their love of travel and boating with their professions of cartography and design, the two have produced one-of-a-kind guides that have helped to inspire new sailors and guide thousands of fellow boaters through the enchanting waters of western Mexico and the Salish Sea.

Heather, Shawn, and their trusty sidekick, Salty Dog, live in the seaside town of Anacortes, Washington, where they keep their Westsail 32, *Om Shanti.* During the summer they enjoy the island-studded waters of the Pacific Northwest, and when the winter rains start falling, they head south to Mexico as much as possible. Find out more about Shawn and Heather and their boating guides at www.bluelatitudepress.com.

About the Boat

O*m Shanti* is a cutter-rigged, Westsail 32, based on the classic designs of Colin Archer. *Om Shanti* was built in 1976, in Costa Mesa, California by the Westsail Corporation who was known for producing sailboats that could sail anywhere in the world under any conditions. *Om Shanti* is a stout 32-foot fiberglass, full keel, double-ender with a five-foot draft. She weighs nearly 25,000 pounds fully loaded.

Shawn and Heather purchased *Om Shanti* in 1998. They cruised the San Juan Islands and southern British Columbia from their homeport in Bellingham, Washington. In 2003, they tossed off the dock lines and cruised down to Mexico where they spent the next seven years. In 2010, *Om Shanti* returned to the Pacific Northwest, and is back to sailing the beautiful waters of the Salish Sea.

Chart Legend

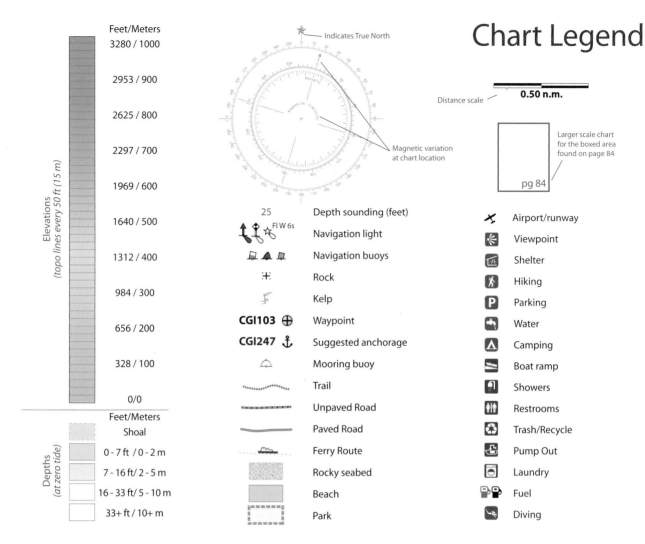

Indicates True North

Magnetic variation at chart location

0.50 n.m.

Distance scale

pg 84

Larger scale chart for the boxed area found on page 84

Feet/Meters

3280 / 1000
2953 / 900
2625 / 800
2297 / 700
1969 / 600
1640 / 500
1312 / 400
984 / 300
656 / 200
328 / 100
0/0

Elevations (topo lines every 50 ft (15 m))

Feet/Meters

Shoal

Depths (at zero tide)

0 - 7 ft / 0 - 2 m
7 - 16 ft / 2 - 5 m
16 - 33 ft / 5 - 10 m
33+ ft / 10+ m

25	Depth sounding (feet)
Fl W 6s	Navigation light
	Navigation buoys
	Rock
	Kelp
CGI103 ⊕	Waypoint
CGI247 ⚓	Suggested anchorage
	Mooring buoy
	Trail
	Unpaved Road
	Paved Road
	Ferry Route
	Rocky seabed
	Beach
	Park

✈	Airport/runway
	Viewpoint
	Shelter
	Hiking
P	Parking
	Water
⛺	Camping
	Boat ramp
	Showers
	Restrooms
♺	Trash/Recycle
	Pump Out
	Laundry
	Fuel
	Diving

How to Use the Book

This book has been created to provide boaters travelling the Gulf Islands with the most up-to-date and complete information currently available. Whether your boat is power or sail, large or small, this guide is designed to help provide mariners with the information needed to confidently and comfortably cruise the Gulf Islands. Because cruising does not end once the boat stops moving, this guide, in addition to the maritime information, will also inform you of things to do once you are swinging on the hook or tied up at a marina. Places to get fuel, water, and provisions are included, as well as favorite spots to stretch your legs, cultural and historical museums to explore, eateries to escape the galley for a meal out, or local haunts to get a cold beverage. The information used to create this guide has been gathered by us during many years of travelling and exploring the Gulf Islands and the nearby San Juan Islands.

The book begins with Victoria and continues north to Nanaimo. Every effort has been made to include all of the popular (and not so popular) anchorages that a boater may travel to while exploring the islands. With over 200 islands and islets, Canada's Gulf Islands offer many more undiscovered gems outside the scope of this book for those adventurers wishing to get off the beaten path and blaze their own trail.

The charts used throughout the book have been created from scratch by combining on-site surveys, satellite and aerial photography, laser and radar topography data, Canadian Hydrographic Service licensed chart data, current digital elevation models and anything else we could get our hands on. The charts use the WGS 84 datum, and all of the GPS waypoints used throughout this guide (unless otherwise noted) are our own rather than secondhand information passed along from cruiser to cruiser.

Shorelines have been drawn and referenced to current satellite photography, digital elevation models data for unparalleled detail.

Mileage table example:

Bedwell Harbour to:		
Ganges Harbour *(Salt Spring Island)*	14 nm
Ladysmith	34 nm
Montague Harbour *(Galiano Island)*	14 nm
Nanaimo	40 nm
Pirates Cove *(De Courcy Island)*	31 nm
Roche Harbor *(USA)*	9 nm
Russell Island	8 nm
Sidney	9 nm
Tod Inlet	20 nm
Victoria	27 nm
Wallace Island	20 nm
Winter Cove *(Saturna Island)*	9 nm

Regarding depths, soundings come from the Canadian Hydrographic Service official charts. Depths are given at lower low water, large tide, or LLWLT. Depth contours indicated on the charts by varying shades of white to blue are included to give mariners a general idea of the bottom contours of a given area. The cover overview contains bathymetric data from the GEBCO dataset and should not be used for navigation.

Mileage tables are provided as a quick reference for distances to possible "next stops" from the anchorage being discussed. With so many "next stop" possibilities, locations used in the tables try to reference a major destination within a general cruising area. For instance, Bedwell Harbour to Ganges Harbour will give you an exact mile count between the two locations, but will also give you an approximate idea on mileage to nearby anchorages on Prevost Island.

Throughout this book, the mileages used for distances over water are given in nautical miles, distances over land are given in statute miles. These distances are not straight-line "as the crow flies," but calculated to reflect the distance one would logically travel in actual circumstances.

For some of the larger cities and towns, a brief history and few of the sights to see are listed. Supplies and services including marine chandleries, grocery stores, and restaurants are also included. Please keep in mind though, that these lists are not exhaustive and more stores or services may be found in that particular town. Our lists are based on ease of access, personal experience, referrals and research. As much as we would like to include all the businesses available throughout the Gulf Islands and Vancouver Island, unfortunately, our guide just is not big enough! We welcome all of you to share any of your experiences and recommendations with us for inclusion in future editions.

As new information becomes available, including updates, changes or errors, we will post the information on our website at **www.bluelatitudepress.com**. We want ev-

eryone to have the most accurate and up-to-date information available and welcome any comments or suggestions.

By using this guide, you will be equipped with the latest, most up to date cruising information available, but nothing will substitute for having a safe and sound vessel, always keeping a good watch, current CHS charts, tide and current tables, and operating your vessel with the utmost respect of the environs you are exploring.

Keep in mind when using this book that while every attempt has been made to ensure this information is as accurate as possible, things change and mistakes are possible. We welcome any corrections, updates or any other information you would like to share with your fellow cruiser. You can contact us at:

Shawn Breeding and Heather Bansmer
Blue Latitude Press, LLC
www.bluelatitudepress.com
info@bluelatitudepress.com

Also Available
San Juan Islands: A Boater's Guidebook

Exploring Washington's stunning San Juan Islands and port towns of Bellingham and Anacortes.

Canada Information

The following list of topics provides information to help facilitate your adventure through Canada's Gulf Islands, from customs clearing procedures to information on local weather and forecasts.

Anchoring and Stern Lines

A number of the anchorages within the Gulf Islands may require reduced swinging room while at anchor due to tight confines by the shoreline, a steeply sloping bottom or making room for fellow boaters in a crowded anchorage. For these situations, it is a good idea to carry on board a stern line for tying to shore.

A stern line tied to shore prevents a boat from swinging at anchor. Once anchored, a line is taken to shore using a dinghy (or kayak, SUP, etc.), and secured to something on shore (tree, chain, ring, etc). Ideally, it is best to loop around a solid object on shore and bring both ends of the line to the boat to secure. This enables an easy and quick recovery of the line when leaving the anchorage without the need to go back ashore to untie knots and retrieve the line.

Shorelines are typically very long, depending on personal preference, between 200 to 600 feet in length. For boats continuing further north through BC and Alaska, the longer the line the better. Most boaters choose to use polypropylene line as it floats on the surface and is lightweight. Lines that sink may get snagged by rocks or underwater debris when slack is in the line. Keeping the line on a drum or spindle is an easy way to store, deploy and retrieve stern lines.

Keep in mind when using a stern line that the distance from boat to shore will change throughout the day and night with the rising and falling of tides. Adjustments in the length of line may be necessary to compensate for the changing distance.

Boat Haul Out and Storage

There are a number of different haul out facilities and storage yards available in the Gulf Islands area which are listed within this guide. Most of the larger ports (Victoria, Sidney, Maple Bay, Ladysmith and Nanaimo) have facilities for hauling vessels for repair and maintenance, with many of the facilities offering short and long term storage as well.

Charts

Charts are one of the single most important items to have on a boat to help you navigate the intricate waterways while avoiding reefs and shallow water dangers within the Gulf Islands. The Canadian Hydrographic Service (CHS) produces and maintains a suite of nautical charts that cover the coastal waters of Canada including the Gulf Islands. The CHS charts are available in a variety of formats, including traditional paper charts, Raster Navigational Charts (RNC) which are bitmap electronic images of paper charts, and Electronic Navigational Charts (ENC) which are vector charts that conform to international standards. For further information or to view the chart catalog online, visit CHS's website at: **www.charts.gc.ca**.

Chart#	Chart Name
3313	Gulf Islands and Adjacent Waterways Atlas
3462	Juan de Fuca Strait to Strait of Georgia
3463	Strait of Georgia, Southern Part
3440	Race Rocks to D'Arcy Island
3441	Haro Strait, Boundary Pass, Satellite Channel
3442	North Pender Island to Thetis Island
3443	Thetis Island to Nanaimo
3412	Victoria Harbor (w/ Portage Inlet)
3424	Approaches to Oak Bay
3479	Approaches to Sidney (Tsehum Harbour, Sidney, Iroquois & John Passes)

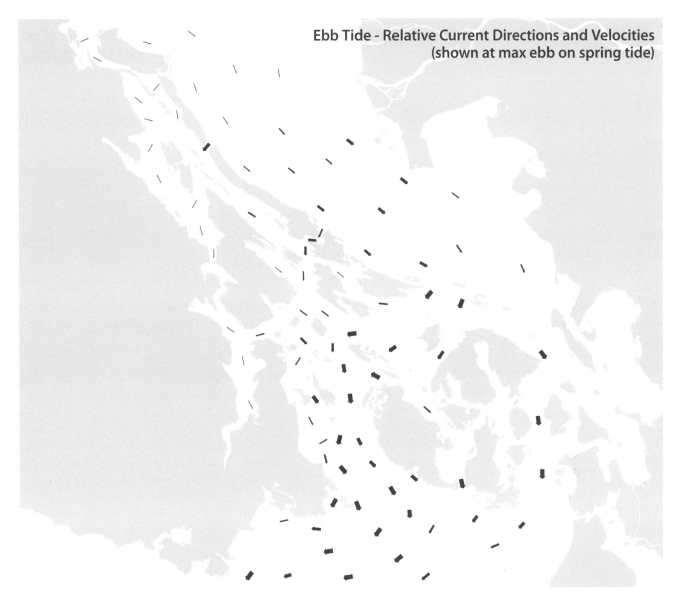

3478   Plans Salt Spring Island
3477   Plans Gulf Islands (Bedwell, Telegraph, Preedy, Pender Canal)
3473   Active Pass, Porlier Pass, Montague Harbour
3475   Plans Stuart Channel (Chemainus, Ladysmith, Dodd Narrows)
3458   Approaches to Nanaimo
3447   Nanaimo Harbor and Departure Bay

Currents and Tides

The maze of islands and reefs, along with the variable bathymetry of the ocean floor, results in a complex flow of currents ebbing and flooding through the Gulf Islands. Tides dictate the times and intensities of these currents with generally two high tides and two low tides occurring each day.

Along with charts, tide tables, current tables, and a current atlas are essential resources to have on board your boat to help you navigate through the Gulf Islands. Knowing when slack and peak current times are throughout the day will help you plan your route and your departure time. Knowing what level the tide is at and what the future level will be, will help you determine a safe location and depth to anchor.

It is also important to keep in mind that weather and currents can greatly change the sea state. When wind opposes current, waves can stack up creating a steep or confused wave state. These conditions can make for an uncomfortable ride, or for smaller boats under severe weather and currents, a dangerous situation.

The tidal range within the islands varies. For example, in Victoria, near the southern end of Vancouver Island, the

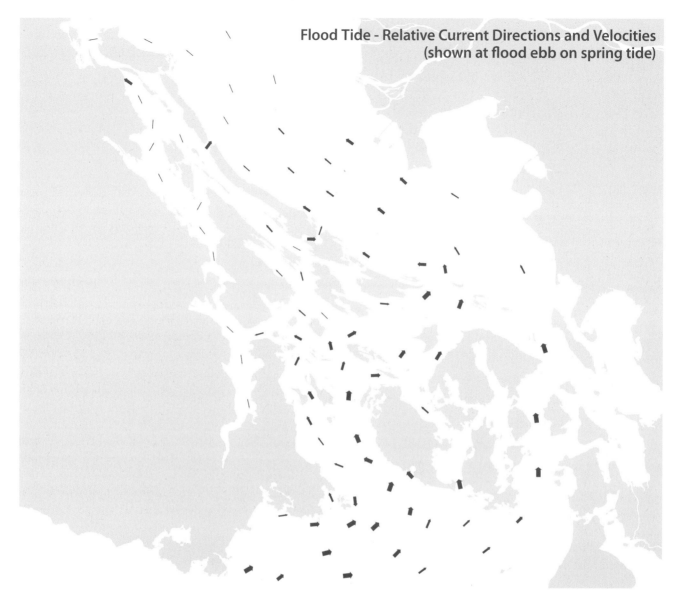

Flood Tide - Relative Current Directions and Velocities
(shown at flood ebb on spring tide)

tidal range can reach over 10 feet on extreme tides. In the north at Silva Bay on Gabriola Island, the tidal range can reach as high as nearly 17 feet on extreme tides.

In areas where land restricts the flow of water, currents can also become quite forceful. Two popular passes for pleasure boats, Dodd Narrows and Porlier Pass, both have currents that can reach nearly 10 knots on extreme tides.

A number of publications are available for tides and currents in the Gulf Islands. The most popular is the Canadian Hydrographic Service's (CHS) *Current Atlas for Juan de Fuca Strait to the Strait of Georgia* and the annual *Canadian Tides and Current Tables Vol. 5*. Other publications include the annual *Ports and Passes* tide and current tables book and the annual *Waggoner Tables* that can be used in conjunction with the CHS *Current Atlas*.

Customs and Immigration

Private boats entering Canadian waters (carrying 29 people or less), are required to report their arrival to the Canada Border Services Agency (CBSA). Upon arrival, go directly to a Telephone Reporting Site-Marine (TRS/M)

Canadian Ports of Entry

- Raymur Point CBSA Boat Dock in Victoria
- Oak Bay Marina
- Port of Sidney Marina
- Van Isle Marina
- Canoe Cove
- Poets Cove
- Nanaimo Port Authority Marina

US Ports of Entry
- Roche Harbor, San Juan Island
- Friday Harbor, San Juan Island
- Anacortes
- Port Angeles
- Point Roberts

and follow the instructions posted on location to contact the CBSA Telephone Reporting Centre (TRC) to request clearance to enter Canada. Only the owner/operator may leave the boat to place the call to the TRC. Everyone else must remain onboard until the CBSA gives authorization.

Requirements for non-residents of Canada include:
- Full name, date of birth and citizenship
- Boat registration or documentation
- Length and purpose of the stay in Canada
- Destination
- Passport
- Visa information (if applicable)

Private vessels crossing from Canada to nearby US San Juan Islands or US mainland ports are required to clear in with US Customs and Border Protection (CBP). For US and Canadian citizens that boat frequently between the two countries, the NEXUS program allows pre-screened travelers expedited processing at marine reporting locations, as well as airports and car border crossings. For further information check: www.cbp.gov/travel/trusted-traveler-programs/nexus. NEXUS card holders are able to check in at the additional Canada ports of Port Browning, Cabbage Island, Horton Bay, Ganges Harbour, and Montague Harbour.

In 2018, CBP launched a new option for reporting your arrival into the US. The Reporting Offsite Arrival-Mobile (CBP ROAM) app. The free CBP ROAM mobile app allows users to notify CBP via personal smart device. There is no application process or pre-registration requirement to use the CBP ROAM app. Once downloaded, travelers input their biographic information, conveyance and trip details and then submit their trip to CBP for review. A CBP officer may then initiate a video chat to further interview travelers. Once the CBP officer reviews the trip, travelers will receive a push notification and an email with their clearance status and next steps, if applicable. In certain circumstances, boaters using the CBP ROAM app may still need to report in person to CBP, including if an I-94 or cruising permit is required, if customs duties must be paid, or in other circumstances as applicable. To download the app search for "CBP ROAM" in the Apple App Store or Google Play Store.

Emergency Contacts
- Police Fire Ambulance: Dial 911*
- Coast Guard 1-800-855-6655
- Rescue Coordination Centre 1-800-567-5111 – Marine or Air Emergencies
- Poison Control Centre 1-800-567-8911
- Ambulance Bookings 1-800-866-5602
- BC Nurse's Line 1-866-215-4700
- Oil Spill Hotline 1-800-663-3456

* Cell phone reception can be spotty in the islands. You may pick up a US-based service at some locations. If making an emergency call to 911, be sure to let operators know you are calling from Canada.

Local Hospitals
Royal Jubilee Hospital, Victoria:	(250) 370-8000
Victoria General Hospital, Victoria:	(250) 727-4212
Saanich Peninsula Hospital, Sidney:	(250) 652-3911
Lady Minto Hospital, Salt Spring Island:	(250) 538-4800
Pender Islands Health Centre:	(250) 629-3233
Cowichan District Hospital, Duncan:	(250) 737-2030
Nanaimo Regional General Hospital:	(250) 755-7691

Ferries

British Columbia operates a number of passenger and vehicle ferries throughout the Gulf Islands. BC Ferries operate daily with the major ferry terminals connecting the mainland and Vancouver Island at Tsawwassen, West Vancouver (Horseshoe Bay), Nanaimo (Departure Point and Duke Bay), and Sidney (Swartz Bay). Interisland ferry service includes terminals at:
- Fulford Harbour, Long Harbour and Vesuvius, Salt Spring Island
- Otter Bay, North Pender Island
- Village Bay, Mayne Island

- Lyall Harbour, Saturna Island
- Sturdies Bay, Galiano Island
- Preedy Harbour, Thetis Island
- Telegraph Harbour, Penelakut Island
- Descanso Bay, Gabriola Island
- Chamainus, Crofton, Mill Bay, and Brentwood Bay, Vancouver Island

On the water, the ferries have regular scheduled routes through the islands. These ferries are large (the Spirit class ferries are nearly 550 feet in length), move quickly, and have limited maneuverability. When sharing the waters with these large ships, it is your duty to stay out of the ferry's path especially around the ferry terminals and narrow channels like Active Pass. Five short blasts of the ferry's horn means the captain is signaling for a boat to move out of the way of the ferry's path. With the law of mass on their side, it is best to alter course to let ferries pass before continuing on your route. Ferries entering the narrow, S-shaped Active Pass from either direction make an announcement on VHF channel 16 prior to entering. BC Ferries stand by on VHF channel 16 and the appropriate

VHF vessel traffic channel for their area - Victoria, VHF 11; Vancouver, VHF 12.

For current ferry sailing schedules or for additional information on BC Ferries, visit their website at: **www.bcferries.com**, or by phone at: 1-888-BC FERRY.

Fishing Licenses

A fishing license is required to fish for any species of finfish and/or shellfish; salt water and/or fresh water in Canada. Licenses for residents and non-residents of Canada can be obtained for 1, 3, or 5 days, along with annual licenses. Children under the age of 16 years old are required to obtain a license, however there is no fee for the license. You must carry your license with you at all times when fishing. All catches of chinook, lingcod, and halibut must be recorded on your licence in ink.

The easiest way to obtain a Tidal Waters Sport Fishing Licence is to go online. Fill out the application online and print your license at: **www.pac.dfo-mpo.gc.ca/fm-gp/rec/licence-permis/application-eng.html**. For further questions contact Fisheries and Oceans Canada at 1-877-535-7307 or by email at: fishing-peche@dfo-mpo.gc.ca.

Deadhead marked by a plastic jug

Logs and Deadheads

Spring tides or storms can float driftwood off beaches, rivers can wash out trees from the mountains, or log booms can lose a log from their tow. This can all result in floating logs, and is something to keep an eye out for while cruising through the Pacific Northwest. Many logs float horizontally on the water making them more visible to spot. Some logs however can float near vertically with just a small amount showing above water or be partially submerged. They are waterlogged and are very heavy. These logs are known as deadheads and can be quite damaging to the hulls of vessels or their propellers. If you spot a deadhead, please contact the Canadian Coast Guard (Pacific Region VHF channel 83A). If possible, try to hammer a bright marker into it to help warn other boaters.

British Columbia Provincial Parks

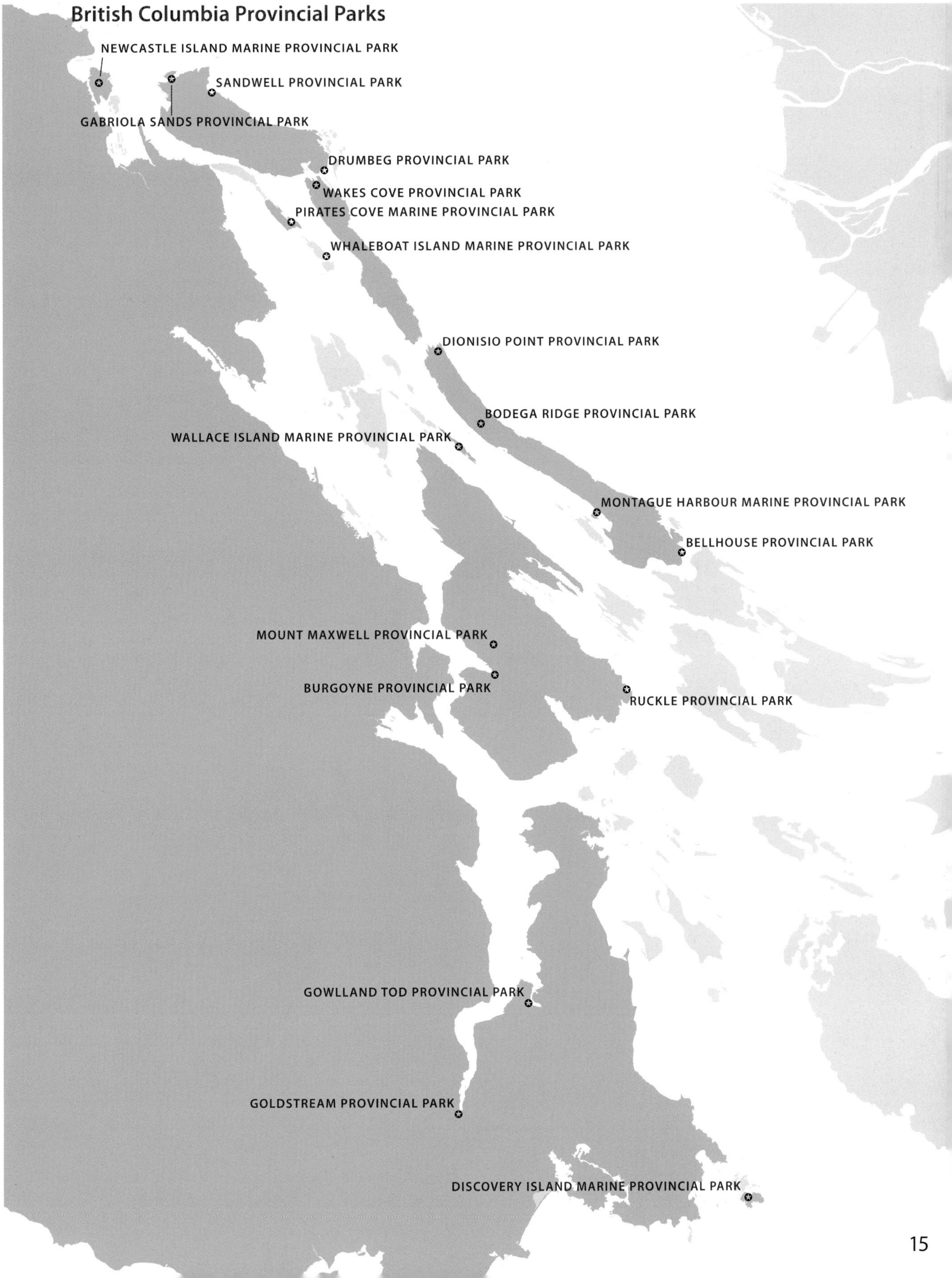

NEWCASTLE ISLAND MARINE PROVINCIAL PARK

SANDWELL PROVINCIAL PARK

GABRIOLA SANDS PROVINCIAL PARK

DRUMBEG PROVINCIAL PARK

WAKES COVE PROVINCIAL PARK

PIRATES COVE MARINE PROVINCIAL PARK

WHALEBOAT ISLAND MARINE PROVINCIAL PARK

DIONISIO POINT PROVINCIAL PARK

BODEGA RIDGE PROVINCIAL PARK

WALLACE ISLAND MARINE PROVINCIAL PARK

MONTAGUE HARBOUR MARINE PROVINCIAL PARK

BELLHOUSE PROVINCIAL PARK

MOUNT MAXWELL PROVINCIAL PARK

BURGOYNE PROVINCIAL PARK

RUCKLE PROVINCIAL PARK

GOWLLAND TOD PROVINCIAL PARK

GOLDSTREAM PROVINCIAL PARK

DISCOVERY ISLAND MARINE PROVINCIAL PARK

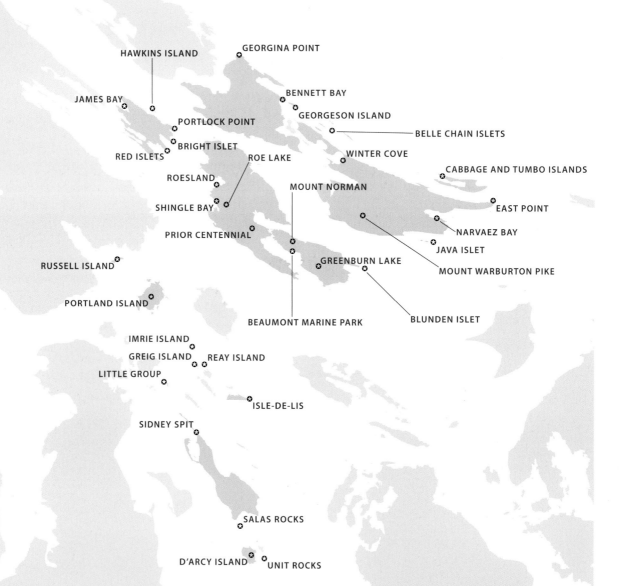

Gulf Islands National Park Reserve

HAWKINS ISLAND

GEORGINA POINT

JAMES BAY

BENNETT BAY

PORTLOCK POINT

GEORGESON ISLAND

BELLE CHAIN ISLETS

BRIGHT ISLET

RED ISLETS

ROE LAKE

WINTER COVE

CABBAGE AND TUMBO ISLANDS

ROESLAND

MOUNT NORMAN

EAST POINT

SHINGLE BAY

NARVAEZ BAY

PRIOR CENTENNIAL

JAVA ISLET

GREENBURN LAKE

MOUNT WARBURTON PIKE

RUSSELL ISLAND

PORTLAND ISLAND

BEAUMONT MARINE PARK

BLUNDEN ISLET

IMRIE ISLAND

GREIG ISLAND

REAY ISLAND

LITTLE GROUP

ISLE-DE-LIS

SIDNEY SPIT

SALAS ROCKS

D'ARCY ISLAND

UNIT ROCKS

Money

The unit of currency for Canada is the Canadian dollar. Coins come in 5¢, 10¢, 25¢, $1 and $2. The one dollar coin is commonly called a "loonie" as it bears the image of a common loon on one side. The two dollar coin is commonly called a "toonie". Paper currency comes in bills of $5, $10, $20, $50 and $100.

For changing currency, banks usually offer the best exchange rate. ATMs (automatic teller machines) are widely used throughout Canada and offer the same rate of exchange the bank has posted. However, some banks will add on an international transaction fee and/or a fee for using another bank's ATM. Call your local bank to find out if they charge any additional fees.

Most businesses will also accept credit cards. Be sure to check with your credit card company to see if international transaction fees apply, and to alert them that you will be using the card in Canada.

Parks

Canada's Gulf Islands, along with Vancouver Island, hold a wealth of protected public park land. British Columbia as a whole has the third largest parks system in North America, following Canada's National Parks and the US National Park Service.

The province of British Columbia has designated a number of Provincial Parks in the islands as well as a number of Marine Provincial Parks (see page 15 for a map of Provincial Parks). While each park may have particular rules for that area, here are a few items to keep in mind when visiting Provincial Parks:

- **No Anchoring** - BC Parks is implementing a policy to encourage boaters to only anchor in waters that are greater than 10 metres (33 feet) in depth. Along shorelines from the low tide level to about 10 metres depth, marine plants provide critical habitats for juvenile fish and shellfish. These habitat forming plants can be large kelps or seagrasses. Boating activities that can damage these habitats include anchoring in water less than 10 metres deep or motoring through kelp beds or seagrass meadows at low tide.
- **Respect Aquatic Life** - The intertidal zone is an environment in constant transition. Twice daily the tides move in and out.
- **Watch Where You Step** - Some intertidal creatures are hard to see. If you move a rock, do so carefully. Return the rock to its original position before you leave. Keep a safe distance from intertidal creatures. They live in a harsh environment, and may protect themselves with claws, spines or sharp shells. Do not remove anything

from the beach. People often collect kelp, driftwood, rocks, sand and gravel. All these materials provide essential habitat for beach dwellers.

- **Be Aware of People, Places and Things** - BC's coastline and inland waterways were and still are pathways and gathering places for First Nations communities. What is a good landing site today has probably been used for thousands of years. Treat these places as culturally sensitive and potential archaeological sites. Do not damage these sites or remove artifacts.

For further information on British Columbia Provincial Parks, check their website at: **www.env.gov.bc.ca/bcparks/**.

The Gulf Islands National Park Reserve was formed by Canada's federal government in 2003 by combining a number of existing ecological reserves, provincial parks, and newly acquired lands across 15 islands and islets (see page 16 for a map of the park). The park headquarters are based in Sidney. For further information check the park website at: **www.pc.gc.ca/en/pn-np/bc/gulf** or by phone at: (250) 654-4000.

Weather

Nestled within the lee of mountain ranges found on both the Olympic Peninsula and Vancouver Island, the Gulf Islands are uniquely protected from the direct force of weather that arrives along the Pacific coast of Washington and British Columbia. These mountain ranges also help to create a rain shadow effect over the islands, resulting in a drier climate than the majority of western and northern Vancouver Island, which can average approximately 120 to 160 inches of rain a year. Average annual rainfall ranges from 25 inches to 31 inches around the Victoria area, with the majority of rain falling in the winter months.

The Gulf Islands are also affected by seasonal conditions. The summer months from June through September are characterized by warmer, drier and calmer conditions with average temperatures ranging in the 50's to 70's F. Daylight at the peak of summer solstice is approximately 16 hours, offering long and warm days throughout the summer. The winter months of November through February are more typically cold, wet and windy, with average temperatures ranging in the 30's to 40's F. Daylight at the peak of winter solstice is approximately 8 hours. During the winter months, storms hitting the Pacific coast create wetter and windier conditions than during the more calm months of summer.

While the surrounding mountain ranges help to shield the islands from large weather systems, the intricate maze of islands and surrounding waterways can create localized weather conditions. Hills, points and the islands themselves can change the wind direction and velocity as it funnels or bends around land masses.

During the prime summer boating months, weather tends to be fairly benign compared to the wetter and windier months of winter. Warm weather and a large North Pacific High generally prevent frontal systems from the Gulf of Alaska from reaching the area. The strongest winds are typically found in the Strait of Georgia and the Strait of Juan de Fuca. Northwesterly winds are common in the Strait of Georgia as wind flows down mainland BC's intricate maze of lengthy inlets and into the Strait of Georgia. In the Strait of Juan de Fuca, westerly winds, including frequent summer gales, are driven by diurnal sea breezes. As warm air heats and rises during the long summer days over mainland Washington and BC, cooler air over the Pacific Ocean rushes into the Strait of Juan de Fuca creating westerly winds.

During the winter months, strong frontal systems can be frequent, bringing wet, windy and cooler temperatures to the islands. As the North Pacific High retreats south for the winter, the Aleutian Low moves into the Gulf of Alaska and begins to grow. This Low dominates the atmospheric pressure system in the North Pacific during the winter, bring mainly southerly winds and rain.

Fog can also affect the area, blanketing the islands and greatly reducing visibility. While fog can happen any time of the year if the conditions are right, fog is more frequently found during the warmer summer and early autumn months. As the moist, cool air of the Pacific Ocean condenses, it creates a morning/evening fog layer. This cool air and fog can be drawn into the Strait of Juan de Fuca affecting land and waterways bordering the strait, including the city of Victoria. More often, the San Juan Islands experience more fog than do the Gulf Islands. As the day heats up, the fog generally burns off.

Waves generated by wind and/or by current is also something to take into account when boating in the Gulf Islands. Large, open stretches of water have a greater distance (fetch) for wind driven waves to build. Open waterways like the Strait of Georgia and the Strait of Juan de Fuca are examples of areas that are unobstructed, where wind and waves can build. Combining these conditions with an opposing current will create waves with increased height and shortened wave length.

The Government of Canada through it's Environment Canada department, produces valuable marine weather forecasts for Canadian waters. These forecasts include the regions of Juan de Fuca Strait (west, central and east), Strait of Georgia - South of Nanaimo, and Haro Strait. Forecasts for these areas are available via VHF weather channels and online at: **weather.gc.ca/marine/index_e.html**

The National Oceanic and Atmospheric Administration's (NOAA) National Weather Service also provides marine weather forecasts, for the Northern Inland Waters. Although this forecast, which includes the San Juan Islands, is for US waters, it provides additional forecasts for neighboring islands and waters. These forecasts are available via VHF weather channels or online at:
www.ndbc.noaa.gov/data/Forecasts/FZUS56.KSEW.html
www.atmos.washington.edu/data/marine_report.html

Whales

Sightings of orca, or killer whales, are one of the true highlights during a visit to the Gulf Islands. A community of orcas return each year to the inland waters of Washington and British Columbia, known as the Southern Resident population. These local residents are made up of three matriarchal family pods - the J, K and L pods. These whales spend the summer months in the Pacific Northwest feeding on fish, including salmon, herring and cod.

The residents are generally found swimming the inland waters from June through September. While the J pod has been observed in Washington and British Columbia year-round, the movement of K and L pods during the winter and spring months is mostly unknown. Tracking studies on the K and L pods have shown the whales offshore of Vancouver Island and Monterrey, California.

Aside from resident whales, transient orca whales are also spotted in the inland waters of Washington and British Columbia. These whales travel in small family groups of three to four, feeding on marine mammals including seals, sea lions, porpoise, dolphins and whales. Residents and transients differ in their diet, the shapes of their dorsal fins, vocalizations, and travel patterns.

Orcas are the largest mammal of the dolphin family, characterized by their black and white markings. Males weigh up to approximately 12,000 pounds and measure between 24 to 31 feet in length. Females generally weigh up to 8,000 pounds and measure up to 26 feet in length. One of the easiest ways to distinguish between mature males and females is by their dorsal fins. Females have small curved fins and males have a long straight fins up to six feet in length.

In the dark waters of the Pacific Northwest, orcas are able to locate food sources by using sonar, or echolocation. Whales can produce a rapid clicking sound which travels through the water in the form of sound waves. These waves bounce off anything in the whale's path and return to sensors within the whale.

According to the Center for Whale Research in Friday Harbor, approximately 75 whales (J Pod=22, K Pod=18, L Pod=35) make up the southern resident community as of January 2019. For further information or to donate to the research of these amazing whales, visit the Center for Whale Research website at: **www.whaleresearch.com**.

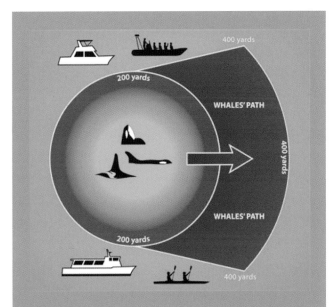

Be Whale Wise

BE CAUTIOUS & COURTEOUS: approach areas of known or suspected marine wildlife activity with extreme caution. Look in all directions before planning your approach or departure.

SLOW DOWN: reduce speed to less than 7 knots when within 400 metres/yards of the nearest whale. Avoid abrupt course changes.

KEEP CLEAR of the whales' path. If whales are approaching you, cautiously move out of the way.

DO NOT APPROACH whales from the front or from behind. Always approach and depart whales from the side, moving in a direction parallel to the direction of the whales.

DO NOT APPROACH or position your vessel closer than 200 metres/yards to any whale.

If your vessel is not in compliance with the 200 metres/yards approach guideline, place engine in neutral and allow whales to pass.

STAY on the **OFFSHORE** side of the whales when they are traveling close to shore.

LIMIT your viewing time to a recommended maximum of 30 minutes. This will minimize the cumulative impact of many vessels and give consideration to other viewers.

DO NOT swim with, touch or feed marine wildlife.

DO NOT drive through groups of porpoises or dolphins to encourage bow or stern-riding.

Should dolphins or porpoises choose to ride the bow wave of your vessel, avoid sudden course changes. Hold course and speed or reduce speed gradually.

Sample Itineraries

The following itineraries are a sample of cruises designed to fit a variety of schedules and interests. These itineraries are easily adjusted for adding or removing various ports of call. Depending on weather, some locations may not be suitable for anchoring, and may end up changing the itinerary.

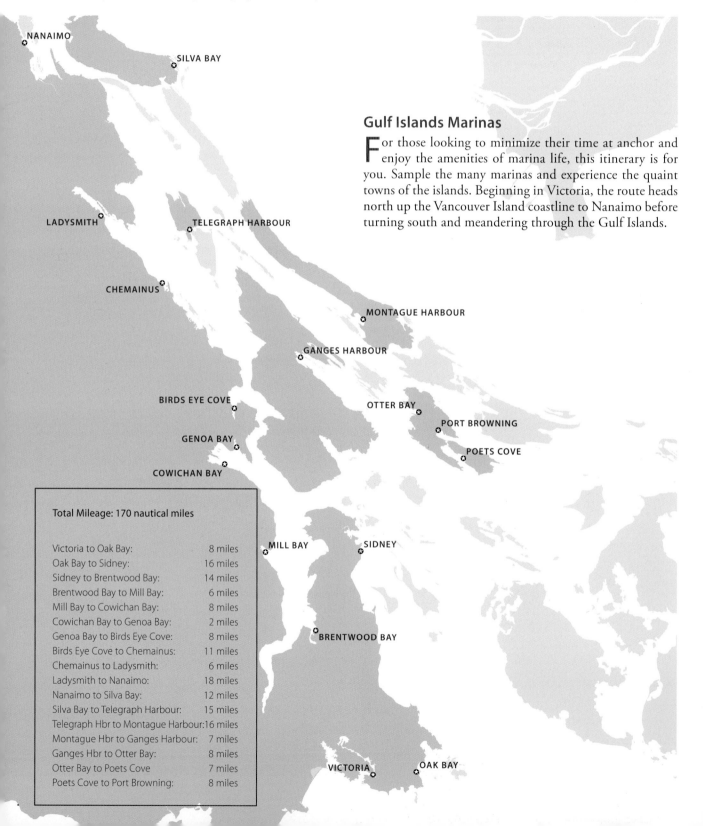

Gulf Islands Marinas

For those looking to minimize their time at anchor and enjoy the amenities of marina life, this itinerary is for you. Sample the many marinas and experience the quaint towns of the islands. Beginning in Victoria, the route heads north up the Vancouver Island coastline to Nanaimo before turning south and meandering through the Gulf Islands.

Total Mileage: 170 nautical miles

Victoria to Oak Bay:	8 miles
Oak Bay to Sidney:	16 miles
Sidney to Brentwood Bay:	14 miles
Brentwood Bay to Mill Bay:	6 miles
Mill Bay to Cowichan Bay:	8 miles
Cowichan Bay to Genoa Bay:	2 miles
Genoa Bay to Birds Eye Cove:	8 miles
Birds Eye Cove to Chemainus:	11 miles
Chemainus to Ladysmith:	6 miles
Ladysmith to Nanaimo:	18 miles
Nanaimo to Silva Bay:	12 miles
Silva Bay to Telegraph Harbour:	15 miles
Telegraph Hbr to Montague Harbour:	16 miles
Montague Hbr to Ganges Harbour:	7 miles
Ganges Hbr to Otter Bay:	8 miles
Otter Bay to Poets Cove	7 miles
Poets Cove to Port Browning:	8 miles

The Perfect Charter

Many get the chance to first experience the beauty of the Gulf Islands by charter boat, and there are numerous companies in the area to assist in outfitting you with the ideal boat for your travels. The Perfect Charter itinerary is designed specifically to help those on a limited time schedule get a real flavor for the islands and to visit a few not-to-be-missed gems. Whether traveling with a family or on a solo adventure, these seven day itineraries take you past lush green islands, amazing wildlife, tours of local towns, and ample shoreside activities.

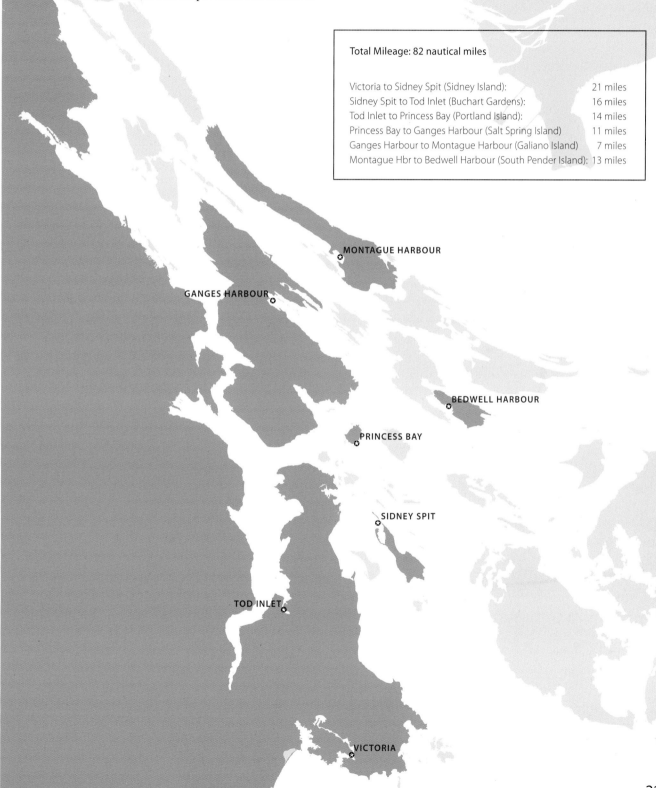

Total Mileage: 82 nautical miles

Victoria to Sidney Spit (Sidney Island):	21 miles
Sidney Spit to Tod Inlet (Buchart Gardens):	16 miles
Tod Inlet to Princess Bay (Portland Island):	14 miles
Princess Bay to Ganges Harbour (Salt Spring Island)	11 miles
Ganges Harbour to Montague Harbour (Galiano Island)	7 miles
Montague Hbr to Bedwell Harbour (South Pender Island):	13 miles

MONTAGUE HARBOUR

GANGES HARBOUR

BEDWELL HARBOUR

PRINCESS BAY

SIDNEY SPIT

TOD INLET

VICTORIA

The Perfect Charter

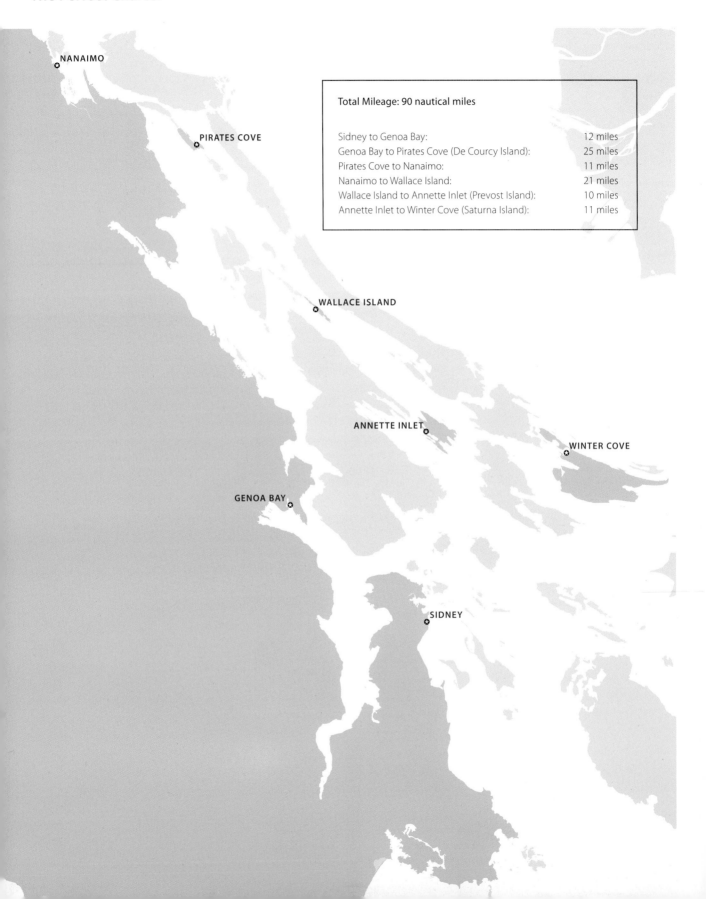

NANAIMO

PIRATES COVE

WALLACE ISLAND

ANNETTE INLET

WINTER COVE

GENOA BAY

SIDNEY

Total Mileage: 90 nautical miles

Sidney to Genoa Bay:	12 miles
Genoa Bay to Pirates Cove (De Courcy Island):	25 miles
Pirates Cove to Nanaimo:	11 miles
Nanaimo to Wallace Island:	21 miles
Wallace Island to Annette Inlet (Prevost Island):	10 miles
Annette Inlet to Winter Cove (Saturna Island):	11 miles

The Day Hiker's Paradise

For those who enjoy getting off the boat and exploring their surroundings by foot, the Day Hiker's Paradise itinerary will keep you well exercised and enjoying the beautiful scenery of the islands. Enjoy the countless miles of trails provided by BC's Provincial Marine Parks and the Gulf Islands National Park Reserve. From climbing the impressive 1,900 foot Mount Maxwell at Burgoyne Bay, or strolling the nearly 14 miles of well groomed trails at Newcastle Island off Nanaimo, there is adventure at every stop. Check with the respective anchorage description to see if digital versions of the trail maps are available for download to your smart phone.

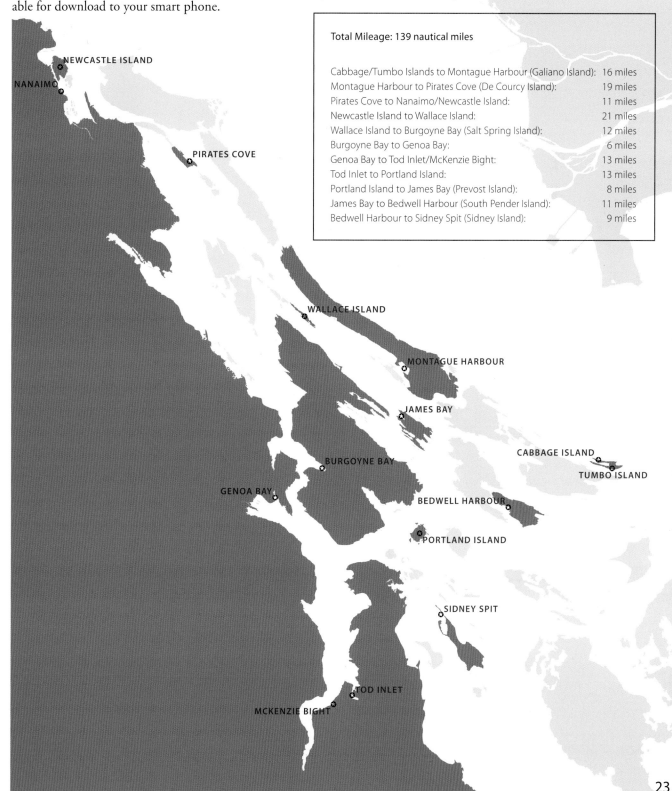

Total Mileage: 139 nautical miles

Cabbage/Tumbo Islands to Montague Harbour (Galiano Island):	16 miles
Montague Harbour to Pirates Cove (De Courcy Island):	19 miles
Pirates Cove to Nanaimo/Newcastle Island:	11 miles
Newcastle Island to Wallace Island:	21 miles
Wallace Island to Burgoyne Bay (Salt Spring Island):	12 miles
Burgoyne Bay to Genoa Bay:	6 miles
Genoa Bay to Tod Inlet/McKenzie Bight:	13 miles
Tod Inlet to Portland Island:	13 miles
Portland Island to James Bay (Prevost Island):	8 miles
James Bay to Bedwell Harbour (South Pender Island):	11 miles
Bedwell Harbour to Sidney Spit (Sidney Island):	9 miles

Chapter 1

Victoria

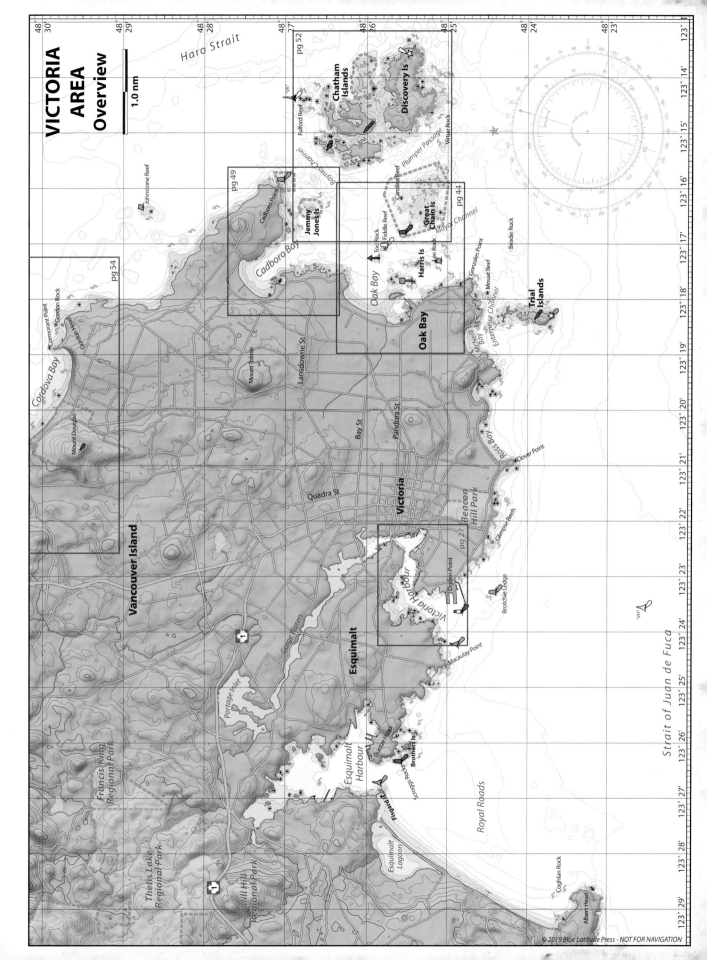

1.0 nm

Haro Strait

pg 52

Chatham Islands

Discovery Is

Fulford Reef

VK

Plumper Passage

Virtue Rock

Baynes Channel

pg 49

Carolina Reef

Great Chain Is

Johnstone Reef

Cadboro Point

Mayor Channel

Jemmy Jones Is

Toc Rock

pg 44

Fiddle Reef

Brodie Rock

pg 54

Cadboro Bay

Harris Is

Lee Rock

Gonzales Point

Cormorant Point

Mouat Reef

Gordon Rock

Gordon Head

Oak Bay

Enterprise Channel

Oak Bay Is

McNeill Bay

Trial Islands

Cordova Bay

Mount Tolmie

Oak Bay

Mount Douglas

Lansdowne St

ROSS BAY

Clover Point

Bay St

Pandora St

Vancouver Island

Quadra St

Victoria

Beacon Hill Park

Glimpse Reefs

pg 27

Ogden Point

Brotchie Ledge

Gorge Waters

Victoria Harbour

Esquimalt

Portage Inlet

Macaulay Point

Strait of Juan de Fuca

Francis King Regional Park

Esquimalt Harbour

Dunize Head

Brothers Is

Scroggs Rocks

Fisgard

Royal Roads

Esquimalt Lagoon

Thetis Lake Regional Park

Mill Hill Regional Park

Coghlan Rock

Albert Head

©Kevin Oke

Victoria

Victoria, also known as the City of Gardens, has a charm and beauty like no other. While its colonial history presents an elegant and stately display of manicured gardens and architecture, its modern restaurants and chic condos blend a lively spirit into the coastal town. Its seemingly never-ending trail systems and miles of protected waterways afford visitors and locals alike an outdoor playground for hikers, bikers, and paddlers. Sweeping views of the Strait of Juan de Fuca and its backdrop of the majestic Olympic Mountain range in nearby Washington state will keep you stuck to the park bench for hours.

Victoria is located at the southern end of Vancouver Island along the Strait of Juan de Fuca. Victoria Harbour is the main marine center for the city. The harbor is a busy working port serving cruise ships, ferries, tugs towing barges, commercial fishing boats, water taxis, whale watch boats, and seaplanes, along with pleasure boats, kayaks, and stand up paddle boards. The Greater Victoria Harbour Authority (GVHA) controls the majority of transient marina slips available within the harbor. The main visitor docks are found at the Causeway Floats, Ship Point Wharf, and Wharf Street Marina. Due to heavy traffic, anchoring is not permitted within Victoria Harbour.

Victoria Harbour is entered between Macaulay Point to the west and the long Ogden Point breakwater to the east. Approaches to the harbor can be made from the east or southerly directions. Approaching the bay from the south is relatively straight forward with open stretches of water. For boats heading eastbound through the Strait of Juan de Fuca and approaching from a southwesterly direction, be sure to give Race Rocks ample room when passing. Wind and current conditions around these rocks can create tide rips, large swells and/or standing waves.

Victoria to:		
Ganges Harbour (*Salt Spring Island*)		36 nm
Ladysmith		51 nm
Montague Harbour (*Galiano Island*)		37 nm
Nanaimo		63 nm
Oak Bay		7 nm
Pirates Cove (*De Courcy Island*)		55 nm
Port Townsend (*USA*)		35 nm
Princess Bay (*Portland Island*)		26 nm
Roche Harbor (*USA*)		20 nm
Sidney Spit (*Sidney Island*)		21 nm
Tod Inlet		36 nm
Winter Cove (*Saturna Island*)		33 nm

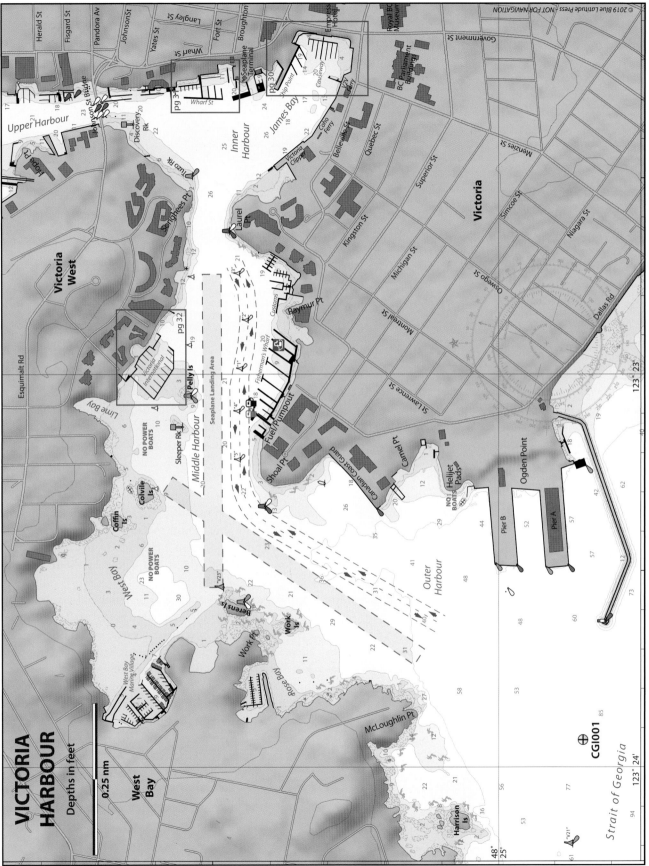

VICTORIA HARBOUR
Depths in feet

0.25 nm

© 2019 Blue Latitude Press – NOT FOR NAVIGATION

CGI001 - 48°24.850'N 123°23.930'W

West Bay

Victoria West

Upper Harbour

Hope Pt

Esquimalt Rd

Lime Bay

Songhees Pt

Tuzo Rk

Discovery Rk

Johnson St Bridge

Herald St
Fisgard St
Pandora Av
Johnson St
Yates St
Fort St
Broughton
Langley St
Wharf St

Seaplane Terminal

Wharf St

pg 31

pg 30

Empress Hotel

Ship Point

Causeway

V2V Ferry

James Bay

Inner Harbour

Victoria Clipper

Coho Ferry

Belleville St

Quebec St

BC Parliament Buildings

Royal BC Museum

Government St

Menzies St

Victoria

Superior St

Simcoe St

Niagara St

Kingston St

Michigan St

Oswego St

Dallas Rd

Laurel Pt

pg 32

Victoria International

Pelly Is

Sleeper Rk

NO POWER BOATS

Middle Harbour

Seaplane Landing Area

Colville Is

Coffin Is

West Bay

NO POWER BOATS

Berens Is

Work Pt

Work Is

West Bay Marina Village

Rose Bay

Customs

Raymur Pt

Fisherman's Wharf

Fuel/Pumpout

Shoal Pt

Camel Pt

Canadian Coast Guard

Helijet Pads

NO BOATS

St Lawrence St

Montreal St

Ogden Point

Pier B

Pier A

Outer Harbour

McLoughlin Pt

Harrison Is

Strait of Georgia

CGI001

123° 23'

123° 24'

48° 25'

When approaching from the east, give Trial Islands ample room when rounding. These islands are mostly low and barren, marked with a lighthouse on the southern end and red and white radio towers near the middle. Passage for smaller boats with local knowledge can be taken north of Trial Islands through Enterprise Channel. The navigable portion of this channel is narrow with strong flowing currents. Mouat Reef lies on the northern side of the east entrance to the channel.

Special note should be taken with currents when approaching Victoria. The areas around Race Rocks, Trial Islands and Discovery Island all can have very strong ebbs and floods, some reaching near 7 knots. Getting caught in a strong current when nearing Victoria can make a long transit day extremely long, especially for slower moving boats. Should the weather pick up, wind opposing these strong currents can make for very steep waves and large tide rips that can be dangerous for small boats especially around Race Rocks, the south end of Trial Islands and the southeast end of Discovery Island.

The coast between Clover Point and the Ogden Point breakwater is rocky with detached reefs and kelp beds. Lying 0.5 miles southeast of the breakwater is the Brotchie Ledge. This small ledge is marked by a navigation light with surrounding kelp beds.

Entrance to Victoria Harbour is taken between Macaulay Point and the Ogden Point breakwater. The harbor is divided into four sections: **Outer Harbour** from the breakwater to Shoal Point, **Middle Harbour** from Shoal Point to Laurel Point, **Inner Harbour** from Laurel Point to the Johnson Street Bridge, and **Upper Harbour** north of the Johnson Street Bridge.

Due to the heavy amount of vessel and seaplane traffic transiting Victoria's harbour, detailed traffic lanes and rules of operation have been created by Transit Canada and are strictly enforced by harbour patrol boats (see page 27). When entering the harbour, be aware of the speed limits found throughout: 7 knots for the Outer Harbour and 5 knots for the Middle, Inner and Upper Harbours. No vessels are allowed to anchor anywhere within the Port of Victoria unless authorized by the Port Official. Sail boats are also NOT permitted to sail within any section of the harbor. All sails need to be lowered before entering the Outer Harbour when arriving to Victoria.

Inbound and Outbound Traffic Lanes for vessels less than 65 feet are found within the Outer and Middle Harbours. These lanes are unmarked in the Outer Harbour, but the division between the inbound and outbound traffic lanes

Trial Islands and Mt. Baker

is marked with five lighted yellow cautionary buoys flashing every 4 seconds in the Middle Harbour. Vessels over 65 feet in length will transit the Middle Harbour via the Seaplane Take Off and Landing Areas, or via the Inbound Traffic Lane and shall transit these areas without stopping or delay.

There are two unmarked Seaplane Take Off and Landing Areas within the Outer and Middle Harbours found to the west and north of the vessel inbound/outbound traffic lanes. White strobe lights located at Shoal Point, Laurel Point, Berens Island and Pelly Island are activated to alert mariners of the imminent takeoff or landing of a seaplane. When these strobe lights are activated, use extreme caution.

A Seaplane Inclement Weather Operating Area in West Bay may be used for takeoff in some high wind conditions. Because of varying weather conditions, boat operators should not count on pilots always being able to operate completely within the designated areas. Therefore, boaters must remain vigilant at all times. Seaplanes operate in Victoria Harbour from 7am to 30 minutes past sunset.

Vessels with engines are not allowed in most of the northern areas of the Middle Harbour. This area is reserved for seaplanes and human powered vessels (kayaks, SUPs, etc). Human powered vessels can also use the Inbound and Outbound Traffic Lanes or paddle close to the north shore, north of the four white information buoys until west of Colville Island.

For vessels needing to transit under the Johnson Street Bridge, be aware the vertical clearance under the bridge at high-water is 19 feet and the width of the channel between pilings is 122 feet. The bridge operator stands by on VHF channel 12. Hours of operation are weekdays, 8am to midnight and weekends 8am to 4pm. Rush hour car traffic prevents the bridge from opening from 7 to 9am and 4 to 6pm weekdays.

Vessels entering Victoria from foreign waters must report to the Canadian Border Services Agency (CBSA) customs dock. The dock is 160 feet in length and located at Raymur Point between Fisherman's Wharf and the Coast Harbourside Hotel marina. Be sure to reference "Raymur Point CBSA Boat Dock" as your reporting site. For vessels over 160 feet contact CBSA at 1-888-226-7277 to make alternate arrangements with CBSA.

A fuel dock is located at Fisherman's Wharf. Both gas and diesel fuel are available from Victoria Marine Fuels. Two of the five diesel pumps are high volume with Cam Lock capability. A small store offers fishing tackle, drinks, snack food, ice and oil. Call (250) 381-5221 or visit their website at: www.victoriamarinefuels.com for hours of operation.

The pumpout station for Victoria is located on Finger B at Fisherman's Wharf. Tokens can be purchased from the marina office or the fuel dock.

Johnson Street Bridge

Customs Dock

Fuel Dock

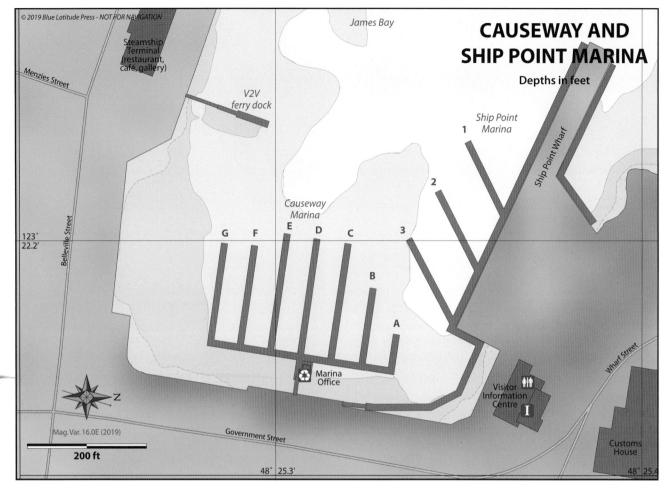

© 2019 Blue Latitude Press - NOT FOR NAVIGATION

James Bay

CAUSEWAY AND SHIP POINT MARINA

Depths in feet

Steamship Terminal (restaurant, café, gallery)

Menzies Street

V2V ferry dock

Ship Point Marina

1

Ship Point Wharf

2

Belleville Street

123° 22.2'

Causeway Marina

G F E D C

3

B

A

Marina Office

Wharf Street

Visitor Information Centre

I

Mag. Var. 16.0E (2019)

Government Street

Customs House

200 ft

48° 25.3'

48° 25.4

Causeway & Ship Point Marinas

The Causeway and Ship Point Marinas are located within the Inner Harbour in front of the picturesque Fairmont Empress Hotel and Parliament Buildings. Both marinas offer year-round transient moorage. The Causeway Marina can accommodate boats up to 60 feet in length with over 2,500 feet of lineal moorage. The Ship Point Marina can accommodate vessels from 60 to 280 feet in length. A float at the south end of Ship Point and a crescent float along the Lower Causeway are used for some commercial and pleasure vessels to pick up and drop off passengers. Potable water and 30amp electricity is available at Causeway Marina. Potable water and 30, 50, and 100 amp (single phase & 3 phase/280V and 480V) electricity is available at Causeway Marina. Secured gated entry is available at both marinas along with free wifi and garbage and recycle services. Restrooms, showers and laundry facilities are located at the Wharf Street Marina. Reservations are accepted for both marinas for any size vessel for free with the exception of holiday weekends in which a fee is charged. Pumpout service is available at Fisherman's Wharf (see page 29).

Greater Victoria Harbour Authority
100-1019 Wharf Street
Victoria, BC V8W 2Y9
(250) 383-8326, Toll-free: 1-877-783-8300
reservations@gvha.ca
www.gvha.ca

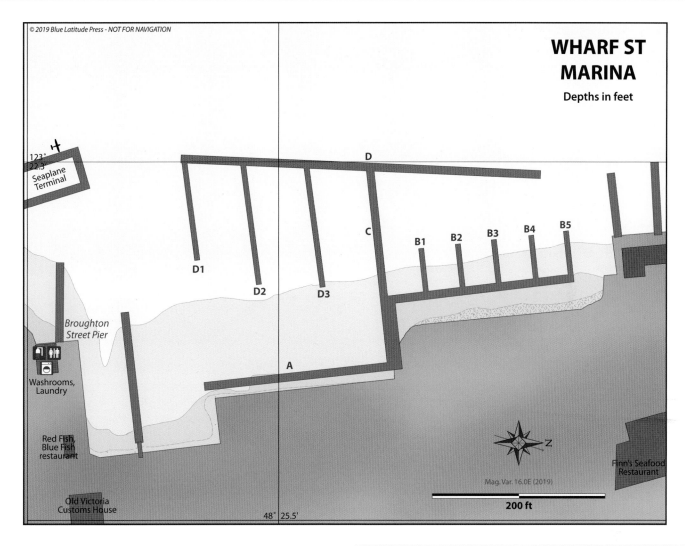

© 2019 Blue Latitude Press - NOT FOR NAVIGATION

WHARF ST MARINA

Depths in feet

123°
22.3'

Seaplane Terminal

D

D1

D2

D3

C

B1 B2 B3 B4 B5

A

Broughton Street Pier

Washrooms, Laundry

Red Fish, Blue Fish restaurant

Old Victoria Customs House

48° 25.5'

Finn's Seafood Restaurant

Mag. Var. 16.0E (2019)

200 ft

Wharf Street Marina

The Wharf Street marina is located north of the seaplane terminal within the Inner Harbour. This marina offers year-round transient and annual moorage for vessels from 20 to 375 feet in length. 30 and 50 amp power, along with potable water is available at each slip. Services include free wifi, secure gated entry, and garbage and recycle services. Bathrooms, showers, and laundry facilities are found next to the marina on the Broughton Street Pier. Pumpout service is available at Fisherman's Wharf (see page 29).

Greater Victoria Harbour Authority
100-1019 Wharf Street
Victoria, BC V8W 2Y9
(250) 383-8326, Toll-free: 1-877-783-8300
reservations@gvha.ca
www.gvha.ca

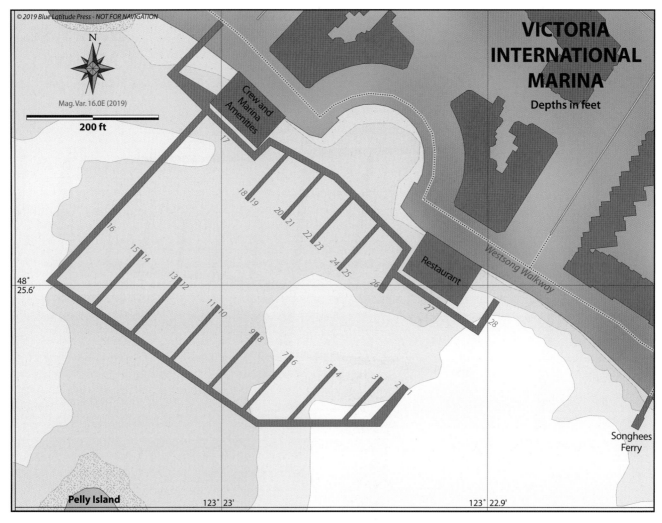

© 2019 Blue Latitude Press - NOT FOR NAVIGATION

N

Mag. Var. 16.0E (2019)

200 ft

VICTORIA INTERNATIONAL MARINA

Depths in feet

Crew and Marina Amenities

Restaurant

Westsong Walkway

Songhees Ferry

48° 25.6'

Pelly Island

123° 23'

123° 22.9'

Victoria International Marina

The Victoria International Marina is located along the shore of Victoria West. This brand new luxury marina is designed for superyachts between 65 and 175 feet in length. The marina offers 28 slips with a mix of transient (3-day minimum) and longer term berthing options.

Slips have 120-volt Single-phase power through one 100 amp and two 50 amp outlets and larger slips have 240-volt three-phase power through two 100 amp outlets. Potable water is available at each slip along with an auto suction sewer connection. Additional services include 24/7 gated security, high speed wifi, a fitness center, shower facilities, land transportation and valet service, reception and crew lounges, and concierge service.

Victoria International Marina
Monitors VHF channel 68A
1 Cooperage Place
Victoria, BC, V9J 7J9
(778) 432-0477
info@vimarina.ca
vimarina.ca

Fairmont Empress Hotel

History of Victoria

The history of Victoria begins back with the Lekwungen People, the original inhabitants of the area. Known today as the Esquimalt and Songhees Nations, these Coast Salish families hunted, foraged, practiced controlled burns, and cultivated the land throughout this area for thousands of years prior to European exploration and settlement. The protected waters of the Inner Harbour, along with a mild year-round climate and abundant wildlife, provided a favorable environment for settlements. Victoria's first name was Camosun (or Camosack), a Lekwungen name meaning "where different waters meet and are transformed."

In the mid 18th-century Spanish, British, French, Russian, and American explorers were scouting the waters of the Pacific Northwest - many looking for the Northwest Passage, others looking for fur trading opportunities. England's Captain James Cook and crew, along with his midshipman George Vancouver, are believed to be the first recorded Europeans to step foot on Vancouver Island in 1778 at Nootka Sound. In order to claim a foothold along the northeast Pacific coast, England sent then Captain George Vancouver in 1791 to survey the coast from 30 to 60 degrees north lati-

Ship Point Marina

Victoria Harbour Ferry ballet

tude. As further exploration of these northern waters increased, word and trading of the rich pelts of sea otters and other animals spread.

In 1824, the English run Hudson's Bay Company (HBC) established Fort Vancouver on the Columbia River of now Washington state. With escalating boundary concerns between England and the US, James Douglas, a chief factor at the HBC, established a new post on Vancouver Island in 1843. Douglas chose the site of present day Victoria and named the settlement Fort Victoria.

In 1849, Vancouver Island became an official Crown Colony of England. While settlement to the area began slowly, the Fraser River Gold Rush of 1858 set Fort Victoria off on a wild development boom. Miners from around the world stopped at the port town before heading east to the Fraser River. To supply the nearly overnight influx of thousands of people, commercial shops and tents sprang up around the fort. In 1862 the town of Victoria was incorporated.

In 1866, the Crown Colonies of Vancouver Island and British Columbia (mainland) merged to become one colony. Six years later in 1871, British Columbia (BC) became the sixth province of the Dominion of Canada. Victoria was made the capital of the province with its political ties, thriving industrial and financial district, and large naval base.

Victoria's reign as BC's largest city began to decline with the construction of the Canadian Pacific Railway (CPR) in the late 1800's. In order to link Canada's vast provinces from east and west coasts, rail lines were used to transport goods and people as well as providing a communication network. With the terminus of the line in Vancouver, shipping and industry slowly shifted from Victoria to the mainland.

Over the decades Victoria has retained its metropolitan and government status, and is the largest city on Van-

Parliament buildings

couver Island. The beautiful waterfront city has evolved into a major tourist destination, education center, and desirable retirement community. In the 1980's, Victoria's 19th-century Old Town and Chinatown districts went through major restorations, breathing new life into these historical landmarks.

Greater Victoria today has a quickly growing population of over 367,000 people. The city is still a major naval center with Canada's Pacific Coast naval base at Canadian Forces Base Esquimalt. Three top rated schools including the University of Victoria, Royal Roads University, and Camosun College provide higher education and research for the area. Tourism is now one of Victoria's top industries, seeing over three million tourists annually. The city showcases its First Nations, British colonial and Asian history through museums, art, landmarks, parks and cuisine, making it a favorite destination.

Sights to See

One of the best highlights of a visit to the beautiful city of Victoria is a tour of the Royal BC Museum. The museum was founded in 1886 and the Archives in 1894. In 2003, these two organizations joined to become British Columbia's

Old Town

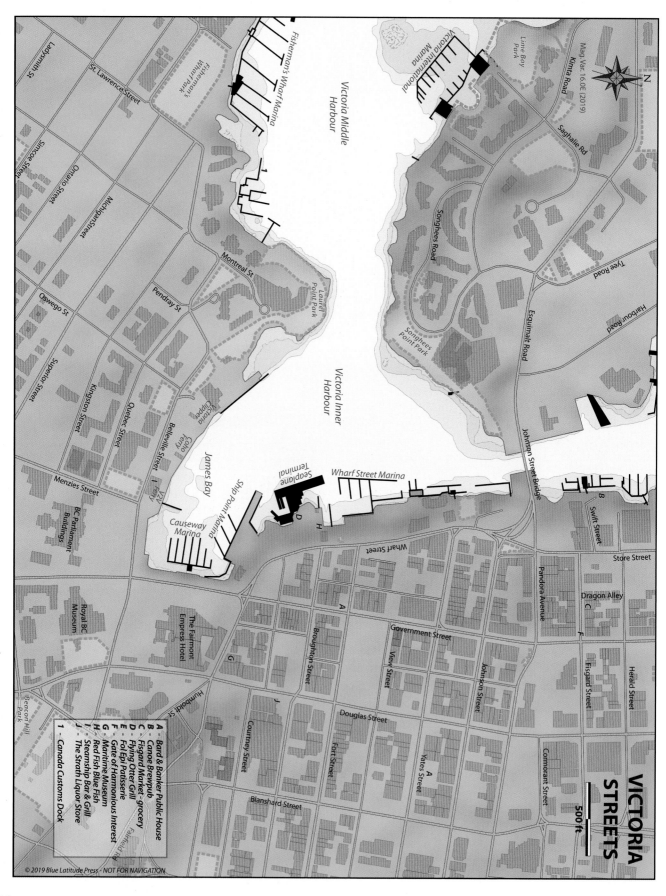

Fisherman's Wharf Marina

Fisherman's Wharf Park

Ladysmith St.

St. Lawrence Street

Simcoe Street

Ontario Street

Michigan St.

Oswego St.

Superior Street

Kingston Street

Quebec Street

Belleville Street

Montreal St.

Pendray St.

Victoria Clipper

Coho Ferry

Victoria Middle Harbour

Laurel Point Park

Victoria Inner Harbour

James Bay

Ship Point Marina

Causeway Marina

Menzies Street

BC Parliament Buildings

Royal BC Museum

The Fairmont Empress Hotel

Humboldt St.

Beacon Hill Park

Fairfield Rd.

Seaplane Terminal

Wharf Street Marina

Wharf Street

D
H

A

G

J

Government Street

Broughton Street

View Street

Fort Street

Johnson Street

Yates Street

Douglas Street

Courtney Street

Blanshard Street

Victoria International Marina

Lime Bay Park

Kinta Road

Saghalie Rd

Mag. Var. 16.0E (2019)

Songhees Road

Songhees Point Park

Esquimalt Road

Tyee Road

Harbour Road

Johnson Street Bridge

N

Swift Street

Store Street

Pandora Avenue

Dragon Alley

B

C

F

Fisgard Street

Herald Street

Cormorant Street

A – Bard & Banker Public House
B – Canoe Brewpub
C – Fisgard Market - grocery
D – Flying Otter Grill
E – Fol Epi Patisserie
F – Gate of Harmonious Interest
G – Maritime Museum
H – Red Fish Blue Fish
J – Steamship Bar & Grill
1 – The Strath Liquor Store
1 – Canada Customs Dock

VICTORIA
STREETS

500 ft

© 2019 Blue Latitude Press - NOT FOR NAVIGATION

Royal BC Museum

combined provincial museum and archives, collecting arti-facts, documents and specimens of British Columbia's natu-ral and human history. The Royal BC Museum is also home to thousands of spectacular photographs, films, recordings and objects showcasing the many First Nations cultures in BC. These items represent up to 10,000 years of history from across the province, celebrating the diversity and resilience of indigenous peoples. Also housed within the museum is BC's largest IMAX movie theater showing both documentaries and Hollywood movies. The museum is located within easy walking distance from the water on the corner of Govern-ment and Belleville Streets, between the Fairmont Empress and the BC Parliament Buildings. For further information on touring the Royal BC Museum visit: royalbcmuseum.bc.ca.

Just across the street from the museum and overlooking the Inner Harbour are the Parliament Buildings. The strik-ingly ornate government buildings are a definite sight to see when visiting Victoria. The buildings are situated on over 12 beautifully manicured acres and have served as a site of government in BC since 1864. The Parliament Buildings are open to the public each weekday, Monday to Friday, from 8:30am to 5pm. Visitors may join one of the free regularly-scheduled guided tours, which last roughly 30 to 45 min-

Royal BC Museum

utes, or visitors may explore the buildings on their own self-guided tour. During the summer months the buildings are also open for free guided tours on weekends and holidays from 9am to 5pm. Guided tours begin from the waiting area inside of the main entrance. For further information on vis-iting and schedules, please visit www.leg.bc.ca.

Fisherman's Wharf

Wyland Wall

Fisherman's Wharf

Next on the list and a short walk away is Beacon Hill Park. Beacon Hill is the gem of Victoria's city parks. The 200 acres of waterfront park land include natural areas, manicured landscape areas, miles of walking trails, playgrounds, a petting zoo, and sports areas for tennis, golf, baseball, cricket and lawn bowling. During the summer months, the park hosts free outdoor concerts from Friday to Monday beginning at 1:30pm from July to September at the Cameron Bandshell. Bring a picnic, your camera and some walking shoes to enjoy the beauty and serenity of this amazing downtown, waterfront park. Although there are numerous entrances to the park, the closest from the Inner Harbor is located southeast of the Royal BC Museum at Douglas and Southgate Streets. Download a copy of the park map at: www.victoria.ca/assets/Departments/Parks~Rec~Culture/Parks/Documents/beacon-hill-park-map.pdf.

For a delightful and unexpected treat, catch a performance of the Victoria Harbour Ferry's water ballet. For over

Beacon Hill Peacocks

Catch an early morning walk through Victoria's not to be missed Beacon Hill Park, and you might hear an unusual bird call through the trees. Resident park peafowl are a familiar sight here with the iridescent birds taking roost in the trees or strutting around the manicured lawns of the park. In the spring and early summer months, the birds go through their mating season where males put on an impressive show for their prospective mates. Fanning out their shimmering tail feathers, males dance and flirt for any female that crosses their path. With a six-foot display, males flaunt their colorful, "eyed" feathers, turning and shaking their backsides in hopes of winning the eye of a peahen. When searching out these beautiful birds, listen for their calls and head towards the petting zoo where water and food are made available for them.

25 years these maneuverable little boats have been putting on 12-minute performances in the Inner Harbour with five boats for tourists and locals alike. The ballets are performed every Sunday at 10:45am beginning after Victoria Day (the last Monday preceding May 25 in honor of Queen Victoria's birthday) to mid September, and every Saturday at 10:45am from July through August. The ballets takes place near the Steamship Terminal. When not gracefully twirling on the water, these boats offer regular, scheduled ferry service around the harbour including stops in Victoria West and Esquimalt. Daily tours of the harbour and gorge can also be arranged at the Empress Dock. The ferries also provide unique tours of harbour in the city now known as the "Cradle of the Craft Beer Revolution of Canada" on their Pickle Pub Crawl tour. For further information check their website at: www.victoriaharbourferry.com.

Another special highlight to Victoria is its historic Chinatown. Centered around Fisgard Street, Victoria's Chinatown is the oldest in Canada and was the gateway for Asian immigration in the mid 1800's for thousands of Chinese gold miners and builders who worked on the construction of the Canadian Pacific Railway. According to records from the University of Victoria library, by 1860, 35% of Vancouver Island's population was Chinese. A must see when visiting Chinatown is The Gate of Harmonious Interest. Built in 1981 on the corner of Fisgard and Government Streets, the gate is situated at the heart of Chinatown. While enjoying and appreciating the architecture, history and culture of this area, be sure to save time to visit the many shops and delicious dining options.

Enjoy a scenic waterfront walking path around the inner harbor and head over to the vibrant Fisherman's Wharf. This eclectic mix of brightly colored houseboats and food kiosks is set amongst a working fishermen's harbor. Sample one of the many floating food vendors or buy seafood fresh off the boat. Walk the docks and watch the hustle and bustle of Victoria's harbor go by from boats of all shapes and sizes to seaplanes, kayaks and more. Pick up the paved walking path near the corner of Belleville Pendray Streets and follow for roughly a half mile to the wharf.

For those looking to stretch their legs a little farther and explore the southern end of Vancouver Island, walk, bike, or hike the 34-mile Galloping Goose Regional Trail. The former railway line turned into trail, begins in downtown Victoria and meanders through city and rural areas where it terminates at the historical gold mining ghost town of Leechtown. The Galloping Goose connects to the Lochside Regional Trail which travels the Saanich Peninsula up to Swartz Bay. Both trails are part of the national, 15,000-mile Trans-Canada Trail system. From the Johnson Street bridge

Chinatown

Gate of Harmonious Interest

in Victoria, the trail is paved for approximately eight miles as it heads west. The trail then turns to gravel as it heads out of the urban area and into more rural areas. For further information and to download maps of the trails visit: www.gallopinggoosetrail.com.

Tilikum

Tilikum, housed by the Maritime Museum of British Columbia (MMBC), is a historic 38-foot red cedar dugout canoe. Captain John Voss purchased the canoe to sail around the world after being inspired by Joshua Slocum's book, *Sailing Alone Around the World*, in which Slocum documents his solo circumnavigation from 1895 to 1898. Voss modified the canoe for open ocean travel by reinforcing the hull, adding an enclosed cabin area, keel and rudder, as well as installing three masts to carry sail.

Voss set sail on his round the world adventure in 1901 with crewman and journalist Norman Luxton. Voss' journey took him from Victoria to their first stop at Penrhyn Island. From there Voss, along with a handful of different crewmen, traveled across the South Pacific to Australia, New Zealand, across the Indian Ocean to South Africa, across the Atlantic to Brazil and back across the Atlantic to London.

Along the way Voss earned money for the extended voyage and repairs by putting his small boat on exhibition at his ports of call and giving lectures on his adventures, making him an international celebrity.

By 1904, Voss had made his way to London where he put *Tilikum* on exhibit at the Naval and Fisheries Exhibition of 1905. Voss ended up selling the famous boat in England where she changed hands numerous times and fell into disrepair. In 1930, *Tilikum* was purchased by the city of Victoria and the BC government, and brought back home. Once back in Victoria, she underwent needed repairs and was put on display for all to see this amazing little canoe that traveled the world's ocean and weathered tremendous storms at sea.

In 1965, the MMBC purchased *Tilikum* and houses her today within the museum. To visit *Tilikum* and learn about BC's maritime heritage, head to MMBC at 634 Humboldt Street or visit: **mmbc.bc.ca**.

Marine Chandleries and Services

Castle Building Centre
Offering a wide range of building and hardware supplies. Located across from the Westside Village Shopping Center at 220 Bay Street. www.castle.ca, (250) 595-1225

Home Depot
Home improvement chain for tools, hardware, plumbing, electrical, lumber, and more. Located in the University Heights Shopping Center at 3986 Shelbourne Street. homedepot.ca, (250) 853-5350

Iron Capital
Begun as a scrap business in 1934, Iron Capital has evolved over the years into a unique, all inclusive general store. Selling hardware, electrical, paints, clothing, housewares, fishing, marine, and camping gear. Near the Wharf Street Marina at 1900 Store Street. www.capitaliron.net, (250) 385-9703

Lowe's Home Improvement
Home-improvement chain for tools, hardware, plumbing, electrical, lumber, and more. Located at 3170 Tillicum Road. www.lowes.ca, (250) 294-8100

Trotac
A family run marine supply store that has been serving Vancouver Island for the past 40 years. Selling a vast array of marine products for all your boating needs. Services include pump rebuilds, splicing and rigging. Located at 370 Gorge Road East. www.trotac.ca, (250) 386-234

Provisioning

BC Liquor Store
BC Liquor Stores offer a great selection of beers, wines and spirits. Located across from Thrifty Foods on Menzies Street.

Fisgard Market
Fresh produce and Asian staples. Located in Chinatown at 550 Fisgard Street.

Save On Foods
Located across the Johnson Street bridge in Victoria West. A large chain grocery supplying fresh produce, meats, dairy, bakery items and all the staples. Located in the Westside Village Shopping Center on Wilson Street.

The Strath Liquor Store
Next to the Strathcona Hotel, the store offers a wide selections of wines, spirits, craft and international beers. Located on Douglas and Broughton Streets.

Thrifty Foods
Located in a shopping center on Simcoe Street. A large chain grocery store open 24/7 supplying fresh produce, meats, dairy, bakery items and all the staples.

Transportation
Airport
Victoria International Airport (YYJ) serves the Victoria and Saanich Peninsula region. The airport is located roughly 16 miles north of downtown Victoria. Car rentals and public buses are available at the airport. Airlines serving the airport include: Air Canada, Air North, Air Transat, Delta, Flair, Horizon (Alaska Airlines), Island Express, Pacific Coastal, Sunwing, United, VivaAerobus, and WestJet.

Buses
BC Transit is the public bus system serving Victoria, west Victoria and Saanich Peninsula regions. Greyhound and Pacific Coach Lines serves the greater Vancouver Island area.

Ferries
A number of ferries serve Victoria and Saanich Peninsula. The largest ferry system is BC Ferries with routes connecting Vancouver Island, the Gulf Islands and the mainland. Ferry service from Port Angeles to Victoria's Inner Harbour is available through the Black Ball Ferry Line. Service from the Inner Harbour to Vancouver is available through V2V Vacations. Ferry service from downtown Seattle to Victoria's Inner Harbour is available through Clipper Vacations.

Seaplanes
Seaplanes are a popular and direct mode of transportation with the Gulf Islands, Vancouver Island and mainland. Victoria's seaplane terminal is located next to the Wharf Street Marina. Airlines serving the airport include: Harbour Air, Kenmore Air and Salt Spring Air.

Restaurants
Bard & Banker Public House
Located on the corner of Government and Fort Streets in a beautiful and historic 1800's bank building. This classic Scottish-style pub has a great selection of local craft beer and premiums imports along with wine and spirits. Open daily for breakfast, lunch and dinner with nightly live music. bardandbanker.com, (250) 253-9993

Canoe Brewpub
Combine a historic (1894) and beautifully restored timber-framed building with excellent housemade craft beer and top it off with one of the city's most premier outdoor patios with a view, and you get Canoe Brewpub. Exceptional beer, food and ambiance, Canoe is a must try. Live music Thursday through Sunday. Located on Swift Street, just north of the Johnson Street Bridge. www.canoebrewpub.com, (250) 361-1940

Flying Otter Grill
Located on the Harbour Air Seaplane docks, the Flying Otter offers amazing views of the Inner Harbour and seaplanes landing and taking off. Excellent salads, burgers, fish and chips, and cold beers and cocktails. Open daily for lunch and dinner. www.flyingottergrill.com, (250) 414-4220

Fol Epi Patisserie
For delicious fresh baked delicacies including buttery croissants and pain au chocolat, danish, cream pastries and cookies, Fol Epi is your place. Fresh baked breads include baguettes, ciabattas, boules, ryes and whole wheats. They

Race to Alaska
Race to Alaska, or R2AK, is an amazing, one-of-a-kind event organized by the Northwest Maritime Center. Begun in 2015, the two stage, self-supported race begins in Port Townsend and ends in Ketchikan. The rules are simple: row, paddle or sail without the help of an engine or supply drops. Get there first and win $10,000, get there second and win a set of steak knives.

Stage one of the race is known as the proving ground. This leg was designed as a qualifier for the full race or as a stand-alone sprint for those who want a brief sample of the race. The 40-mile leg from Port Townsend to Victoria is open water, crossing the windy Strait of Juan de Fuca.

Stage two departs Victoria under much fan fare and celebration. From a standing start, racers run down the docks to their vessels and using human power to leave the harbor, they race to Ketchikan. Other than passing two waypoints along the way at Seymour Narrows and Bella Bella, racers are free to choose their own course.

For current race dates and further information on this unique event, check their website at: **r2ak.com**.

Canoe Brewpub

Bastion Square

Seaplane terminal

even have a charcuterie with house cured salamis and pates. Open daily. Located at 732 Yates Street. www.folepi.ca, (778) 265-6311

Red Fish Blue Fish

For some classic fish and chips on the wharf, look no further than the Red Fish Blue Fish stand. A very popular lunch stop especially in the summer months. Located on the wharf near the corner of Wharf and Broughton Streets. Open daily for lunch. www.redfish-bluefish.com, (250) 298-6877

Steamship Bar & Grill

After exploring the city, enjoy a cold drink or a bite to eat with an amazing view of the harbor in their outdoor 2nd floor patio. Located at the Steamship Terminal at the Victoria to Vancouver (V2V) Ferry dock. steamshipgrill.com, (778) 433-6736

Tea at the Empress

Afternoon tea at the Fairmont Empress is an experience not to be missed while in Victoria. Served in their Lobby Lounge, house-made signature Empress scones, pastries, clotted creams, strawberry preserves with fresh lavender and 21 of the finest loose leafs teas are served. During the summer, tea is served daily from 11am to 4pm. Located on the waterfront on Government Street. www.fairmont.com, (250) 389-2727

©Kevin Oke

Oak Bay

The quaint seaside suburban village of Oak Bay offers a quiet alternative to the hustle and bustle of Victoria Harbour. Lying a mere 2.5 miles east of downtown Victoria, Oak Bay affords visitors close proximity to all the sights and attractions of the big city, while providing a peaceful, park-like setting to spend the night. Complete with a marina, fuel dock, customs dock, and room to anchor, Oak Bay is the perfect option for those looking for a bit of tranquility with the ease of travel to the exciting urban center of Victoria.

Oak Bay is located at the southeast end of Vancouver Island and two miles west of Discovery and Chatham Islands. The water between these islands and Oak Bay is scattered with numerous drying reefs and rocky islets requiring very careful navigation upon approach. Currents in this area can also be very strong, as much as 6 knots. Be sure to check the tide tables and plan your transit accordingly.

From the south, there are two main channels: Mayor Channel west of Great Chain Island, and Plumper Passage east of the Chain Islets. From the northeast the main channel is Baynes Channel, which separates Vancouver Island and the Chatham Islands group.

For boats approaching from the south and heading to the marina, passage can be taken between Vancouver Island and Harris Island. Lying just south of Harris Island is Lee Rock. Lee Rock is marked close south by buoy "V25." Be aware that shallow areas are found on either side of the approach to the marina and careful navigation should be used. Currents through this area can be over 3 knots.

Approaching from the north, passage can be taken through Baynes Channel. Keep in mind that currents

Oak Bay		
	Bedwell Harbour (South Pender Island)	21 nm
	Ganges Harbour (Salt Spring Island)	30 nm
	Genoa Bay	28 nm
	Ladysmith	45 nm
	Montague Harbour (Galiano Island)	30 nm
	Nanaimo	56 nm
	Pirates Cove (De Courcy Island)	49 nm
	Port Townsend (USA)	31 nm
	Roche Harbor (USA)	13 nm
	Sidney	16 nm
	Tod Inlet	30 nm
	Victoria	7 nm

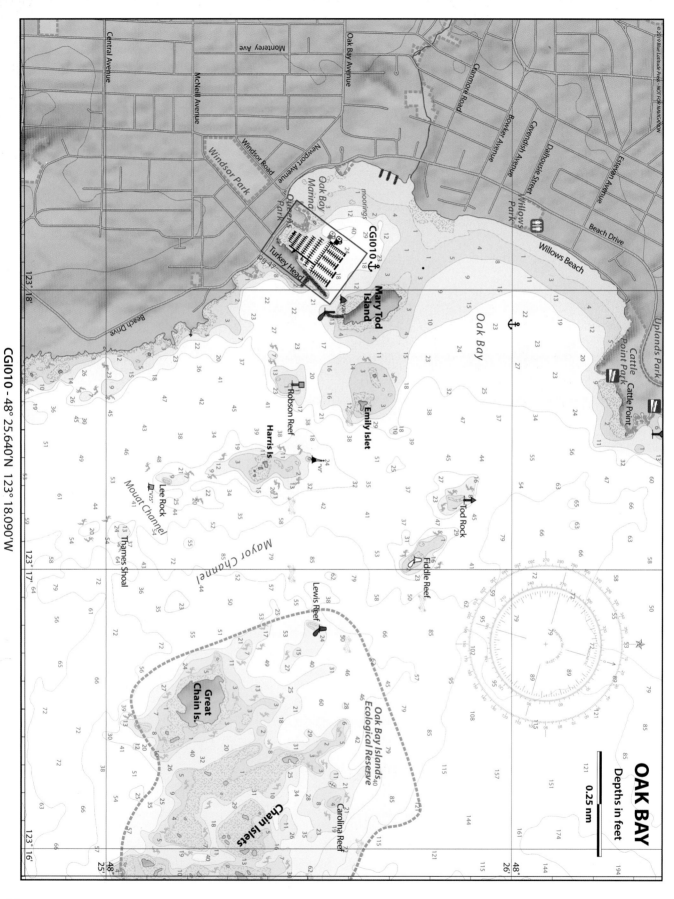

OAK BAY
Depths in feet

0.25 nm

CGI010 - 48° 25.640'N 123° 18.090'W

Willows Beach

through this pass can exceed 6 knots. Stronger winds opposing this current will cause heavy tide rips with short, steep seas in this area. Continuing southwest, pass between Fiddle Reef and Lewis Reef, both marked with navigation lights. Pass north of the Harris Island cardinal buoy, and then between Robson Reef and Emily Islet.

Entrance to the marina is taken only between the breakwater at Turkey Head and the breakwater from Mary Tod Island. Access to the marina should not be taken north of Mary Tod Island. Once inside the breakwaters, buoy "V26" marks the outer end of a reef extending west from Mary Tod Island near the entrance.

The water surrounding the marina is filled with numerous private moorings. Anchorage can be taken outside of the moorings and west of Mary Tod Island. The bottom shallows quickly so be sure you have adequate depth within your swinging radius at low tide. While the holding is mostly mud, the bottom has a heavy layer of seaweed and can cause some anchors to drag. Given the proximity to Juan de Fuca Strait, this area may be affected by winds blowing through this large body of water, including summer time southwesterlies.

Vessels entering Oak Bay from foreign waters must report to the Canadian Border Services Agency (CBSA) customs dock. The customs dock is located at Oak Bay Marina at the end of F Dock at the fuel dock.

For trips to shore, dinghies can be landed at Queens Park, located just west of the Oak Bay Marina, or for a daily fee, dinghies can also be landed at the Oak Bay Marina. Be sure to check the tide table if landing at Queens Park as low tide can be quite a hike to carry the dinghy to/from the water.

Once ashore, there are a number of activities to keep you busy with many sights to explore. For exercise, Oak Bay has numerous beachside quiet residential streets for a nice stroll or bike ride. True to its name sake, the town is surrounded by towering giant oak trees providing nice shade and natural beauty. The city has put together a number of walking and cycling maps available at: www.oakbay.ca/explore-oak-bay/getting-around/walking-cycling.

For those looking to experience the sights of downtown Victoria, convenient public bus service is available. Direct downtown Victoria buses can be caught near the corner of Windsor Road and Newport Avenue (one block from Queens Park). A bus stop is also located at the entrance to the Oak Bay Marina, which will require a transfer to get to downtown Victoria. For current routes and schedules, check BC Transit at: bctransit.com.

A short half mile walk up Beach Drive to Oak Bay Avenue leads you to the delightful village of Oak Bay. Shops and eateries line the main street, enticing visitors with delectable food and drink, as well as alluring galleries and boutiques.

During the summer months from June through September on the second Wednesday of each month, Oak Bay Village is transformed into a lively open air market from 4 to 8pm. With the main street closed to vehicle traffic, vendors set up tents to sell their wares including farmers, artisans, and chefs.

No trip to Oak Bay is complete without visiting Willows Beach and Uplands Park. The beach's beautiful crescent of sand overlooks the island-studded back drop of the bay. Willows Beach is a popular swimming area. If arriving by boat, keep a careful watch and use paddles to approach the beach (no engines). Keep in mind during the summer, from May 1 to September 30, dogs are not permitted on the beach. Willows Beach is also home to the annual Oak Bay Tea Party. For over 50 years the Tea Party has been entertaining visitors with midway rides, a parade, air show, bathtub race, live music and food vendors. Check their website for dates and schedules: www.oakbayteaparty.com. Adjacent Uplands Park is roughly 75 acres of natural park land with a stunning Garry Oak meadow and spring blooming native wildflowers. Cattle Point offers a boat ramp and the park offers miles of walking trails.

Nearby Mary Tod Island offers a nice destination for dinghy, kayak or SUP exploration. The western shore of the island offers a landing beach with a few unimproved trails crisscrossing the small island. Small bushes of Garry Oak and native wildflowers can be seen on the island.

Provisioning

COBS Bread
Offering a variety of freshly baked breads and pastries. Located in the village at 2178 Oak Bay Avenue. www.cobsbread.com, 250 592 8687

Cork and Barrel Spirit Merchants
A nice liquor store offering spirits, wine and beer. Located within the shopping center next to Fairway Market at 2187 Oak Bay Avenue. (250) 592-9463

Fairway Market
A chain grocery store supplying fresh produce, meats, dairy, bakery items and all the staples. Conveniently located in the Athlone Court shopping village at 2187 Oak Bay Avenue. fairwaymarkets.com, (250) 592-8191

Village Butcher and The Whole Beast
One space, two amazing meat shops. The Village Butcher offers locally raised, high quality, healthy, and humanely treated meats and sausages. The Whole Beast is an artisanal salumeria offering excellent locally cured and smoked meats. Located within the village at 2032 Oak Bay Avenue. villagebutcher.ca, 250-598-1115; www.thewholebeast.ca, (250) 590-PORK

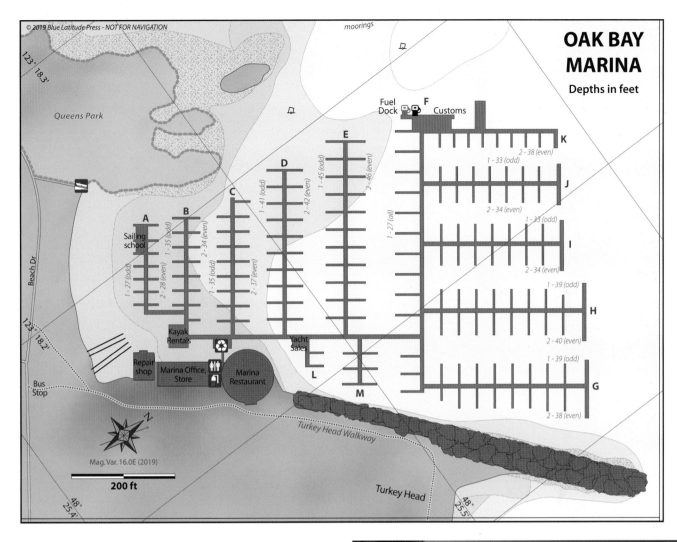

© 2019 Blue Latitude Press - NOT FOR NAVIGATION

OAK BAY MARINA

Depths in feet

Oak Bay Marina

The Oak Bay Marina is one of four marinas under the management of the Oak Bay Marine Group. The marina offers both transient (reservations recommended) and permanent slips to boats from 20 to 70 feet in length. Each slip has access to power and water hookups. Additional services include a fuel dock, customs dock, restrooms, showers, bike and kayak rentals, garbage and recycling, small marine chandlery, and a restaurant and coffee bar with wifi access. A public bus stop is conveniently located at the marina.

Oak Bay Marina
Monitors VHF channel 66A
1327 Beach Drive
Victoria, BC V8S 2N4
(250) 598-3369
obm@obmg.com
oakbaymarina.com

Customs and Fuel Dock

©Kevin Oke

Cadboro Bay

Nestled just north of Oak Bay is the small village of Cadboro Bay. Home to the regal Royal Victoria Yacht Club, Cadboro Bay is alive with boats taking advantage of the calm waters and sailing breezes. A large protected anchorage headed by an enticing sandy beach park welcome visitors to this peaceful beachside community. A small village hosts a handful of shops and eateries for a night away from the galley. Just up the hill is the extensive campus for the University of Victoria (UVic).

Cadboro Bay is located on the southeastern end of Vancouver Island, approximately 2 miles north of Oak Bay. Discovery and Chatham Islands and the Chain Islets create hazards to navigation in the form of numerous reefs, rocky islets and strong currents so careful attention to the charts and current atlas is required when approaching Cadboro Bay.

Approaches to Cadboro Bay can be taken from the south via Mayor Channel or Plumper Passage, or from the east via Baynes Channel. Mayor Channel is entered from the south between Thames Shoal and the reefs extending off Great Chain Island. The channel continues north past Harris Island and between Lewis Reef and Fiddle Reef,

all marked with navigation aids. Mayor Channel can have currents up 2 or 3 knots. Plumber Passage is entered from the south between Virtue Rock and Commodore Point on Discovery Island. The passage continues northeast past the Chain Islets and Chatham Islands. Plumber Passage can experience strong currents, between 3 to 5 knots. Baynes Channel is entered from the north between Cadboro Point on Vancouver Island and Fulford Reef off Chatham Is-

Cadboro Bay		
Bedwell Harbour (South Pender Island)	20 nm
Cowichan Bay	27 nm
Ganges Harbour (Salt Spring Island)	29 nm
Montague Harbour (Galiano Island)	30 nm
Nanaimo	57 nm
Pirates Cove (De Courcy Island)	47 nm
Roche Harbor (USA)	13 nm
Sidney Spit (Sidney Island)	14 nm
Telegraph Harbour (Thetis Island)	40 nm
Tod Inlet	29 nm
Victoria	10 nm
Winter Cove (Saturna Island)	26 nm

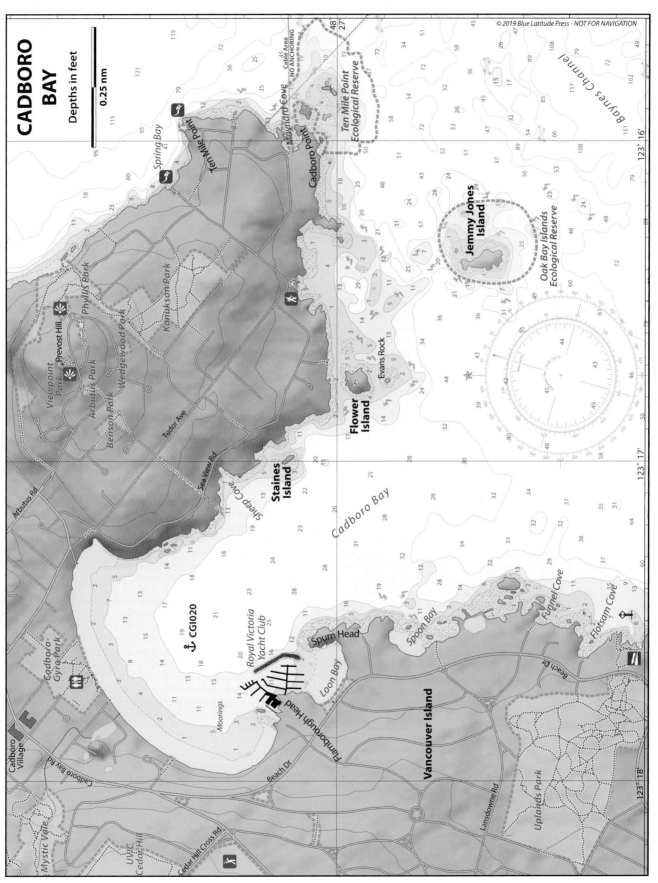

© 2019 Blue Latitude Press - NOT FOR NAVIGATION

CADBORO BAY

Depths in feet

0.25 nm

Spring Bay

Ten Mile Point

Maynard Cove

Cadboro Point

Cable Area
NO ANCHORING

Ten Mile Point
Ecological Reserve

Baynes Channel

Jemmy Jones
Island

Oak Bay Islands
Ecological Reserve

Phyllis Park

Koniukson Park

Prevost Hill

Viewpoint
Park

Arbutus Park

Wedgewood Park

Benson Park

Tudor Ave

Sea View Rd

Sheep Cove

Staines
Island

Evans Rock

Flower
Island

Cadboro Bay

Arbutus Rd

Cadboro
Gyro Park

CGI020

Royal Victoria
Yacht Club

Moorings

Spurn Head

Loon Bay

Spoon Bay

Funnel Cove

Flotsam Cove

Beach Dr

Cadboro
Village

Flamborough Head

Beach Dr

Vancouver Island

Cadboro Bay Rd

Mystic Vale

UVIC
Cedar Hill

Cedar Hill Cross Rd

Lansdowne Rd

Uplands Park

CGI020 - 48° 27.310'N 123° 17.590'W

lands. The shoreline west of Cadboro Point is shallow with numerous reefs and detached rocks.

Entrance to Cadboro Bay is open with a fairly uniform bottom throughout. The private Royal Victoria Yacht Club is located on the west shore behind a rock breakwater. Private moorings are found near the head of the bay and north of the yacht club. Anchorage can be taken near the head of the bay in 3 to 5 fathoms over a good holding mud bottom.

For trips to shore, dinghies can be taken to the beautiful sand beach at the Cadboro-Gyro Park. The park offers an amazing playground, complete with zipline, picnic tables and plenty of sand. The village is a short two block walk for provisioning or a bite to eat. Provisioning stops at the village include Peppers Foods - a well stocked grocery store, Caddy Bay Liquor Store, and Weidu Market - a small Asian specialty grocery store.

Loon Bay Park, tucked in behind the yacht club, is also a nice spot for a dinghy landing, although somewhat muddy at low tide. Walkers can stretch their legs on nearby UVic's Mystic Vale and Alumni Chip trails, and visit the beautiful Finnerty Gardens. For boats traveling with dogs, the UVic Cedar Hill Corner property offers an informal dog walk area for your best friend to stretch his/her legs too. Keep in mind that during the summer months, the Cadboro-Gyro Park and public beach are closed to dogs from May 1 to August 31.

©Kevin Oke

Discovery and Chatham Islands

Discovery and Chatham Islands lie roughly two miles east of Oak Bay. The low, wooded islands comprise a maze of reefs and islets with shallow water passages between. A portion of Discovery Island is a Marine Provincial Park that is open to the public for picnicking and overnight camping. The northern portion of Discovery Island, Chatham Island, and some of the smaller islets are First Nations Reserve lands and are closed to the public.

Discovery Island Marine Provincial Park is centered around the southern portion of the island at Rudlin Bay. A nearly mile-long trail meanders the southern shoreline, linking Commodore Point with the camping area and eastern lighthouse area (access is not permitted to the lighthouse compound). A pit toilet is available for visitors and campers. Strictly enforced rules for the park include no pets of any kind allowed ashore, no campfires, mandatory use of food caches while camping for food and fragrant items, and to stay within park boundaries and trails.

Unfortunately Rudlin Bay has no safe or protected anchorage. The bay is rocky with detached reefs, and is open to the exposed waters and currents of Juan de Fuca and Haro Straits. Those who visit Discovery Island usually come by small boat or kayak, and have thorough local

Staqeya

In 2012, reports of a lone wolf on Chatham and Discovery Islands began to filter into authorities. A rarity in this heavily populated section of Vancouver Island, this coastal gray wolf, named Staqeya by the Songhees, is now a permanent resident of the island group. It is unclear where or why the wolf swam to the islands and stayed, but he now enjoys a solitary island life set under the glow of suburban Victoria. Through scat analysis, Staqeya feasts mostly on harbour seals and the occasional water fowl. To insure Staqeya's healthy survival, please respect his privacy, do not leave food for him, and follow park rules for his and your safety.

knowledge of the area. Keep in mind that these islands are set amongst an area with very strong currents and frequent winds that can create dangerous rip tides and steep waves.

Chatham Island, the northern portion of Discovery Island, and a number of the surrounding islets are First Nations Reserve land and under the control of the Songhees First Nation. Several of the nearby islets are also a part of the Oak Bay Island's Ecological Reserve. To be respectful of these private islands and islets, please do not enter into these sensitive areas. These islands are surveilled and regularly patrolled with strict enforcement and steep fines.

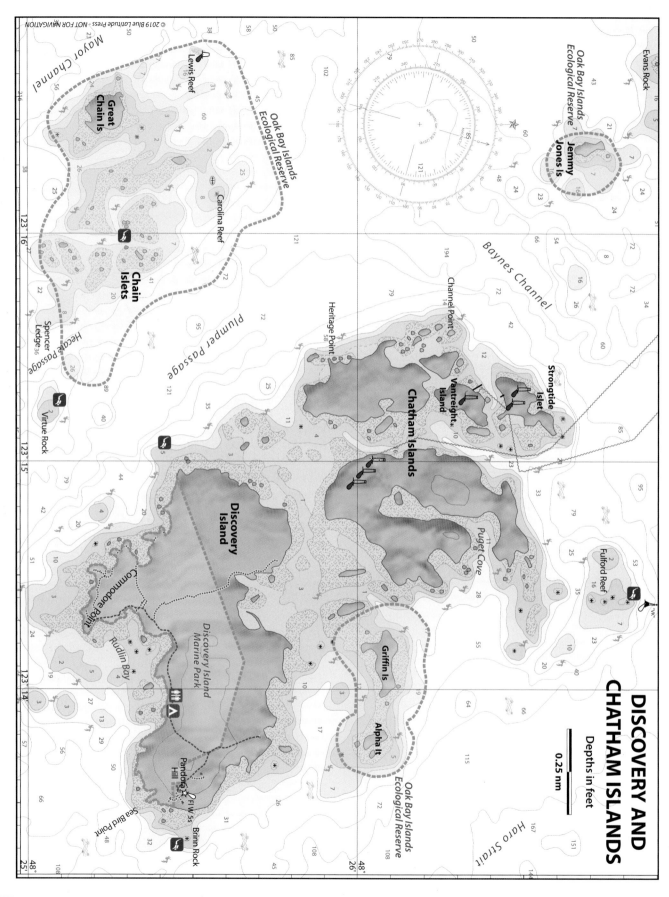

© 2019 Blue Latitude Press – NOT FOR NAVIGATION

Mayor Channel

Lewis Reef

Great
Chain Is

Oak Bay Islands
Ecological Reserve

Carolina Reef

Chain
Islets

Spencer
Ledge

Hecate Passage

Plumper Passage

Virtue Rock

Heritage Point

Channel Point

Baynes Channel

Evans Rock

Oak Bay Islands
Ecological Reserve

Jemmy
Jones Is

Strongtide
Islet

Vantreight
Island

Chatham Islands

Puget Cove

Fulford Reef

Discovery
Island

Commodore Point

Rudlin Bay

Discovery Island
Marine Park

Griffin Is

Alpha It

Pandora
Hill

Sea Bird Point

Brinn Rock

Fl W 5s

Oak Bay Islands
Ecological Reserve

Haro Strait

DISCOVERY AND CHATHAM ISLANDS

Depths in feet

0.25 nm

©Kevin Oke

Cordova Bay

Tree-filled cliff tops and the 460 acre Mount Douglas Park shield the unassuming anchorage at Cordova Bay from the nearby urban corridor stretching north from Victoria. This quiet bay, tucked in behind Cormorant Point, offers a pleasant stop for boats traveling north or southbound. Thirteen miles of trails traverse the beach-side Mount Douglas Park, offering scenic vistas of the surrounding island-strewn landscape and the metropolitan area of Victoria.

Cordova Bay is located approximately 10 miles south of the town of Sidney on Vancouver Island. The bay is formed by Gordon Head and Cormorant Point to the southeast. The far northern portion of the bay up to Cordova Spit is part of Military Exercise Area WC.

Approaching from the south, boats should be aware of Johnstone Reef, which lies 1 mile east of Finnerty Cove. Port hand buoy "V29" marks the north end of the reef. Once approaching the bay and rounding Gordon Head, be

sure to locate Gordon Rock, which lies roughly 0.15 miles off the headland. For boats approaching from the north, be sure to locate the rock hazards known as Zero Rock and Little Zero Rock. These reefs lie nearly 2 miles north-northeast of Cormorant Point. Zero Rock is marked by a

Cordova Bay	Bedwell Harbour (South Pender Island)	16 nm
	Ganges Harbour (Salt Spring Island)	25 nm
	Genoa Bay	22 nm
	Montague Harbour (Galiano Island)	25 nm
	Nanaimo	52 nm
	Oak Bay	7 nm
	Saanichton Bay	7 nm
	Sidney Spit (Sidney Island)	10 nm
	Telegraph Harbour (Thetis Island)	35 nm
	Victoria	13 nm
	Winter Cove (Saturna Island)	22 nm

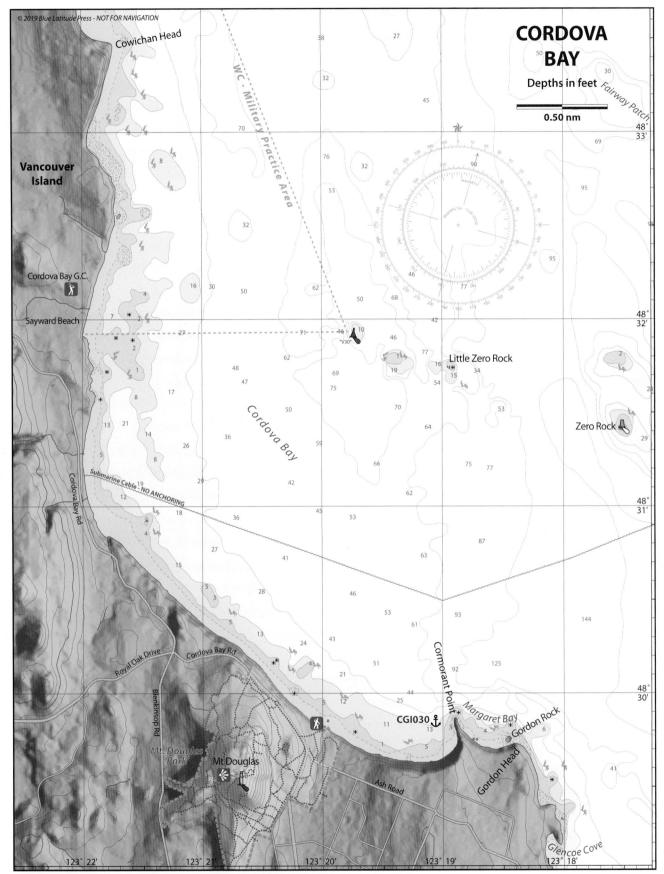

© 2019 Blue Latitude Press - NOT FOR NAVIGATION

Cowichan Head

WC - Military Practice Area

CORDOVA BAY

Depths in feet

Fairway Patch

0.50 nm

Vancouver Island

Cordova Bay G.C.

Sayward Beach

Little Zero Rock

Cordova Bay

Zero Rock

Cordova Bay Rd

Submarine Cable - NO ANCHORING

Cormorant Point

CGI030 ⚓

Margaret Bay

Gordon Rock

Royal Oak Drive

Cordova Bay Rd

Blenkinsop Rd

Gordon Head

Mt. Douglas Park

Mt. Douglas

Ash Road

Glencoe Cove

123° 22'   123° 21'   123° 20'   123° 19'   123° 18'

CGI030 - 48° 29.805'N 123° 19.086'W

View from the top of Mount Douglas

navigation light, as well as the eastern extent of Little Zero Rock's reef area.

Anchorage can be taken in the southern portion of Cordova Bay, west of Cormorant Point. This anchorage provides westerly to southerly wind protection, but is open to the north and east. During stronger southerly winds, waves can wrap around the point into the anchorage. Anchor in 3 to 5 fathoms over a mostly mud bottom. Near shore, kelp and seaweed beds are found, especially during the summer months.

To access the trails at Mount Douglas Park, dinghies and kayaks can be landed at the beach near the outflow of a small stream. From here, a trail can be picked up that heads towards park facilities including picnic tables, restrooms and park information signs. The park has conveniently labeled their maps with trails being either easy, moderate or difficult for the novice to experienced hiker. The peak of Mount Douglas stands at 750 feet and affords amazing views, well worth the exhilarating hike to the top! For pet owners, be aware that dogs are not permitted on the beach or playground areas at the park.

Mount Douglas viewing platform

Beach at Mount Douglas Park

Chapter 2

Sidney Area

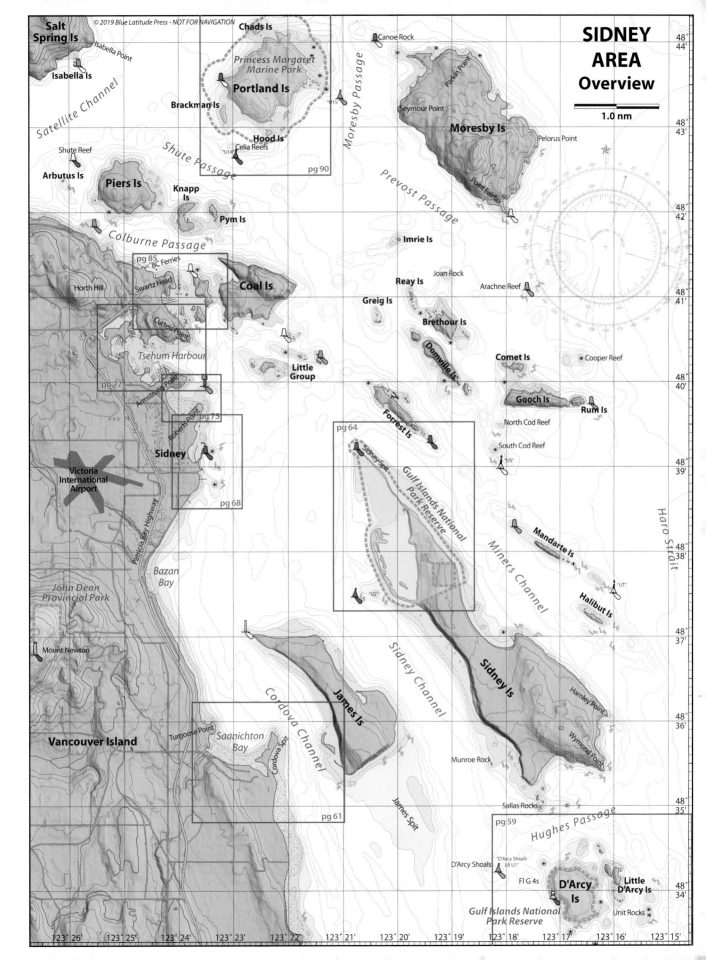

Salt Spring Is

Isabella Point

Isabella Is

Shute Reef

Arbutus Is

Piers Is

Knapp Is

Pym Is

Colburne Passage

pg 85

BC Ferries

Horth Hill

Swartz Head

Coal Is

Curteis Point

Tsehum Harbour

pg 77

Armstrong Point

Roberts Point

pg 73

Sidney

pg 68

Victoria International Airport

Patricia Bay Highway

Bazan Bay

John Dean Provincial Park

Mount Newton

Vancouver Island

Turgoose Point

Saanichton Bay

Cordova Spit

Cordova Channel

pg 61

Satellite Channel

Shute Passage

Chads Is

Princess Margaret Marine Park

Portland Is

Brackman Is

Hood Is

"U14"

"U15"

Celia Reefs

Little Group

pg 90

Canoe Rock

Moresby Passage

Parkin Point

Seymour Point

Moresby Is

Pelorus Point

Point Fairfax

Prevost Passage

Imrie Is

Joan Rock

Reay Is

Greig Is

Brethour Is

Domville Is

Arachne Reef

Comet Is

Cooper Reef

Gooch Is

Rum Is

North Cod Reef

South Cod Reef

"US"

Forest Is

pg 64

Sidney Spit

Gulf Islands National Park Reserve

"U2"

Mandarte Is

"UT"

Halibut Is

Miners Channel

Haro Strait

James Is

Sidney Channel

Sidney Is

Harney Point

Munroe Rock

Wymond Point

James Spit

Sallas Rocks

Hughes Passage

pg 59

D'Arcy Shoals

"D'Arcy Shoals" LB U1"

Fl G 4s

D'Arcy Is

Little D'Arcy Is

Unit Rocks

Gulf Islands National Park Reserve

SIDNEY AREA Overview

1.0 nm

© 2019 Blue Latitude Press - NOT FOR NAVIGATION

48° 44'
48° 43'
48° 42'
48° 41'
48° 40'
48° 39'
48° 38'
48° 37'
48° 36'
48° 35'
48° 34'

123° 26' 123° 25' 123° 24' 123° 23' 123° 22' 123° 21' 123° 20' 123° 19' 123° 18' 123° 17' 123° 16' 123° 15'

©Kevin Oke

D'Arcy Island

D'Arcy Island, bordering the western side of Haro Strait, is part of the Gulf Islands National Park Reserve. Primarily used by kayakers due to its lack of protected anchorage sites and surrounding reefs, the island offers seven walk-in campsites, along with picnic tables and a pit toilet (no campfires allowed).

D'Arcy Island lies one mile south of Sidney Island and is flanked by numerous rocks, shoals and reefs including Kelp Reefs, Unit Rocks, and D'Arcy Shoals. Reefs, kelp, a rocky bottom and lack of wind and wave protection make the island a less than favorable anchorage. A park ranger buoy is located on the eastern side of the island, but is not for public use. Shells of former buildings can still be seen today reminding visitors of the island's somber history as a leper colony.

Chinese Leper Colony

Up until recent times, Hansen's Disease, or leprosy, was believed to be a highly contagious disease and held a definite social stigma world-wide. It was once common for lepers to be separated and placed into far removed "colonies." Today, it is known that Hansen's Disease is not highly contagious and is curable through treatment with antibiotics.

In the late 1800's however, leprosy was still greatly feared, and discrimination of Chinese immigrants was rampant. In the spring of 1891, five Chinese men were discovered in Victoria to have been suffering from leprosy. City government officials worked quickly to find a location to quarantine the men. They selected remote D'Arcy Island to be the official leprosarium for the area. Although Canada already had a federally run leprosarium in New Brunswick, complete with hospital and medical care, the federal government declined to take Victoria's suffering men. The hospital in New Brunswick provided care to Caucasians, not Chinese.

In May of 1891, the five men were forcibly removed from the city and taken to D'Arcy Island. The men were dropped at the island with meager accommodations and supplies. Every three months a steam ship would arrive with the medical health officer who provided the bare necessities in food and clothing, but no real medical treatment. For years, the men suffered alone, in pain, and in dire living conditions.

Numerous reports were sent to the provincial government describing the deplorable living conditions and lack of medical treatment. In 1905, the BC government assumed control from the city, and increased food and supply shipments to once every month. In 1906, Canada passed the Leprosy Act, in which the federal government assumed control over all leprosariums, including D'Arcy Island. Medical staff providing treatment and pain management, better living structures and supplies were finally made available to those exiled on the island.

From 1891 to 1924, 49 men were banished to D'Arcy, 43 of which were Chinese. Of these 49, 20 Chinese men and 1 Japanese man were deported. In 1924, the remaining 6 men were moved to Bentinck Island and D'Arcy was officially closed. Bentinck remained in operation until its closure in 1957.

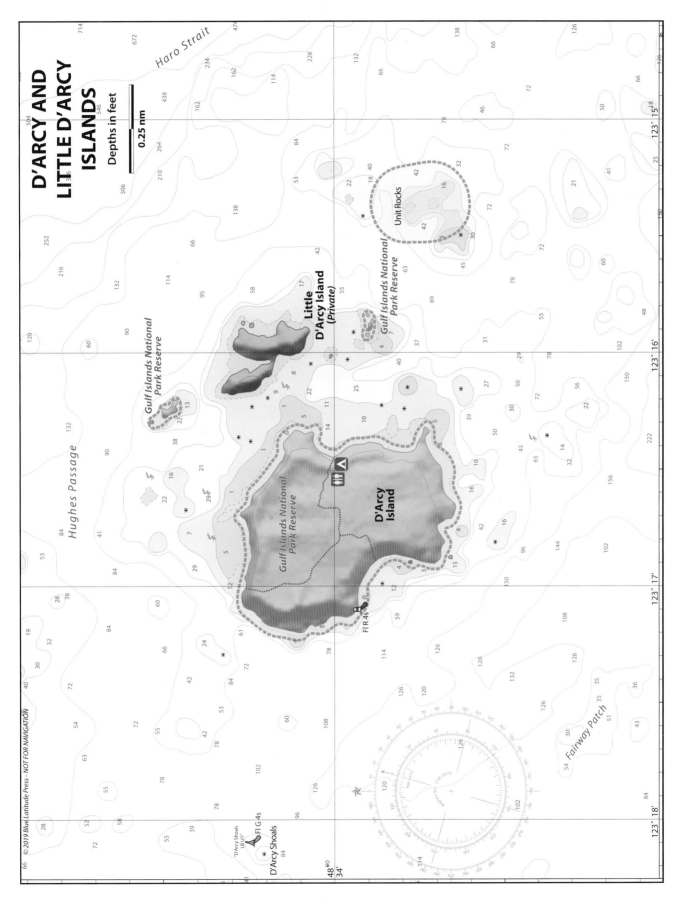

D'ARCY AND LITTLE D'ARCY ISLANDS

Depths in feet

0.25 nm

Haro Strait

Hughes Passage

Gulf Islands National Park Reserve

Little D'Arcy Island (Private)

Gulf Islands National Park Reserve

Unit Rocks

Gulf Islands National Park Reserve

D'Arcy Island

Gulf Islands National Park Reserve

Fl R 4s

Fairway Patch

D'Arcy Shoals

"D'Arcy Shoals LB U1"

Fl G 4s

123° 15'

123° 16'

123° 17'

123° 18'

48° 34'

© 2019 Blue Latitude Press - NOT FOR NAVIGATION

Saanichton Bay

With miles of beautiful sand beach to stroll and a large protected bay for a comfortable night's sleep, Saanichton Bay is a welcome stop for boaters. Located a mere three and a half miles south of the quaint seaside town of Sidney, the bay offers a quiet anchorage with close proximity to the luxuries of town. Much of Saanichton Bay and Cordova Spit are part of the Tsawout First Nations Reserve, and was one of the main historic winter village sites of the Saanich people.

Saanichton Bay is located on the east side of Saanich Peninsula and one mile west of James Island. Access to the bay is taken via Cordova Channel, which separates James Island from the peninsula. For boats approaching from the south, be sure to locate the reefs of Zero Rock and Little Zero Rock, as well as the extensive shallow water off the south end of James Island. Give the sandy point of Cordova Spit ample room when rounding into the bay. Approaching from the north is relatively free from obstructions.

Once inside the bay, be aware that the head of the bay is quite shallow with extensive mud flats at low water. Anchorage can be taken throughout the bay in 3 to 6 fathoms over a mud bottom. A few private moorings are found in the bay for local island residents as well commercial moorings for the occasional barge. This anchorage provides shelter from most winds except northerly. Due to the low sand spit, little wind abatement will be had during southeast winds, but the anchorage will afford good wave protection.

The western shore of Saanichton Bay provides a public wharf at Turgoose Point for easy trips to shore. The 30 foot long public dock is located on the southwest side of the wharf. To walk Cordova Spit and the beach south, dinghies and kayaks can be landed on the sandy shore. This is First Nations Reserve land, and in order to protect the delicate clam, oyster and eelgrass beds, boaters are asked to land/

Saanichton Bay to:		
Birds Eye Cove		19 nm
Friday Harbor (USA)		20 nm
Ganges Harbour (Salt Spring Island)		19 nm
Nanaimo		45 nm
Oak Bay		13 nm
Pirates Cove (De Courcy Island)		37 nm
Port Browning (North Pender Island)		18 nm
Roche Harbor (USA)		11 nm
Russell Island		10 nm
Sidney		4 nm
Tod Inlet		18 nm
Victoria		19 nm

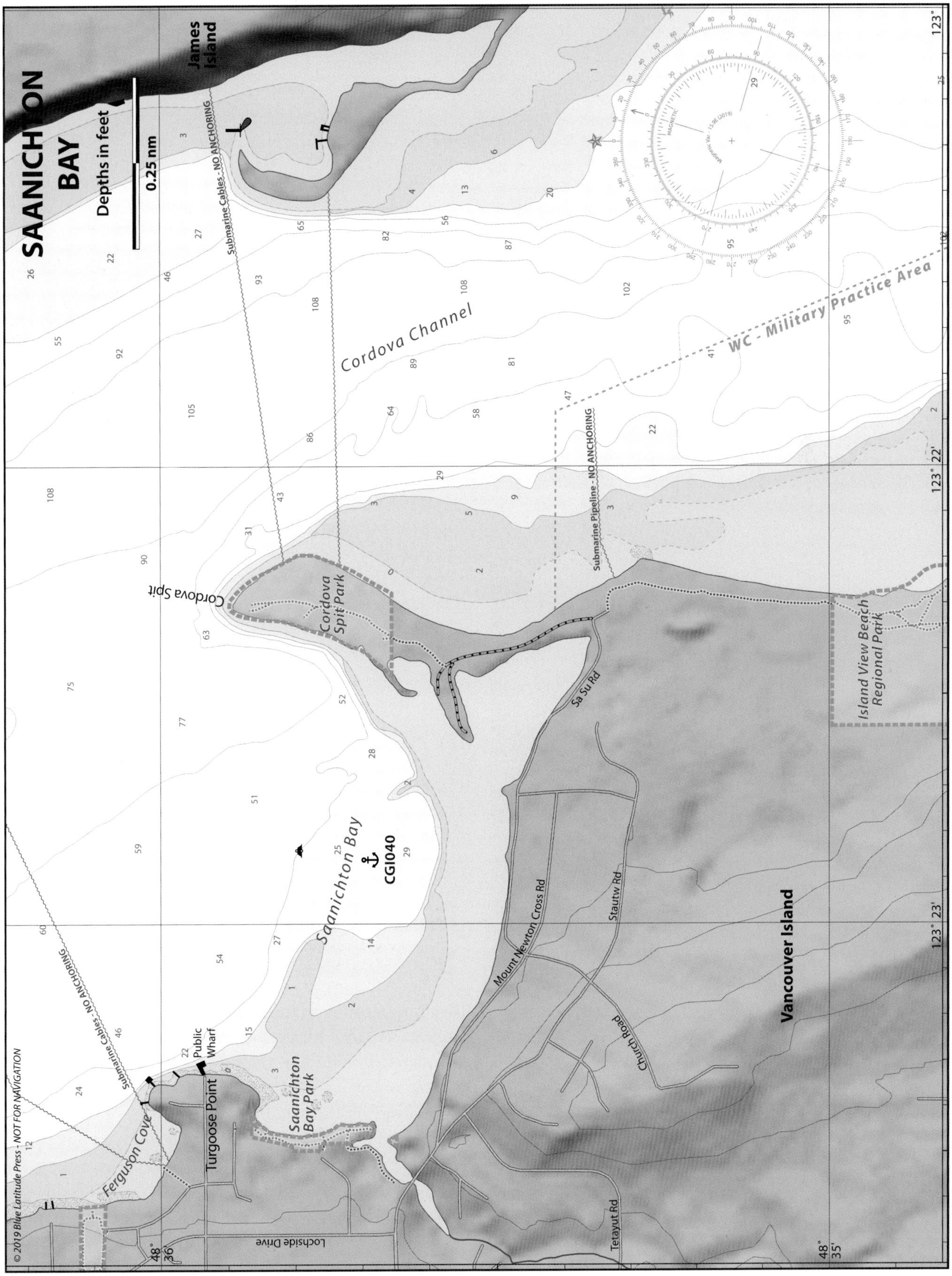

SAANICHTON BAY

Depths in feet

0.25 nm

James Island

Submarine Cables - NO ANCHORING

3

65

27

46

93

108

26

22

55

92

105

86

108

43

31

90

63

75

77

51

59

60

54

27

1

15

22

24

46

12

1

Cordova Channel

82

56

87

102

108

81

58

64

89

29

9

5

3

2

0

2

3

2

28

52

Cordova Spit

Cordova Spit Park

Saanichton Bay

⚓
CGIO40

25

29

14

Saanichton Bay Park

3

Public Wharf

Turgoose Point

Ferguson Cove

Submarine Cables - NO ANCHORING

WC – Military Practice Area

41

47

2

22

Submarine Pipeline - NO ANCHORING

Island View Beach Regional Park

Sa Su Rd

Mount Newton Cross Rd

Stautw Rd

Church Road

Vancouver Island

Tetayut Rd

Lochside Drive

4

6

13

20

Saanichton Bay Park

123°

35'

123° 22'

123° 23'

48°
36'

48°
35'

CGIO40 - 48° 35.690'N 123° 22.860'W

61

Cordova Spit and James Island

Yellow Sand Verbena

southern BC. Together with the lagoon and wetlands, the spit provides refuge and nesting sites to over 120 species of birds. The spit is also one of the rare homes to the endangered sand verbena moth. The moth's only known host plant is the Yellow Sand Verbena, which is found growing on the sandy dunes.

Further down Cordova Channel is the Island View Beach Regional Park. This waterfront park is also part of the coastal dune system and offers a nice loop trail through the dunes and marshland. Camping, picnic tables, drinking water and pit toilets are available at the park and campground. Keep in mind dogs are not allowed on the beach at the park above the natural boundary of the sea from June 1 to September 15, except to pass through on a leash.

James Island

James Island lies between Sidney Island to the east and the Saanich Peninsula on Vancouver Island to the west. The island has striking white cliffs on its southern end, and long stretches of sandy spits off its northern, western, and southern shores. In 1913 the island was purchased by Canadian Explosives Ltd. who constructed a munitions plant and company village on the island. During the company's peak, the village held more than 50 residences, a store and post office, a school, and a sports field. By 1961 the company shut the village down, transporting workers to the island from nearby Saanichton Bay. In 1978 the plant was permanently closed on the island and eventually demolished. Today James Island is in private ownership with no public access.

launch only at high tides. Due to the sensitive ecosystem on this very special coastal dune, dogs are not allowed and visitors are asked to stick to the trails.

According to the Tsawout, Cordova Spit or ȾIXEN, is one of the few intact coastal dune ecosystems left in

©Kevin Oke

Sidney Spit

With its Caribbean hues of white beaches and turquoise waters, Sidney Spit evokes a sense of the tropics in the middle of the Pacific Northwest. Located at the northern end of Sidney Island, there is no question why Sidney Spit is part of the Gulf Islands National Park Reserve. At low tide, the spit emerges offering over a mile of sand beach to stroll and tidal flats to investigate. South of the spit, trails meander around the park and through the forested campground. The large lagoon is a bird watchers paradise with resident and migrating birds taking safe haven in the protected waters. During the summer months, a

©Kevin Oke

Sidney Spit to:		
Friday Harbor (USA)	18 nm
Ganges Harbour (Salt Spring Island)	16 nm
Genoa Bay	14 nm
Nanaimo	43 nm
Pirates Cove (De Courcy Island)	32 nm
Princess Bay (Portland Island)	5 nm
Roche Harbor (USA)	9 nm
Sidney	2.5 nm
Silva Bay (Gabriola Island)	38 nm
Tod Inlet	16 nm
Victoria	22 nm

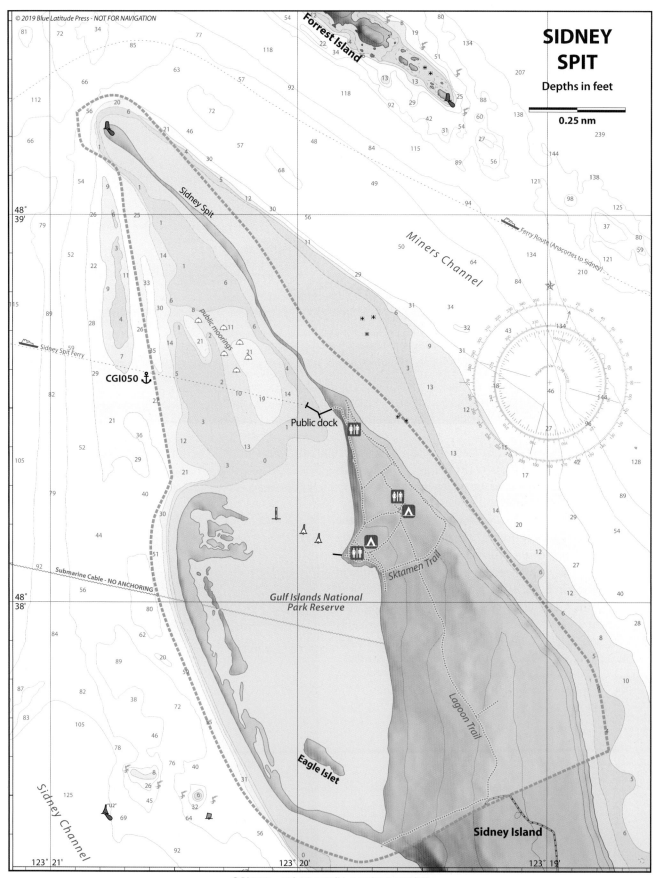

© 2019 Blue Latitude Press - NOT FOR NAVIGATION

Forrest Island

SIDNEY SPIT

Depths in feet

0.25 nm

Sidney Spit

Miners Channel

Ferry Route (Anacortes to Sidney)

MAGNETIC

Sidney Spit Ferry

CGI050

Public moorings

Public dock

Gulf Islands National Park Reserve

Sktamen Trail

Lagoon Trail

Submarine Cable - NO ANCHORING

Eagle Islet

Sidney Channel

"U2"

Sidney Island

CGI050 - 48° 38.570'N 123° 20.600'W

foot ferry from Sidney provides transportation to tourists and campers for all to enjoy this beautiful park.

Sidney Island is located approximately 2.5 miles east of the town of Sidney, and is bordered on either side by Miners Channel and Sidney Channel. The southeast portion of the island lies along Haro Strait, separating Canadian and US waters. Sidney Spit is found at the far northern end of the island, with the northern point marked by a red and white light tower.

For boats approaching from the south via Sidney Channel, be sure to locate Sidney Channel light buoy "U2." This buoy marks the western extent of shoals stretching out from Sidney Island near the north end of Sidney Channel. Currents in Sidney Channel can be quite swift so plan your travel accordingly.

For boats approaching via Miners Channel, be aware of the shallows found southwest of Halibut Island near the southern entrance to the channel. The green and white tower of Mandarte Island North light marks the detached reef lying off the northwest end of Mandarte Island.

If approaching from the north, be aware that currents near the Sidney area can be strong, flowing in a north (flood) and south (ebb) direction. Be sure to locate the Little Group, which is a group of islands, reefs and shoals approximately one mile northwest from the tip of Sidney Spit. Dock Island, the eastern most island in the Little Group is marked by a white and green light tower.

Once near the Sidney Spit anchorage, be sure to follow the Canadian government chart closely as shallow areas are scattered throughout the approach and can lead to groundings without careful attention. Do check your tide tables before entering and anchoring as a good anchor spot at high tide maybe a poor location at low tide.

Sidney Spit offers ample room for boats at anchor. The park also provides mooring buoys and dock space for visitors. Be sure to check the chart before approaching the mooring field as it has shallow areas to the west and north. Be aware the public park dock is shallow and meant for shallow draft boats and dinghies. The end tie of the dock is reserved for the summertime foot ferry from Sidney. The dock is removed in the fall and winter months.

Anchorage can be taken throughout the area in 2 to 6 fathoms over a sand and mud bottom. This anchorage is best suited for periods of light wind. Better southerly and westerly protection can be taken at nearby Saanichton Bay or at the marinas in Sidney or Tsehum Harbour.

For trips to shore, dinghies and kayaks can be landed on the beach at the spit or at the park dock. Please be aware that water craft of any kind, including kayaks, SUPs, and row boats, are not allowed within the lagoon. The lagoon

Sidney Island Brick and Tile Co. bricks

Lagoon pier

Yellow Sand Verbena

Sidney Spit Light

is closed to all boats except authorized personnel to protect the water fowl within the salt marsh.

Once on shore, the park offers miles of walking either on the sand spit at low tide or on one of the park's many trails. Be sure to take the walk down to the pier overlooking the lagoon. This was once the site of Sidney Island Brick and Tile Company which operated on the island from 1906 to 1915. Using the island's fine clay deposits, bricks were made from this location to support the region's construction boom. Piles of whole and broken bricks are still scattered throughout the area, some even turned into elaborate cairns from visiting campers.

From the lagoon pier, visitors have an amazing view of the of the salt marsh, perfect for bird watching. Along with being a perfect habitat for shorebirds, Sidney Island is also part of the Pacific Flyway, making it an important food and rest stop along the birds' migration path. In March and April, Brant geese can be seen, and during July and August, hundreds of Rhinoceros auklets and Heermann's gulls can be found.

Sidney Spit offers campsites from May 15 to September 30 (from November 1 to February 29 Sidney Island is closed to facilitate traditional hunting by first nations). Currently the water system at the park is undergoing repairs and potable water is unavailable until further notice.

©Kevin Oke

Sidney

The idyllic seaside town known as "Sidney by the Sea," boasts some of the islands' most incredible views and a true welcoming spirit. With a population of only 11,000, this quaint coastal town is centered around the waterfront and its main thoroughfare of Beacon Street. Waterside parks and walking paths line the shore offering sweeping views of Mt Baker and the Gulf and San Juan Islands. Inviting shops, educational museums, and delicious eateries provide endless entertainment options for visitors.

Located on the northern end of Saanich Peninsula, Sidney is near the main hub of transportation to and from Vancouver Island. The Victoria International Airport lies a mere 2.5 miles from the marina, and the immense Swartz Bay Terminal for BC Ferries is only 3.5 miles to the north. Ferry transport to and from the US via the Washington State Ferries is available from a terminal located less than a half mile south of the marina.

Sidney is located on the eastern shore of north Saanich Peninsula on Vancouver Island, and roughly two miles west from the popular anchorage at Sidney Spit. Two large

rock breakwaters lie off the town and provide shelter to the Port Sidney Marina.

When approaching Sidney, caution should be taken as two shoals lie just off the approach to town and the entrance to the marina. One shoal is located 0.2 miles southeast of the public wharf and is marked by port hand buoy "U5." The other shoal is located 0.2 miles northeast

Sidney to:		
	Bedwell Harbour *(South Pender Island)*	9 nm
	Friday Harbor *(USA)*	19 nm
	Ganges Harbour *(Salt Spring Island)*	16 nm
	Ladysmith	30 nm
	Montague Harbour	16 nm
	Nanaimo	42 nm
	Pirates Cove *(De Courcy Island)*	34 nm
	Princess Bay *(Portland Island)*	4 nm
	Roche Harbor *(USA)*	10 nm
	Sidney Spit *(Sidney Island)*	2.5 nm
	Tod Inlet	15 nm
	Victoria	23 nm

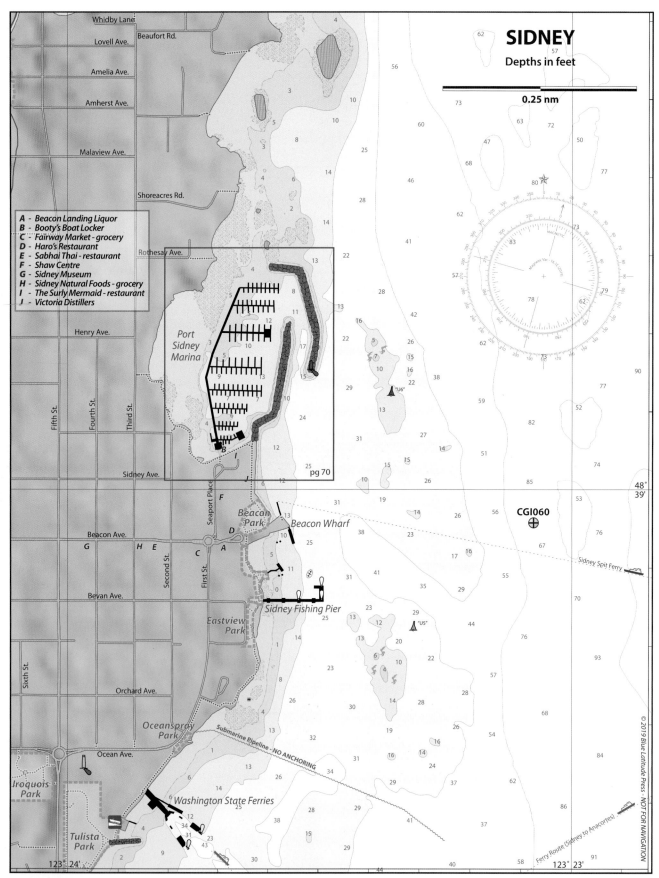

SIDNEY
Depths in feet

0.25 nm

A - Beacon Landing Liquor
B - Booty's Boat Locker
C - Fairway Market - grocery
D - Haro's Restaurant
E - Sabhai Thai - restaurant
F - Shaw Centre
G - Sidney Museum
H - Sidney Natural Foods - grocery
I - The Surly Mermaid - restaurant
J - Victoria Distillers

Port Sidney Marina

pg 70

Beacon Park

Beacon Wharf

Sidney Fishing Pier

Eastview Park

Oceanspray Park

Iroquois Park

Tulista Park

Washington State Ferries

Submarine Pipeline - NO ANCHORING

Ferry Route (Sidney to Anacortes)

Sidney Spit Ferry

CGI060

© 2019 Blue Latitude Press - NOT FOR NAVIGATION

CGI060 - 48° 38.960'N 123° 23.080'W

Sidney waterfront

of the public wharf and is marked by starboard hand buoy "U6." As most vessel traffic to Sidney is entering or leaving the marina, it is important for boats to locate these shoals, especially "U6," prior to approach.

It is also important to keep in mind that the currents off Sidney can be quite strong. Be sure to check the current atlas when approaching the Sidney area.

For boats entering the marina, access can only be taken through the rock breakwaters immediately south of the Sidney Breakwater light. Due to rocks and shoal water, access cannot be taken north of the marina. The entrance between the two rock breakwaters is approximately 100 feet wide. Boats entering Sidney from foreign waters must report to the Canadian Border Services Agency (CBSA) customs dock which is located just inside the marina's breakwaters at the end of G dock. The customs dock is approximately 95 feet in length.

The public wharf is located off Beacon Avenue and houses a fish market and small walk-up restaurant. A newer 70 foot dock has been added to the north side of the wharf where foot ferries pick up and drop off passengers. Due to the open nature of the water surrounding the Sidney waterfront, anchorage is best suited for daytime lunch or provisioning stops in settled weather.

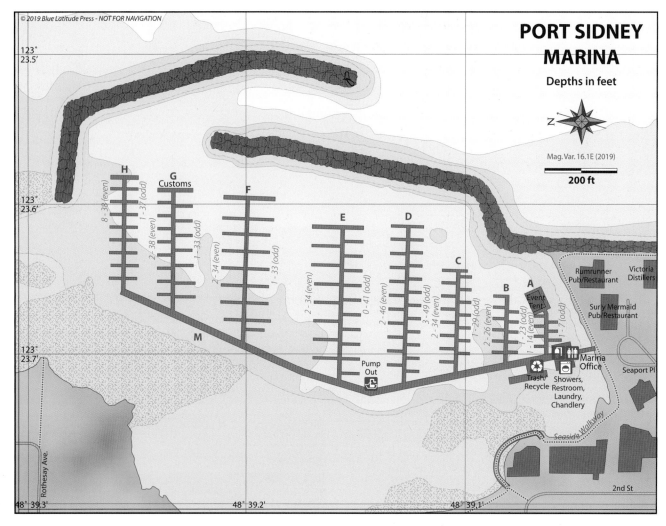

Port Sidney Marina

The Port of Sidney Marina is located in the heart of the seaside town of Sidney. The marina can accommodate vessels up to 125 feet in length with potable water and electrical hook ups (30/50 and 100 amp) for each slip. The Port of Sidney Marina is also a Port of Entry for vessels needing to clear into Canada with a customs dock located near the entrance. Services at the marina include restrooms, showers, laundry facilities, gated entry, free wifi, a pumpout station for boats up to 38 feet in length, and garbage and recycling areas.

For provisioning, the Fairway Market is located about two blocks from the marina. Shopping carts can be taken back to your boat and returned to the pick-up area at the top of the dock ramp.

Port Sidney Marina
Monitors VHF channel 66A
9835 Seaport Place
Sidney, BC V8L 4X3
(250) 655-3711
admin@portsidney.com
www.portsidney.com

Sidney Spit ferry with Mt. Baker

Sights to See

No trip to Sidney would be complete without a visit to the Shaw Centre for the Salish Sea. This aquarium and learning center has over 160 species of marine life, a marine mammal artifact exhibit, and a unique Coast Salish art collection. The Centre opened in 2009 and is an award winning aquarium and learning center dedicated exclusively to the Salish Sea Bioregion of British Columbia. 28 aquarium habitats hold over 3,500 animals including a giant pacific octopus, wolf eels, and pacific salmon. Exhibits also include a 'hands-on' touch pool experience, and a fully intact killer whale skeleton and marine mammal artifact display. The Shaw Centre is located at the Sidney Pier Hotel and Spa on the corner of Beacon Avenue and Seaport Place. For further information on visiting the Centre check their website at: www.salishseacentre.org.

After a visit to the Shaw Center, check out the Sidney Museum and Archives located on Beacon Avenue and 4th Street. Established in 1971, the museum collects, preserves and displays significant historical artifacts and materials from Sidney and the North Saanich area. The museum is home to 7,000 permanent artifacts, along with monthly rotating displays. For further information on the museum, including hours and rates, check their website at: www.sidneymuseum.ca

Sidney Street Market

If you're lucky enough to be in Sidney on a Thursday night during the summer, the Street Market is an entertaining, family friendly must see. Each Thursday evening from June through August, Sidney's Beacon Avenue closes to car traffic as over 150 vendors set up displays and tents. Beginning at 5:30pm, local farmers, artisans, chefs and gardeners offer an amazing array of fresh produce, cheeses, jewelry, clothing, flowers, handmade soaps, breads, and much more. Come hungry to enjoy the many delicious food vendors and live music while shopping, eating and enjoying the market. For further information on the market's seasonal dates and times check: www.sidneystreetmarket.ca.

For those looking for a little exercise and exploration, check out the Lochside Regional Trail. Great for bikers and walkers, this 18 mile trail stretches from Swartz Bay to Victoria, where it connects with the Galloping Goose Regional Trail, extending an additional 34 miles. The former railway line turned paved and gravel trail, begins in Victoria at the Switch Bridge and travels north through urban areas, past beaches, farmlands, and wetlands. To pick up the southbound trail in Sidney, head down 5th Street to the round-about at Ocean Avenue. The trail heads south from the roundabout on 5th and connects with Lochside Drive where it mirrors the shoreline for approximately three miles. For northbound travel, connect with the trail on Beacon Avenue on the east side of Highway 17 (Patricia Bay Highway).

For a quick day trip (or overnight camping) for those who missed the sights at Sidney Island, jump on the foot ferry at Beacon Pier and head over to Sidney Spit. Part of the Gulf Islands National Park Reserve, Sidney Spit (see page 63) offers beautiful sandy beaches for strolling and wooded trails for hiking. The 25-minute summer only ferry, offers multiple sailings daily. For further information including schedules and fares check: www.alpinegroup.ca.

Cocktail enthusiasts will enjoy a tour of the new Victoria Distillery located waterfront, immediately south of the Port Sidney Marina. View the process of distilling fine gins and vodka in beautifully ornate copper stills, along with the blending and bottling process. During the summer months enjoy these craft spirits in their cozy waterfront lounge. For further information on their spirits, tours and hours check: victoriadistillers.com.

Provisioning, Marine Chandleries and Services

BC Liquor Store

A government chain liquor store selling wine, beer, cider and liquor. Located on Beacon Avenue, behind Save-on-Foods.

Beacon Landing Liquor Store

Located next to near the roundabout at Beacon Avenue and 1st Street. Selling a nice selection of beer, cider, wine and liquor.

Booty's Boat Locker

Booty's is a marine chandlery store located at the Port Sidney Marina. The store offers a range of supplies including electronics, cleaning products, fishing gear, docking and mooring supplies, and gifts. www.bootysboatlocker.com, (778) 351-2955

Fairway Market

Located just a block south of the marina, Fairway Market offers fresh produce, meats, dairy, bakery items and all the staples. Located on the corner of Beacon Avenue and 1st Street.

Save-on-Foods

Located in a shopping center on Beacon Avenue, six blocks from the marina. A large chain grocery store supplying fresh produce, meats, dairy, bakery items and all the staples.

Sidney Natural Foods

Specializing in vitamins and natural foods with a nice bulk foods and spices section. Located at 2473 Beacon Avenue.

Thrifty Foods

A chain grocery store selling fresh produce, meats, dairy, bakery items and all the staples. Located in a shopping center on the corner of James White Boulevard and 7th Street.

Restaurants

Haro's Restaurant and Bar

Enjoy sweeping waterfront views and daily happy hours at Haro's with indoor and outdoor patio seating. Fresh, local seafood and produce are used to create excellent meals. Live music on Thursdays. Located in the Sidney Pier Hotel & Spa next to Beacon Park.

Sabhai Thai

A family-owned Thai restaurant serving traditional delicious Thai recipes using wholesome fresh ingredients. Located on Beacon Avenue between 2nd and 3rd Street.

The Surly Mermaid

Located at the Port Sidney Marina, the Surly Mermaid has outdoor and indoor seating with an exceptional view. Serving tasty and fresh pub fare.

Victoria Distillers

Booty's Boat Locker

Shaw Centre for the Salish Sea

Roberts Bay

Bird enthusiasts will welcome a stop at Roberts Bay which is part of the federal Shoal Harbour Migratory Bird Sanctuary. The mostly shallow bay is an annual stop over for a variety of migratory birds including green-winged teal ducks, American wigeon ducks, bufflehead ducks, horned grebes and great blue herons.

Roberts Bay is located on the Saanich Peninsula between Sidney and Tsehum Harbour on Vancouver Island. The bay lies between Roberts Point to the south and Armstrong Point to the north. When approaching Roberts Bay, be sure to locate Graham Rock which lies near the middle of the entrance to the bay. The rock is marked by a port hand daymark from a metal tower.

Much of Roberts Bay is shallow, limiting the area where most can approach or anchor. Mud tidal flats extend out from the shoreline, especially in the southern end of the bay. Shallow anchorage can be taken in 1½ to 2 fathoms over a mostly mud bottom. Be sure to keep a careful eye on the depth sounder when approaching and check the tide tables to make sure you have enough water throughout the changing of the tides.

Public beach access is available at the end of Ardwell Avenue and Bowden Road for trips to shore. These are also popular launch sites for local kayakers. From Bowden Road, it is a one block walk to Van Isle Marina and the Sea Glass Waterfront Grill. When anchoring in the bay and trips to shore, keep in mind that this is a sensitive bird sanctuary. Make sure dogs are always on leashes and do not disturb nesting sites.

Roberts Bay to:		
Bedwell Harbour (South Pender Island)	9 nm
Ganges Harbour (Salt Spring Island)	16 nm
Ladysmith	29 nm
Montague Harbour (Galiano Island)	16 nm
Nanaimo	41 nm
Pirates Cove (De Courcy Island)	32 nm
Roche Harbor (USA)	10 nm
Russell Island	7 nm
Sidney Spit (Sidney Island)	3 nm
Victoria	23 nm
Wallace Island	22 nm

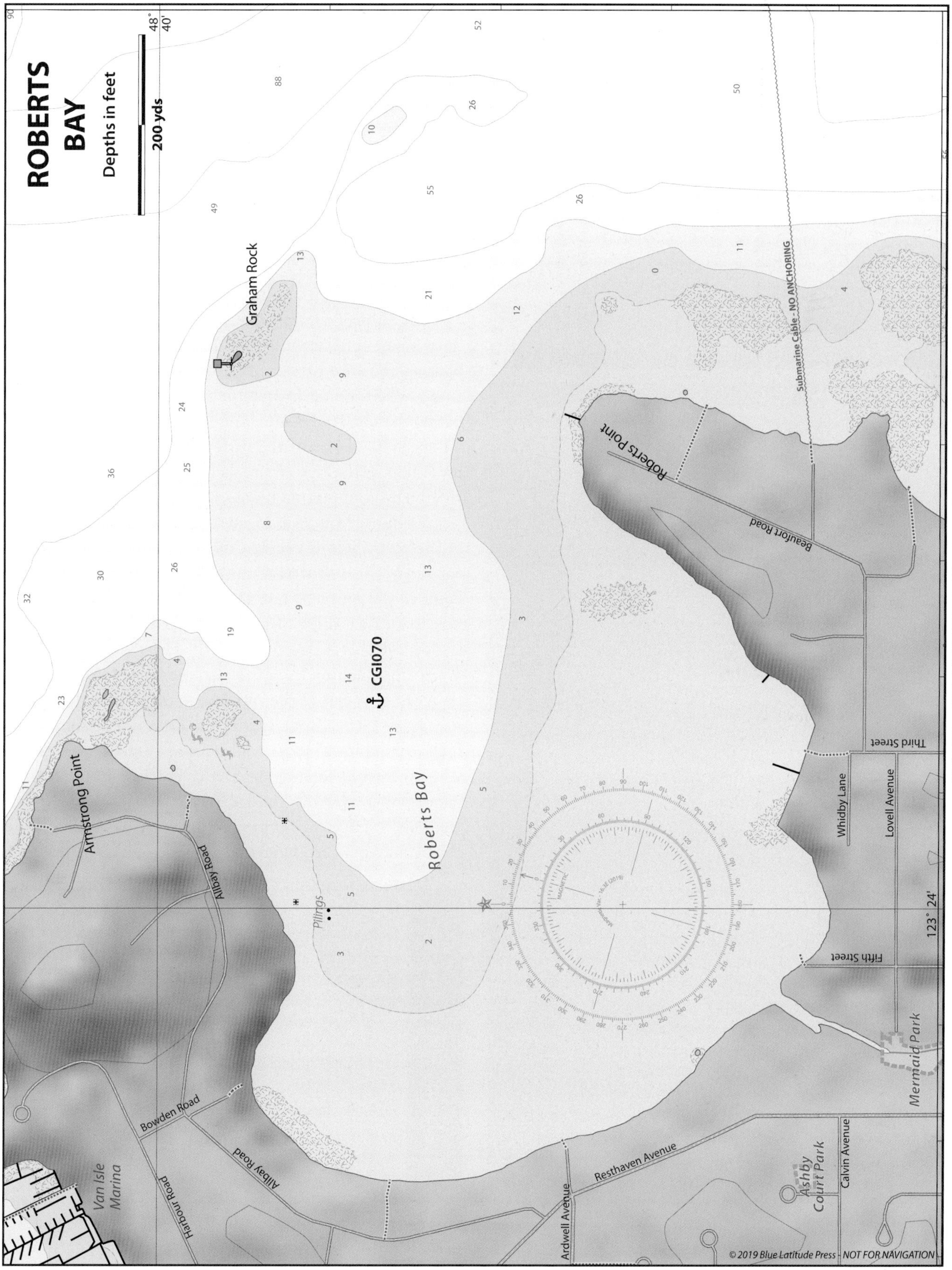

ROBERTS BAY

Depths in feet

200 yds

48°
40'

90

52

88

26

10

55

49

26

50

Graham Rock

13

21

26

11

24

2

9

12

0

25

2

6

Submarine Cable - NO ANCHORING

36

8

9

3

4

30

26

13

9

Roberts Point

32

19

13

Beaufort Road

7

23

14 ⚓ CGI070

13

4

0

Armstrong Point

11

13

11

5

Third Street

Allbay Road

11

5

Whidby Lane

Pilings

5

Roberts Bay

Lovell Avenue

3

2

5

123° 24'

Fifth Street

Bowden Road

Mermaid Park

Harbour Road

Van Isle Marina

Allbay Road

Resthaven Avenue

Ardwell Avenue

Ashby Court Park

Calvin Avenue

© 2019 Blue Latitude Press - NOT FOR NAVIGATION

CGI070 - 48° 39.875′N 123° 23.820′W

©Kevin Oke

©Kevin Oke

Tsehum Harbour

Tsehum Harbour, also known locally as Shoal Harbour, is a boat haven for southern Vancouver Island. Six marinas and yacht clubs are tucked into the naturally protected basins of the harbor. With less than a mile walk from the Swartz Bay ferry terminal, many people from the mainland moor their boats in the marinas at Tsehum Harbour to be closer to the incredible cruising grounds of the Gulf Islands. Fuel docks, marine chandleries, haul out yards, ample marina space, and even a Canada Customs dock make Tsehum Harbour the perfect one stop dock.

The name Tsehum comes from the Tseycum First Nations' name for clay which was found on the bottom of the harbor. The well protected harbor was used by the Tseycum as their winter home. The harbor was also previously known as Shoal Harbour due to the extensive tidal flats found at the heads of the various basins. Today, much of these flats and a few channels have been dredged to provide access and marina moorage.

Tsehum Harbour is located a little over one mile north of the town Sidney on Vancouver Island. The harbour is entered between Curteis Point to the north and Armstrong Point to the south. When approaching from the south, be sure to locate Graham Rock, which lies just east of the entrance to Roberts Bay and is marked by a navigation light. When approaching from the east, the Little Group lies less than one mile east of the entrance to the harbor. True to its name, the Little Group is a formation of small islands and rocks surrounded by drying ledges and shoals.

When approaching from the north, passage can be taken either side of Goudge Island via John Passage or Iroquois Passage, or by passing east of Coal Island. John Passage lies between Coal and Goudge Islands. A few rock

Tsehum Harbour to:		
Birds Eye Cove		19 nm
Ganges Harbour (Salt Spring Island)		19 nm
Ladysmith		33 nm
Nanaimo		45 nm
Oak Bay		13 nm
Pirates Cove (De Courcy Island)		36 nm
Port Browning (North Pender Island)		18 nm
Roche Harbor (USA)		11 nm
Russell Island		10 nm
Sidney		4 nm
Tod Inlet		18 nm
Victoria		19 nm

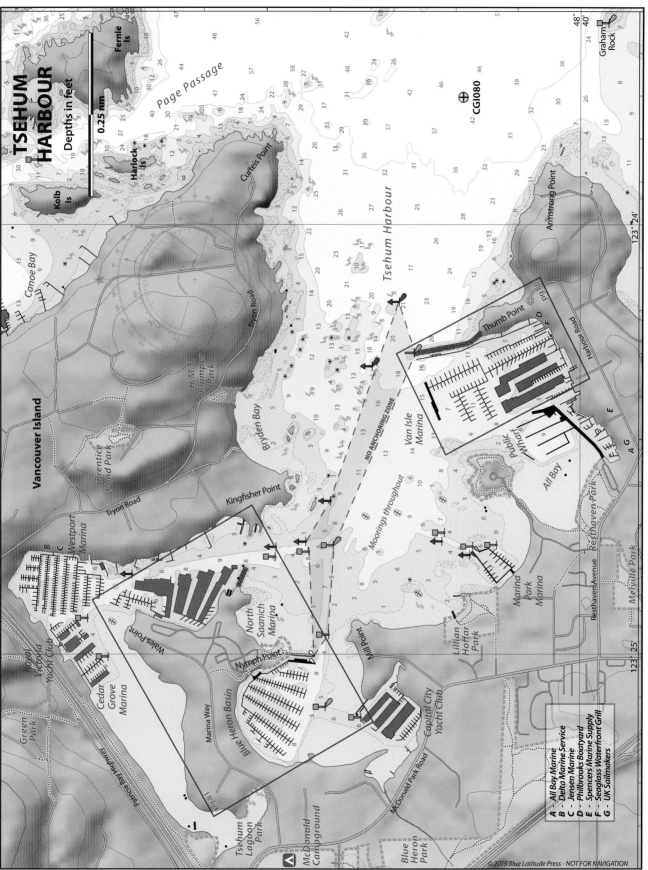

TSEHUM HARBOUR

Depths in feet

0.25 nm

Fernie Is

Kolb Is

Harlock Is

Page Passage

Curteis Point

Vancouver Island

Canoe Bay

H.M.S. Plumper Park

Prentice Pond Park

Tryon Road

Bryden Bay

Kingfisher Point

Tsehum Harbour

Armstrong Point

Graham Rock

⊕ CGI080

NO ANCHORING ZONE

Moorings throughout

Van Isle Marina

Thumb Point

Public Wharf

All Bay

Harbour Road

Resthaven Park

Resthaven Avenue

Melville Park

Marina Park Marina

Lillian Hoffar Park

Mill Point

Nymph Point

Capital City Yacht Club

Blue Heron Basin

Wales Point

North Saanich Marina

Marina Way

Westport Marina

Cedar Grove Marina

Royal Victoria Yacht Club

Green Park

Patricia Bay Highway

McDonald Park Road

McDonald Campground

Tsehum Lagoon Park

Blue Heron Park

A – All Bay Marine
B – Delta Marine Service
C – Jensen Marine
D – Philbrooks Boatyard
E – Spencers Marine Supply
F – Seaglass Waterfront Grill
G – UK Sailmakers

© 2019 Blue Latitude Press - NOT FOR NAVIGATION

CGI080 - 48° 40.190'N 123° 23.700'W

Public Wharf

hazards are found within the pass including John Rock, lying off the southeast side of Goudge Island. On a drying reef immediately north of John Rock is the John Passage daybeacon marked by a port hand daymark. Further up the pass is the Coal Island daybeacon on a drying reef marked by a starboard hand daymark. Drying reefs can also be found extending off Carney Point on Coal Island. For Iroquois Passage, see page 84 for detailed information on transiting the channel.

Once at the entrance to Tsehum Harbour, channel markers direct boats to the inner harbor and marina basins. There are three areas within the harbor: All Bay, Blue Heron Basin, and Tsehum Harbour North. All Bay is in the south of Tsehum Harbour, west of Thumb Point and the extending breakwater off the point. Blue Heron Basin is located on the west side of the harbor. Tsehum Harbour North is on the north side.

To enter the harbor, channel markers can be found off the breakwater at Thumb Point. North of these channel markers and between Kingfisher Point and Curteis Point are shallow areas with a number of detached rocks. Be sure to stay within the designated channel to avoid these hazards.

Van Isle Marina

Tsehum Harbour is operated by the Tsehum Harbour Authority. A 4 knot speed limit is enforced throughout the harbor. A "no anchoring or mooring" area lies between the Tsehum Harbour light and a private light off Nymph Point. Outside of this area, anchoring is permitted, however be cautioned of debris littering the bottom which can snag anchors and chains. Private moorings are also found in this area northwest of All Bay, which has left very little room remaining for visiting boats to anchor. Most visiting boats to Tsehum Harbour will moor at one of the marinas.

A large public wharf is located on the west side of All Bay. Many commercial fishing boats can be found at the wharf, with a number selling freshly caught seafood off the dock. This dock is used primarily by fishing boats and a few long term pleasure boats, many rafted two to three deep. Transient moorage for visiting boats is not typically found at the public wharf. Better options for dock space can be found at Van Isle Marina.

Due to the shallow nature of the harbor, it is important to pay close attention to the tide tables when entering or leaving. This is especially true for the Tsehum Har-

bour North basin. The marked channel leading into this popular basin (home to the large Westport Marina and haulout yard) is narrow and shallow. Unsuspecting boats run aground here every year on their way to or from the marinas and haulout yard. To avoid a grounding, especially for sailboats with deep keels, make sure the tide is high enough for your boat's draft to transit the channel.

Much of the shoreside businesses at Tsehum Harbour are located near All Bay and Westport Marina in Tsehum Harbour North. Marine chandleries and services, haulout yards, marinas, and eateries can be found near these locations. For provisioning, the best grocery stores can be found roughly one mile south in the town of Sidney (see page 73). Transport to Sidney or other locations like Butchart Gardens or Victoria, is offered via the public bus system, cabs or car rentals (see the transport section on page 83).

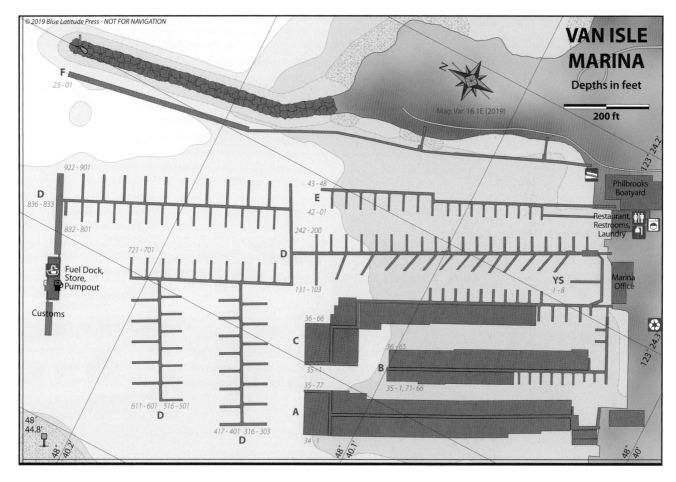

Van Isle Marina

Van Isle Marina is located in the southeast portion of Tsehum Harbour. The 500-slip marina offers transient and permanent mooring options for boats up to 200 feet in length. Each slip has potable water and power hookups (15/30/50/100 amp). A 180-foot, conveniently located, fuel dock offers diesel and ethanol-free gas with fuel flow control to accommodate slow and fast flow (up to 250 liters per minute). The fuel dock also provides a holding tank pumpout station and small marine store selling oils, charts, snacks, beverages and fishing tackle. Services at the marina include restrooms, showers, laundry facilities, free wifi, business center facility, courtesy bicycles, launch ramp, and garbage/recycling disposal. Thrifty Foods offers grocery drop off service to the marina from nearby Sidney. The marina is also a port of entry for Canadian Border Services Agency (CBSA) with a customs dock conveniently located next to the fuel dock.

Van Isle also offers a haul out yard and maintenance/repair services. Their hydraulic trailer is capable of hauling up to 45-tons or vessels up to 70 feet in length to their work yard or long term storage yard. 200 feet of dock space is reserved for service work on boats.

Van Isle Marina
Monitors VHF channel 66A
2320 Harbour Road
Sidney, BC V8L 2P6
(250) 656-1138
info@vanislemarina.com
vanislemarina.com

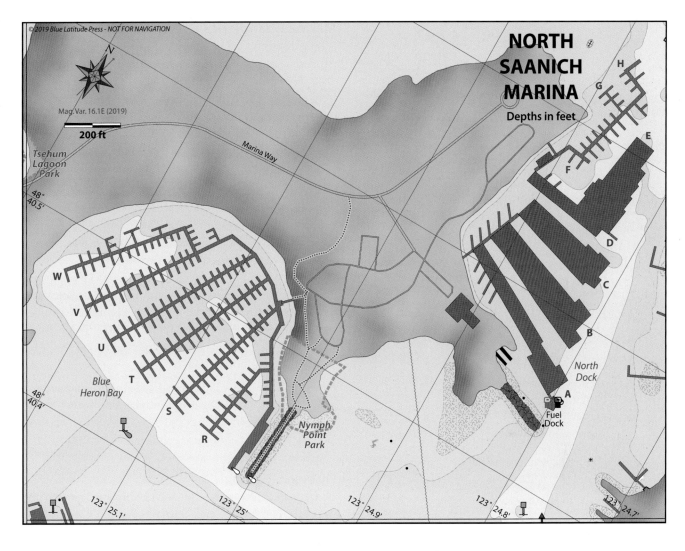

North Saanich Marina

North Saanich Marina, operated by the Oak Bay Marine Group, offers both transient and permanent moorage for boats up to 70 feet in length. Each slip has access to water and power hookups (15, 30 or 50 amp). Services include restrooms, showers, wifi available at the Marina office, and free parking. The marina has a 50 foot fuel dock found at the end of A dock with a small store selling ice, oil, snacks, and tackle. The marina is also home to the Sidney North Saanich Yacht Club. The yacht club and marina is located in Blue Heron Basin.

North Saanich Marina
Monitors VHF channel: 66A
1949 Marina Way
Sidney, BC
(250) 656-5558
nsm@obmg.com
northsaanichmarina.com

Resthaven Park

Marine Chandleries and Services

All Bay Marine

All Bay Marine is a chandlery found at the southern end of Tsehum Harbour near Van Isle Marina. Carrying a nice selection of marine chandlery items and a custom splicing center. The store also offers a dinghy dock for shoppers between 9am and 4pm Monday through Friday. Located at 2204 Harbour Road. www.allbaymarine.com, (250) 656-0153

Delta Marine Service

Operating out of Westport Marina, Delta Marine has over 40 years of experience with high quality yacht repair, haul out services, and custom metal fabrication. Along with a large maintenance shop, Delta has 70 and 65 foot floating boat sheds where work can be carried out while in the water. Delta is also an official Fleming Yachts and Grand Banks Yachts authorized repair and service center. Delta boats over 65 feet in length are hauled at Ocean Pacific in Campbell River. Located at Westport Marina at 2075 Tryon Road. www.delta-marine.com, 250.656.2639

Jensen Marine

Jensen Marine is a chandlery specializing in supplies and services for boats during haul out including paints, cleaners, varnishes, filters, fittings and more. Located at Westport Marina at 2075 Tryon Road. www.jensenmarine.ca, (250) 656-1114

Philbrooks Boatyard

Philbrook's Boatyard is a full-service shipyard, specializing in repair, conversion, and new construction projects. The shipyard's two marine ways can accommodate vessels up to 150 tons or 130 feet. Support shops and services include machine, paint, metal, fiberglass, electrical, engineering, joinery, finishing and upholstery. Located next to Van Isle Marina at 2324 Harbour Road. www.philbrooks.com, (250) 656-1157

Spencers Marine Supply & Consignment

Spencers is a well stocked marine chandlery located near Van Isle Marina. Items include electronics, paints, hardware, gifts and more. Located at 2240 Harbour Road. www.spencersmarinesupply.com, (778) 351-1400

UK Sailmakers

UK Sailmakers Northwest Loft is the largest full production and repair loft in Western Canada. The loft provides dock space to fit new sails or repair sails. Located at 2212 Harbour Road. www.uksailmakers.ca, 1-800-563-7245

Westport Marina

Westport Marina offers a full service marine haul out yard operating a 50 ton travel lift for boats up to 70 feet in length. Boat owners can work on the boat themselves or hire qualified on or off site tradespeople. Services include pressure washing, mast lift, engine crane, water and power use, and more. Westport also operates a 520 slip marina for annual or monthly rates. Located at 2075 Tryon Road. www.thunderbirdmarine.com, (250) 656-2832

Restaurants

Seaglass Waterfront Grill

A beautiful waterfront setting overlooking the Van Isle Marina. Offering savory local harvest meals including fresh seafood and produce. Serving breakfast, lunch, and dinner daily. Located at the head of E dock at Van Isle Marina. www.sgwg.ca , (778) 351-3663

Stonehouse Restaurant & Pub

The Stonehouse is a classic English style manor in a wooded setting offering a tasty pub menu including burgers, fish and chips, pizzas and more. Open for lunch and dinner everyday. Located near the Swartz Bay ferry terminal. stonehousepub.ca, (778) 351-1133

Transportation

BC Transit

BC Transit is the public transit system for Saanich Peninsula, Victoria, and west Victoria. Convenient stops and frequent buses makes for easy travel in this area. Check their website for maps and schedules. bctransit.com, (250) 382-6161

Rental Cars

With Tsehum Harbour located only four miles from the Victoria International Airport, numerous car rental companies are available including National (250-654-0068), Enterprise (250-655-7368), and GSA (250-655-5038).

Sidney Taxi

Sidney Taxi offers convenient taxi service for the Sidney area. Their fleet of five mini vans offer ample space and are dog friendly. Summer is the busy time and advance reservations are recommended. www.sidneytaxiltd.com, (250) 656-6666

Sea Glass Restaurant and Philbrooks Boatyard

Westport Marina

Philbrooks Boatyard

Canoe Bay (Canoe Cove)

Once a safe haven and shipping port for rumrunners delivering banned liquor to the San Juan Islands during the prohibition era, Canoe Cove today supports a thriving, modern marine industry. The naturally protected harbor is home to a large marina, haulout yard and numerous businesses catering to the installation, service, and repair of boats and their systems. Set amidst lush forest land and an island dotted landscape, Canoe Bay, known locally as Canoe Cove, makes a delightful stop for exploring, or for needed repairs or maintenance.

Canoe Cove is located between Tsehum Harbour and Swartz Bay on the northeastern end of Saanich Peninsula on Vancouver Island. Numerous islands, islets, and reefs surround the entrance to the cove so careful attention to the chart is necessary on approach. Currents can also be strong through the maze of islands and reefs so plan your trip accordingly.

Entrance to Canoe Cove can be taken through either Iroquois Passage or Page Passage. Page Passage is used primarily by small boats with local knowledge due to the number of mid-channel rocks, narrow waterways and strong currents. Iroquois Passage is the more common approach and can be used for approaches from either the north or the south. The passage is entered from the south between Goudge and Fernie Islands. When approaching from the south, be aware of the submerged one-fathom rock lying mid-channel off the north end of Fernie Island. Approaching from the north, Iroquois Passage is entered between Goudge Island and Swartz Head, passing east of Musclow Islet. A speed limit of 4 knots is set for Page Passage, Iroquois Passage, and Canoe Cove.

Once in the cove, be aware of rocks found just northeast of the marina and west of Musclow Islet. A one-fathom shallow area is located just north of Kolb Island. In the southern part of the cove, anchorage may be available between the marina and Kolb Island, however private moorings take up most of the available space in this area of the cove. Check with Canoe Cove Marina for moorage.

Vessels entering Canoe Cove from foreign waters must report to the Canadian Border Services Agency (CBSA) customs dock. The customs dock is located at Canoe Cove Marina at the fuel dock.

Canoe Cove to:		
Bedwell Harbour (South Pender Island)		9 nm
Ganges Harbour (Salt Spring Island)		14 nm
Genoa Bay		10 nm
Ladysmith		28 nm
Nanaimo		40 nm
Roche Harbor (USA)		11 nm
Russell Island		4 nm
Sidney		2 nm
Tod Inlet		13 nm
Victoria		43 nm
Wallace Island		20 nm
Winter Cove (Saturna Island)		16 nm

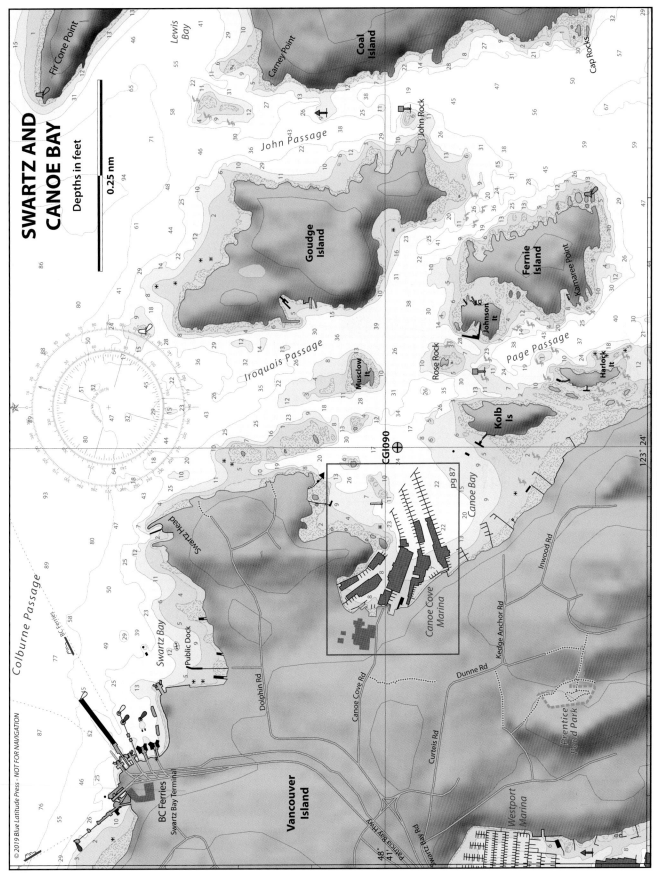

SWARTZ AND CANOE BAY

Depths in feet

0.25 nm

Fir Cone Point

Lewis Bay

Carney Point

Coal Island

John Rock

Cap Rocks

John Passage

Goudge Island

Fernie Island

Kamaree Point

Johnson It

Iroquois Passage

Musclow It

Rose Rock

Page Passage

Harlock It

Kolb Is

CGI090

Colburne Passage

BC Ferries

Swartz Head

Swartz Bay

Public Dock

Canoe Bay

pg 87

Canoe Cove Marina

Canoe Cove Rd

Dolphin Rd

Dunne Rd

Kedge Anchor Rd

Inwood Rd

Curteis Rd

Prentice Pond Park

Vancouver Island

BC Ferries
Swartz Bay Terminal

Westport Marina

Swartz Bay Rd

Patricia Bay Hwy

48° 41.1'

123° 24'

© 2019 Blue Latitude Press - NOT FOR NAVIGATION

CGI090 - 48° 40.980'N 123° 24.000'W

85

Marine Chandleries and Services

All Things Marine Thrift Store

All Things Marine sells donated used marine items year-round as a fund raiser for the Maritime Museum of BC. Donated books and marine items are gladly accepted. Located at #14 - 2300 Canoe Cove Road. mmbc.bc.ca/atm/, (778) 351-0011

Blackline Marine

Blackline Marine is located at Canoe Cove Marina. The haul out yard specializes in fiberglass fabrication and repairs, metal fabrication, yacht rigging, painting and maintenance. Located at #22 - 2300 Canoe Cove Road. www.blacklinemarine.com, (250) 656-6616

Canoe Cove Manufacturing

Offering service and installs including engines, heaters, and electronics. Also a service center for Ranger Tugs and Cutwater Boats. Located at Canoe Cove Marina. canoecovemanufacturing.com, (250) 656-3915

Pacifica Paddle

Pacifica Paddle offers kayak, canoe, and SUP board rentals, lessons and tours. Located at the head of the dock at Canoe Cove Marina. www.pacificapaddle.com, (250) 665-4548

Raven Marine

Raven Marine offers services including maintenance, repairs, yacht monitoring and yacht detailing. They also offer global yacht transportation, providing shipping and logistics support to destinations around the world. Located Canoe Cove Marina at #18 - 2300 Canoe Cove Road. ravenmarine.ca, (250) 655-3934

Vector Yacht Services

Vector Yacht Services operates a haul out yard, a re-power specialty shop, and provides marine services and repairs. Canoe Cove Marina operates the travel lift. Located at Canoe Cove Marina at 2300 Canoe Cove Road. www.vectoryacht.com, (250) 656-5515

Restaurants

Canoe Cove Joe's

Canoe Cove Joe's serves excellent breakfast dishes, coffee and espresso drinks, and great burgers for lunch. Joe's is open everyday for breakfast and lunch. Conveniently located at the marina. canoecovejoes.com, (250) 656-5557

Stonehouse Restaurant & Pub

The Stonehouse is a classic English style manor in a wooded setting offering a tasty pub menu including burgers, fish and chips, pizzas and more. Open for lunch and dinner everyday. Located just up the road from the marina. stonehousepub.ca, (778) 351-1133

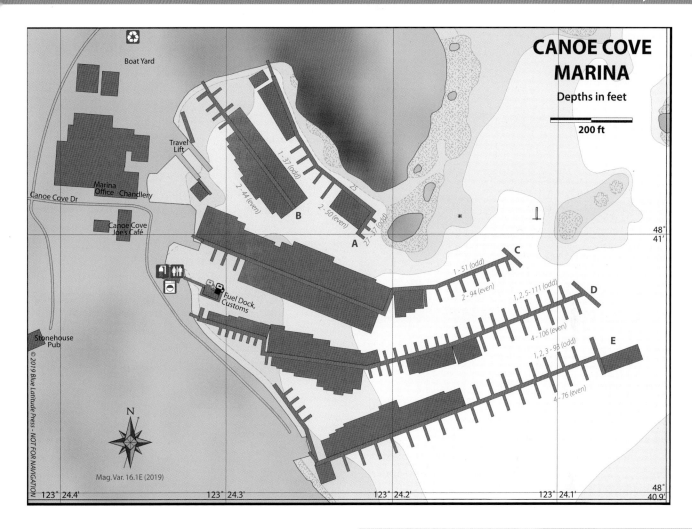

Canoe Cove Marina

Canoe Cove Marina is tucked within a picturesque cove between Tsehum Harbour and Swartz Bay. The marina offers 450 slips including 140 boathouses and 28 covered slips. The majority of slips are for permanent moorage. Transient boats are assigned unoccupied slips as available. Each slip has access to water and power, along with garbage and recycle disposal. A 50-foot fuel dock is located near shore between docks C and D selling gas, diesel, oil, propane and ice. Be aware that maneuvering room near the fuel dock is limited for larger vessels. Onshore amenities include a fully stocked marine chandlery, Canoe Cove Joe's restaurant and coffee bar, laundry facilities, showers, and restrooms.

Canoe Cove Marina also operates a large haulout and storage yard. The new 75-ton Marine Travelift is capable of hauling boats up to 80 feet in length, 22.5 feet in beam, and weighing 186,000 pounds. Service and repairs for the yard is performed by Vector Yacht Services.

Canoe Cove Marina
Monitors VHF channel: 66A
2300 Canoe Cove Road
North Saanich, BC V8L 3X9
(250) 656-5566
info@canoecovemarina.com
www.canoecovemarina.com

Swartz Bay

Rum Island (Isle-de-Lis)

Rum Island, as it is commonly known on the charts, achieved its name from the rumrunners of the 1920's who shuttled alcohol to nearby Stuart Island during the US prohibition era. More recently, the island has become known as Isle-de-Lis, in honor of the island's donor who bequeathed the land. Today it is part of the Gulf Islands National Park Reserve and open to the public.

The island is located immediately east of Gooch Island, which at low tide, is connected by a narrow isthmus of land. A navigation light is found on a small islet just east of Tom Point bordering the west side of Haro Strait. A half mile north of Tom Point is the unmarked Cooper Reef.

Rum Island is used primarily by kayakers due to the lack of good anchorage and strong currents in the area. The park offers three campsites, a pit toilet, picnic tables and a trail circling the island. The isthmus between Gooch and Rum is the best place to land when exploring or camping on the island.

Swartz Bay

Swartz Bay, located at the northeast end of Saanich Peninsula, is most known for its BC Ferries terminal. The five-berth terminal is the second largest and busiest in BC behind the mainland's Tsawwassen terminal. Swartz Bay is also home to Seaspan Ferries, which operates scheduled freight transportion between Vancouver Island and the mainland. Southeast of the ferry terminal is a public wharf and launch ramp used primarily by local island residents.

Swartz Bay is located on the south side of Colburne Passage on Saanich Peninsula. Due to the frequent traffic of large ferries and their accompanying wake, Swartz Bay is not a popular destination for visiting boats. Anchorage near the public wharf is mostly filled with private moorings.

Swartz Bay offers a public wharf through the Capital Regional District (CRD). The wharf has approximately 130 feet of dock space, most of which is used primarily by daily commuters from nearby islands. Due to its heavy use, moorage is limited to a maximum of three days. The wharf also serves as the destination point for all Gulf Islands' marine medical evacuations. The yellow outer float is reserved for emergency use and loading. Those using this area for loading must remain with the boat and be prepared to move in case of an emergency. The maximum time allowed in this area is 15 minutes. For further information on CRD public wharfs check their website at: www.crd.bc.ca, or call the wharfinger at (250) 655-3256.

Rum Island

Portland Island (Princess Margaret Marine Park)

Portland Island is a must stop for any cruise through the Gulf Islands. This magical marine park includes beautiful beaches, lush forest land, and miles of walking trails linking each section of the island. Two intimate anchorages, each with convenient dinghy docks, allow boaters the chance to explore this one of a kind island.

Several midden beaches dot the shoreline, telling of the island's rich history with the First Nations people. Dating back to over 3,000 years ago, these middens were once thick layers of shells that helped to feed centuries of families. These areas are now archaeological sites, protected under BC law and may not be disturbed.

The island was named after Fairfax Moresby's flagship, the *HMS Portland*. Morseby was a British Royal Navy officer who became the Commander in Chief of the Pacific Station in 1850. During his time in the Pacific, he proposed the building of the Esquimalt Naval Base on Vancouver Island.

In the later 1800's, Hawaiians began to settle in the area including Portland, Russell and Salt Spring Islands.

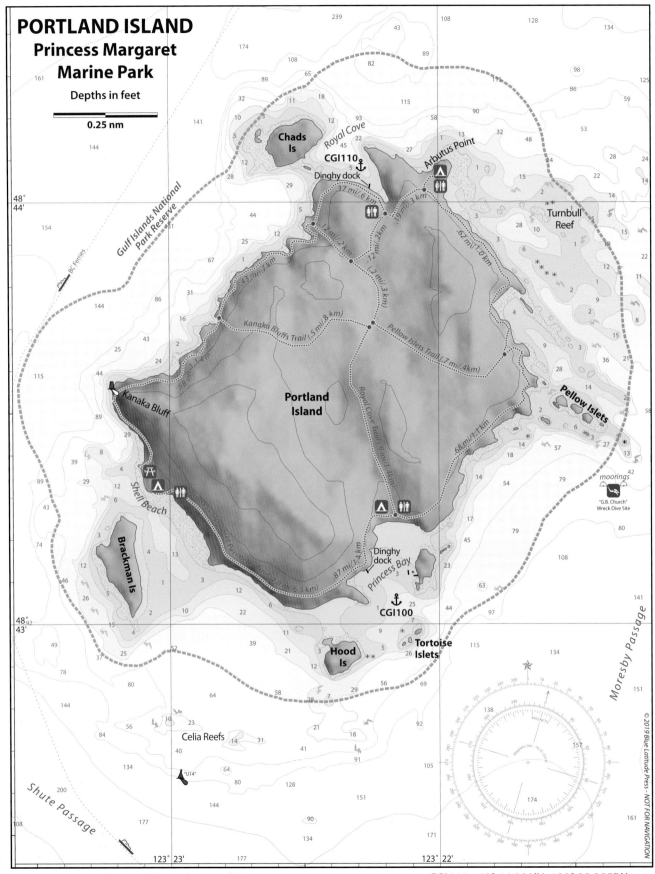

PORTLAND ISLAND
Princess Margaret
Marine Park

Depths in feet

0.25 nm

Chads
Is

Royal Cove

CGI110

Dinghy dock

Arbutus Point

.37 mi/.6 km

.19 mi/.3 km

.12 mi/.2 km

.62 mi/1.0 km

Turnbull
Reef

.12 mi/.2 km

(.2 mi/.3 km)

Gulf Islands National
Park Reserve

.43 mi/.7 km

BC Ferries

Kanaka Bluffs Trail (.5 mi/.8 km)

Pellow Islets Trail (.7 mi/.4 km)

Portland
Island

Pellow
Islets

.28 mi/1.4 km

Kanaka Bluff

Royal Cove Trail (.9 mi/1.4 km)

.68 mi/1.1 km

Shell Beach

moorings

"G.B. Church"
Wreck Dive Site

Brackman Is

Princess Margaret Peninsula Trail (4.0 mi/6.5 km)

Dinghy
dock

.87 mi/1.4 km

Princess Bay

CGI100

Celia Reefs

Hood
Is

Tortoise
Islets

Moresby Passage

"U14"

Shute Passage

MAGNETIC

Magnetic Var. 16.1E (2019)

© 2019 Blue Latitude Press - NOT FOR NAVIGATION

CGI100 - 48° 43.050'N 123° 22.160'W   CGI110 - 48° 44.090'N 123° 22.285'W

The Hawaiians, or Kanakas as they are known in their language, became seamen and laborers on merchant ships stopping over in Hawaii. The Hudson's Bay Company was a large employer of Hawaiians, especially with the fur trade between North America and Asia. Hawaiians, William Naukana and his good friend and later son-in-law, John Palua, applied to preempt land on Portland Island. It is believed that the apple trees at the head of Princess Bay were likely planted by these families.

In 1958, Princess Margaret toured British Columbia during its centennial celebration. To commemorate her special visit to the province, Portland Island was gifted to the princess. In 1967, the princess returned the island back to the province for preservation as a marine park, in which it was named Princess Margaret Marine Park. Portland Island, along with a 400 meter protection zone surrounding the island, are now part of the Gulf Islands National Park Reserve.

In 1989, the Artificial Reef Society of British Columbia (ARSBC) began its very first project within the boundaries of Princess Margaret Marine Park. The *G.B. Church*, a 175-foot coastal freighter, was chosen as the artificial reef to be sunk just south of the Pellow Islets on the east side of Portland Island. In 1991, the ship was sunk where she now lies in 90 feet of water.

One of the best attractions at Portland Island is the hiking trails. Over six miles of trails envelop Portland, taking visitors on an adventurous tour around the shoreline or crossing the middle of the island. Trails lead to striking midden beaches, homesteaders' fruit orchards, and through thick forests of madrones, cedars, oaks and firs. With no native black-tailed deer, plants and trees thrive on the island. Along the way, the trails pass through the island's three camping areas at Princess Bay, Arbutus Point, and Shell Beach. In total, there are 24 campsites with each campground offering pit toilets and food caches (no potable water available).

If you're lucky enough to be visiting during April or May, the island offers a beautiful display of native wildflowers. Meadows of sea blush, chocolate lilies, fawn lilies, and shooting stars are a few of the gems you can find growing on the island. Be sure to stick to the trail during these bloom times to avoid trampling the blossoms and thereby regenerating seeds.

While at Portland Island, keep in mind the island is part of the Gulf Islands National Park Reserve. No campfires are permitted at the island and dogs must remain on leashes at all times. Nearby Brackman Island and Pellow Islets are closed to the public. For campers, be sure to lock your food away in the campgrounds' designated food caches, as there is a healthy population of hungry raccoons on the island.

KANAKA TRAIL CONSTRUCTED BY 1979 YOUTH CREW

©Kevin Oke

Princess Bay

Picturesque Princess Bay is a favorite stop on any itinerary through the islands. Headed by a beautiful pebble beach and fringed by a rugged and rocky shoreline, the small anchorage at Princess Bay is a welcome destination for boaters and kayakers alike. A convenient dinghy dock allows easy access to the island and its miles of scenic hiking trails. One of the island's campgrounds, along with picnic tables, are found at the old homesteaders' orchard site and overlook the alluring beach and anchorage. During the summer months, this popular anchorage can fill to a surprising capacity.

Princess Bay is located on the southeastern side of Portland Island and east of Moresby Island. The two islands are separated by Moresby Passage, which is used to approach the island from the north or south. The pass is relatively free of hazards with the exception of Canoe Rock located at the north entrance to the pass. Currents through Morseby Passage can reach 2 to 3 knots. BC Ferries use Moresby Passage on their approach and departure to and from the terminal at Swartz Bay. If approaching Princess Bay from the north, be sure to locate Pellow Islets, which

are located of Portland Island's east side. These reefs are marked by a lighted navigation buoy that sits roughly 0.25 miles southeast of the islets. Just south of the islets lies the artificial reef dive site, the *G.B. Church*. Be aware that there may be divers in the water in this area.

Entrance to Princess Bay should be taken east and north of Tortoise Islets to avoid the detached rocks off

Princess Bay to:		
Bedwell Harbour (*South Pender Island*)	7 nm
Ganges Harbour (*Salt Spring Island*)	12 nm
Genoa Bay	11 nm
Ladysmith	28 nm
Montague Harbour (*Galiano Island*)	12 nm
Nanaimo	40 nm
Pirates Cove (*De Courcy Island*)	29 nm
Roche Harbor (*USA*)	11 nm
Russell Island	4 nm
Sidney	4 nm
Tod Inlet	13 nm
Victoria	26 nm

Hood Island. Keep in mind that Princess Bay shoals rapidly near the head of the bay towards the pebble beach, as well as north of Hood Island. Anchorage can be taken within the bay in 2 to 3 fathoms over a mostly mud bottom. During the summer months, when the anchorage fills, some boats will use stern lines to shore in order to reduce their swing in a tight anchorage. Be sure to check the tide tables before setting the anchor to make sure there is ample water under the boat in this fairly shallow anchorage.

While the bay is protected from west and north winds, it is exposed to southerly winds. Better southerly wind protection is available at Royal Cove on the island's north end. Due to ferry traffic in Moresby Passage, some ferry wake may be experienced in the anchorage.

For trips to shore, a convenient dinghy dock is available within the bay. At the head of the ramp is a park kiosk listing island information along with a map of the island's trails. Taking a photo of the map, along with trail distances, is handy to have on hand when hiking the island's many trails. For those traveling with pets, dogs are welcome on the island as long as they are leashed and picked up after.

At the head of the bay is Princess Bay campground and the historic homesteader's orchard. Picnic tables and a composting toilet are available here. For those interested in diving, the *G.B Church* artificial reef site is a short dinghy ride away. Two mooring buoys that also act as decent/ascent lines are available at the wreck site.

©Kevin Oke

Royal Cove

Royal Cove is one of two very popular anchorages within the marine park on Portland Island. Notched into the island's northern shore, Royal Cove offers boaters a quiet refuge to drop the anchor and explore this special island. Hiking, kayaking, tide pooling, and beach lounging are some of the favorite pastimes here. A convenient dinghy dock make shore-side excursions easy, and a nearby campground offers space for sleeping out under the stars.

Royal Cove is located on the north end of Portland Island, roughly 1.5 miles southeast of Russell Island and the entrance to Fulford Harbour on Salt Spring Island. The approach to Royal Cove is taken via Satellite Channel which separates Portland and Salt Sprint Islands. Currents through Satellite Channel run roughly 1 to 2 knots.

If approaching Royal Cove via Moresby Passage on the east side of Portland Island, be sure to locate both Pellow Islets and Turnbull Reef. These reefs and rocky islands extend up to 0.4 miles off the eastern shore of Portland Island. Be sure to stay well offshore when rounding the east and northeast end of the island.

Royal Cove has a unique V-shape and is nearly connected to Chads Island by drying rocks. Entrance to the cove can only be taken via the east side of Chads Island to avoid this extensive reef. Once inside the cove, anchorage can be taken in 2 to 6 fathoms, usually with a stern line to shore. A shallow ledge lines the edge of the cove so be sure you have ample water before tying to shore.

Royal Cove affords southerly and westerly wind protection, but is open to winds from the north. Due to ferry traffic through Moresby and Swanson Channels, some ferry wake may be experienced in the anchorage.

Royal Cove to:		
Bedwell Harbour (South Pender Island)	7 nm
Ganges Harbour (Salt Spring Island)	12 nm
Genoa Bay	11 nm
Ladysmith	28 nm
Montague Harbour (Galiano Island)	12 nm
Nanaimo	40 nm
Pirates Cove (De Courcy Island)	29 nm
Roche Harbor (USA)	12 nm
Russell Island	2 nm
Sidney	7 nm
Tod Inlet	13 nm
Victoria	27 nm

For trips to shore, a dinghy dock is located near the head of the cove. A kiosk at the top of the ramp has island information along with a map of the island's trails. A short walk to the east takes visitors to the Arbutus Point campground where picnic tables and a composting toilet are available. True to its name, campers can set up their tents under a beautiful canopy of arbutus, or madrone, trees.

For those traveling with kayaks or SUPs on board, Portland Island is the perfect spot for a circumnavigation of a truly pristine island. Enjoy a quiet morning paddle and explore the marine park by water. Glide past the Kanaka Bluffs, stretch your legs at Shell Beach, and "kayak snorkel" the reefs at Turnbull Reefs. The island offers exceptional views and a wealth of nooks to explore by a shallow draft boat.

For those needing a long walk or an exhilarating trail run, Royal Cove is perfectly situated to join trails that round or bisect the island. Take a camera and a picnic lunch to spend the day exploring the island by foot and enjoying each beach Portland has to offer. During the warm summer months be sure to bring water as there is no potable water available on island.

Chapter 3

Saanich Inlet

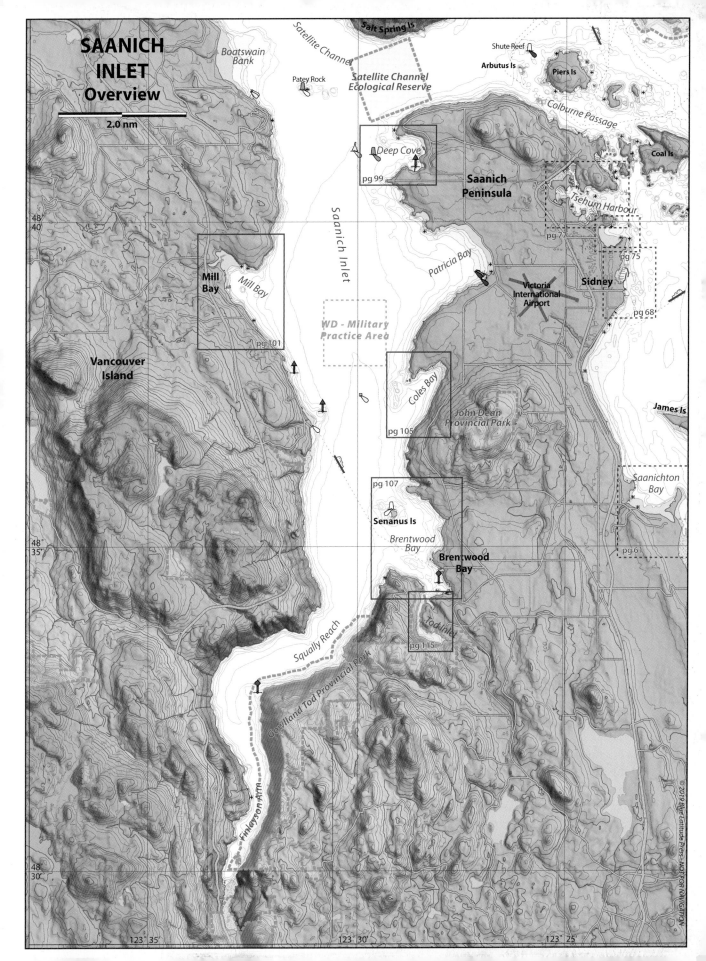

SAANICH INLET
Overview

2.0 nm

Boatswain Bank

Satellite Channel

Salt Spring Is

Shute Reef

Arbutus Is

Piers Is

Patey Rock

Satellite Channel Ecological Reserve

Colburne Passage

Coal Is

Deep Cove

Saanich Peninsula

Tsehum Harbour

pg 99

Patricia Bay

pg 77

48°
40′

Mill Bay

Mill Bay

Victoria International Airport

Sidney

pg 75

pg 68

Saanich Inlet

Vancouver Island

WD - Military Practice Area

pg 101

Coles Bay

John Dean Provincial Park

James Is

pg 105

Saanichton Bay

pg 107

Senanus Is

Senanus Is

Brentwood Bay

Brentwood Bay

pg 61

48°
35′

Squally Reach

Tod Inlet

pg 115

Gowlland Tod Provincial Park

Finlayson Arm

48°
30′

123° 35′

123° 30′

123° 25′

© 2019 Blue Latitude Press - NOT FOR NAVIGATION

Deep Cove

Deep Cove, located near the northwestern tip of Saanich Peninsula, is often overshadowed by its nearby neighbors of Brentwood Bay and Tod Inlet. Deep Cove offers a small private marina in its southeast end.

Deep Cove is located at the northeast end of Saanich Inlet. The cove lies between Moses Point to the north and Coal Point to the south. When approaching Deep Cove, be aware of both Wain Rock, which lies 0.2 miles southwest of Moses Point, and Patey Rock which lies 0.7 miles northeast of Hatch Point. Both rocks are marked by navigation lights. Once inside the cove, anchorage can be taken near the head in 4 to 9 fathoms. A small creek drains into the cove near the middle of the bay forming a shallow delta area. This area is also marked by old pilings and a small rock berm. This anchorage is best suited during periods of calm weather as it is a fairly exposed.

In the southern portion of the bay, numerous private moorings and the Deep Cove Marina are found. This portion of the cove also has a number of below and above water rocks, with the largest marked by a daybeacon in front of the marina (see above photo). The Deep Cove Marina is a small private marina with mostly permanent moorage, however they may have occasional space for transient boats. Call or check their website at (250) 656 -7070 or www.deepcovemarina.net.

Deep Cove to:		
Bedwell Harbour (South Pender Island)	12 nm
Brentwood Bay	7 nm
Ganges Harbour (Salt Spring Island)	14 nm
Genoa Bay	7 nm
Ladysmith	25 nm
Nanaimo	35 nm
Pirates Cove (De Courcy Island)	27 nm
Roche Harbor (USA)	15 nm
Russell Island	5 nm
Sidney	6 nm
Tod Inlet	8 nm
Victoria	28 nm

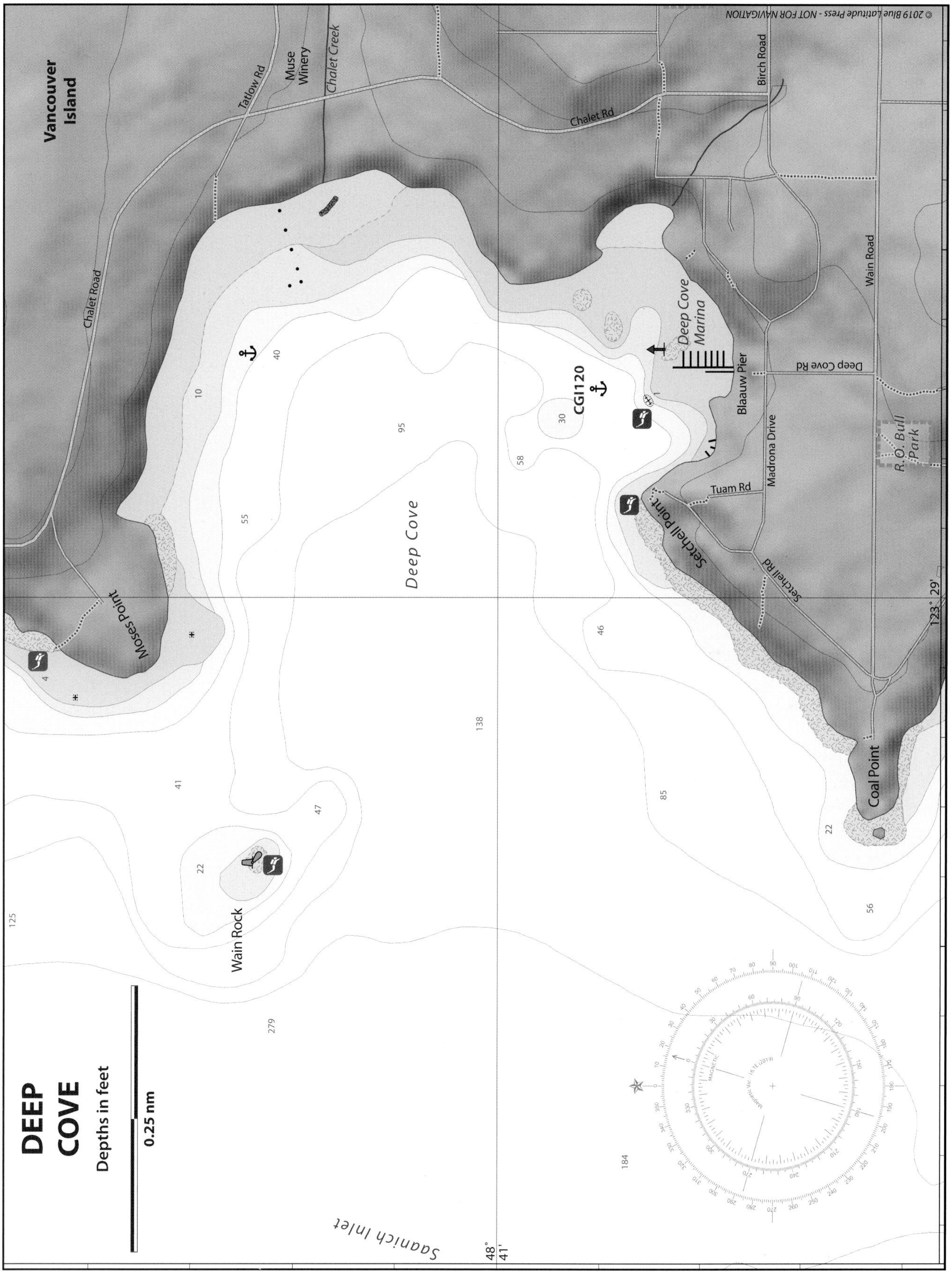

DEEP COVE

Depths in feet

0.25 nm

Vancouver Island

Tatlow Rd

Muse Winery

Chalet Creek

Chalet Rd

Birch Road

Chalet Road

Wain Road

Chalet Road

Deep Cove Marina

Deep Cove Rd

Blaauw Pier

Madrona Drive

R.O. Bull Park

CGI120

40

10

95

55

30

58

Moses Point

Deep Cove

Tuam Rd

Sechelt Point

Sechelt Rd

46

138

85

22

Coal Point

56

Wain Rock

22

41

47

125

279

184

Saanich Inlet

48° 41'

48°

123° 29'

CGI120 - 48° 40.900'N 123° 28.700'W

©Kevin Oke

Mill Bay

Mill Bay achieved its identity back in the 1860's when a water-powered sawmill was built at the mouth of Shawnigan Creek. Today this quaint coastal town has grown to a population of roughly 3,200 people and is home to a modern 100+ slip marina. Fishing, hiking, and kayaking are a few of the area's top activities at both Mill Bay and nearby Shawnigan Lake. A short quarter mile walk to the local shopping center provides convenient provisioning, and a beautiful restaurant at the marina makes for delicious and easy dining out options.

Mill Bay is located on the northwestern shore of Saanich Inlet, just south of Whisky Point and due west of Patricia Bay. The approaches to Mill Bay are relatively free of hazards. A shallow pinnacle is located just south of the center of the bay with 15 feet of water covering it. The Mill Bay Marina is located near the middle of the bay. Just south of the marina is the public wharf with nearly 230 feet of pier and a 50 foot dock attached.

Anchorage can be taken within the bay in 5 to 7 fathoms over a mostly mud bottom. A number of private moorings are located around the public wharf and south of the marina. Mill Bay provides protection from north and west winds, but is open to the south and east. Better southeasterly protection can be found in Brentwood Bay or Tod Inlet.

For trips to shore, the public wharf provides a nice location to tie up the dinghy or kayak, or land on the beach near the launch ramp north of the marina. Mill Bay Road

Mill Bay to:		
Bedwell Harbour (South Pender Island)		16 nm
Ganges Harbour (Salt Spring Island)		18 nm
Genoa Bay		8 nm
Montague Harbour (Galiano Island)		19 nm
Nanaimo		38 nm
Pirates Cove (De Courcy Island)		30 nm
Royal Cove (Portland Island)		9 nm
Roche Harbor (USA)		18 nm
Sidney		10 nm
Telegraph Harbour (Thetis Island)		22 nm
Tod Inlet		6 nm
Victoria		32 nm

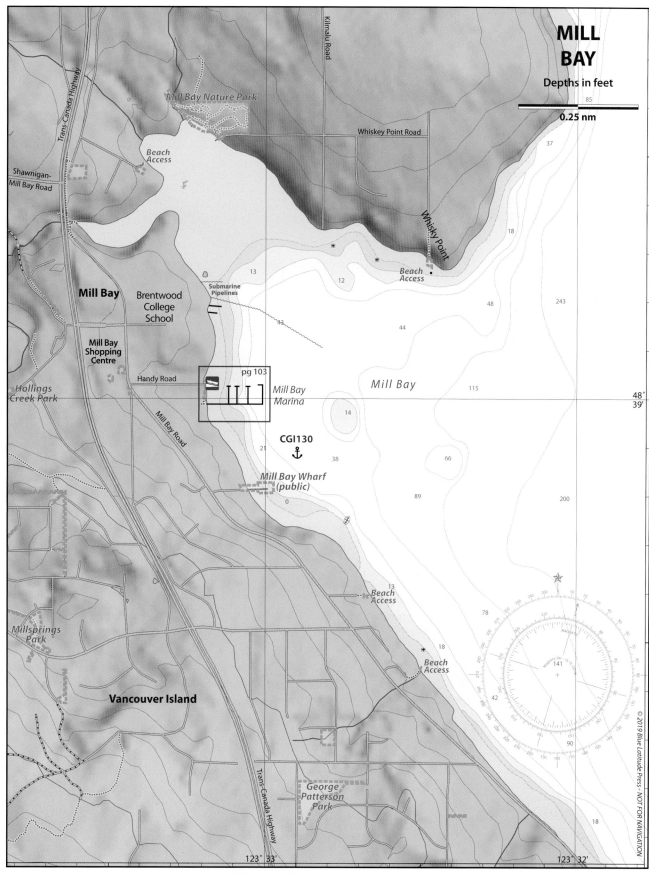

MILL BAY

Depths in feet

0.25 nm

Trans-Canada Highway

Kilmalu Road

Mill Bay Nature Park

Whiskey Point Road

Beach Access

Shawnigan-Mill Bay Road

Whisky Point

85

37

18

Beach Access

13

12

48

243

Mill Bay

Brentwood College School

Submarine Pipelines

43

44

Mill Bay Shopping Centre

Handy Road

pg 103

Mill Bay Marina

Mill Bay

115

Hollings Creek Park

48° 39'

14

Mill Bay Road

21

CGI130
⚓

38

66

200

Mill Bay Wharf (public)

0

89

13
Beach Access

78

Millsprings Park

141

18
Beach Access

Vancouver Island

42

90

Trans-Canada Highway

George Patterson Park

18

123° 33'

123° 32'

CGI130 - 48° 38.890'N 123° 32.890'W

Bridgemans Bistro

is the main road through town and leads to the shopping center where a variety of stores and dining options are available. Provisioning and supply stores at the center include Thrifty Foods, BC Liquor, Mill Bay Paint & Hardware, and Pharmasave. Banks and Canada Post are also located within the shopping center. A handful of restaurants including fast food options and coffee shops are located at the center as well as on the west side of the highway.

A few of the top activities at Mill Bay include kayaking and fishing. For those traveling without kayaks, rentals are available at the Mill Bay Marina. The estuary north of the marina provides a great spot for shallow draft kayaks to explore and watch the variety of birds and marine life within the estuary. Paddlers can also explore the shoreline and beaches found south of the marina.

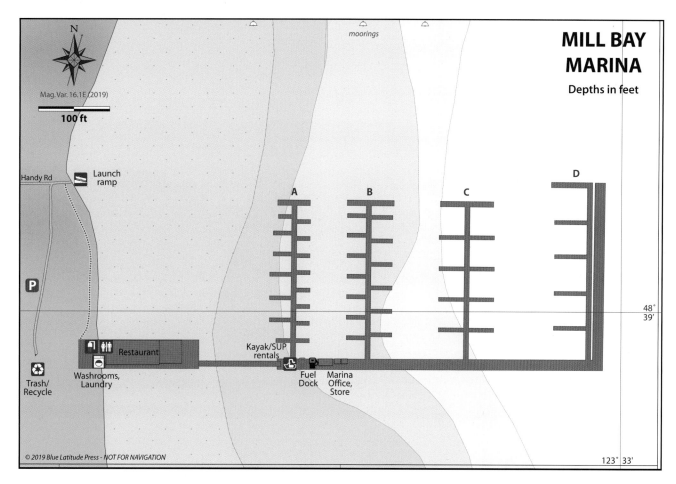

Mill Bay Marina

Mill Bay Marina is a modern full service marina within the picturesque Saanich Inlet. The marina can accommodate boats up to 200 feet in length. Each slip has access to power and water hookups. Services at the marina include restrooms, showers, laundry facilities, free wifi, gated entry with cameras, and garbage and recycle disposal. The marina also operates a large fuel dock and marine pumpout facility. A small store sells ice, snacks, and fishing supplies.

With an amazing view of the marina, bay, and Mt Baker, the marina's restaurant, Bridgemans Bistro, offers delicious meals for breakfast, lunch, and dinner. Set over the water with floor to ceiling glass, the casual restaurant offers sweeping views with fresh, Pacific Northwest style menus.

Mill Bay Marina
Monitors VHF Channel 66A
740 Handy Road
Mill Bay, BC V0R 2P1
(250) 743-4303
contact@millbaymarina.ca
www.millbaymarina.ca

Coles Bay

Quiet Coles Bay is tucked into the western shore of Saanich Peninsula amidst a small residential community. A regional park located at the head of the bay offers easy beach access along with a short loop nature trail. A small creek empties into the bay forming a perfect sand and pebble beach for tidal life exploration.

Coles Bay is located on the east side of Saanich Inlet between Patricia Bay to the north and Brentwood Bay to the south. The northern entrance point to the bay is Yarrow Point with Dyer Rocks lying close, southwest of the point. A rock located 0.3 miles southwest of Yarrow Point lies in 6 feet of water and is marked by port hand buoy "U23." When approaching the bay from the north, be sure to given this submerged rock ample room when rounding into the bay.

Anchorage can be taken within the bay in 5 to 7 fathoms over a mostly mud bottom. The anchorage offers protection in north and east winds but is open to the south and west. Better southerly and northwest wind protection can be found at nearby Tod Inlet.

For trips to shore the Coles Bay Regional Park offers a nice beach for landing dinghies and kayaks. A short half mile loop nature and beach trail follows a small creek through the forest. Picnic tables and pit toilets are available at the park.

For those with bikes and an extra sense for adventure, be sure to check out the nearby John Dean Provincial Park. From Coles Bay to the main park is just under 4 miles. The park is at the top of Mount Newton with amazing views of Saanich Peninsula and the Gulf Islands. The park includes one of the last stands of old-growth Douglas fir and Garry oak on the peninsula. There are approximately 4 miles of trails winding through the forest, along with picturesque overlooks, and restrooms. For further information and maps, visit: www.env.gov.bc.ca/bcparks.

Coles Bay to:		
Bedwell Harbour (South Pender Island)	17 nm
Brentwood Bay	4 nm
Ganges Harbour (Salt Spring Island)	19 nm
Genoa Bay	10 nm
Nanaimo	40 nm
Pirates Cove (De Courcy Island)	32 nm
Roche Harbor (USA)	20 nm
Russell Island	10 nm
Sidney	11 nm
Telegraph Harbour (Thetis Island)	24 nm
Tod Inlet	5 nm
Victoria	33 nm

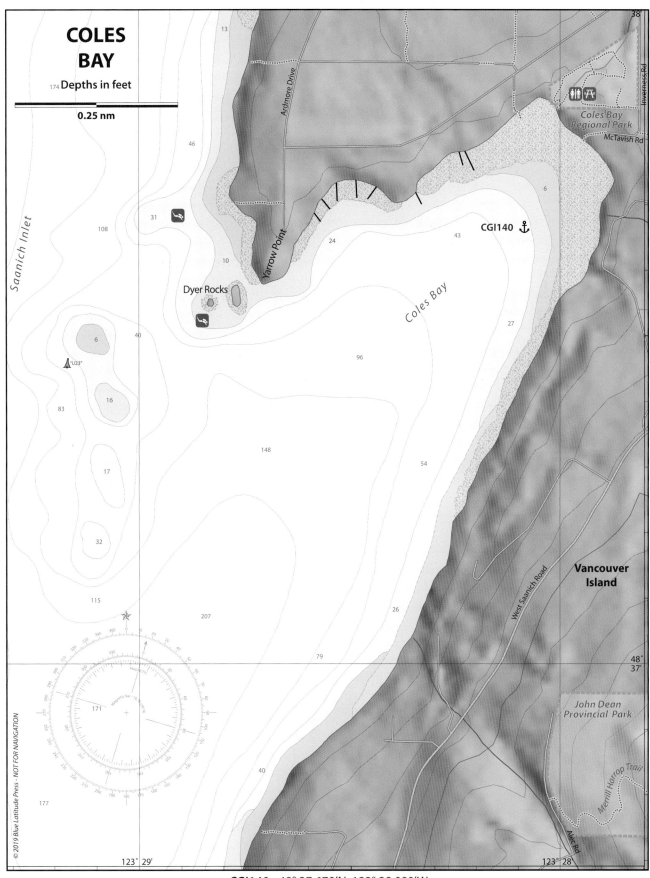

COLES BAY

174 Depths in feet

0.25 nm

Saanich Inlet

Ardmore Drive

Inverness Rd

♿ 🪑

Coles Bay
Regional Park

McTavish Rd

6

CGI140 ⚓

Yarrow Point

46

31

108

10

24

43

Coles Bay

27

Dyer Rocks

40

6

"U23"

96

16

83

148

54

17

Vancouver
Island

32

115

207

26

48°
37'

John Dean
Provincial Park

79

West Saanich Road

MAGNETIC

Magnetic Var - 16.5 (2019)

171

Merrill Harrop Trail

177

Alec Rd

© 2019 Blue Latitude Press - NOT FOR NAVIGATION

40

123° 29'

123° 28'

CGI140 - 48° 37.670'N 123° 28.080'W

©Kevin Oke

Brentwood Bay

Beautiful, sheltered Brentwood Bay is a popular stop for most boats heading to Butchart Gardens. The small seaside village offers three comfortable marinas and a handful of ocean side eateries. Kayakers and stand up paddle boarders are a common sight as they set off to explore the placid waters of Tod Inlet and Gowlland Tod Provincial Park. A short dinghy ride around the corner to Butchart Cove delivers ocean-side visitors to the Butchart Gardens dock and dock entrance to the stunning park.

Brentwood Bay is located within Saanich Inlet, between Henderson Point to the north and Willis Point to the south. The village of Brentwood Bay, along with the majority of mooring options, is located in the southeast portion of the bay. Senanus Island lies near the entrance to the bay, and southwest of Henderson Point. BC Ferries operates a small car and passenger ferry from Brentwood Bay to Mill Bay with the terminal located just south of Sluggett Point.

In the southeast portion of Brentwood Bay lie a couple of rock hazards to be aware of when approaching the marinas. Close southwest of the ferry landing and west of the Brentwood Bay Resort Marina lies a drying rock which is marked by starboard hand buoy "U22." From buoy "U22," the reef extends southeast nearly 400 feet. Do not approach this area or the marina from the south to avoid these rocks, and pay careful attention to the chart. A second drying rock is located 0.1 miles north of Daphne Islet. This rock is marked by a daybeacon.

Brentwood Bay to:		
Bedwell Harbour (South Pender Island)		20 nm
Birds Eye Cove		17 nm
Ganges Harbour (Salt Spring Island)		22 nm
Nanaimo		43 nm
Pirates Cove (De Courcy Island)		35 nm
Roche Harbor (USA)		23 nm
Russell Island		12 nm
Sidney		14 nm
Telegraph Harbour (Thetis Island)		27 nm
Tod Inlet		1 nm
Victoria		36 nm

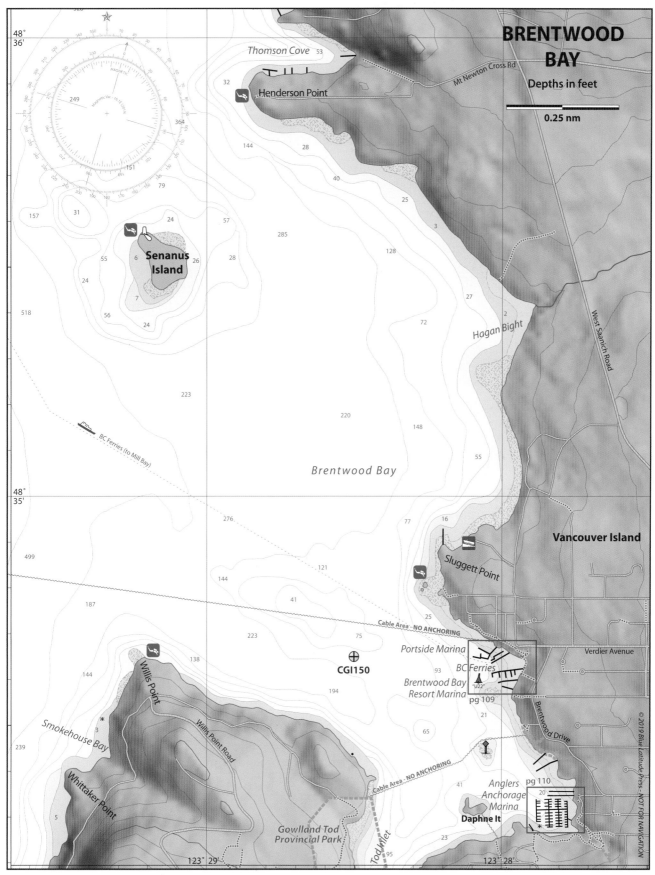

BRENTWOOD BAY

Depths in feet

0.25 nm

48° 36'

249

364

151

79

Thomson Cove 53

Henderson Point

Mt Newton Cross Rd

32

144

28

157

31

24

57

40

Senanus Island

285

25

55

6

26

28

3

24

7

128

56

27

72

24

2

Hagan Bight

518

223

220

148

Brentwood Bay

BC Ferries (to Mill Bay)

55

48° 35'

276

77

16

Vancouver Island

499

121

Sluggett Point

144

187

41

25

Cable Area - NO ANCHORING

223

75

Portside Marina

Verdier Avenue

⊕
CGI150

BC Ferries

93

Willis Point

138

194

Brentwood Bay Resort Marina

U22

pg 109

144

21

Smokehouse Bay

3

65

Brentwood Drive

239

Willis Point Road

Whittaker Point

Cable Area - NO ANCHORING

41

Anglers Anchorage Marina

pg 110

20

5

Daphne It

Gowlland Tod Provincial Park

Tod Inlet

23

95

123° 29'

123° 28'

© 2019 Blue Latitude Press - NOT FOR NAVIGATION

CGI150 - 48° 34.650'N 123° 28.050'W

Brentwood Bay Resort & Spa

Seahorses Cafe

While anchorage may be possible in Brentwood Bay, better anchoring options are available in nearby Tod Inlet. The main anchorage in the southeast portion of Brentwood Bay is deep and is filled by private moorings. Anglers Anchorage Marina, Brentwood Bay Resort Marina, and Portside Marina are good marina options for overnight stays in the bay. For those anchoring in Tod Inlet, it is a short and protected skiff ride or paddle in to Brentwood Bay for exploring, shopping and dining.

For trips to shore, a public wharf is located just north of Anglers Anchorage Marina. The long pier and 65-foot dock is a popular dinghy dock for locals and the privately moored boats in the bay. Keep in mind when transiting this area by boat or dinghy, that a 4 knot speed limit is enforced. A number of kayak and SUP rentals are available in Brentwood Bay so keep your eyes open for novice paddlers, and keep your wake to a minimum.

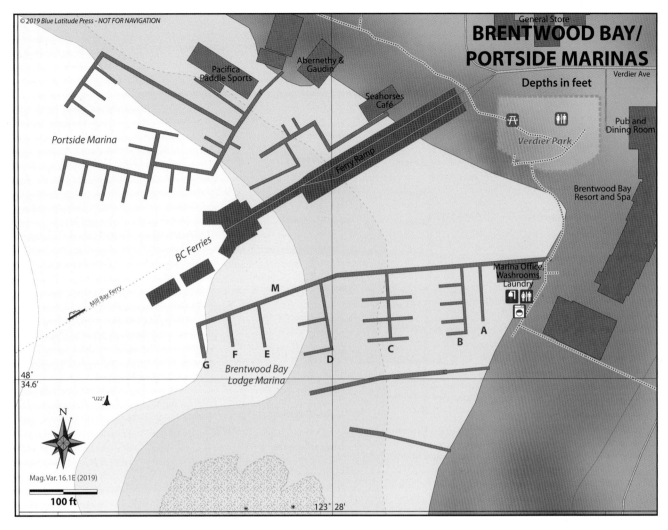

Portside Marina

Originally named Gilbert's Boathouse, Portside Marina has been in operation since 1927. The marina has recently come under new management and is in the progress of updating the infrastructure, including new docks and new slips. The marina is located just north of the BC Ferry Terminal. Currently the marina can accommodate boats up to 50 feet in length. Services include restrooms, showers and laundry facilities.

Portside Marina
789 Saunders Lane
Brentwood Bay, BC V8M 1C5
(250) 652-2211
portsidemarina@shaw.ca
www.portsidemarina.net

Brentwood Bay Resort & Spa Marina

The elegant Brentwood Bay Resort & Spa marina is located just south of the BC Ferry Terminal. The 50-slip marina caters to transient boats exploring Saanich Inlet. Services include restrooms, showers, and laundry facilities. Marina guests also have use of the resort's fitness room, pool, and hot tub (adults only). Other services include cable, water, and power (15, 30 & 50 amp) hook ups at each slip. The marina office closes during the winter months from November 1st to March 31st.

Brentwood Bay Resort & Spa
849 Verdier Avenue
Victoria, BC, V8M 1C5
(250) 544-2079
info@brentwoodbayresort.com
www.brentwoodbayresort.com/marina

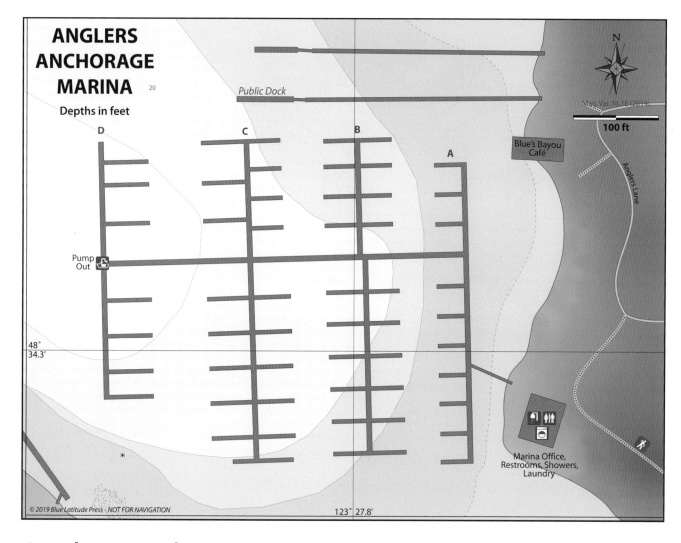

ANGLERS
ANCHORAGE
MARINA 20

Depths in feet

D   C   B   A

Public Dock

Blue's Bayou
Café

Pump
Out

48°
34.3'

Marina Office,
Restrooms, Showers,
Laundry

N

Mag. Var. 16.1E (2019)

100 ft

Anglers Lane

© 2019 Blue Latitude Press - NOT FOR NAVIGATION

123° 27.8'

Anglers Anchorage Marina

Anglers Anchorage Marina is located at the entrance to Todd Inlet and is less than a half mile dinghy run to Butchart Gardens. Recently under new management, the marina is continually adding upgrades to the marina's infrastructure and grounds. The marina can accommodate boats up to 160 feet in length with water and power (15, 30 and 50 amp) hookups available at each slip. Services include restrooms, showers, laundry facilities, free wifi, garbage and recycling disposal, and a pump out facility.

Angler Anchorage Marina
905 Grilse Lane,
Brentwood Bay, BC V8M 1B5
(250) 652-3531
info@anglersanchoragemarina.com
anglersanchoragemarina.com

Sights to See

The main highlight for most visiting this area is a day spent wandering the immaculate and colorful gardens at Butchart Gardens. Over 900 plant varieties spread over 55 acres are meticulously landscaped into a variety of special gardens. With a number of its one million annual visitors arriving by boat, Butchart Gardens provides five mooring buoys, a dinghy dock, and a special entrance for boaters within Butchart Cove. During the popular summer months, nightly live music concerts are played on their outdoor stage, and every Saturday features a fireworks show choreographed to music.

While venturing out by dinghy, kayak, or SUP, be sure to check out Tod Inlet and Gowlland Tod Provincial Park. The park provides a convenient dinghy dock and well-groomed forest lined walking trails. For a bigger adventure, dinghy or paddle around Willis Point to explore McKenzie Bight and a larger portion of the Gowlland Tod Provincial Park (see page 97). From McKenzie Bight, additional trails traverse the thickly forested park.

Marine Chandleries and Services

Abernethy & Gaudin Boatbuilders

A&G are restorers and builders of fine wooden craft. They

Moodyville General Store

Brentwood Bay Resort & Spa

Blue's Bayou Café

Anglers Anchorage Marina

Public Wharf

specialize in sail, power, and rowing vessels from 6 to 120 feet in length. They also perform other services such as mechanical, welding, interior, plumbing and electrical. www.agboats.com, (250) 652-7921

Pacifica Paddle Sports

Pacifica Paddle offers kayak, canoe, and stand up paddle board rentals, lessons and tours. Located at the head of the dock at Portside Marina. www.pacificapaddle.com, (250) 665-7411

Provisioning

BC Liquor

BC Liquor Stores offer a great selection of beers, wines and spirits. Located in the shopping center next to Canada Post on the corner of Wallace Drive and West Saanich Road.

Carnivore Meats & More

A butcher shop located next to BC Liquor selling local, grass fed and GMO free meats. www.carnivoreandmore.com

Fairway Market

A grocery store offering fresh produce, meats, dairy, and all the staples. Located at the shopping center on the corner of Wallace Drive and West Saanich Road.

Restaurants

Brentwood Bay Resort & Spa Dining Room and Pub

Brentwood Bay Resort offers two dining options: the casual Brentwood Bay Pub, and the Brentwood Bay Dining Room. The Pub has a great selection of local craft beers and regional wines, along with a menu of grilled burgers, local seafood, and wood oven flatbreads. The Pub is open for lunch and dinner each day. The Dining Room offers seasonally inspired, local and fresh northwest meals paired with the region's finest wines. The Dining Room is open for breakfast and dinner with reservations recommended. www.brentwoodbayresort.com

Blue's Bayou Café

Blue's Bayou is located next to the Anglers Anchorage Marina with sweeping bay views and outdoor deck seating. The menu specializes in Creole and Cajun-style food. Open for lunch and dinner, closed Sundays during the summer, and Sunday and Monday in the winter. www.bluesbayoucafe.com

Seahorses Café

Located next to the BC Ferry terminal, Seahorses Cafe sits over the water with nice outdoor seating. A delicious menu including burgers, sandwiches, soups, salads, and even baked treats for dessert. Closed Tuesdays and Wednesdays. www.seahorsescafe.com

Butchart Gardens

In 1904, Robert and Jennie Butchart, pioneers in the cement industry, moved out west to found British Columbia's first Portland cement plant. The Butcharts settled along the shores of Tod Inlet, building their home and limestone quarry. Ships were able to access Tod Inlet and the quarry's pier, supplying the burgeoning development of North America's west coast cement needs. By the following decade, the limestone deposits were depleted, and Jennie Butchart turned her attention to beautifying the open pits near their home. Between 1906 and 1929, the Butcharts expanded their gardens, creating the Japanese Garden overlooking Butchart Cove, the Italian Garden on their former tennis court, and the regal Rose Garden. She also began the immense task of bringing in yard upon yard of top soil to the former pit now known today as the Sunken Garden.

In 1939, Ian Ross, grandson of Robert and Jennie, was gifted the gardens on his 21st birthday. Over the years, Ian transformed his grandparents private gardens into the enchanting garden display we see today. 50 full-time gardeners manage the 55 acres of gardens with 26 greenhouses, 900 varieties of bedding plants, and 300,000 bulbs planted for spring.

To visit Butchart Gardens by boat, a 150 foot dinghy dock is provided for visitors in Butchart Cove (dinghies only and all dinghies must leave the dock by closing time). Visitors are also welcome to tie up overnight (24 hour maximum stay) to one of five complimentary buoys in Butchart Cove. One buoy is for boats less than 18 feet in length, and the other four buoys are for boats under 40 feet in length. Stern ties are mandatory while tied to the buoys.

One million people visit Butchart Gardens each year, with the majority arriving by charter buses or cars during July and August. During these peak times, the paths and overlooks can become very congested with visitors between 10:30am to 3:30pm. The Gardens recommend visiting either before or after these times to enjoy prime natural light and a more peaceful walk. Your admission ticket allows you to leave and come back on the same day of purchase. This especially advantageous for boaters who can dinghy back to their boats for a break, and return to catch an evening concert, fireworks show, or quieter crowds. For further information check their website at: www.butchartgardens.com, or phone at: (250) 652-4422.

Tod Inlet

Nearly landlocked Tod Inlet is a must stop, especially for first time boaters exploring the Gulf Islands. Surrounded by the Gowlland Tod Provincial Park and minutes from the enchanted Butchart Gardens, Tod Inlet is a place like no other in the islands. Tucked deep into the forest, the inlet has more of a look and feel of anchoring on a quiet, peaceful pond rather than an ocean. Tree-lined walking trails, protected paddling excursions and exploratory trips to the nearby village of Brentwood Bay will keep visitors happily active at Tod Inlet.

Tod Inlet is located on the western shore of Saanich Peninsula within Saanich Inlet. Entrance to Tod Inlet can be found at the southeast end of Brentwood Bay near Butchart Cove. When approaching from the north, passage can be taken either side of Senanus Island when entering Brentwood Bay. Be aware that a couple of rock hazards lie within Brentwood Bay. The first lies close southwest of the ferry landing marked by starboard hand buoy "U22." The second lies 0.1 miles north of Daphne Islet and is marked by a daybeacon. Numerous private moorings are found in the southeast end of Brentwood Bay and near the entrance to Tod Inlet. Brentwood Bay also has a speed limit of 4 knots.

The entrance to the main anchorage within the inlet is narrow, less than 300 feet in some sections. Near the entrance and just south of Butchart Cove is the port hand buoy "U21." This buoy marks a rock on the outer edge of a small gravel spit and should be avoided. When transiting the narrow portion of the inlet, be aware that boats will occasionally anchor in this section with stern ties to shore. Kayaks, stand up paddle boards, dinghies and other boats frequent this area as well so be sure to keep a careful watch.

Tod Inlet to:		
Bedwell Harbour (South Pender Island)		20 nm
Ganges Harbour (Salt Spring Island)		23 nm
Genoa Bay		13 nm
Ladysmith		31 nm
Montague Harbour (Galiano Island)		23 nm
Nanaimo		43 nm
Pirates Cove (De Courcy Island)		35 nm
Roche Harbor (USA)		23 nm
Russell Island		13 nm
Sidney		15 nm
Victoria		36 nm

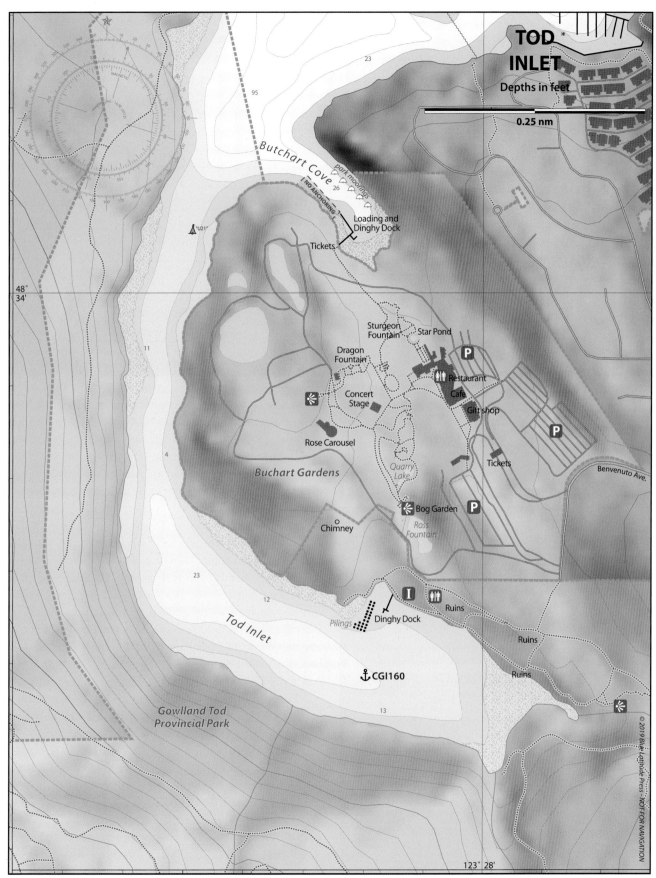

TOD INLET

Depths in feet

0.25 nm

23

95

26

park moorings

Butchart Cove

"U21"

NO ANCHORING

Loading and
Dinghy Dock

Tickets

48°
34'

11

Sturgeon
Fountain

Star Pond

Dragon
Fountain

P

Restaurant

Cafe

Concert
Stage

Gift shop

Rose Carousel

4

Buchart Gardens

*Quarry
Lake*

P

Tickets

Benvenuto Ave.

Bog Garden

Chimney

*Ross
Fountain*

P

23

12

Tod Inlet

Pilings

Dinghy Dock

I

Ruins

Ruins

⚓ CGI160

Ruins

13

*Gowlland Tod
Provincial Park*

123° 28'

CGI160 - 48° 33.600'N 123° 28.220'W

Purple Martins

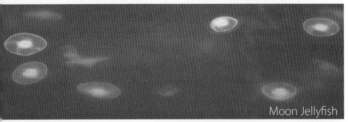

Moon Jellyfish

Pea Flowers

Quarry Remnants

Anchorage can be taken within the inlet in 2 to 4 fathoms over a solid holding mud bottom. During the summer months, this popular anchorage can become quite full, especially on weekends. Certain areas of the inlet, mainly near shore and shallow areas, are marked with white buoys as "No Anchor" zones. These areas are eelgrass restoration sites, and boats should not anchor within or near these areas to protect the fragile grasses.

While Tod Inlet is nearly landlocked and provides great wave protection, a small gap at the head of the inlet can allow winds to funnel through the anchorage. For those planning to visit Butchart Gardens, five complimentary 24-hour mooring buoys are provided in Butchart Cove (see page 115). Due to the lack of swinging room and commercial traffic (seaplanes and Butchart Garden tour boats), anchoring is not recommended in Butchart Cove, but better suited for Tod Inlet.

For trips to shore, a convenient dinghy dock is located at the park near the head of the inlet. On shore, remnants of the old quarry and later, tile and clay pot factory, can still be seen. Concrete footprints of old buildings, steel mooring bollards, and wood pilings from an old pier still linger in the landscape. Two trails, the Tod Inlet and Tod Creek Trails, lead from the inlet up to Wallace Drive, a roughly 20 minute walk. The Tod Creek Trail is mostly a single path trail leading through a mossy forest along the ravine of Tod Creek. The Tod Inlet Trail is mostly the dirt and gravel access road and connects with the Tod Creek Trail.

Gowlland Tod Provincial Park Trails

While at the dinghy dock, be sure to check out the eclectic mix of Purple Martin nest boxes on the nearby pilings. Their chirpy inhabitants migrate from South America to the Salish Sea each summer to breed. Purple Martins have suffered a great decline in population due to loss of nesting sites by both human encroachment and competing non-native birds. Thanks to volunteers building nest boxes throughout the Georgia Basin, Purple Martin populations are on a steady rise (see page 281 for further Purple Martin information).

Tod Inlet and nearby Saanich Inlet provide excellent areas for a peaceful and protected paddle. For those without a kayak or SUP, the village at Brentwood Bay offers rental options (see page 112). A three mile paddle or dinghy ride down to McKenzie Bight provides access to more trails traversing Gowlland Tod Provincial Park.

Through decades of industrial use and dumped trash, the health of Tod Inlet's underwater habitat has suffered. Moon jellyfish, which thrive in low oxygen areas and debris-filled ocean floors, are numerous in Tod Inlet. Today, the inlet is continually undergoing huge efforts to clean and encourage healthy growth. In 2000, roughly 1,800 shoots of eelgrass were planted. In 2017, contaminated topsoil and industrial beach debris were removed from the area around the dinghy dock, and replaced with clean sand and gravel. Dumped metal and concrete debris, along with sunken boats and garbage was also removed from the seafloor. To help aid in the continued improvements and health of Tod Inlet, please respect the no dumping rule and do not anchor within the "No Anchor" zones.

Dinghy Dock

Quiet Anchorage

Quarry Mooring Bollard

Chapter 4

Pender Islands

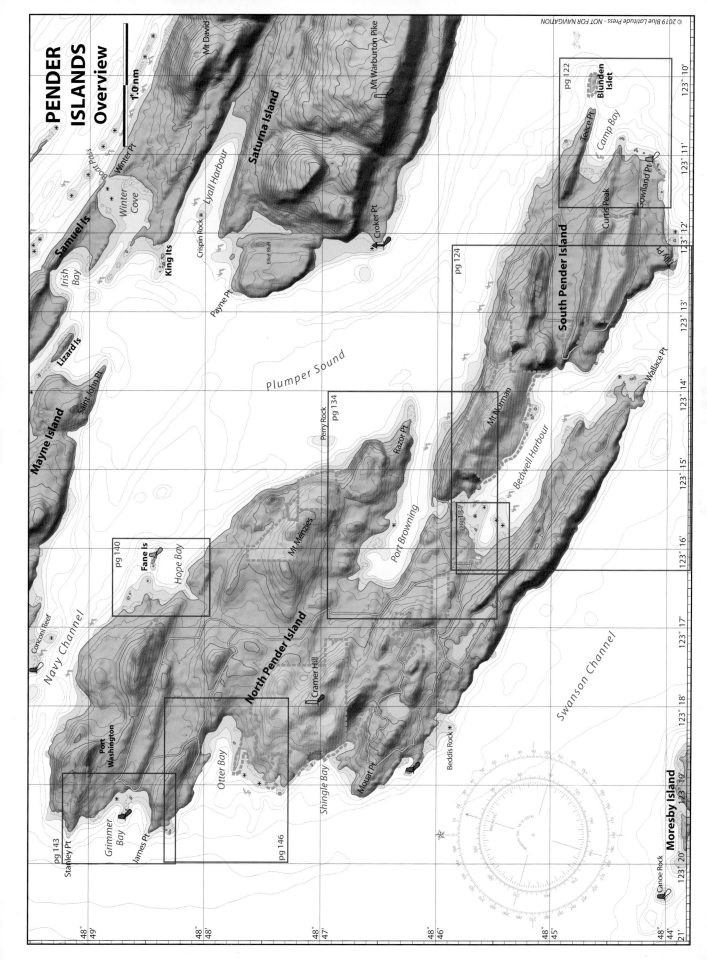

PENDER ISLANDS
Overview

1.0 nm

© 2019 Blue Latitude Press - NOT FOR NAVIGATION

pg 122

Blunden Islet

Teece Pt

Camp Bay

Gowlland Pt

Curtis Peak

South Pender Island

Mill Pt

Wallace Pt

pg 124

Mt Norman

Bedwell Harbour

pg 137

Swanson Channel

Samuel Is

Boot Pass

Winter Pt

Winter Cove

King Its

Lyall Harbour

Crispin Rock

Payne Pt

Elliot Bluff

Croker Pt

Saturna Island

Mt David

Mt Warburton Pike

Plumper Sound

Perry Rock

pg 134

Razor Pt

Port Browning

Mt Menzies

Fane Is

pg 140

Hope Bay

Irish Bay

Lizard Is

Saint John Pt

Mayne Island

Navy Channel

Conconi Reef

North Pender Island

Cramer Hill

Port Washington

Stanley Pt

pg 143

Grimmer Bay

James Pt

pg 146

Otter Bay

Shingle Bay

Mouat Pt

Beddis Rock

Moresby Island

Canoe Rock

48°
49'

48°
48'

48°
47'

48°
46'

48°
45'

48°
21'

123° 20'

123° 19'

123° 18'

123° 17'

123° 16'

123° 15'

123° 14'

123° 13'

123° 12'

123° 11'

123° 10'

©Kevin Oke

Pender Islands

The Penders are comprised of North Pender Island and the smaller of the two, South Pender Island. The islands, once joined by a narrow isthmus, were separated in 1902 when a canal was dug between Bedwell Harbour and Port Browning. In 1955, a bridge was built over the canal, reconnecting the two islands to vehicles. Today, the Penders are the third most populated of the Gulf Islands with a population over 2,200 people. Ferry service from the mainland (Tsawwassen) and Vancouver Island (Swartz Bay) provide easy access for people and vehicles to reach the islands.

Boasting the most public beach access points of any of the Gulf Islands, North and South Pender Islands allow visitors the chance to explore much of the island, both by land and sea. Large patches of Gulf Islands National Park land can be found on both islands. Beaumont Marine Park, Mount Norman, and Greenburn Lake national park lands comprise over 30 percent of the land on South Pender Island. National park land on the north island includes Roe Lake, Roesland, Shingle Bay campground, Mount Menzies, and Prior Centennial campground.

For boaters, the islands offer protected anchorages as well as a number of full service marinas. For boats coming to the islands from foreign waters, a convenient Canadian Border Services Agency (CBSA) customs dock is located in Bedwell Harbour. Provisioning, shopping, and dining is made easy at the Driftwood Centre near Port Browning. The Penders also have a wealth of onshore activities including a 9-hole golf course, a 27-hole disc golf course, miles of hiking trails, and plenty of country roads for cycling.

Exploring the islands by road is simple with the informal Car Stop program. Numerous stops can be found on the major roads of the islands, marked by signs and usually a small chair or bench. Island rules for the ride are simple: "Drivers don't have to take the first in line, You're not obliged to accept a ride, that's fine. You accept a ride at your own risk, But the ride is free, so consider it a gift."

Centrally located Pender Islands also make an easy jumping off point for many nearby popular destinations. Ganges Harbour, Winter Cove, Sidney Spit, and even Roche Harbor are all within a comfortable 15 mile radius of the Penders.

Camp Bay

Camp Bay on South Pender Island offers a quiet alternative to nearby Bedwell Harbour and Port Browning. The anchorage offers sweeping views of Boundary Pass and the interesting commercial traffic passing by. On clear days, the 10,781-foot Mount Baker can be seen to the east. Public access for shoreside exploration and a nice beach are found around the corner at Gowlland Point and Brooks Point Regional Park.

Camp Bay is located on the eastern shore of South Pender Island, bordering Boundary Pass. The bay is entered between Higgs Point to the south and Teece Point to the north. When approaching Camp Bay, be aware that strong currents and tide rips can be experienced through Boundary Pass and off Blunden Islet. Passage can be taken between Blunden Islet and Teece Point with a mid-channel depth of 40 feet.

Anchorage can be taken within the bay in 3 to 7 fathoms. At the head of the bay rocky ledges extend out and should be avoided when anchoring. Camp Bay offers protection from north and west winds, but is open to predominate southeasterly wind and waves. This anchorage is best suited during periods of calm weather. Due to its proximity to Boundary Pass, wake from passing ships may also be experienced.

For trips to shore, the nearby beach at Gowlland Point offers a nice spot to land the dinghy or kayak, and public access to Gowlland Point Road for island exploration. While ashore, be sure to walk the wooded and grassland trails at Brooks Point Regional Park. If you're lucky to visit during the spring months, be sure to visit the grassy point to catch the field blooming with native chocolate lilies.

Camp Bay to:		
	Bedwell Harbour *(South Pender Island)*	3 nm
	Ganges Harbour *(Salt Spring Island)*	15 nm
	Ladysmith	33 nm
	Montague Harbour *(Galiano Island)*	16 nm
	Nanaimo	41 nm
	Port Browning *(North Pender Island)*	5 nm
	Roche Harbor *(USA)*	9 nm
	Sidney	11 nm
	Victoria	28 nm
	Wallace Island	21 nm
	Winter Cove *(Saturna Island)*	6 nm

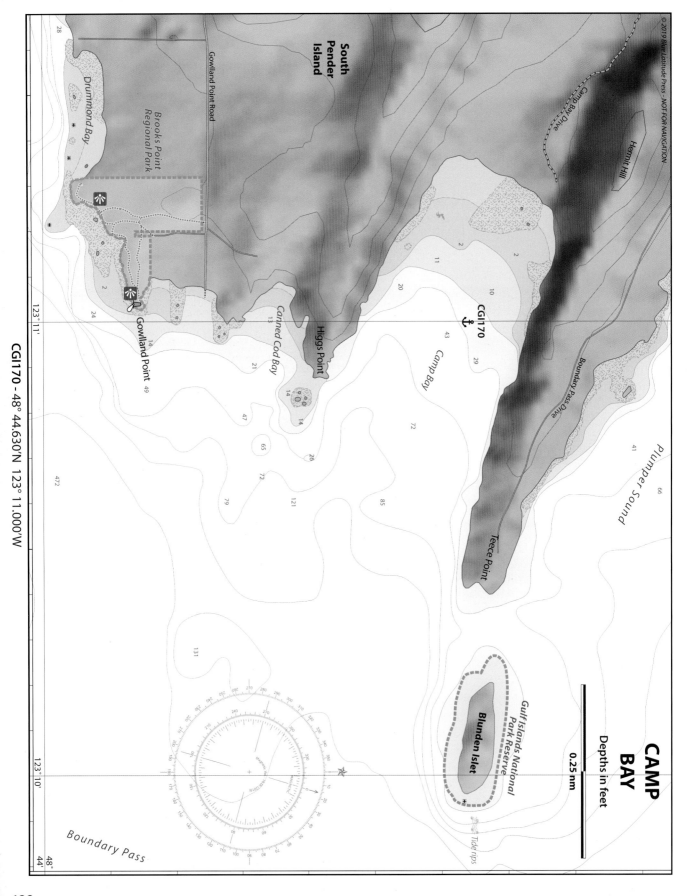

South
Pender
Island

Gowlland Point Road

Brooks Point
Regional Park

Drummond Bay

28

24

2

Gowlland Point

14

49

Canned Cod Bay

13

Higgs Point

21

14

14

47

65

26

72

79

121

472

131

Camp Bay

20

11

43

29

10

2

2

11

⚓ CGl170

85

72

Teece Point

Hermit Hill

Camp Bay Drive

Boundary Pass Drive

Plumper Sound

41

66

© 2019 Blue Latitude Press – NOT FOR NAVIGATION

Blunden Islet

Gulf Islands National
Park Reserve

Tide rips

Boundary Pass

CAMP
BAY

Depths in feet

0.25 nm

123° 11'

123° 10'

48°
44'

CGl170 - 48° 44.630'N 123° 11.000'W

©Kevin Oke

Bedwell Harbour

Bedwell Harbour is home to the very popular Beaumont Marine Park and the stylish Poets Cove Resort & Spa. With ample anchorage and marina slips, a beautiful national park and a convenient customs dock, Bedwell Harbour is a haven for boats of all shapes and sizes. Hikes ranging from easy to energetic through the national parks, along with miles of protected paddling offer visitors a variety of activities to the explore the Pender Islands. After a day of exertion, the resort's relaxing spa or heated pools provide the perfect way to wind down for the day.

Bedwell Harbour is located off Boundary Pass, between North and South Pender Islands. The nearly two and a half mile inlet is formed by the entire western shore of South Pender Island and the narrow southern peninsula of North Pender Island. Entrance to the harbor is found between Wallace Point on North Pender and Tilly Point on South Pender.

On the approach to Bedwell Harbour, keep in mind that the major commercial shipping lanes of Haro Strait and Boundary Pass lie nearby. If crossing Boundary Pass from US waters, northbound traffic in Haro Strait is obscured by islands until vessels make a sharp turn around

Bedwell Harbour to:		
Ganges Harbour (Salt Spring Island)	14 nm
Ladysmith	34 nm
Montague Harbour (Galiano Island)	14 nm
Nanaimo	40 nm
Pirates Cove (De Courcy Island)	31 nm
Roche Harbor (USA)	9 nm
Russell Island	8 nm
Sidney	9 nm
Tod Inlet	20 nm
Victoria	27 nm
Wallace Island	20 nm
Winter Cove (Saturna Island)	9 nm

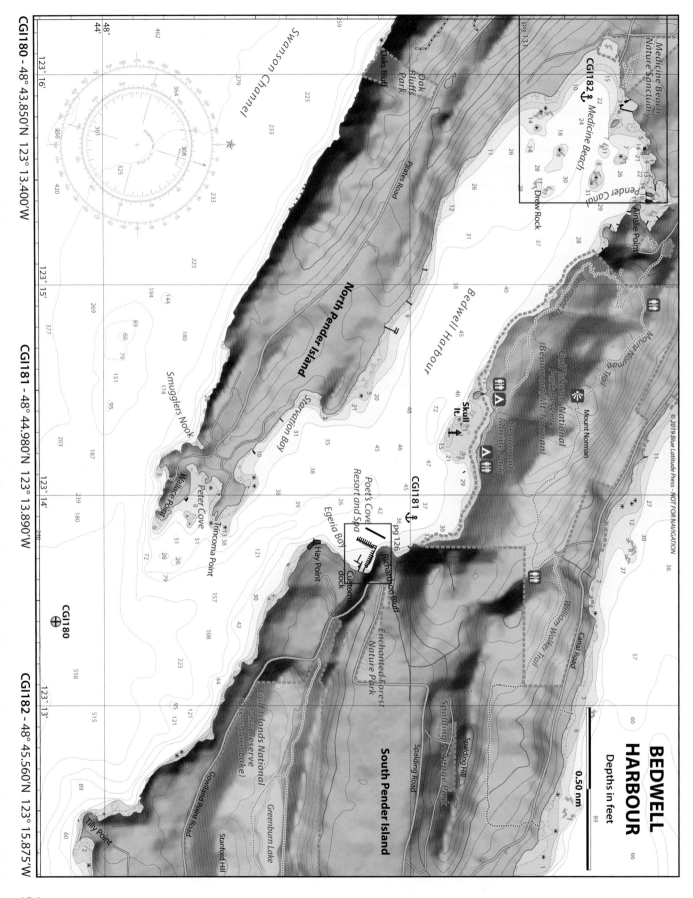

Stuart Island at aptly named, Turn Point. Having an AIS (Automatic Identification System) receiver or marine traffic app on a smart phone is a useful tool when crossing these shipping lanes. Both Haro Strait and Boundary Pass also experience strong tidal streams with rates of 3 to 4 knots so plan your crossing accordingly.

The entrance to Bedwell Harbour is wide, deep and relatively free of hazards. Because of the popularity of the harbor and customs dock, traffic for boats and seaplanes can be heavy at times so be sure to keep a careful eye out. For boats approaching via Pender Canal, see page 129 for further information.

Both Beaumont Marine Park and Poets Cove Marina are located north of Hay Point on South Pender Island, also known as Egeria Bay. Ample anchorage can be found within Beaumont Marine Park and northwest of the marina. Anchor in 4 to 10 fathoms over a mostly mud bottom. Park mooring buoys are available for a nightly fee. Bedwell Harbour offers protection from most winds, but is open to wind and waves from the southeast. Keep in mind some current does ebb and flow through the harbor which can affect anchoring and docking.

Boats entering Bedwell Harbour from foreign waters may clear in at the Canadian Border Services Agency (CBSA) customs dock. This CBSA station is only open seasonally from May 1 to September 30. The three-fingered customs dock is located in Egeria Bay next to Poets Cove Marina. As Bedwell Harbour is a very popular clearance location, the customs dock is one of the largest in the area. A small office and phones are located at the top of the ramp. This is also a popular clearance location for seaplanes flying between Canada and the US. The end of the diagonal finger is reserved for seaplanes only.

For trips to shore, dinghies can be landed on the pebble beaches at Beaumont Marine Park. Although nearby Skull Islet is within the park, the islet not open to public access. A staircase leads from the beach to a park kiosk, payment box for moorings, and trailheads. Camping is also available at the park with 13 primitive sites scattered near the shoreline. For additional park information, a volunteer marine host is located on a float near the beach during the summer months. For those looking for meal off the boat, spa day or liquor store, a dinghy dock is located at Poets Cove Marina near the ramp on the northeast side of the main dock.

Beaumont Marine Park

Mt Norman Overlook

Poets Cove Marina

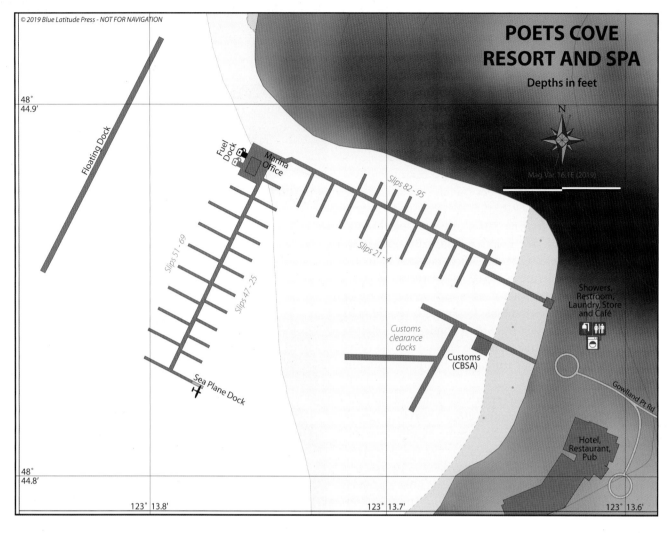

POETS COVE RESORT AND SPA

Depths in feet

Mag. Var. 16.1E (2019)

Floating Dock

Fuel Dock

Marina Office

Slips 51 - 69

Slips 47 - 25

Slips 82 - 95

Slips 21 - 4

Sea Plane Dock

Customs clearance docks

Customs (CBSA)

Showers, Restroom, Laundry, Store and Café

Gowlland Pt Rd

Hotel, Restaurant, Pub

Poets Cove Resort & Spa

The beautiful Poets Cove Resort & Spa is located on South Pender Island within the protection of Bedwell Harbour. The resort offers 110 slips for boats up to 100 feet in length. Each slip has access to water and power (15 and 30 amp) hook ups. Additional moorage is available on the floating dock (no power or water). For boats entering Canada, a customs dock is located immediately adjacent to the marina that is open from May 1 to September 30. Services at the marina include a 60-foot fuel dock (diesel and gas), restrooms, showers, laundry facilities, and free Wifi. Marina guests also have use of the resort's luxury facilities including two heated pools, a hot tub, three restaurants, a children's play area, tennis court, spa, paddle sport rentals, and a liquor and convenience store.

Poets Cove Resort & Spa
Monitors VHF Channel 66A
9801 Spalding Road
Pender Island, BC V0N 2M3
1-888-512-7638
marina@poetscove.com
poetscove.com

Poets Cove Resort at Sunset

Sights to See

The highlight of Bedwell Harbour and South Pender Island is, by far, the magnificent Gulf Islands National Park which includes Beaumont Marine Park and Mount Norman. This 143 acre park is located along the shores of Bedwell Harbour and includes the island's highest peak of Mount Norman, standing at 800 feet. Nearly four miles of trails connect the park from sea to sky, varying from easy to difficult walking paths. The shoreline of the park includes beautiful crescents of sand and pebble beaches as well as stunning rock formations.

For those looking for an amazing overlook of the Gulf Islands and Vancouver Island, be sure to save energy and pack your camera for a hike up to the Mount Norman overlook platform. This ambitious hike will keep your heart pumping as you climb from sea level to the peak at 800 feet. At the top of the mountain is a stunning overlook platform, complete with telescope for sighting all the distant islands and waterways. During the summer months, this hike can induce a lot of sweat so be sure to bring plenty of water as the park does not have any sources of potable water.

Another popular nearby hike is the Greenburn Lake trail. Also part of the Gulf Islands National Park, Greenburn Lake is located near the top of a small hill with a nice looping trail around the lake. The trailhead for the lake lies just up the road from Poets Cove Resort on Gowlland Point Road, near the fire station.

©Kevin Oke
Greenburn Lake

Sedimentary Rock

Beaumont Marine Park

Beaumont Marine Park Trails

Poets Cove Resort

Poets Cove Marina

For a lazy day at the beach, take the dinghy or kayak out and enjoy the beautiful park at Mortimer Spit. On warm summer days, Mortimer Spit is also a popular swimming locale for those brave enough to endure the chilly ocean water. The journey to the spit takes you through the unique man-made canal separating the islands and under the bridge that was later built to reconnect the islands. The sight of the isthmus and surrounding shoreline was once a historical camp for the Coast Salish known as "Xelisen," meaning "lying between". In the mid 1980's, a three year joint excavation project was undertaken by Simon Fraser University and Heritage Conservation Branch. During this study, it was found through radiocarbon dating of the middens that camps at the isthmus date back roughly 5,000 years ago.

Be sure to save time to visit South Pender Island's Enchanted Forest Park. This nature walk is an easy, pleasant walk through lush forests and ferns with boardwalks, bridges and informative signs. During the wet season, a small waterfall surrounded by greenery can be seen. A few trailheads for the park are located on Spalding Road, just up from Poets Cove Resort.

Restaurants

Aurora

Aurora is a fine dining restaurant at Poets Cove Resort. Serving a West Coast inspired menu with local ingredients, Aurora offers diners delicious meals along with the finest views of Bedwell Harbour. The restaurant is open daily from May through early October. poetscove.com/dining/, 1-888-512-POET

Moorings Café

Moorings Café at Poets Cove Resort offers espresso, baked goods, sandwiches, and ice cream for breakfast and lunch. Indoor and outdoor seating options are available overlooking the pool and marina. The cafe also houses a small convenience and liquor store. Open daily during the summer season.

Syrens Bistro & Lounge

Syrens Bistro at Poets Cove Resort offers casual pub-style dining. The bistro is open daily for lunch and dinner from May through early October.

Pender Canal looking south

Pender Canal

In 1902, a narrow isthmus was dredged on Pender Island to create a more protected route for the local ferry. This man-made waterway, known as Pender Canal, separated the island in two, forming North and South Pender Islands. Later, in 1955, a one-lane bridge was constructed over the canal to provide vehicle and pedestrian access to both islands.

Pender Canal lies north to south and links Bedwell Harbour with Port Browning. The canal is roughly 75 feet wide with a minimum depth of just under 6 feet. The bridge over the canal has a width of 39 feet between the piers and a vertical clearance of 27 feet. Just north of the bridge lies overhead cables with a vertical clearance of 36 feet. Pender Canal and adjacent Shark Cove, have a speed limit of 5 knots.

The south entrance (Bedwell Harbour side) contains a drying rock and a rock awash. The entrance is marked by starboard hand buoy "U54" and port hand buoy "U53". Be sure to check the chart when approaching and stay within the navigation buoys to avoid the rock dangers. Current does run through the canal, up to 4 knots, so check the current tables before entering.

To avoid encountering a boat mid-channel, make a call on VHF channel 16 (**low power**) prior to entering Pender Canal. For example, "Sécurité, Sécurité, Sécurité. This is vessel *Om Shanti* entering Pender Canal northbound. *Om Shanti* standing by on channel 16."

Pender Canal looking north

Pender Canal buoys looking north

Medicine Beach

Perched at the head of Bedwell Harbour lies Medicine Beach, a delightful and quiet anchorage fronted by a unique wetlands nature sanctuary. Along with a beautiful sand and pebble beach for strolling, the bluffs north of the beach offer hiking trails and scenic vistas. After a day of hiking and beach combing, a small shopping center provides homemade pizzas and thirst quenching local ciders, beers, wines, spirits, and even fresh coffee drinks.

Medicine Beach is found at the northern end of Bedwell Harbour on North Pender Island. Bedwell Harbour lies between North and South Pender Islands, with the narrow man-made Pender Canal separating the two islands. On approach to Medicine Beach, be aware of covered rocks, including Drew Rock, and shallow areas lying out from the beach near the anchorage area. Drew Rock lies in nearly 7 feet of water, with other nearby rock hazards lying in less so be sure to check the chart before approaching.

Anchorage can be taken off the beach and well clear of any rock dangers in 4 to 5 fathoms over a mostly mud bot-tom. Medicine Beach affords good protection from most winds, but is open to the area's predominate southeasterly winds and waves. For trips to shore, dinghies and kayaks are easily landed on the sand and gravel beach.

One of the best pastimes at Medicine Beach is to explore the 20 acres of protected land at the Medicine Beach Nature Sanctuary. The Sanctuary, which was formed in

Medicine Beach to:		
Ganges Harbour (Salt Spring Island)		15 nm
Ladysmith		34 nm
Montague Harbour (Galiano Island)		15 nm
Nanaimo		42 nm
Pirates Cove (De Courcy Island)		33 nm
Roche Harbor (USA)		11 nm
Russell Island		10 nm
Sidney		11 nm
Victoria		29 nm
Wallace Island		21 nm
Winter Cove (Saturna Island)		10 nm

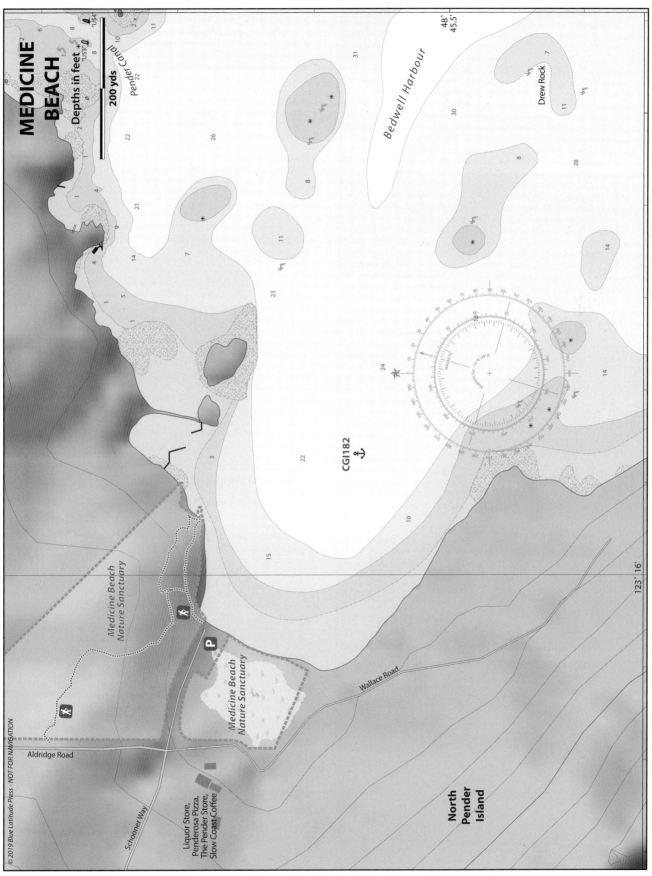

MEDICINE BEACH

2 Depths in feet *

200 yds

Pender Cove

"U54"
"U53"

MEDICINE BEACH

Bedwell Harbour

48°
45.5'

Drew Rock

CGI182 ⚓

Medicine Beach
Nature Sanctuary

P

Medicine Beach
Nature Sanctuary

Wallace Road

Aldridge Road

Schooner Way

Liquor Store,
Penderosa Pizza,
The Pender Store,
Slow Coast Coffee

North
Pender
Island

123° 16'

© 2019 Blue Latitude Press - NOT FOR NAVIGATION

CGI182 - 48° 45.560'N 123° 15.875'W

131

1995, is owned by the Islands Trust Conservancy, and managed by the Pender Islands Conservancy Association (PICA). Beginning at the beach, sand, gravel, and crushed shells, along with a thick layer of drift wood act as a berm to the marshy wetlands behind. Archeological excavations have dated indigenous peoples in this area to roughly 5,000 years ago. A shell midden stretches the length of Medicine Beach, with its name referencing it as a medicinal plant collecting site or as a place of spiritual healing.

Behind the beach lies the unique brackish marsh lands which are uncommon in the Gulf Islands. Fresh water run-off from the surrounding hills combines with ocean water from the twice daily incoming tides to provide a diluted saltwater environment. Rare plants like the colorful Henderson's checker mallow can be found in the marsh along with skunk cabbage, seagrasses and more. The marsh also provides an excellent habitat for coastal and migratory birds including the Great Blue Heron, Virginia Rail, and Western Grebes.

A trailhead near the beach explores the coastal bluffs and forest of the sanctuary. The trail, roughly a quarter of a mile in length, provides scenic vistas of the beach and anchorage before turning to head inland. The forest is comprised of Douglas firs, madrones, cedars, and the protected Garry oak. The trail ends at Aldridge Road.

For those looking for a little more adventure on a warm summer day, take the 2 mile walk up Schooner Way to Pirates Road and follow it down to the south end of Magic Lake to Swimming Hole park. This park is a favorite with locals who come to enjoy the warmer lake waters and soak up the sunshine on the wood dock and floating dive platform.

Just behind the marsh land and sanctuary is a small building housing the Medicine Beach Liquor Store, Penderosa Pizza, and The Pender Store. The Medicine Beach Liquor Store offers a variety of locally brewed beers and ciders, wine, and spirits, as well as region and international varieties. Penderosa Pizza bakes delicious classic and original pizzas using their own fresh leavened pizza dough and house-made sauces (penderosapizza.com). The Pender Store is a convenience/grocery selling a small selection of staples as well as some incredible homemade takeout meals including meat pies, pasta dishes, enchiladas and more (250-217-6641). Across the parking lot is Slow Coast Coffee serving a fine selection of coffee, tea, and espresso drinks along with fresh bakery items and an eclectic mix of daily food specials (250-629-3619).

©Kevin Oke

Port Browning

Small enough to give the feel of quaint island living, yet large enough to have the luxuries of town life, Port Browning is a charming stop on any Gulf Islands itinerary. Port Browning offers lots of room to anchor, a full service marina, restaurants with a view, and a nearby shopping center to indulge island visitors. And for those with a disc golf passion or interest in learning to play, the excellent 27-hole, Golf Islands Disc Park, is located nearby.

The long inlet of Port Browning is located along both North and South Pender Islands. The inlet, which is accessed via Plumper Sound, can be entered south of Razor Point on North Pender Island. When approaching Razor Point, be aware of a drying reef and shoal spit extending 0.2 miles east of the point. Once inside the inlet, a shallow area with minimum depths of 16 feet lies roughly 0.25 miles southeast from the head of the inlet.

For those entering Port Browning Marina, be aware of rocks off the northern entrance point to the marina. These rocks are marked by starboard hand buoy "U52." A floating breakwater for the marina lies off the southern entrance point to the marina and is marked by a green light. Enter the marina between buoy "U52" and the floating breakwater. Do not enter north of buoy "U52."

Anchorage can be taken throughout the bay in 3 to 5 fathoms over a mud bottom. A number of private moor-

Port Browning to:		
	Ganges Harbour (Salt Spring Island)	15 nm
	Ladysmith	40 nm
	Montague Harbour (Galiano Island)	12 nm
	Nanaimo	39 nm
	Pirates Cove (De Courcy Island)	30 nm
	Princess Bay (Portland Island)	13 nm
	Roche Harbor (USA)	11 nm
	Sidney	15 nm
	Tod Inlet	26 nm
	Victoria	32 nm
	Wallace Island	19 nm
	Winter Cove (Saturna Island)	5 nm

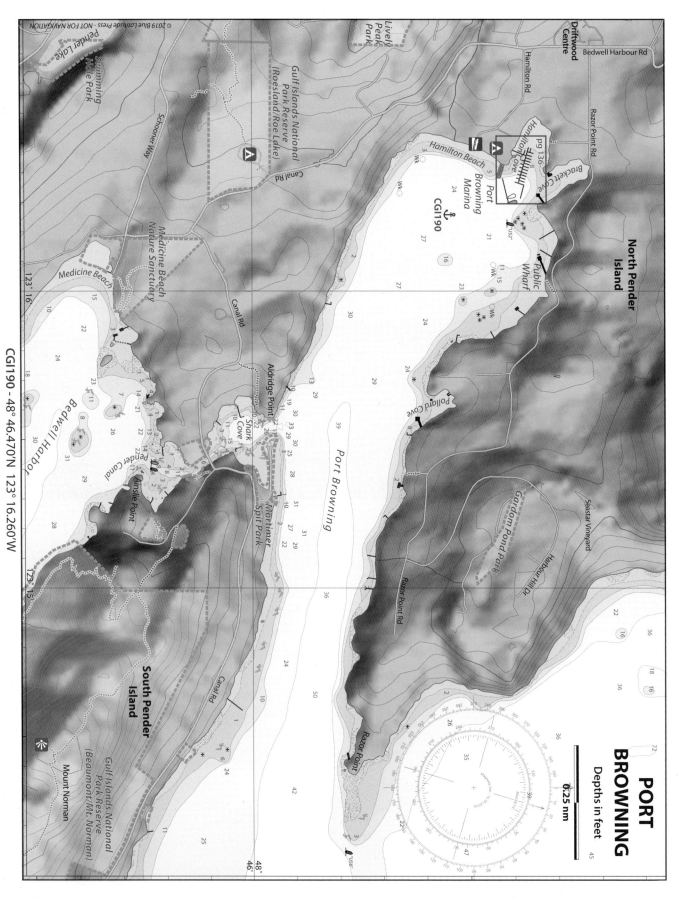

© 2019 Blue Latitude Press - NOT FOR NAVIGATION

PORT BROWNING

Depths in feet

0.25 nm

CGI190 - 48° 46.470'N 123° 16.260'W

North Pender Island

South Pender Island

Port Browning Marina

CGI190

Port Browning

Bedwell Harbour

Medicine Beach

Medicine Beach Nature Sanctuary

Gulf Islands National Park Reserve (Roesland/Roe Lake)

Lively Peak Park

Swimming Hole Park

Pender Lake

Schooner Way

Canal Rd

Canal Rd

Canal Rd

Pender Canal

Ainslie Point

Mortimer Spit Park

Shark Cove

Aldridge Point

Hamilton Beach

Public Wharf

Pollard Cove

Gardom Pond Park

Seastar Vineyard

Harbour Hill Dr

Razor Point Rd

Razor Point Rd

Razor Point

Mount Norman

Gulf Islands National Park Reserve (Beaumont/Mt. Norman)

Driftwood Centre

Bedwell Harbour Rd

Hamilton Rd

Hamilton Rd

Hamilton Cove

Bracket Cove

pg 136

Port Browning Resort campground

ings are scattered throughout the inlet, although there is plenty of room to anchor. Port Browning offers protection from most directions except for the area's predominate southeasterlies in which it is open to wind and waves. Better southeast wind protection can be found on nearby Saturna Island at Boot Cove or Lyall Harbour (see page 158).

Port Browning also offers a public wharf through the Capital Regional District (CRD). Two floats are available totalling 120 feet, however most of the float space is taken up by long-term resident moorage, the Coast Guard Auxiliary vessel, and dinghies from boats moored in the harbor. Visitors are welcome, but rafting may be required. The wharf also provides a tidal grid for boats needing access below the waterline. For further information on CRD public wharfs check their website at: www.crd.bc.ca, or call the wharfinger at (250) 881-2019.

For trips to shore, dinghies and kayaks can be landed on the beach at the head of the inlet near the boat ramp. The boat ramp provides public access and connects to Hamilton Road. From the beach, it is less than a half mile walk to Driftwood Centre for shopping a dining options.

Port Browning Marina

Port Browning Marina Pub and office

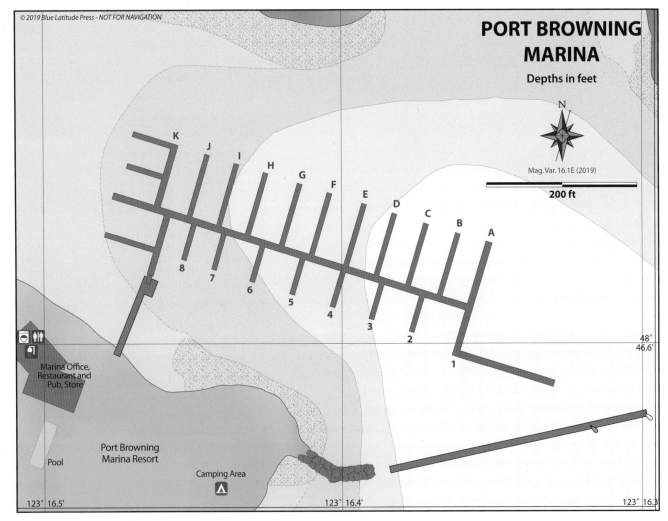

© 2019 Blue Latitude Press - NOT FOR NAVIGATION

PORT BROWNING MARINA

Depths in feet

Mag. Var. 16.1E (2019)

200 ft

Marina Office, Restaurant and Pub, Store

Pool

Port Browning Marina Resort

Camping Area

Port Browning Marina

Port Browning Marina is part of the Mill Bay Marine Group which includes Mill Bay Marina, Port Sidney Marina and others. The marina has just recently upgraded with new docks and a breakwater. Port Browning Marina can accommodate boats up to 80 feet in length with power hookups available. Services at the marina include restrooms, showers, laundry facilities, camping, Wifi, an ATM, and use of the seasonal pool. The marina is home to the Bridgemans Bistro, the Port Browning Marina Pub, and a convenience store with snacks, ice, coffee drinks and more are available.

Port Browning Marina
Monitors VHF channel 66A
4605 Oak Road
Pender Island, BC V0N 2M0
(250) 629-3493
contact@portbrowning.ca
www.portbrowning.ca

Port Browning Marina and anchorage

CRD public wharf (foreground boat on the tidal grid)

Sights to See

Port Browning is centrally located, providing easy exploration of both North and South Pender Islands. For visitors traveling with bikes, the rural roads offer prime cycling territory to check out the islands' various parks. The Penders also have a unique rideshare option with various "Car Stops" throughout the two islands (see page 120).

If you are lucky enough to visit on a Saturday, be sure to bring your grocery bags and take a trip to the farmer's market. Held at the local community hall, the market hosts local farmers, craftspeople and food vendors. Saturdays, from Easter to Thanksgiving, the market is open from 9:30am to 1pm at the Pender Island Community Hall. The hall, which is located at 4418 Bedwell Harbour Road, is a 1.8 mile walk from the Port Browning Marina.

For the sporting enthusiast, North Pender Island is home to two courses, one for golf and one for disc golf. The Pender Island Golf and Country Club is a 9-hole course located on Otter Bay Road. The Golf Island Disc Park is a unique 27-hole course found off Galleon Way, north of Magic Lake. The course is free, and if you are lacking discs on board, they can be purchased at Pender Pharmacy, Pender Island Kayak Adventures (at Port Browning) and The Driftwood Auto Centre. For further information, check their website at: www.discgolfisland.com

Driftwood Centre

Marine Services and Provisioning

BC Liquor
BC Liquor Stores offer a great selection of beers, wines and spirits. Located in the Driftwood Centre. (250) 629-3413

Driftwood Auto & Marine Centre
The Driftwood Auto & Marine Centre is a general store with auto parts, marine parts, hardware, fishing gear and fuel. Located in the Driftwood Centre along Bedwell Harbour Road. (250) 629-3002

Pender Island Pharmacy
Pender Island Pharmacy offers a bit of everything including prescriptions, cosmetics, office supplies, gifts, golf discs, and toys. Located in the Driftwood Centre. (250) 629-6555

Tru Value Foods
A locally owned grocery providing quality and healthy, foods including fresh produce, meats, dairy, bakery and a deli. Located in the Driftwood Centre along Bedwell Harbour Road. truvaluefoods.com, (250) 629-8322

Restaurants

Bridgemans Bistro
The Bistro serves meals using locally sourced ingredients in a beautiful setting overlooking the marina. Open for lunch and dinner. Located at Port Browning Marina.

Jo's Place
Jo's Place is a favorite on the Penders, serving delicious breakfast and lunch meals. Be sure to try one of the many eggs benedict options. Open 8am to 2pm daily. Located in the Driftwood Centre along Bedwell Harbour Road. www.josplacepender.com, (250) 629-6033

Port Browning Marina Pub
Newly remodeled, the pub overlooks the marina and harbor. Serving a good selection of craft beers and pub food using local products and seafood.

Vanilla Leaf Bakery Café
The Vanilla Leaf Bakery serves excellent coffee, homemade baked goods including gluten-free and vegan options, soups, and lunch items. Indoor and outdoor seating with free wifi. Located in the Driftwood Centre. Open daily from 7am to 5pm. (250) 629-6453

©Kevin Oke

Hope Bay

Historic Hope Bay is reminiscent of the early home-steading days when life revolved around the water. People, goods, and mail were brought to the island via the ferry landing at Hope Bay, however in 1966 a new ferry terminal was constructed across the island at Otter Bay. Today a public wharf takes the place of the ferry landing and leads up to newly rebuilt waterfront buildings.

Hope Bay is located on the northeastern end of North Pender Island. The bay lies at the northern end of Plumper Sound and south end of Navy Channel. The bay is entered between Auchterlonie Point and Fane Island. The eastern end of Fane Island is marked by a navigation light. When approaching Hope Bay from the north, pass east of Fane Island to avoid a drying reef lying between North Pender and Fane Island.

Anchorage can be taken at Hope Bay south of Fane Island in 7 to 9 fathoms. Be sure to check the chart prior to entering as the bathymetry around Hope Bay is fairly irregular. A small, yet very steep sided 145-foot hole lies southwest of Fane Island. Extending from shore north of

the public wharf, depths become are quite shallow. This anchorage is best suited during periods of calm weather as it is somewhat exposed to wind and waves with the exception of weather from the west. The anchorage may also be affected by boat and ferry traffic transiting Navy Channel and Plumper Sound.

Hope Bay is home to a public wharf through the Capital Regional District (CRD). The CRD dock has ap-

Hope Bay to:		
	Ganges Harbour *(Salt Spring Island)*	11 nm
	Montague Harbour *(Galiano Island)*	9 nm
	Nanaimo	35 nm
	Pirates Cove *(De Courcy Island)*	27 nm
	Roche Harbor *(USA)*	15 nm
	Russell Island	9 nm
	Sidney	15 nm
	Telegraph Harbour *(Thetis Island)*	23 nm
	Victoria	35 nm
	Wallace Island	15 nm
	Winter Cove *(Saturna Island)*	3 nm

139

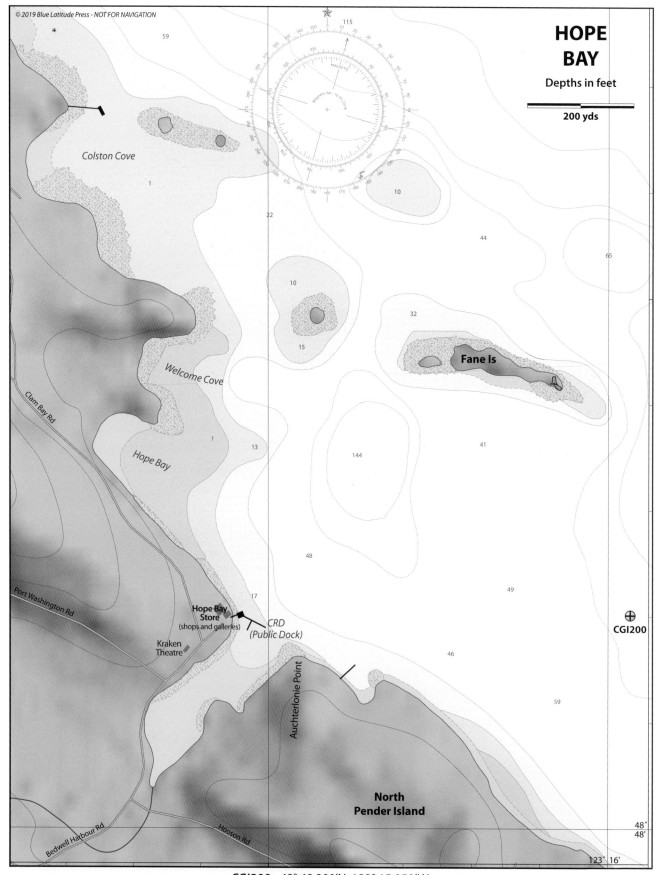

© 2019 Blue Latitude Press - NOT FOR NAVIGATION

HOPE BAY

Depths in feet

200 yds

Colston Cove

59

1

22

10

10

15

Welcome Cove

1

13

Hope Bay

32

Fane Is

44

65

41

144

48

49

59

46

17

Clam Bay Rd

Port Washington Rd

Hope Bay Store
(shops and galleries)

CRD (Public Dock)

Kraken Theatre

Auchterlonie Point

North Pender Island

⊕
CGI200

115

MAGNETIC

48° 48'

123° 16'

Bedwell Harbour Rd

Hooson Rd

CGI200 - 48° 48.200'N 123° 15.950'W

proximately 150 feet of moorage space. During the summer months, much of the dock space is used by local boaters, however the east side of the main float can usually accommodate one or two visiting boats. During the winter months or during periods of strong east to southeast winds, the docks are exposed to waves and wind from Plumper Sound. The dock does not provide power or water hookups. Restrooms are available in the Hope Bay store building during business hours. For further information on CRD public wharfs check their website at: www.crd. bc.ca, or call the wharfinger at (250) 813-3321.

On shore is the newly rebuilt Hope Bay Store. The original general store and post office was established in 1905 by Robert Corbett. Sadly, in 1998, the historic waterfront building caught fire. With 27 dedicated local islanders, the Hope Bay Store was rebuilt and opened for office and commercial space in 2005. Today the space holds shops including home designs and decorations, jewelry, an art gallery, vet clinic, gourmet chocolate shop and more. Check the Hope Bay Store website for a current listing of shops and eateries. Just down from the store building, be sure to check out the Kraken Theatre. The intimate theater hosts a variety of musicians, and shows weekly movies. Check their website for current events at: www.thekrakentheatre.com.

S.S. Iroquois

The *S.S. Iroquois* was an 82-foot passenger and cargo ship that served southern Vancouver Island and the Gulf Islands. Launched in 1900, the *Iroquois* transported people, supplies and mail from Sidney to Nanaimo with stops at various Gulf Islands including the dock at Hope Bay.

On April 10, 1910, the *Iroquois* left the Beacon Avenue dock in Sidney amidst strong winds and seas. The ship, heavily loaded with unsecured cargo, began to list shortly after leaving the dock as some of the cargo shifted. Within minutes, the listing ship turned over and sank. With poor passenger list record keeping on board, it is believed that at least 20 people perished in the accident. Of the 10 or 11 people who were saved, three were rescued by William Tzouhalem, Donat Charlie and Bob Klutwhalem of the Cowichan First Nations. For their bravery they were awarded the Government of Canada Medal For Gallant and Humane Services. The captain, Albert A. Sears, was found guilty of negligence and failure to perform his duty to save his passengers.

©Kevin Oke

Grimmer Bay

Grimmer Bay is home to the small housing settlement of historic Port Washington. Like Hope Bay, Port Washington was once a landing site for passenger and cargo ferries, boasting a general store and post office. Today the quiet bay is home to a public wharf and a handful of privately moored boats.

Grimmer Bay is located on the northwestern end of North Pender Island. The bay lies along the northern end of Swanson Channel and faces nearby Prevost Island. Two lobes of the bay are formed by above water and drying rocks extending 0.2 miles northwest from the middle of the head of the bay. The western most rocky islet, Boat Islet, is marked by a navigation light on its western end.

When approaching Grimmer Bay from the north be aware that strong current can be experienced in Swanson Channel near the vicinity of Enterprise Reef and the entrance to Active Pass (3 to 7 knots). Swanson Channel is also one of the main channels used by BC Ferries, including the large 550-foot ferries coming from the mainland. Keep a careful watch and check the current tables when transiting this area.

Once in Grimmer Bay, be aware of a rock with less than 6 feet covering it, lying roughly 150 feet southeast from the end of the Capital Regional District (CRD) dock. Anchorage can be taken within the bay in 6 to 9 fathoms. Private moorings can be found throughout the bay, but ample anchor room is still available. The anchorage provides good easterly wind and wave protection, but is open to westerly weather. Grimmer Bay is also subject to

Grimmer Bay to:		
Ganges Harbour *(Salt Spring Island)*	8 nm
Ladysmith	25 nm
Montague Harbour *(Galiano Island)*	6 nm
Nanaimo	33 nm
Pirates Cove *(De Courcy Island)*	24 nm
Princess Bay *(Portland Island)*	7 nm
Roche Harbor *(USA)*	15 nm
Sidney	11 nm
Victoria	32 nm
Wallace Island	13 nm
Winter Cove *(Saturna Island)*	6 nm

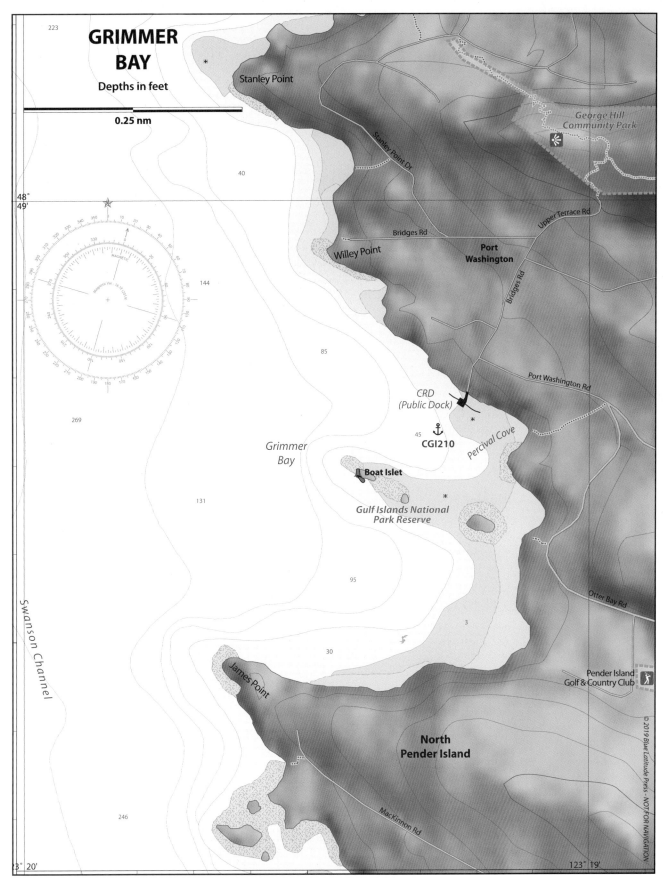

GRIMMER BAY

Depths in feet

0.25 nm

Stanley Point

223

40

Stanley Point Dr

George Hill
Community Park

48°
49'

Bridges Rd

Upper Terrace Rd

Willey Point

Port
Washington

144

Bridges Rd

85

Port Washington Rd

269

CRD
(Public Dock)

*Grimmer
Bay*

45
CGI210

Percival Cove

Boat Islet

131

*Gulf Islands National
Park Reserve*

95

3

Otter Bay Rd

30

James Point

Pender Island
Golf & Country Club

North
Pender Island

Swanson Channel

246

MacKinnon Rd

48° 20'

123° 19'

© 2019 Blue Latitude Press – NOT FOR NAVIGATION

CGI210 - 48° 48.725'N 123° 19.275'W

frequent wakes from passing BC Ferries making this a bit of a rolly anchorage.

Moorage may also be taken at the public CRD dock on the north side of Grimmer Bay. The dock has two sets of floats on either side of the wharf with roughly 200 feet of moorage space. Several local boats have regular moorage here and visitors are welcome to either raft up or use any available space. Keep in mind there is a 45 foot section on the northern section of the dock that is reserved for emergency vessels, school water-taxis and other service providers. Seaplanes also frequent the reserved area, as well as the very end of the dock. The CRD dock does not provide power or water hook ups, and there are no land based facilities. For further information on CRD public wharfs check their website at: www.crd.bc.ca, or call the wharfinger at (250) 629-6111.

For trips to shore, dinghies and kayaks can be landed at the CRD dock. There is little in the way of services at Grimmer Bay, but be sure to check out George Hill Community Park once ashore. The trailhead is located roughly one mile from the dock on Walden Road. The trail to the top is fairly short, only 0.6 miles, but it is steep to reach the 500 foot summit. Bring good shoes and a camera to capture the sweeping views of Swanson and Trincomali Channels.

Otter Bay

Otter Bay is a popular stop on North Pender Island with room for anchoring as well as a full service marina, complete with two heated swimming pools. Otter Bay is also centrally located to a number of nearby favorite destinations like Montague Harbour, Ganges Harbour and Prevost Island. The bay is adjacent to the Gulf Islands National Park Reserve with public trails out to Roe Islet, Roe Lake and the historical compound of Roesland. For golfers, a 9-hole course is located less than a mile north of the Otter Bay Marina.

Otter Bay is located on the northwestern side of North Pender Island along Swanson Channel. The Pender Island BC Ferries terminal is located near the northern entrance to the bay. When approaching from the south, be aware of rocky reefs extending out from shore north of Shingle Bay up to and including Roe Islet. Give this shoreline ample room when passing.

As with Grimmer Bay, when approaching Otter Bay from the north be aware that strong current can be experienced in Swanson Channel near the vicinity of Enterprise Reef and the entrance to Active Pass (3 to 7 knots). Swanson Channel is also one of the main channels used by BC Ferries, including the large 550-foot ferries coming from the mainland. Keep a careful watch and check the current tables when transiting this area.

The northern portion of Otter Bay is known as Hyashi Cove and includes the marina, private moorings, and room to anchor. When approaching Hyashi Cove, port hand buoy "U57" lies close southeast off the point south

Otter Bay to:		
	Clam Bay *(Thetis Island)*	18 nm
	Ganges Harbour *(Salt Spring Island)*	9 nm
	Montague Harbour *(Galiano Island)*	7 nm
	Nanaimo	34 nm
	Pirates Cove *(De Courcy Island)*	25 nm
	Princess Bay *(Portland Island)*	6 nm
	Roche Harbor *(USA)*	14 nm
	Sidney	10 nm
	Tod Inlet	18 nm
	Victoria	31 nm
	Wallace Island	14 nm
	Winter Cove *(Saturna Island)*	8 nm

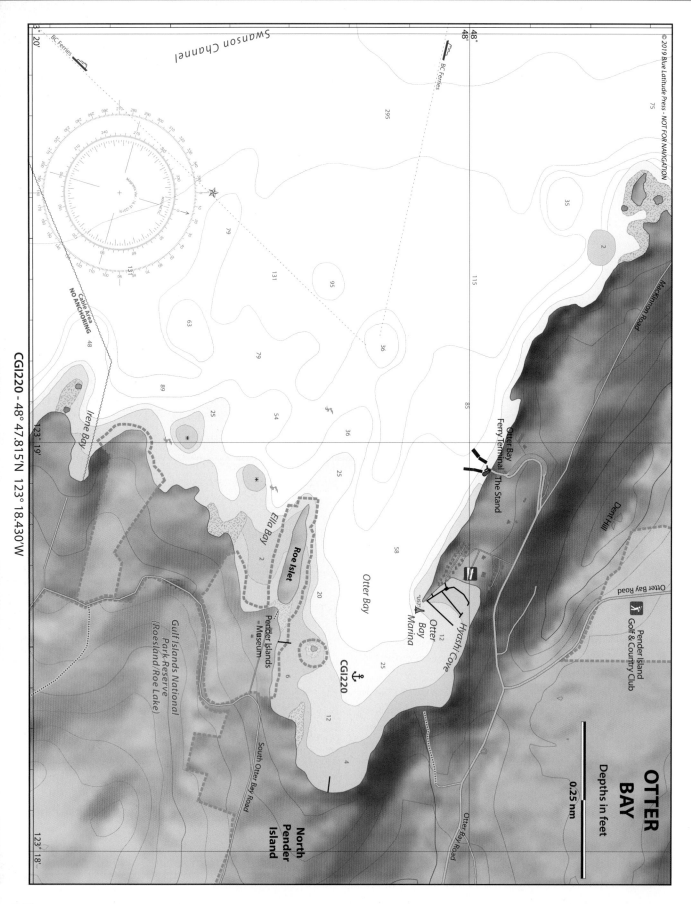

OTTER BAY

Depths in feet

0.25 nm

Swanson Channel

BC Ferries

BC Ferries

© 2019 Blue Latitude Press - NOT FOR NAVIGATION

75

295

35

2

115

95

131

79

36

63

85

79

89

54

25

36

25

58

Cable Area
NO ANCHORING

Irene Bay

48

Ella Bay

Roe Islet

2

20

Otter Bay

25

12

Hyashi Cove

Otter Bay Marina

USD

Otter Bay
Ferry Terminal
The Stand

MacKinnon Road

Dent Hill

Otter Bay Road

Pender Island
Golf & Country Club

Pender Islands
Museum

Gulf Islands National
Park Reserve
(Roesland/Roe Lake)

6

CGI220

12

4

South Otter Bay Road

Otter Bay Road

North
Pender
Island

CGI220 - 48° 47.815'N 123° 18.430'W

of the marina. Pass south of this buoy to avoid shoal areas between the buoy and the point.

Anchorage can be taken within the bay in 3 to 6 fathoms over a mud bottom. The anchorage provides good protection from weather with the exception of winds from the west. Due to ferry traffic in Swanson Channel, boat wake may be experienced in the anchorage. A number of private moorings are also scattered throughout the bay.

For trips to shore, dinghies can be landed at the dinghy dock at Roesland within the Gulf Islands National Park Reserve. While at the park, enjoy a piece of Pender Island history with the preserved farmland and resort.

The story of Roesland begins with Robert and Margaret Roe immigrants from Scotland whom arrived in Victoria in 1896. After moving to Pender Island, they purchased 650 acres along Otter Bay in 1906, and named the farm Roesland. After renting out a small cottage on the property, the Roe's saw a niche and decided to supplement their income by offering stays at the "Farm Resort." Over the decades, the farm and resort continued, with operations eventually being handed down to the Roe's son, Bert. In 1971, the property was sold to a long time guest of the resort who continued its operation until 1991.

Parks Canada acquired the land and sought to save the original Roe home. Parks Canada offered use (along with

Roesland and Roe Islet (note photo was taken prior to new park dock installation)

Roe Lake

Today the museum is open to the public from Easter through Thanksgiving each weekend from 1pm to 4pm, except during July and August when it is open from 10am to 4pm. For further information about the Pender Islands Museum, see there website at: www.penderislandsmuseum.ca.

The park also offers two walking trails. During low tide, visitors can cross over to Roes Islet and walk the length of the island. Expansive views of Swanson Channel and Salt Spring Island can be had from the western tip. The second trail is picked up near the western portion of the park and takes visitors to Roe Lake. The trailhead is found off the dirt road, Shingle Bay Road. The forest lined trail eventually opens to the lake fringed with thick with lily pads.

For the golf enthusiast, the Pender Island Golf and Country Club is open to the public. The 9-hole course is located a little more than a half mile up the road from the marina. For those staying at the marina, shuttle service to the course is available. The golf shop offers rentals, clothing and accessories. For further information check their website at: www.penderislandgolf.ca

a nominal lease agreement) of the Roe home to the Pender Islands Museum Society in exchange for restoring the rotting building to its former glory. After two years of work, the museum opened in 2005.

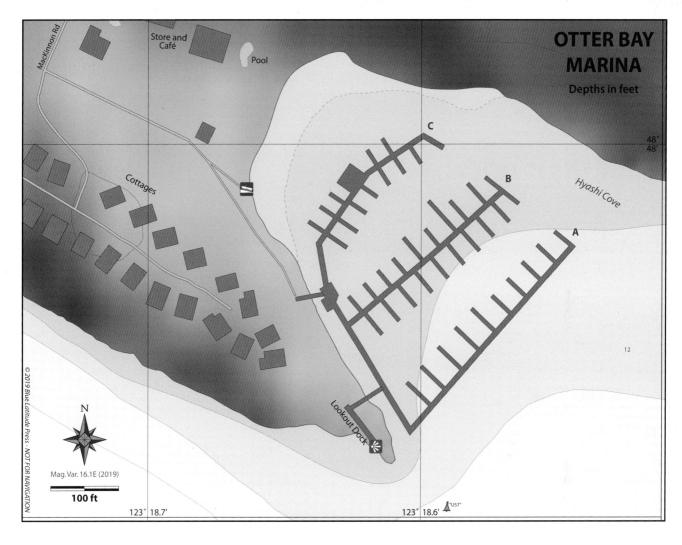

Otter Bay Marina

The Otter Bay Marina is part of The Currents at Otter Bay resort. The marina offers 100 slips for boats with power (15 and 30 amp) and water hook ups at each slip. Services at the marina include restrooms, showers, laundry facilities, free Wifi, a boat ramp, cafe and store.

Guests of the marina also have use of the resort's facilities including two heated pools, propane barbecues, children's playground and shuttle service to the Pender Island Golf and Country Club (public course). The marina also offers a small grocery store and cafe, open daily from May to September. Boats at anchor can use the marina's dinghy dock for a daily fee.

Otter Bay Marina
Monitors VHF channel 66A
2311 MacKinnon Road
Pender Island, BC V0N 2M1
(250) 629-3579
info@otterbaymarina.ca
www.otterbaymarina.ca

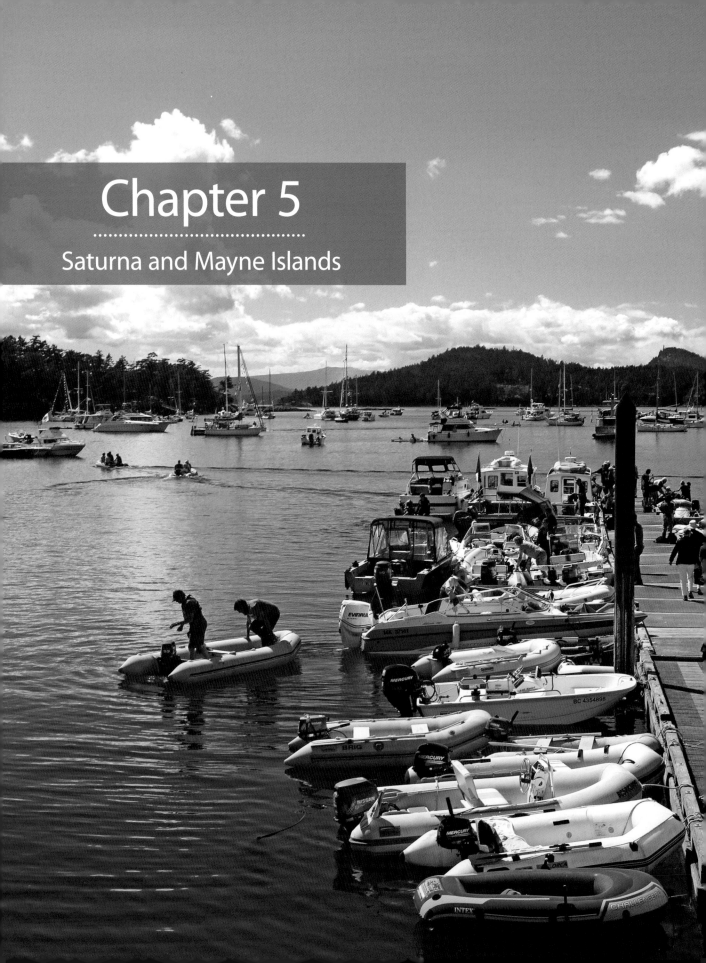

Chapter 5

Saturna and Mayne Islands

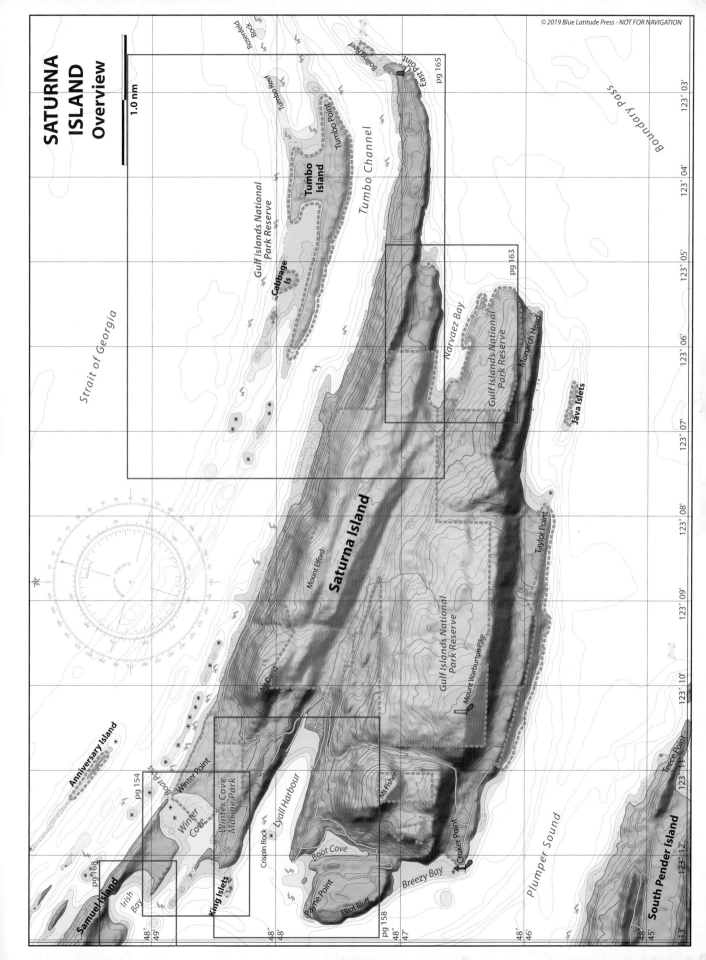

SATURNA
ISLAND
Overview

1.0 nm

© 2019 Blue Latitude Press - NOT FOR NAVIGATION

Strait of Georgia

Boundary Pass

123° 03'

123° 04'

123° 05'

123° 06'

123° 07'

123° 08'

123° 09'

123° 10'

123° 11'

123° 12'

123° 13'

Rosenfeld Rock

Boiling Reef

East Point

pg 165

Tumbo Reef

Tumbo Point

Tumbo Island

Tumbo Channel

Gulf Islands National Park Reserve

Cabbage Is

Narvaez Bay

pg 163

Monarch Head

Gulf Islands National Park Reserve

Java Islets

Saturna Island

Mount Elford

Mt David

Mount Warburton Pike

Gulf Islands National Park Reserve

Taylor Point

Anniversary Island

pg 154

Boot Pass

Winter Point

Winter Cove

Winter Cove Marine Park

Crispin Rock

Lyall Harbour

Boot Cove

Payne Point

Mt Fisher

Croker Point

Breezy Bay

Elliot Bluff

pg 158

pg 168

Samuel Island

Irish Bay

King Islets

Plumper Sound

Teece Point

South Pender Island

48° 49'

48° 48'

48° 47'

48° 46'

48° 45'

©Kevin Oke

Mount Warburton Pike

Saturna Island

Beautiful and rugged Saturna Island sits at the very eastern edge of the Gulf Islands. Although a fairly large island at roughly 12 square miles, Saturna has a very modest year round population of roughly 350 residents. A small selection of shops and eateries supply the island, including the historic Saturna General Store. In 2003, existing park, Crown, and reserve land on Saturna was combined and federally protected under the Gulf Islands National Park Reserve. This combined park land now totals nearly half of the entire island.

In 1791, Spanish explorer, José María Narváez, was sent to document the waters from Nootka Island to the Strait of Georgia. With his schooner, *Santa Saturnina,* Narváez traveled through the Strait of Juan de Fuca and Haro Strait, rounding what is now known as Saturna Island.

East Point

Today the island is known for its mountainous landscape, prime whale watching position, and remote feel. The tourism board boasts friendly residents that equal in number to the unique feral goats roaming the island. BC Ferries serves the island from both the mainland and Vancouver Island.

One of the top events is the July 1st Canada Day Lamb Barbecue (see page 156). Visitors from far and wide descend on Saturna in the hundreds to attend the annual community event that began back in 1950. The event includes live music, local crafts, children's races, raffles, food vendors, beer garden, and much more.

A true highlight of the island is the East Point Park. Part of the Gulf Islands National Park Reserve, East Point offers visitors a prime waterfront vista for enjoying the view and the area's marine mammal stars, the orca whales. The surrounding sculpted sandstone of the point creates interesting tide pools that provide hours of entertainment. Housed in the historic Fog Alarm Building at the East Point Light Station, the Saturna Heritage Centre educates visitors on the history and stories of Saturna Island (www.saturnaheritage.ca).

While Saturna can be explored by boat, dinghy, or kayak, shoreside transport comes in the form of walking, cycling, and thumbing rides from passing residents in cars. The local Lions Club chapter also operates a volunteer shuttle service in exchange for donations (www.saturnalionsclub.net).

Winter Cove

Idyllic Winter Cove is tucked in between Saturna and Samuel Islands, offering boaters a unique and nearly landlocked anchorage. The park at the head of the cove is part of the Gulf Islands National Park Reserve, and offers a large dinghy dock, walking trails and an open ballpark field. Winter Cove is also the site of the widely popular Saturna Island Lamb Barbecue held annually on Canada Day.

Winter Cove is located between the northwestern end of Saturna Island and the southeastern end of Samuel Island. The Strait of Georgia lies northeast of the cove with Plumper Sound lying to the southwest.

Approaches to Winter Cove from the south can be taken via Plumper Sound. Approaching from the north, passage can be taken via Navy Channel between North Pender and Mayne Islands. If transiting through Navy Channel, be sure to locate the expansive Conconi Reef on the chart. For smaller boats, occasionally Georgeson Passage between Samuel and Mayne Islands is used (see page 169). If using Georgeson Passage, be aware that currents run strong through the narrow pass which has a least depth of 34 feet. Dangerous shoals and rocks lie near the northern entrance to the pass.

Lying between Ralph Grey Point and Winter Point at the northeast side of Winter Cove is Boat Passage. From Winter Cove this pass leads into the Strait of Georgia. Due to the strong currents, which can reach 7 knots, dangerous rocks, and shallow depth (15 feet), Boat Passage is best left to small craft and dinghies at slack water. This passage is not recommended for larger boats.

The entrance to Winter Cove is guarded by a long reef extending 0.3 miles northwest from Mikuni Point known

Winter Cove to:		
	Bedwell Harbour (South Pender Island)	9 nm
	Ganges Harbour (Salt Spring Island)	13 nm
	Genoa Bay	21 nm
	Ladysmith	29 nm
	Montague Harbour (Galiano Island)	11 nm
	Nanaimo	38 nm
	Pirates Cove (De Courcy Island)	29 nm
	Roche Harbor (USA)	15 nm
	Sidney	16 nm
	Tod Inlet	24 nm
	Victoria	33 nm
	Wallace Island	17 nm

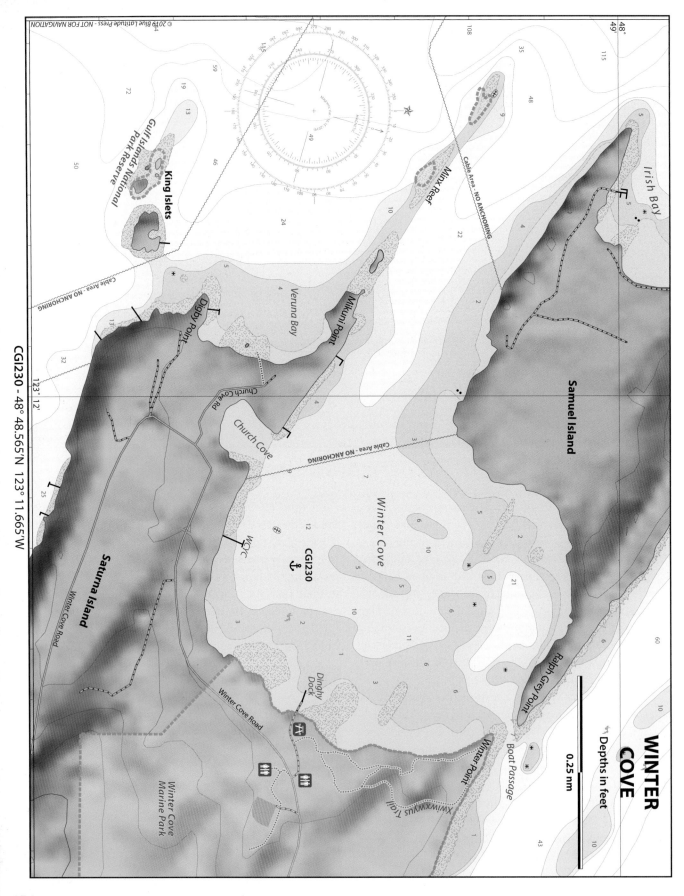

WINTER COVE

Depths in feet

0.25 nm

as Minx Reef. Upon approach, be sure to give Minx Reef ample room when rounding, and do not attempt to cut through sections of the reef.

Winter Cove is shallow with sections of shoal water and reefs so keep close attention to the chart and depth sounder. Prior to anchoring, check the tide tables to make sure there is ample water under the keel for the length of your stay at Winter Cove. An underwater cable extends across the western portion of the cove. Anchorage can be taken within sections of cove in 1 to 2 fathoms over a mostly mud bottom. Current does flow through the anchorage and entrance so be sure to set your anchor well. Winter Cove provides protection from most winds, but is open to weather and waves from the northwest.

For trips to shore, a large floating dinghy dock is provided for access to the national park land. Up from the ramp is a kiosk with park information and maps. A one mile loop trail leads north from the kiosk to Winter Point and Boat Passage. Winter Point provides a very scenic vista of the southern end of the Strait of Georgia and the lower BC mainland. It also provides a good view of the narrow and rocky Boat Passage, and the currents that flow through. Up the gravel drive from the ramp and across Winter Cove Road is the open field ballpark for a toss of the frisbee or kick of the soccer ball.

For those traveling with bikes, it is a 7 mile ride, of mostly flat terrain, out to the East Point national park. Be sure to bring plenty of water and your camera to see the sights of the park including the Saturna Heritage Centre and the beautiful vistas. And maybe even a few orca whales passing by.

by David Stanley

Boat Pass

Lamb Barbecue

The Saturna Island annual Lamb Barbecue began as a simple picnic event in 1950. A local resident moving off island wanted to host a barbecue with his last remaining lambs to celebrate the end of the school year. With great success, the community decided to hold the event annually in celebration of Dominion Day (now called Canada Day) and the end of school. For decades now, locals and visitors alike have been celebrating Canada Day at Saturna and enjoying a wonderful community summer event.

Following annual tradition, the menu consists of local Argentinean-style barbecued lamb, Spanish rice, coleslaw, buns, coffee, tea, and cookies. Locally raised lambs are skillfully butchered by island volunteers and fastened to metal crosses with maple sticks and wire. The meat is then slow roasted over an open firepit for a number of hours before being carved for hungry picnickers.

The event features an outdoor stage with live musicians playing throughout the day. Childrens' relay and sack races, balloon tosses, nail driving contests, and even a dunk tank provide fun for all ages. Booths include face painting, local crafts, used book sales, bingo, and more. Additional food vendors are also at the event including hamburgers, hotdogs, beverages, and a beer garden.

Entrance to the event is free, however tickets are sold for the barbecue meal (cash only). All proceeds help to fund the Saturna Island Community Club. The club provides services and activities such as health care, an ambulance, library, a singing group, groundwater protection, and a children's Christmas party for island residents.

The barbecue is held every July 1st from 10am to 4:30pm at Hunter Field next to Winter Cove. The anchorage and dinghy dock can fill up as hundreds of people come to the island to celebrate Canada Day. Volunteer "water taxis" help to shuttle people from their boats to the congested dinghy dock. While some seating is available, it is a good idea to bring a blanket or folding chair to enjoy the ample grass area for picnicking and listening to the bands. For those traveling with dogs, it is best to leave them onboard as no pets are allowed within the event.

For further information on the Saturna Island Lamb Barbecue festivities, visit their website at: www.saturnalambbarbeque.ca

Lyall Harbour

Lyall Harbour is an amply sized inlet offering prime anchor locations throughout, along with a convenient public wharf near the entrance. Lyall Harbour provides easy access to Saturna Island's local eateries and well-equipped general store. The harbor and nearby coves also provide a protected and scenic location for quiet morning paddles. For those traveling without kayaks, a perfectly placed kayak rental is located alongside the public wharf.

Lyall Harbour is located on the west side of Saturna Island and is entered between Payne Point to the south and King Islets to the north. Approaches to the harbor can be taken from the south via Plumper Sound and from the north via Navy Channel. If transiting through Navy Channel, be sure to locate the expansive Conconi Reef on the chart. For smaller boats, occasionally Georgeson Passage between Samuel and Mayne Islands is used (see page 169). If using Georgeson Passage, be aware that currents run strong through the narrow pass which has a least depth of 34 feet. Dangerous shoals and rocks lie near the northern entrance to Georgeson Passage.

Upon entrance to Lyall Harbour, be aware of two rocks, both marked by navigation buoys. The first rock lies between Payne and Saturna Points, roughly 0.2 miles north of Trevor Islet. This rock has 11 feet of water over it. The second rock is known as Crispin Rock and lies 0.2 miles northeast of Saturna Point, nearly mid-channel. Crispin Rock has roughly 6 feet of water covering it.

Anchorage can be taken throughout Lyall Harbour in 3 to 6 fathoms over a mud bottom. Be aware that submerged cables cross the harbor from approximately King Islets to the public wharf. Lyall Harbour provides wind and wave protection from nearly all directions, although it is open to weather from the northwest. During periods

Lyall Harbour to:		
	Bedwell Harbour *(South Pender Island)*	8 nm
	Ganges Harbour *(Salt Spring Island)*	14 nm
	Montague Harbour *(Galiano Island)*	11 nm
	Nanaimo	38 nm
	Pirates Cove *(De Courcy Island)*	29 nm
	Princess Bay *(Portland Island)*	13 nm
	Roche Harbor *(USA)*	13 nm
	Sidney	15 nm
	Telegraph Harbour *(Thetis Island)*	25 nm
	Tod Inlet	24 nm
	Victoria	33 nm
	Wallace Island	17 nm

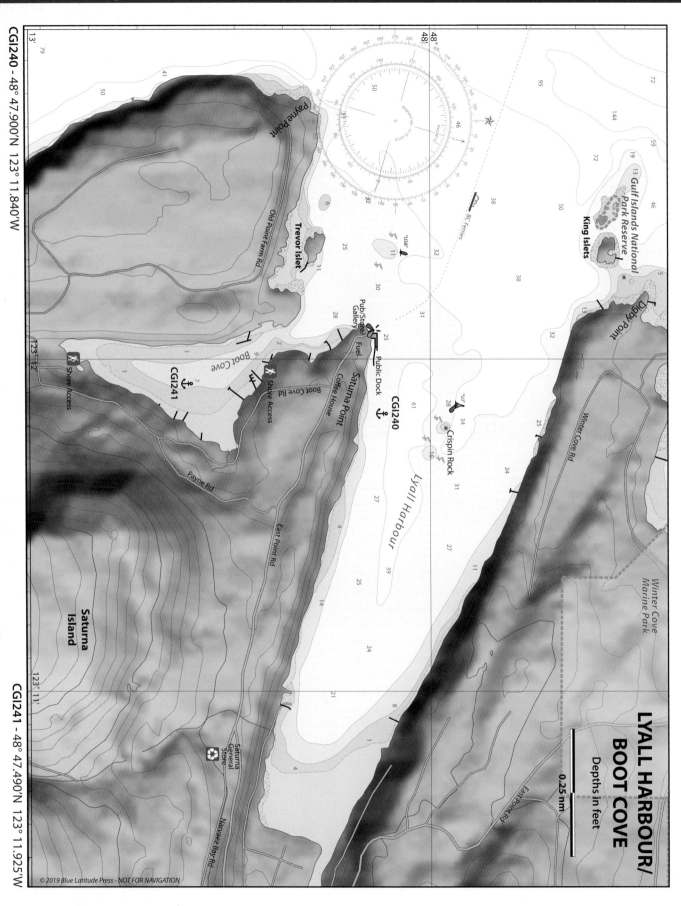

LYALL HARBOUR/
BOOT COVE

Depths in feet

0.25 nm

CGI240 - 48° 47.900'N 123° 11.840'W

CGI241 - 48° 47.490'N 123° 11.925'W

Saturna
Island

Trevor Islet

Payne Point

Old Point Farm Rd

Shore Access

CGI241

Boot Cove

Shore Access

Payne Rd

East Point Rd

Boot Cove Rd

Pub/Store/
Gallery

Fuel

Public Dock

Saturna Point

Coffee House

CGI240

Lyall Harbour

Crispin Rock

Gulf Islands National
Park Reserve

King Islets

Digby Point

Winter Cove Rd

Winter Cove
Marine Park

East Point Rd

Saturna
General
Store

BC Ferries

Narvaez Bay Rd

Lyall Harbour public wharf and ferry terminal

of strong southeasterlies, wind can funnel through the low saddle of land found at the head of the harbor. Private moorings can be see throughout harbor, with most found near the east end. A small private marina is located in the southeast portion of the harbor.

Moorage may also be taken at the public CRD dock which is adjacent to the BC Ferries dock located on Saturna Point. A few local boats moor here and in the summer months, rafting is often necessary. A portion of the dock is reserved for emergency vessels, school water-taxis and other service providers. Seaplanes also frequent the reserved area, as well as the very end of the dock. A fuel dock is located here, however it has been closed indeterminately. For further information on CRD public wharfs check their website at: www.crd.bc.ca, or call the wharfinger at (250)539-0624.

For trips to shore, the public wharf provides a convenient landing location. At the top of the ramp, a handful of shops can be found including the Saturna Lighthouse Pub for a night away from the galley. A one mile walk up Narvaez Bay Road takes you to the Saturna General Store and Cafe. As Narvaez Bay Road is a main road across the island, it is possible to catch a ride with passing cars for longer journeys around the island.

Provisioning and Services
Saturna General Store
Open daily, the General Store offers organic, local fresh produce, a liquor store, deli, post office, café, ice, pet food,

Saturna General Store and Cafe

hardware, garden supplies, gluten-free, candy, newspapers and locally made Haggis Farm Bakery goods. Located at 101 Narvaez Bay Road. (250) 539-2936

Saturna Lions Shuttle
The shuttle bus or minivan can be scheduled for island transport. A minimum of 48 hours notice should be given to allow for arrangement of volunteer drivers. While the shuttle is free, it is highly recommended to make a donation to the Lions Club for their valuable service.

The Point
The Point is located at the head of the public dock. The store provides convenience items including fishing gear, ice, beverages, snacks, local artwork, and books. Addi-

Wild Thyme Coffee House

Saturna Lighthouse Pub

tional services include free wifi, paid garbage disposal, a campground, shower and laundry facilities.

Saturna Recycling Centre and Free Store

The Centre is open Wednesday and Saturday from 10 am to noon. It is located at the corner of Harris and Narvaez Roads, near the Saturna General Store.

Restaurants

Saturna Cafe

The Saturna Cafe is located at the Saturna General Store. The cafe makes fresh sandwiches and breakfast wraps daily that are available through the General Store. On Saturdays and Wednesdays the cafe opens for breakfast and lunch featuring locally sourced products. Friday and Saturday nights the cafe opens for dinner (reservations recommended). Indoor and outdoor garden patio seating is available as well as free wifi.

Saturna Lighthouse Pub

Saturna Lighthouse Pub offers true waterside seating with traditional pub fare food. Local beers are on tap and as well as a selection of BC wines. Live music and free wifi is also offered. Located at the ferry dock in Lyall Harbor. www.saturnapub.com, (250) 539-5725

Wild Thyme Coffee House

Wild Thyme is housed within a vintage Leyland double-decker bus. Once a public transport bus from 1963 to 1976, it was transformed into a unique coffee house and restaurant in 2012. Open daily during the summer for coffee, espresso, tea, breakfast and lunch. Located on East Point Road near the ferry terminal.

Boot Cove

Boot Cove provides a wonderful, nearly landlocked anchorage inside a peaceful, shallow cove. Short dinghy rides provide easy access to Saturna Island's popular stops including the shops and eateries near the ferry terminal in Lyall Harbour, and the national park at Winter Cove. Two public access points within the cove provide convenient trips to shore for quiet walks on the surround rural roads.

Boot Cove is located on the western end of Saturna Island along Plumper Sound. The cove is entered between Saturna Point and Trevor Islet. Before entering the cove, keep in mind it is shallow and may not be suitable for deep draft boats. According to the Canadian Sailing Directions, when entering favor the starboard side to avoid a rock with 2 feet over it. Once inside the cove anchorage can be taken in 1 to 2 fathoms over a good holding mud bottom. A number of private mooring buoys can be found in the cove, but there is room for a handful of boats to anchor. Boot Cove provides good all-round weather and wave protection. A gap in the hills at the head of the cove does tend to funnel winds through the anchorage from the aptly named Breezy Bay on the opposite side of the gap.

For trips to shore, there are two public access points within Boot Cove. One is located near the head of the bay. The other is located near the "heel" of Boot Cove, and can be a bit overgrown at times. Both locations can be a muddy walk at low tide.

Boot Cove to:		
	Ganges Harbour (Salt Spring Island)	14 nm
	Ladysmith	30 nm
	Montague Harbour (Galiano Island)	11 nm
	Nanaimo	38 nm
	Pirates Cove (De Courcy Island)	29 nm
	Port Browning (North Pender Island)	4 nm
	Roche Harbor (USA)	13 nm
	Sidney	15 nm
	Victoria	33 nm
	Wallace Island	17 nm

©Kevin Oke

Narvaez Bay

Narvaez Bay is an off the beaten path anchorage found near the meeting of Boundary Pass and the Strait of Georgia. Much of the land surrounding the bay is part of the Gulf Islands National Park Reserve and features thick forests of firs and madrones. Very little of the land has been developed, bestowing a sense of remoteness and isolation at the far end of Saturna Island.

Narveaez Bay is a large bay located on the eastern side of Saturna Island. Approaches to the island are taken via Boundary Pass. The bay is entered between Monarch Head to the south and East Point to the north. Approaching from the north, be aware of heavy tide rips and overfalls around East Point and Boiling Reef.

Anchorage can be taken near the small cove on the south shore of the bay in 4 to 5 fathoms. Due to the open nature of the bay and its proximity to the large bodies of water of Boundary Pass and the Strait of Georgia, Narvaez Bay is only suited for anchoring during periods of calm weather. Be sure to check the marine forecast if staying overnight.

Narvaez Bay makes for a nice lunch stop to enjoy the beautiful scenery of the park. For trips to shore, dinghies and kayaks can be landed on the beach at the small cove. Campsites and picnic tables are found just up from the beach. A few trails lead out from the campground to a nice overlook at Monarch Head and Echo Bay. Fruit trees mark the remnants of an old homestead found along the trail.

Narvaez Bay to:		
Bedwell Harbour *(South Pender Island)*	8 nm
Cabbage Island	7 nm
Ganges Harbour *(Salt Spring Island)*	20 nm
Ladysmith	36 nm
Montague Harbour *(Galiano Island)*	17 nm
Nanaimo	44 nm
Pirates Cove *(De Courcy Island)*	35 nm
Princess Bay *(Portland Island)*	13 nm
Roche Harbor *(USA)*	13 nm
Sidney	15 nm
Victoria	33 nm

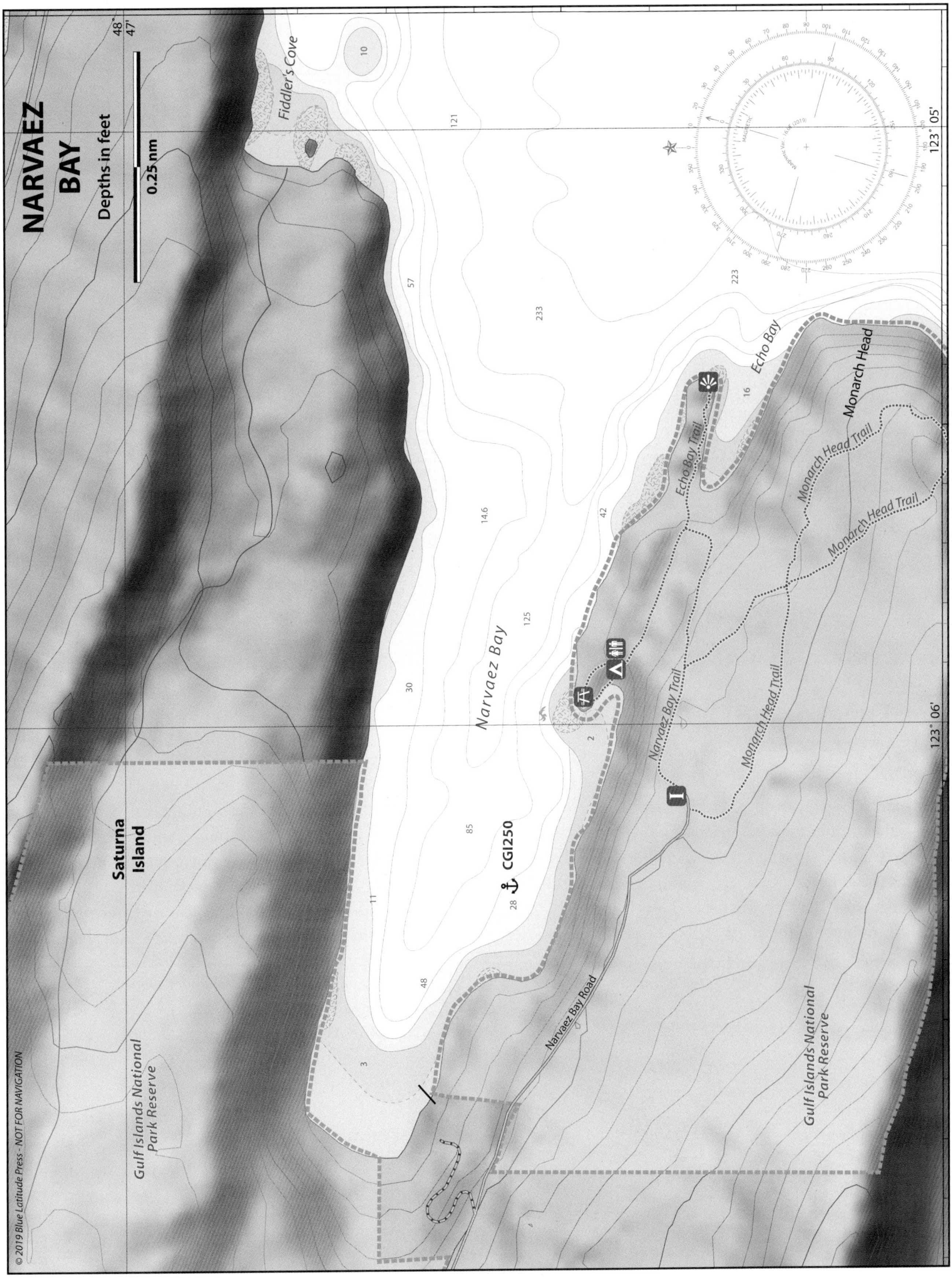

NARVAEZ BAY

Depths in feet

0.25 nm

Fiddler's Cove

10

121

57

233

223

Echo Bay

16

Monarch Head

42

Echo Bay Trail

Monarch Head Trail

Monarch Head Trail

14.6

125

Narvaez Bay

Narvaez Bay Trail

Monarch Head Trail

30

⚓ CGI250

85

2

28

11

Saturna
Island

48

3

Narvaez Bay Road

Gulf Islands National
Park Reserve

Gulf Islands National
Park Reserve

48° 48'
47'

123° 05'

123° 06'

© 2019 Blue Latitude Press - NOT FOR NAVIGATION

CGI250 - 48° 46.535'N 123° 06.265'W

Tumbo & Cabbage Islands

Tumbo and Cabbage Islands are part of the Gulf Islands National Park Reserve. The anchorage found between the islands, known as Reef Harbour, is very popular during the peak summer months. A rare sandy beach provides the perfect spot for soaking up the sun and taking refreshing dips into the ocean. Cabbage Island offers campsites and for those with NEXUS Passes and a cell phone, it is also a check in location for boats arriving from foreign waters.

Cabbage and Tumbo Islands are located at the eastern edge of the Gulf Islands and north of Saturna Island. The islands lie at the southwestern end of the Strait of Georgia. Approaches to Reef Harbour can be taken from the north via the Strait of Georgia or from the south via Tumbo Channel. If approaching from the north, be aware that reefs extend almost one mile northwest from the western tip of Tumbo Island. For boats approaching via Tumbo

Cabbage Island to:		
Bedwell Harbour *(South Pender Island)*	13 nm
Clam Bay *(Thetis Island)*	27 nm
Ganges Harbour *(Salt Spring Island)*	25 nm
Ladysmith	35 nm
Montague Harbour *(Galiano Island)*	16 nm
Nanaimo	43 nm
Pirates Cove *(De Courcy Island)*	34 nm
Roche Harbor *(USA)*	17 nm
Russell Island	20 nm
Sidney	20 nm
Tod Inlet	30 nm
Victoria	39 nm

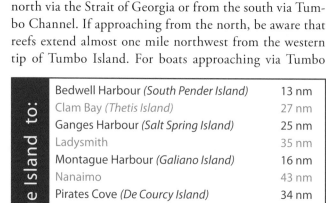

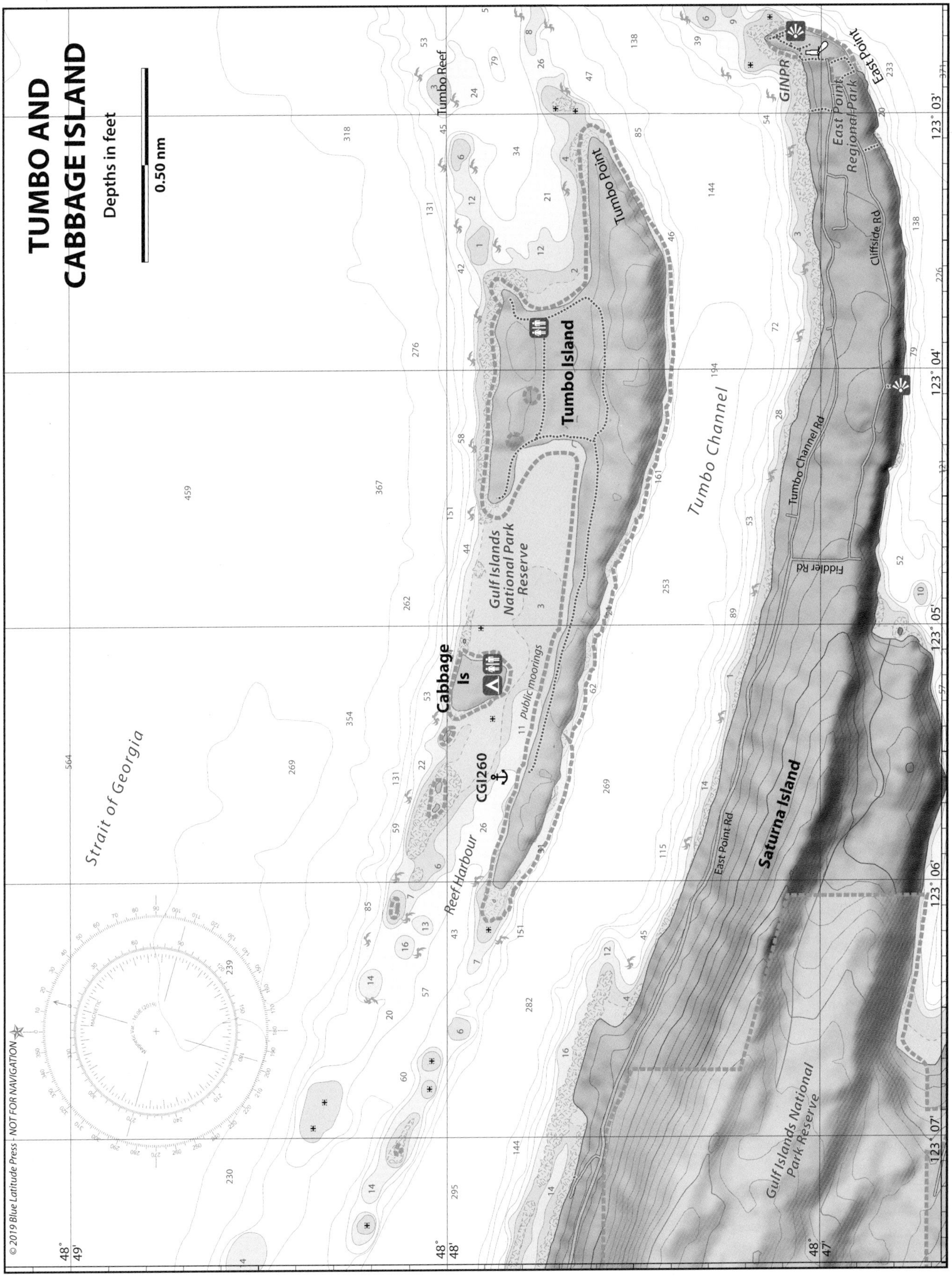

TUMBO AND CABBAGE ISLAND

Depths in feet

0.50 nm

Strait of Georgia

Tumbo Reef

Tumbo Point

Tumbo Island

Gulf Islands National Park Reserve

Tumbo Channel

Cabbage Is

CGI260

Reef Harbour

Public moorings

GINPR

East Point

East Point Regional Park

Cliffside Rd

Tumbo Channel Rd

Fiddler Rd

East Point Rd

Saturna Island

Gulf Islands National Park Reserve

CGI260 - 48° 47.840'N 123° 05.580'W

© 2019 Blue Latitude Press · NOT FOR NAVIGATION

48° 49'

48° 48'

48° 47'

123° 07'

123° 06'

123° 05'

123° 04'

123° 03'

Dinghy landing at Tumbo Island

Channel, be sure to locate Boiling Reef off East Point on Saturna Island. This area, including the eastern entrance to Tumbo Channel can experience heavy tide rips, overfalls and eddies. Be sure to check the current table prior to approaching and give the point ample room when rounding. When entering Reef Harbour from Tumbo Channel, pay close attention to the chart due to numerous reefs extending off the western tip of Tumbo Island.

Anchorage can be taken within the harbor in 2 to 5 fathoms over a mostly mud bottom. Park mooring buoys are also available for a nightly fee. This anchorage is best suited during periods of calm weather. Due to its proximity to the Strait of Georgia and its exposure to wind and waves from the northwest, alternative anchorage should be found during periods of northwesterly winds.

For trips to shore, the gently sloping sand beach on Cabbage Island provides a perfect dinghy or kayak landing location. Camping is available on the island with a pit toilet provided (no water is available). Tide pooling at Cabbage Island is some of the best with the expanse of reefs surrounding the island. Bring a picnic or cold beverage and enjoy the view of the strait and mainland BC.

While there are no trails on Cabbage Island, Tumbo Island provides an excellent tree-lined walk. A roughly 3 mile partial loop trail travels most of the island, taking visitors past historical wood cabins. There is no official dock or dinghy landing on Tumbo Island. Getting from the dinghy to the trail can be a bit challenging so prepare for a scramble up seaweed covered rocks. Previous boaters have occasionally left lengths of line tied to trees to aid in tying up dinghies. Be sure to bring a long dinghy painter or extra line.

Irish Bay (Samuel Island)

Irish Bay provides a quiet alternative to the nearby and popular anchorage of Winter Cove. The small bay offers good protection and a pleasant scenic vista for a handful of boats. While Samuel Island does not provide any public access, it is just a short paddle or dinghy ride over to the park at Winter Cove.

Samuel Island is located between Mayne and Saturna Islands with Irish Bay found on its western shore. Approaches to Irish Bay can be made via Plumper Sound to the south or Georgeson Passage to the north. When approaching via Plumper Sound, be cautious of Minx Reef which lies southeast of the entrance to Irish Bay. Minx Reef extends rougly 0.3 miles northwest from Mikuni Point on Saturna Island.

For those approaching via Georgeson Passage and the Strait of Georgia, be aware of the extensive reefs off Georgeson Island. Reefs and shoals extend nearly 2 miles southeast from Georgeson Island, blocking the north entrance to Georgeson Passage. The narrow pass is also affected by current and is best transitted during or close to slack. See page 169 for a detailed description of Georgeson Passage.

Anchorage can be taken within Irish Bay in 3 to 5 fathoms over a mostly mud bottom. The bay offers good protection from wind and waves from most directions. The land surrounding Irish Bay, including the dock near the entrance, are private. For trips to shore and trail options, dinghies can be landed at the park float in Winter Cove.

Irish Bay to:		
Ganges Harbour (Salt Spring Island)		13 nm
Montague Harbour (Galiano Island)		10 nm
Nanaimo		37 nm
Pirates Cove (De Courcy Island)		28 nm
Port Browning (North Pender Island)		5 nm
Russell Island		11 nm
Sidney		16 nm
Telegraph Harbour (Thetis Island)		24 nm
Tod Inlet		24 nm
Victoria		33 nm
Wallace Island		17 nm

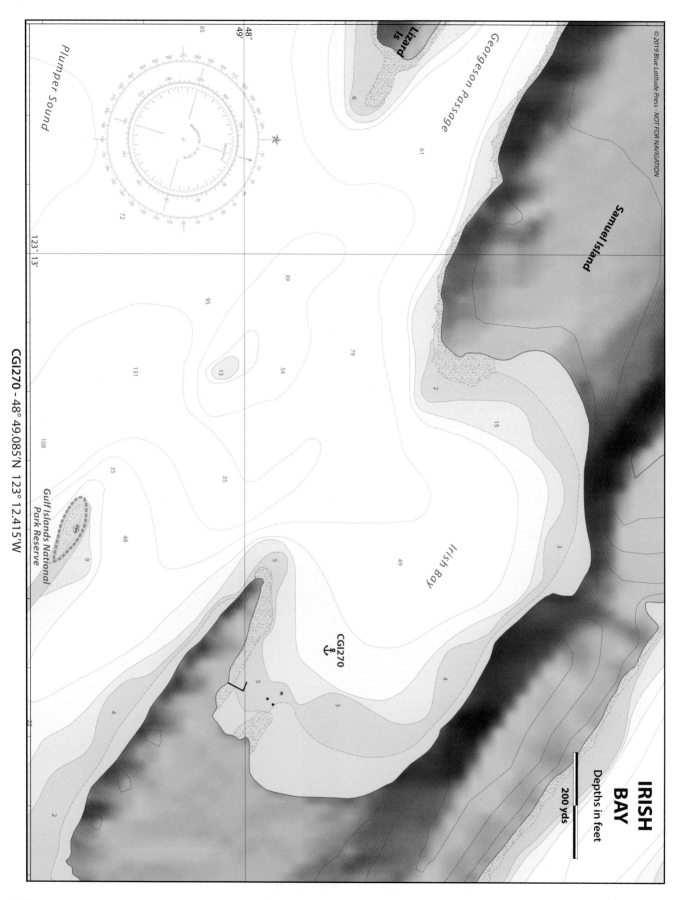

IRISH
BAY

Depths in feet

200 yds

CGI270 - 48° 49.085'N 123° 12.415'W

Plumper Sound

Gulf Islands National
Park Reserve

CGI270

Irish Bay

Samuel Island

Georgeson passage

Lizard
Is

© 2019 Blue Latitude Press · NOT FOR NAVIGATION

Mayne Island

Peaceful Mayne Island lies within the heart of the Gulf Islands, offering sweeping views of the mainland to the east and the island studded waters to the west. Bordering the northwest end of the island is Active Pass, one of the main channels funneling marine traffic between the Strait of Georgia and the Gulf Islands. While being one of the smaller of the ferry served islands, Mayne Island provides a host of activities for visitors including public parks, a small museum, shops, restaurants, and more.

The island's human history begins roughly 5,000 years ago. Archeological finding from Helen Point has documented one of the earliest Coast Salish settlements in the Gulf Islands. The today, the Tsartlip First Nations continue to care for this sacred land.

In 1794, Captain George Vancouver and his crew visited the island near Georgina Point. A coin and a knife were left behind and found over a century later by island homesteaders. When gold was found in the Fraser River area in 1857 and later with the Cariboo gold rush, Miners Bay became a popular port of call for prospectors traveling from Vancouver Island to the mainland. In 1892, the Springwater Lodge was established in Miners Bay, and continues to host travelers today.

Many early homesteaders who came to the island began farming with apples and greenhouse tomatoes being key crops. Early settlers and farmers included many Japanese families. With the start of World War II, these families were forced to move to internment camps located within the interior of BC, losing their land and most of their possessions. In rememberance of these families and their hardship, a park and Japanese garden were created on a former Japanese family farm near Dinner Bay.

Today, Mayne Island is home to seasonal vacationers and long time island residents alike with a population of roughly 1,000 people. BC Ferries provides regular service to the island with a ferry terminal located in Village Bay. For getting around the island, there is voluntary ride share on the island similar to that of the Pender Islands (see page 120). There are 25 "Car Stops" around the island noted by green and white signs. Simply wait at one of these stops and passing drivers may (or may not) offer to give you a ride.

Georgeson Passage

Georgeson Passage is a small, narrow pass linking Plumper Sound with the Strait of Georgia. The pass leads between Samuel Island and Lizard, Mayne, and Curlew Islands. Current flows through the pass requiring

©Kevin Oke

Mayne Island farmland

slower boats to navigate at or near slack. Due to the maze of unmarked rocks and shoals found at the north entrance, this pass is not as commonly used as Active Pass, and is best suited for smaller boats with local knowledge. Careful attention to the chart and tide and current tables is necessary when transiting this pass.

Robson Channel

Robson Channel lies between Mayne and Curlew Islands, linking Georgeson Passage with Horton Bay. The channel is narrow and shallow, and is best suited for smaller boats with shallow drafts and local knowledge. The east entrance of the channel has a rock with less than 3 feet of water covering it. Drying ledges extend from Mayne Island and the southern tip of Curlew Island. Careful attention to the chart and tide and current tables is necessary when transiting this pass.

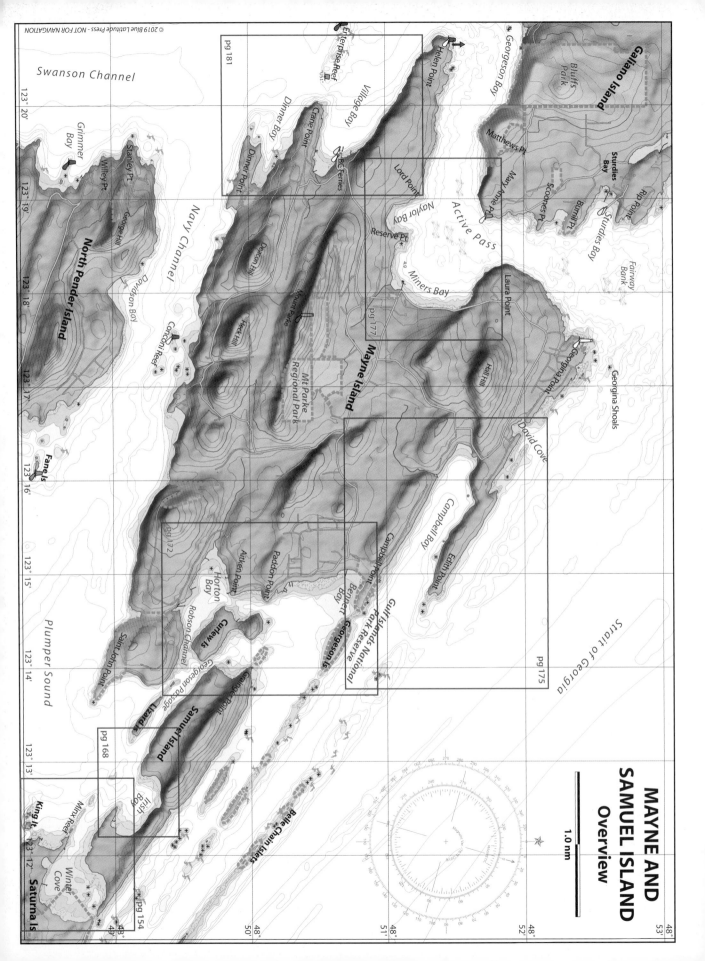

MAYNE AND
SAMUEL ISLAND
Overview

1.0 nm

Horton Bay

Horton Bay is a snug harbor tucked into the protection of Mayne, Curlew, and Samuel Islands. Due to its all-round protection and public wharf, it is a popular mooring location for island residents. The pleasant bay is surrounded by island homes and farmland with quiet country roads perfect for exploring the island by foot or bike.

Horton Bay is located on the southeast end of Mayne Island with Curlew Island lying at the entrance to the bay. Approaches can be taken either north or south of Curlew Island through Georgeson Passage or Robson Channel (see page 169). Approaching from the north, between the north end of Curlew Island and Paddon and Aitken Points on Mayne Island, the channel into the bay is wider and deeper than Robson Channel. Approaching from the south through Robson Channel, be aware of the underwater rock found at the east entrance, the drying ledges between Curlew and Mayne Islands, and the shallow water. Both approaches experience current.

Anchorage can be taken within the bay in 3 to 4 fathoms over a mostly mud bottom. Most of the bay that is out of the main stream of the current is filled with private mooring buoys. When anchoring, be aware of the current that flows between Curlew and Mayne Islands.

Moorage may also be taken at the public CRD wharf in the southeast portion of the bay. The roughly 80 foot dock offers limited space as it is primarily used by local island residents, and rafting may be required. A portion of the dock is reserved for emergency vessels and other service providers. For further information on CRD public wharfs, check their website at: www.crd.bc.ca, or call the wharfinger at (778) 835-2004.

For trips to shore, dinghies can be landed at the public wharf. A short walk south on Beechwood Drive leads to a trailhead taking visitors down to Kadonga Bay. The bay was named after the first Japanese family to settle on Mayne Island in 1903.

Public Wharf

Horton Bay to:		
Annette Inlet *(Prevost Island)*	11 nm
Chemainus	25 nm
Clam Bay *(Thetis Island)*	22 nm
Ganges Harbour *(Salt Spring Island)*	14 nm
Montague Harbour *(Galiano Island)*	11 nm
Pirates Cove *(De Courcy Island)*	29 nm
Port Browning *(North Pender Island)*	6 nm
Princess Bay *(Portland Island)*	13 nm
Sidney	17 nm
Wallace Island	18 nm
Winter Cove *(Saturna Island)*	3 nm

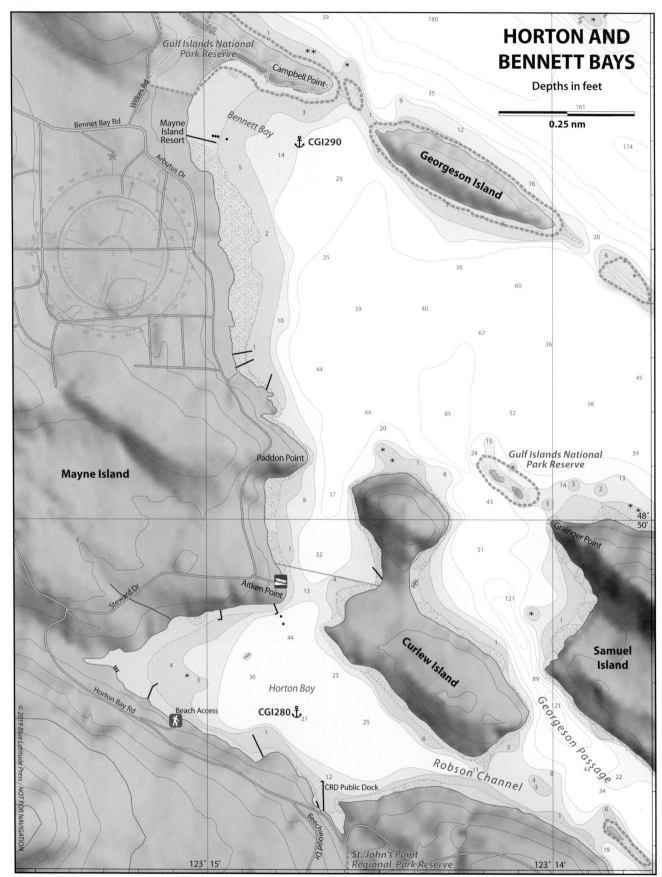

HORTON AND BENNETT BAYS

Depths in feet

0.25 nm
161

Gulf Islands National Park Reserve

Wilkes Rd

Bennet Bay Rd

Mayne Island Resort

Arbutus Dr

Campbell Point

Bennett Bay

⚓ CGI290

Georgeson Island

Mayne Island

Paddon Point

Steward Dr

Aitken Point

Horton Bay Rd

Beach Access

CGI280 ⚓ 21

Horton Bay

Gulf Islands National Park Reserve

Grainger Point

48° 50'

Curlew Island

Samuel Island

Georgeson Passage

Robson Channel

CRD Public Dock

Beechwood Dr

St. John's Point Regional Park Reserve

123° 15'

123° 14'

CGI280 - 48° 49.640'N 123° 14.730'W

CGI290 - 48° 50.695'N 123° 14.730'W

Bennett Bay

Bennett Bay provides easy access to the Gulf Island National Park Reserve found at the head of the bay. The park offers a wonderful beach and walking trails to enjoy the surrounding views and wildlife. Kayak rentals are available at the Mayne Island Resort for exploring the nearby shoreline and islands.

Bennett Bay is located on the eastern shore of Mayne Island along the Strait of Georgia. Approaches to the bay can be taken via Georgeson Passage from the south, or the Strait of Georgia from the north or east. For detailed information on Georgeson Passage see page 169.

For boats approaching from the Strait of Georgia, be aware that this area has extensive unmarked reefs, shoals, and shallow areas, requiring extremely careful attention to the chart. These reefs lie northeast and parallel to Samuel Island, with some stretching over 2 miles in length. The nearly 2 mile long Belle Chain Islets and Anniversary Island lie 0.6 miles northeast of Samuel Island. Additional underwater rocks lie between the northern end of the chain and Edith Point on Mayne Island. Parallel to the Belle Chain Islets, additional islets and reefs extend roughly 2 miles southeast of Georgeson Island.

Anchorage can be taken near the head of the bay in 2 to 4 fathoms over a mud bottom. Bennett Bay provides good northwest wind protection, however it is exposed to southeast wind and waves from the Strait of Georgia.

For trips to shore, dinghies can be landed on the beach at the head of the bay within the park. From the beach, a loop trail heads out to scenic vistas at Campbell Point. Another trail heads from the beach to the parking area along Wilkes Road.

After working up an appetite at the park, check out the Bennett Bay Bistro for lunch or dinner. The bistro is located at the Mayne Island Resort, and offers incredible bay views with indoor and patio seating. The bistro has a nice selection of meals including seafood, sandwiches, , salads, and a variety of entrees. The bistro is located near the southwest end of the bay, and is open daily (www.bennettbaybistro.com).

Bennett Bay to:		
Chemainus		26 nm
Ganges Harbour *(Salt Spring Island)*		15 nm
Montague Harbour *(Galiano Island)*		12 nm
Nanaimo		39 nm
Port Browning *(North Pender Island)*		7 nm
Russell Island		13 nm
Sidney		18 nm
Telegraph Harbour *(Thetis Island)*		26 nm
Tod Inlet		25 nm
Victoria		37 nm
Wallace Island		18 nm
Winter Cove *(Saturna Island)*		3 nm

Bennett and Campbell Bays

Campbell Bay

Campbell Bay is found on the northeast side of Mayne Island, offering shelter from northwesterly winds in the Strait of Georgia. The long bay has a number of homes and private docks dotting its shoreline, and offers easy access to the parks at both Bennett Bay and nearby Cabbage and Tumbo Islands.

Campbell Bay is found on Mayne Island near the southern end of the Strait of Georgia. Entrance to the bay is taken between Edith Point to the north and Campbell Point to the south. Be aware that the area southeast of Campbell Bay has extensive unmarked reefs, shoals, and shallow areas, requiring extremely careful attention to the chart. These reefs lie northeast and parallel to Samuel Island, with some stretching over 2 miles in length. The nearly 2 mile long Belle Chain Islets and Anniversary Island lie 0.6 miles northeast of Samuel Island. Ad-

ditional underwater rocks lie between the northern end of the chain and Edith Point on Mayne Island. Parallel to the Belle Chain Islets, additional islets and reefs extend roughly 2 miles southeast of Georgeson Island.

Anchorage can be taken near the head of the bay in 5 to 9 fathoms over a mostly mud bottom. Campbell Bay provides good northwest wind protection, however it is entirely open to the southeast.

For trips to shore, dinghies can be landed at the Gulf Islands National Park Reserve at the far southern end of Campbell Bay. Dinghies and kayaks can also be taken through the pass between Georgeson Island and Campbell Point to land at the sand and pebble beach at Bennett Bay. This pass has a least depth of 1 foot and is only suitable for shoal draft boats. A loop trail heads out to scenic vistas at Campbell Point, and another trail heads from the beach to the parking area along Wilkes Road.

Campbell Bay to:		
Cabbage Island	8 nm
Ganges Harbour (Salt Spring Island)	14 nm
Ladysmith	31 nm
Montague Harbour (Galiano Island)	11 nm
Nanaimo	38 nm
Pirates Cove (De Courcy Island)	29 nm
Princess Bay (Portland Island)	17 nm
Silva Bay (Gabriola Island)	27 nm
Sidney	21 nm
Tod Inlet	28 nm
Victoria	42 nm

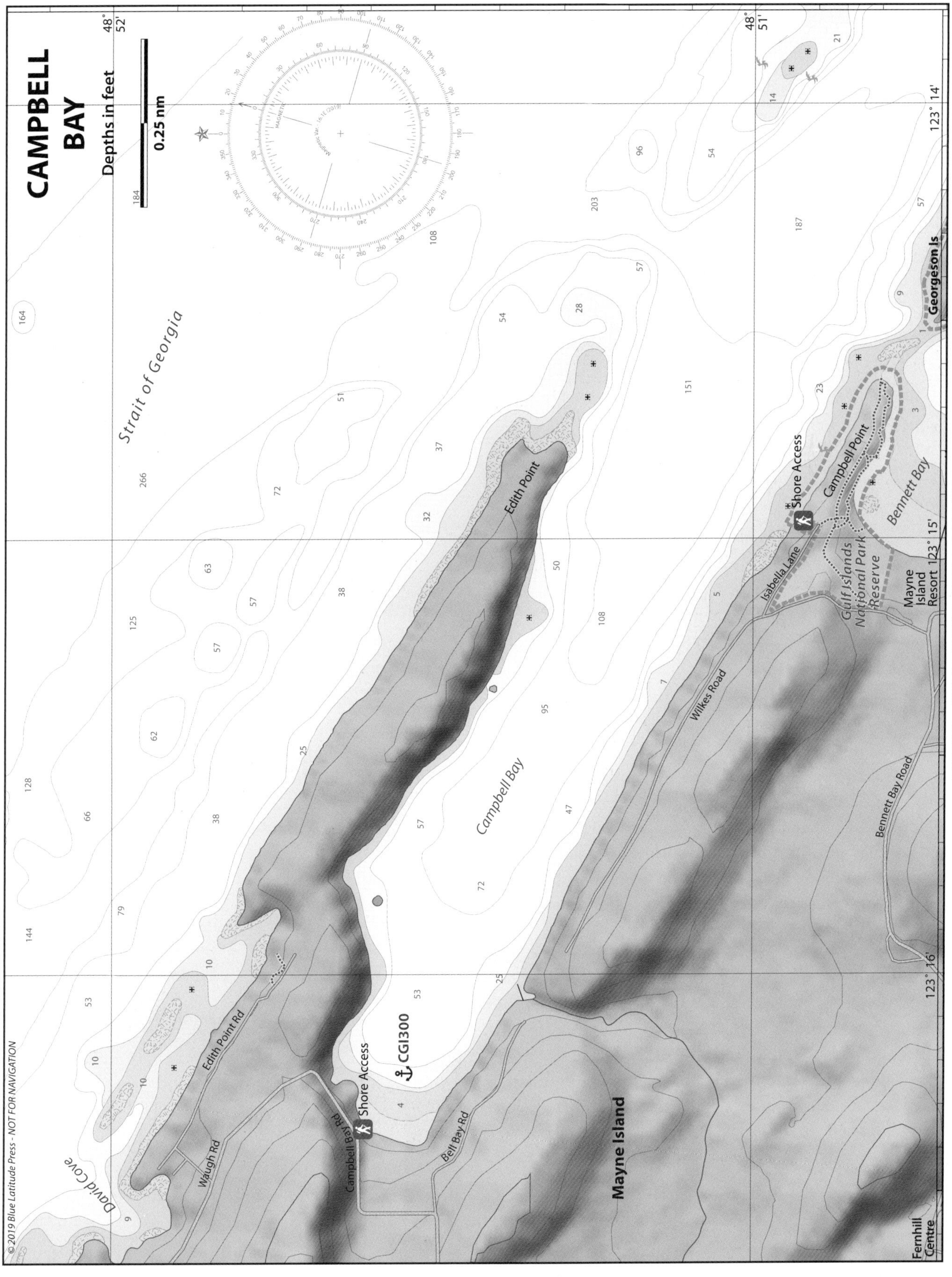

CAMPBELL BAY

Depths in feet

0.25 nm

Strait of Georgia

184

164

108

203

96

54

266

51

57

37

72

32

50

Edith Point

54

28

151

57

*

*

*

125

63

57

62

128

66

38

95

108

47

*

Campbell Bay

57

72

79

144

53

10

10

10

*

*

Edith Point Rd

Waugh Rd

David Cove

6

Campbell Bay Rd

⚓ CGI300
⚓ Shore Access

4

53

25

Bell Bay Rd

5

Wilkes Road

1

25

Mayne Island

Fernhill Centre

Bennett Bay Road

Georgeson Is

57

9

3

*

*

*

23

*

Shore Access

Campbell Point

Bennett Bay

Isabella Lane

Gulf Islands National Park Reserve

Mayne Island Resort

21

14

CGI300 - 48° 51.545'N 123° 16.230'W

© 2019 Blue Latitude Press - NOT FOR NAVIGATION

123° 14'

123° 15'

123° 16'

48° 52'

48° 51'

Miners Bay and Active Pass

Miners Bay

Miners Bay was once a popular stop for many early prospectors traveling between Victoria and the mainland during the Fraser River and Cariboo gold rushes of the mid 1800's. Situated along the current-filled waters of Active Pass, Miners Bay made for a convenient stop before crossing the open waters of the Strait of Georgia. Today, many of the commercial businesses and historical sights are still centered around the area. A small public wharf within the bay offers visitors the chance to explore the sights of Mayne Island.

Miners Bay is located on the northern shore of Mayne Island within Active Pass. Due to the strong currents flowing through Active Pass, strong eddies form and set into the bay. These strong eddies, constant wake from passing boats and ferries, and a deep bay make Miners Bay a very challenging, and sometimes less than pleasant, destination for boats. To opt for a less challenging anchorage, visitors may choose one of the island's other bays, and walk or take advantage of the island's "Car Stop" ride share to explore the amenities around Miners Bay.

Approaches to Miners Bay are taken via Active Pass from either the west or the north. Detailed information for Active Pass is found in Chapter 7 on page 207.

Active Pass is known for its strong currents, which can attain rates of 8 knots, heavy tide rips, and its considerable boat traffic including commercial ships and ferries. Transiting the pass should be taken with great caution and careful attention to the charts, current tables, and marine traffic.

Within Miners Bay, a flood tide in Active Pass produces a clockwise eddy with currents off the wharf reaching 2.5 knots. On ebb tides, a counter-clockwise eddy forms with currents reaching 2 knots off the wharf.

Miners Bay to:		
	Bedwell Harbour (South Pender Island)	13 nm
	Ganges Harbour (Salt Spring Island)	9 nm
	Lyall Harbour (Saturna Island)	10 nm
	Montague Harbour (Galiano Island)	6 nm
	Nanaimo	33 nm
	Pirates Cove (De Courcy Island)	24 nm
	Princess Bay (Portland Island)	11 nm
	Roche Harbor (USA)	19 nm
	Sidney	16 nm
	Tod Inlet	23 nm
	Victoria	37 nm
	Wallace Island	12 nm

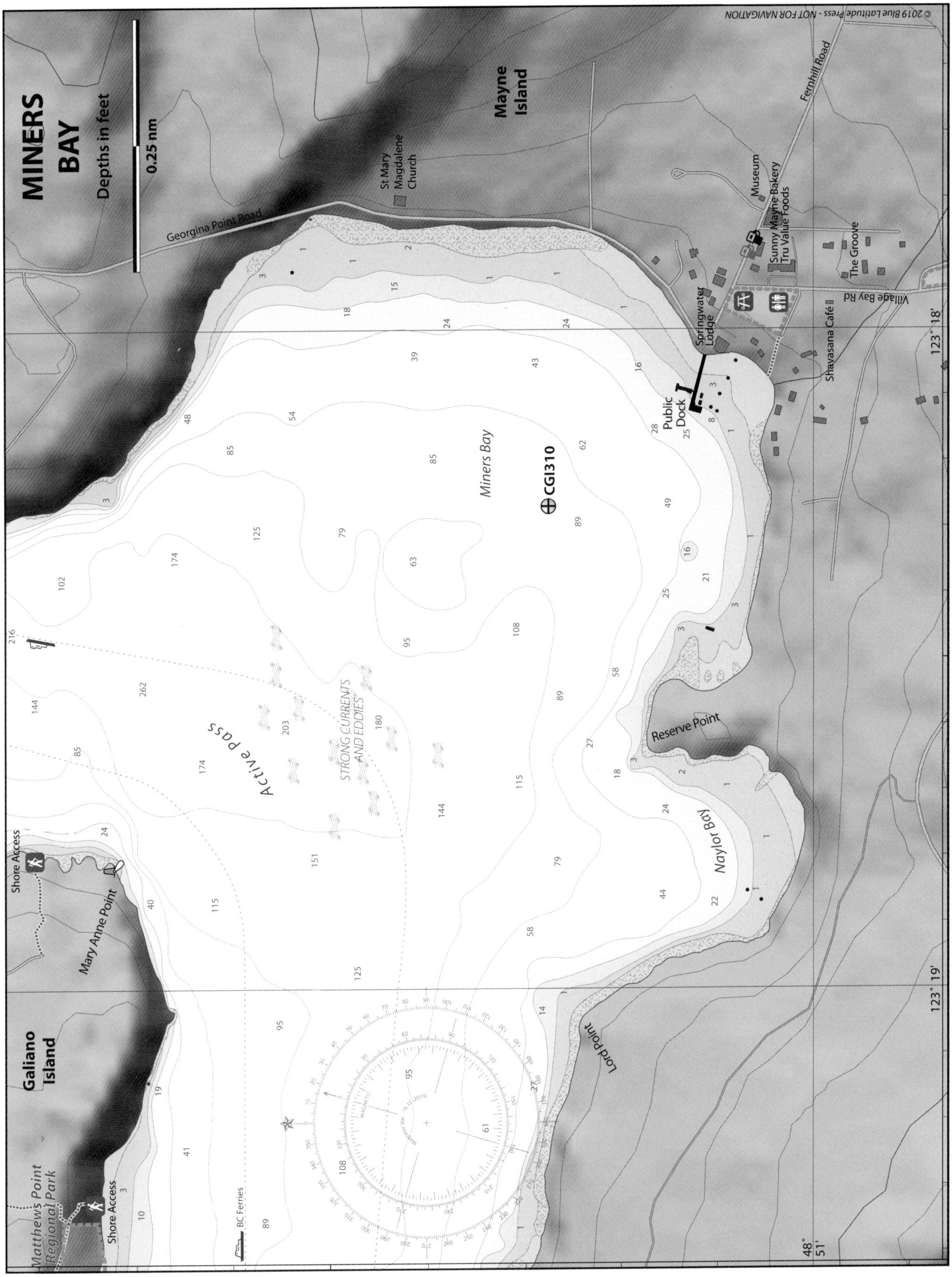

© 2019 Blue Latitude Press – NOT FOR NAVIGATION

MINERS BAY

Depths in feet

0.25 nm

Mayne Island

Georgina Point Road

St Mary Magdalene Church

Fernhill Road

Museum

Sunny Mayne Bakery
Tru Value Foods

The Groove

Springwater Lodge

Shavasana Café

Village Bay Rd

Public Dock

1
2
3
15
18
24
24
39
43
16
62
49
16
21
25
3
3
8
3
28
25
8
1
1
3

48
54
85
85
63
79
125
174

Miners Bay

⊕ **CGI310**
89

95
108
102
262
89
58
203
180
89
27
3
27
18
3
2
1
24
79
44
22

STRONG CURRENTS
AND EDDIES

Active Pass

216
144
85
174
151
115
144
115
125
58
14

Reserve Point

Naylor Bay

Lord point

Shore Access

Mary Anne Point

Galiano Island

24
40
19
95
61
95
41
10
3

Matthews Point
Regional Park

Shore Access

BC Ferries

3

123° 18'

123° 19'

48°
51'

CGI310 – 48° 51.270'N 123° 18.270'W

Public wharf

Due to the depth of Miners Bay, anchorage is found closer to shore. Numerous private moorings are found in this area. A submarine cable lies between Galiano Island and the Miners Bay public wharf. Anchoring is not permitted in this area. Keep in mind this anchorage experiences current and frequent wake from passing boats and ships.

Moorage may be taken at the public CRD wharf in the southern portion of the bay. Two floats are found on either side of a large pier. A portion of the dock is reserved for emergency vessels, water taxis, and seaplanes. These areas are marked in yellow and are not available for general moorage. According to the CRD, the dock is exposed to ferry wake causing the floats to roll extensively, especially during lower tides or northerly winds. For further information on CRD public wharfs, check their website at: www.crd.bc.ca, or call the wharfinger at (778) 835-2004.

Sights to See

As Miners Bay was the original hub for island transportation, a number of historical sights can be found in the area. A first stop is the legendary Plumper Pass Lock-up, which is now home to the island's museum. The Lock-up was built in 1896, and for a number of years, was the only jail in the islands. Today the museum and surrounding grounds hold interesting island artifacts, farming equipment, photos, and more. The museum is located on Fernhill Road, across from the Mayne Island Agricultural Hall.

A short walk across the road is the Mayne Island Agricultural Hall. The hall, which is still in use today, was built in 1900, and is operated by the Mayne Island Agricultural

Society. The society also operates the museum and Thrift Shop, and stages the annual Fall Fair. The fair, which began in 1925, is held the third Saturday of every August. Events include a parade, farmers market, food vendors, and wonderful displays of island art, produce, flowers, baking, canning, sewing, and more. The hall is also the site of the Mayne Island farmer's market. The market is open each Saturday from 10am to 1pm, from the end of May to early October. For further information on the society and their events, visit: www.mayneagriculturalsociety.com.

Located along the bay on Georgina Point Road, is Saint Mary Magdalene Church. Built in 1897, Saint Mary Magdalene Church is the only church on the island. Aside from a few minor revisions, the church today remains as it was built well over a century ago. A cross on the side of the church reads "God and Ocean," carved in Japanese characters by an early island resident, noting the church's location along the bay. North of the church is the historical cemetery.

For those looking for a little exercise and a beautiful park setting, take the 2 mile walk out to the Georgina Point Lighthouse and Gulf Island National Park Reserve. The lighthouse was originally built in 1885 to mark the entrance and nearby reefs of Active Pass. The park is a popular spot to picnic, view the historic lighthouse (now fully automated), and watch the marine traffic transiting the swirling waters of the pass. At low tide, the rocky ledges of the point are exposed and allow visitors to explore the tide pools. To reach the park from the public wharf in Miners Bay, follow Georgina Point Road north for roughly 2 miles to the lighthouse.

Provisioning and Services

Farm Gate Store
Farm Gate Store is a wonderful small island grocery specializing in local and organic produce, meats, and a variety of other food items. A deli counter offers fresh baked treats. Located at 568 Fernhill Road. www.farmgatestore.com

Home Hardware
Home Hardware is a chain hardware store offering hardware, plumbing, electrical, home, and gardening supplies. Located at 652 Fernhill Road. homehardware.ca

Miners Bay Trading Post
The Miners Bay Trading Post is a grocery offering produce, meats, dairy, and a variety of pantry staples. The Trading Post also has a liquor store with beer, wine, and liquor. Located near the bay at 413 Fernhill Road.

Tru Value Foods
Tru Value Foods is a small local chain grocery providing produce, meats, dairy, a deli counter, and more with an emphasis on local and organic. Located at 472 Village Bay Road. truvaluefoods.com

Restaurants

The Groove Island Kitchen
The Groove offers gourmet burgers, pizzas, and tapas made in house with locally sourced ingredients. They also offer a nice selection of local craft beers and BC wines. The restaurant is open seasonally for lunch and dinner with indoor and patio seating. Located at 454 Village Bay Road. www.thegroove.kitchen

Mayne Island Brewing Company
Mayne Island Brewing Company is a small batch brewery specializing in old world style ales. The store is open Fridays and Saturdays from 1pm to 5pm. Located at 490 Fernhill Road. www.mayneislandbrewingco.com

Springwater Lodge
The Springwater Lodge was originally established in 1892. Enjoy a meal and a cold beverage on their beautiful deck overlooking Active Pass. The menu features classic pub fare including fish and chips, burgers, and beer from Mayne Island Brewing Company. Open for lunch and dinner. Located at 400 Fernhill Road. springwaterlodge.com

Sunny Mayne Bakery Cafe
Sunny Mayne Bakery offers freshly baked treats including muffins, pastries, cookies, croissants, and much more. They also offer espresso drinks, soups, sandwiches, pizzas (baked or unbaked for takeout), and custom cakes. Open daily from 6am to 6pm. Located at 472 Village Bay Road, www.sunnymaynebakery.com

Museum

Sweetwater Lodge

Georgina Pt Lighthouse

Mayne Island Brewing

Farm Gate Store

Village Bay

Village and Dinner Bays

Village and Dinner Bays are found on the west side of Mayne Island, separated by the peninsula of land known as Crane Point. Village Bay is home to the BC Ferries terminal for the island, while Dinner Bay remains a more quiet destination with a wonderful community park found at the head of the bay. Both bays provide alternative anchorage to the current-filled waters of Miners Bay, while still being within walking distance of the island village's amentities.

Village and Dinner Bays on Mayne Island are located near the convergence of several main channels including Trincomali, Swanson, and Navy Channels, along with Active Pass. On flood tides, current flows north through Swanson Channel and then splits with lighter currents flowing northwest through Trincomali Channel, and stronger current flowing through the narrow Active Pass. Keep in mind that the closer to Active Pass you get, the stronger the current flow.

Village Bay is entered between Helen Point to the north and Crane Point to the south. Dinner Bay is entered between Crane Point to the north and Dinner Point to the south. Enterprise Reef lies roughly 0.3 miles west-northwest of Crane Point. The west side of the reef is marked by a light on a tower, and the east side of the reef is marked by port

hand buoy "U51." For those approaching Dinner Bay from the south, be aware of detached reefs lying off Dinner Point.

Anchorage can be taken in Dinner Bay in 2 to 4 fathoms near the head. Keep in mind this small bay is very steep with the head becoming quite shallow. A number of private moorings are found within the bay, greatly reducing the room for anchoring.

Anchorage in Village Bay can be taken in 2 to 9 fathoms over a mostly mud bottom. The head of the bay is shoal. A number of private moorings are found throughout the bay. No anchoring is allowed near the underwater cable or in the path of the ferry.

Village Bay to:	Bedwell Harbour *(South Pender Island)*	10 nm
	Chemainus	19 nm
	Clam Bay *(Thetis Island)*	16 nm
	Ganges Harbour *(Salt Spring Island)*	8 nm
	Montague Harbour *(Galiano Island)*	5 nm
	Nanaimo	32 nm
	Pirates Cove *(De Courcy Island)*	23 nm
	Russell Island	7 nm
	Sidney	13 nm
	Tod Inlet	20 nm
	Winter Cove *(Saturna Island)*	7 nm

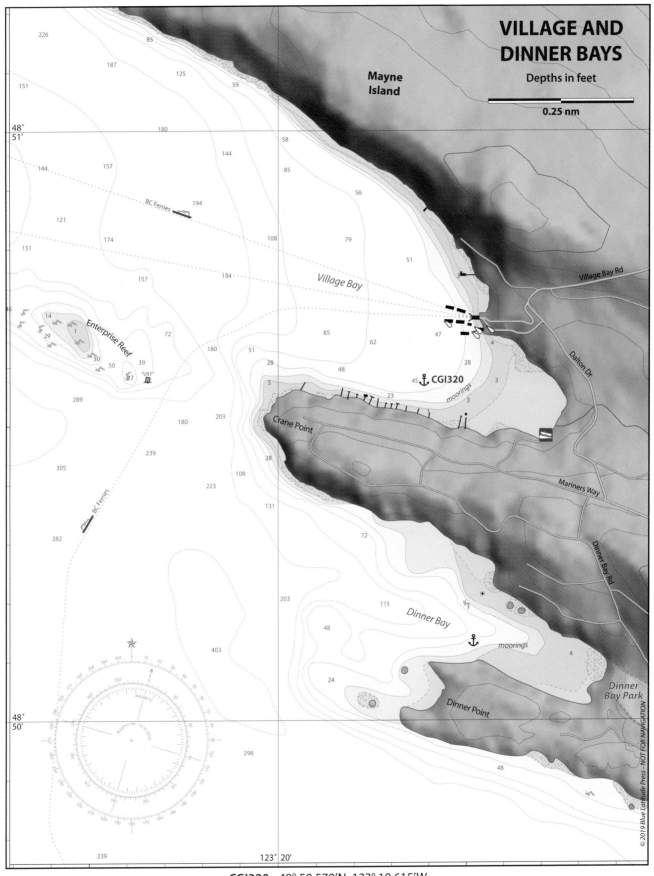

VILLAGE AND
DINNER BAYS

Depths in feet

0.25 nm

226

85

187

125

59

Mayne
Island

151

180

58

144

144

157

144

BC Ferries

194

85

121

56

174

108

79

151

51

157

194

194

Village Bay

Enterprise Reef

14

1

72

3

72

Village Bay Rd

29

30

50

39

180

85

62

47

4

27

"U51"

289

203

48

28

3

CGI320

45

moorings

Dalton Dr

5

23

28

3

180

Crane Point

239

28

305

108

Mariners Way

282

223

131

72

203

115

Dinner Bay

moorings

4

48

Dinner Bay Rd

403

24

*Dinner
Bay Park*

298

48

Dinner Point

239

123° 20'

48° 51'

48° 50'

48° 50'

© 2019 Blue Latitude Press - NOT FOR NAVIGATION

CGI320 - 48° 50.570′N 123° 19.615′W

Dinner Bay

Dinner Bay Community Park

Japanese Garden

Japanese Garden

Both Dinner and Village Bays provide protection from southeast winds, however they are exposed to winds from the northwest. As nearby Active Pass is a main channel for marine traffic, including BC Ferries, wakes from passing boats can affect these anchorages.

For trips to shore in Dinner Bay dinghies can be landed at the head of the bay near the park. It's a bit of a steep climb up to the park. In Village Bay, dinghies can be landed at the southern head of the bay near the boat launch.

One of the highlights to visiting Dinner Bay are the nearby public parks offering a host of activities and beautiful views. At the head of the bay is the Dinner Bay Community Park. The park, which over looks the bay, provides picnic tables, a picnic shelter, a playground, putting green, disc golf course, baseball field, and plenty of open grass area for a game of frisbee or tossing a football.

Located next to the Dinner Bay Community Park is the Mayne Island Japanese Garden. This impressive garden was created by local island volunteers, and is dedicated to the early Japanese families who lived and worked on the island. At the start of World War II, Japanese families were removed from coastal BC and placed in internment camps located in the interior of the province. Today, this lush memorial garden features spring blooming cherry trees, a pond, streams, bridges, a meditation hut, and various shrubs, trees, and blooming flowers.

Chapter 6

Prevost Island

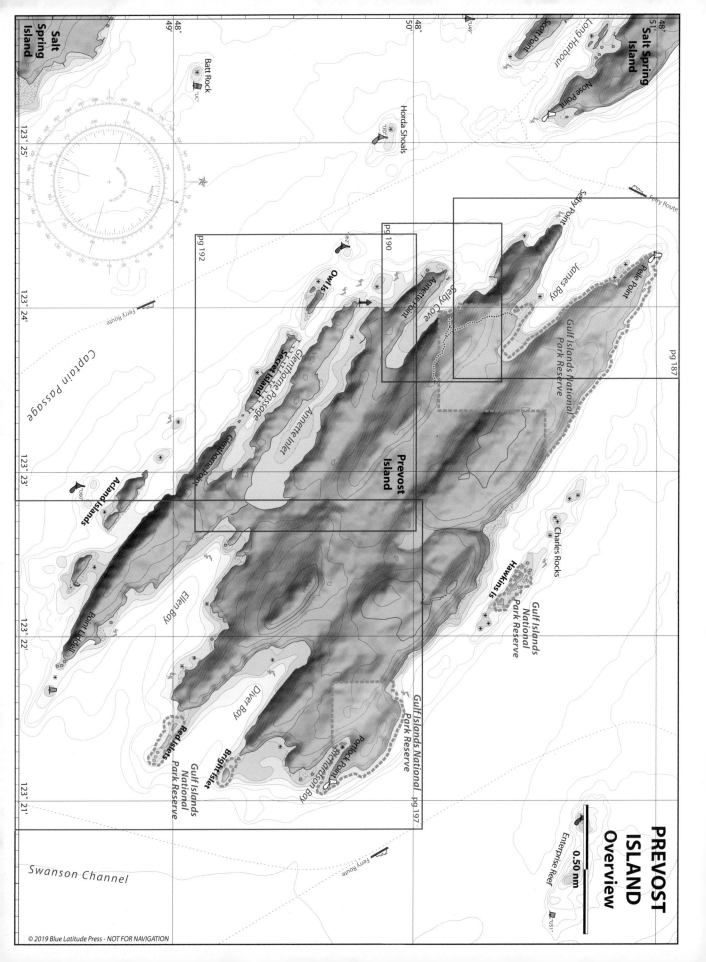

PREVOST ISLAND Overview

Salt Spring Island

Salt Spring Island

Long Harbour

Scott Point

Nose Point

Ferry Route

Batt Rock

Horda Shoals

Selby Point

James Bay

Pelle Point

Selby Cove

Annette Point

Gulf Islands National Park Reserve

pg 190

pg 187

pg 192

Owl Is

Glenthorne Passage

Secret Island

Annette Inlet

Captain Passage

Ferry Route

Glenthorne Point

Prevost Island

Adams Islands

Charles Rocks

Ellen Bay

Hawkins Is

Gulf Islands National Park Reserve

Point Liddell

Diver Bay

Portlock Point

Richardson Bay

Red Islets

Bright Islet

Gulf Islands National Park Reserve

Gulf Islands National Park Reserve

pg 197

Swanson Channel

Enterprise Reef

0.50 nm

© 2019 Blue Latitude Press - NOT FOR NAVIGATION

©Kevin Oke

Prevost Island

Prevost Island lies in the heart of the Gulf Islands, and nearby the popular ports of call like Ganges Harbour on Salt Spring Island and Montague Harbour on Galiano Island. The island's dramatic fingers of land provide excellent anchoring opportunities as well as prime paddling locales for exploration by kayak and stand up paddle boards. No ferries stop at this island which helps maintain it's quiet and peaceful setting.

In 1925, Prevost Island was purchased by Irish nobleman, Digby de Burgh, who used the island for farming. Today, his descendants continue to raise sheep and cattle on the island, maintaining the majority ownership of the island for nearly the past 100 years. In 2012, Parks Canada acquired two pieces of land on both the northwest and east ends of Prevost Island to be incorporated into the Gulf Islands National Park Reserve. Ten primitive camping sites are now offered at the park, and are very popular with visitors arriving by kayak.

Although Prevost Island is relatively small, it boasts six large anchorages scattered around the island. The prime anchorages are located on the island's west and northwestern shore, away from Swanson Channel and the wake of passing ferries. James Bay, the northwestern most anchorage is nearly surrounded by national park land and offers hiking trails and campsites.

Prevost Island is also a historical rarity, as an inland shell midden was discovered on the island in the 1970's. While the majority of midden sites are located along the water's edge, Prevost Island contains a unique inland site that contains solely shells with no fish or mammal bones. From 2013 to 2014, the University of Victoria, First Nations representatives, and representatives from Parks Canada carefully excavated the site to record and preserve the findings. As development continues in the islands, it is important for organizations to study and protect these valuable links to the rich history of the Salish Sea.

©Kevin Oke

James Bay

James Bay is one of the most popular anchorages on Prevost Island. With a large bay, sweeping views of Trincomali Channel, and shoreside access to national park land, its popularity is for good reason. Park campsites also make this a favored stop for kayakers. Nearby Ganges Harbour on Salt Spring Island offers easy provisioning runs to town.

James Bay is located on the northwestern end of Prevost Island. Entrance to the bay is found between Peile Point and Selby Point. Approaches to James Bay can be taken via Captain Passage from the south, or Trincomali Channel to the north. If approaching via Captain Passage, be aware of a few hazards, some of which lie mid channel. Near mid-channel at the southern entrance to Captain Passage lies Channel Islands. These three islands are part of the Gulf Islands National Park Reserve. Deep Ridge is a shoal spit extending 0.4 miles southeast from the Channel Islands. The southern portion of this spit is marked with a light buoy. Batt Rock, which lies 1.8 miles northwest of Channel Islands, has less than 6 feet of water over it. Batt Rock is marked by a navigation buoy. Horda Shoals lie 0.8 miles north-northeast of Batt Rock, and also has less than 6 feet of water over

it. Horda Shoals is marked with a lighted navigation buoy. Southeast of Horda Shoals is the Captain Passage light buoy "U62." Passage can be taken mid-channel between Horda Shoals and buoy "U62." Keep in mind that 2 to 4 knots of currents can ebb and flow through Captain Passage, with tide rips near Nose Point on Salt Spring Island.

For boats approaching from the north, Trincomali Channel is mostly wide, deep and has few navigational haz-

James Bay to:		
	Ganges Harbour (Salt Spring Island)	4 nm
	Ladysmith	21 nm
	Montague Harbour (Galiano Island)	3 nm
	Nanaimo	29 nm
	Pirates Cove (De Courcy Island)	21 nm
	Princess Bay (Portland Island)	9 nm
	Roche Harbor (USA)	18 nm
	Sidney	13 nm
	Tod Inlet	20 nm
	Victoria	34 nm
	Wallace Island	9 nm
	Winter Cove (Saturna Island)	10 nm

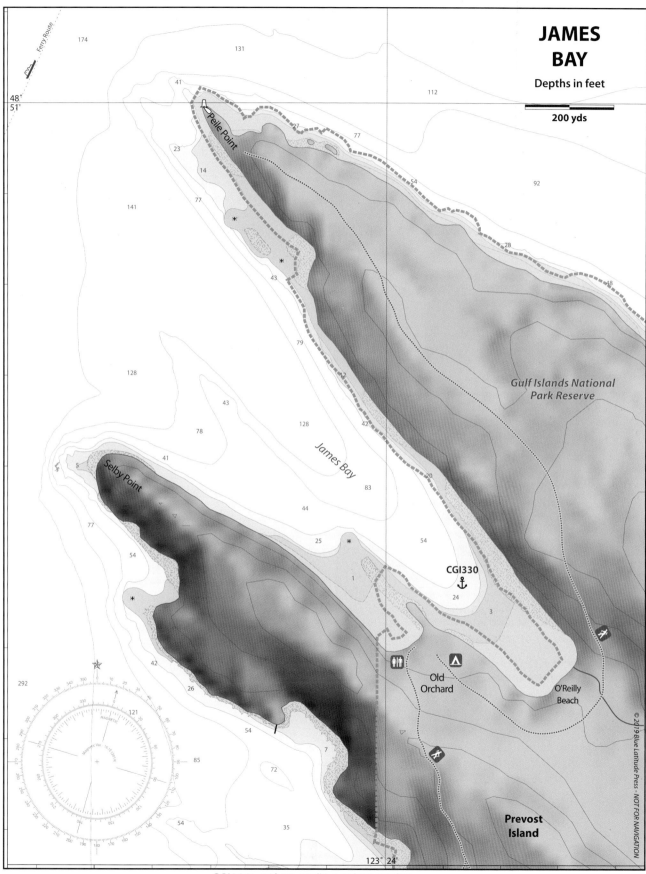

JAMES BAY

Depths in feet

200 yds

Ferry Route

174

131

112

92

48° 51'

41

Pelle Point

23

77

77

14

54

77

141

28

48

43

79

128

43

Gulf Islands National Park Reserve

42

78

128

James Bay

41

Selby Point

5

20

83

77

44

25

54

1

CGI330
⚓

24

54

3

42

26

121

MAGNETIC
Magnetic Var. 16.1E (2019)

292

85

54

Old Orchard

O'Reilly Beach

7

54

72

Prevost Island

35

54

123° 24'

© 2019 Blue Latitude Press - NOT FOR NAVIGATION

CGI330 - 48° 50.475'N 123° 23.870'W

Small beach near campground

Cedar grove

Orchard

ards. Currents at the southern end of the channel can reach 1.5 knots, but north of Wallace Island currents can double in velocity. BC Ferries also transit this area as well, traveling through Active Pass to Long Harbour on Salt Spring Island. At the southern end of the channel is Ben Mohr Rock which lies 0.8 miles northeast of Peile Point. Ben Mohr Rock has 13 feet of water over it and is marked by a lighted buoy.

Once within the bay, be aware of reefs lying south off Peile Point. A second reef extends into the bay from the small beach near the head of the bay. Anchorage can be taken in 5 to 8 fathoms over a mostly mud bottom. The anchorage provides good southerly protection, but is open to wind and waves from the northwest.

For trips to shore, dinghies can be landed within the park at the head of the bay or at the small beach near the campground. Keep in mind both of these beaches are shallow and can be a long ways from the water when the tide goes out. Check the tide table before landing and secure your dinghy or kayak for the appropriate tide change. At the campground, a trail leads through an old heritage orchard and along the shoreline. Keep an eye out for deer who like to eat fallen apples from the trees. A pit toilet is located at the campground, but no water is available. At the head of the bay, a trail leads through beautiful forests of cedars, firs and madrones up the ridge and towards Peile Point. Be sure to bring a camera for sunset photos overlooking the anchorage.

Selby Cove

Selby Cove lies just south of James Bay with the long peninsula of Selby Point separating the two anchorages. A couple of houses and their private docks are found along the shoreline, but otherwise the cove remains quiet and peaceful. A portion of the peninsula is within of the Gulf Islands National Park Reserve.

Selby Cove is located on the west side of Prevost Island, between James Bay to the north and Annette Inlet to the south. Approaches to Selby Cove can be made via Captain Passage which separates Prevost and Salt Spring Islands. When approaching from the south, be aware of a few navigations hazards within Captain Passage listed on page 186. For those entering from the north, give the shoreline around Selby Point ample room to avoid a rock lying south of the point.

Anchorage can be taken within the cove in 2 to 5 fathoms over a mostly mud bottom. The narrowest portion of the cove up to the head is mostly drying mud flats so watch your tide tables and depth sounder before anchoring. Selby Cove provides protection from most winds with the exception of wind and waves from the northwest.

For trips to shore to enjoy the trails of the national park, the easiest place to land a dinghy or kayak is around Selby Point in James Bay. While there is a short trail from Selby Cove over to James Bay, the shoreline here is steep and rocky making it very difficult to disembark and secure a dinghy to shore. Along the way be sure to check out the lattice-like sandstone formations along the way.

Selby Cove to:		
	Ganges Harbour (Salt Spring Island)	4 nm
	Ladysmith	22 nm
	Montague Harbour (Galiano Island)	3 nm
	Nanaimo	29 nm
	Pirates Cove (De Courcy Island)	21 nm
	Princess Bay (Portland Island)	9 nm
	Roche Harbor (USA)	18 nm
	Sidney	13 nm
	Tod Inlet	20 nm
	Victoria	34 nm
	Wallace Island	9 nm
	Winter Cove (Saturna Island)	10 nm

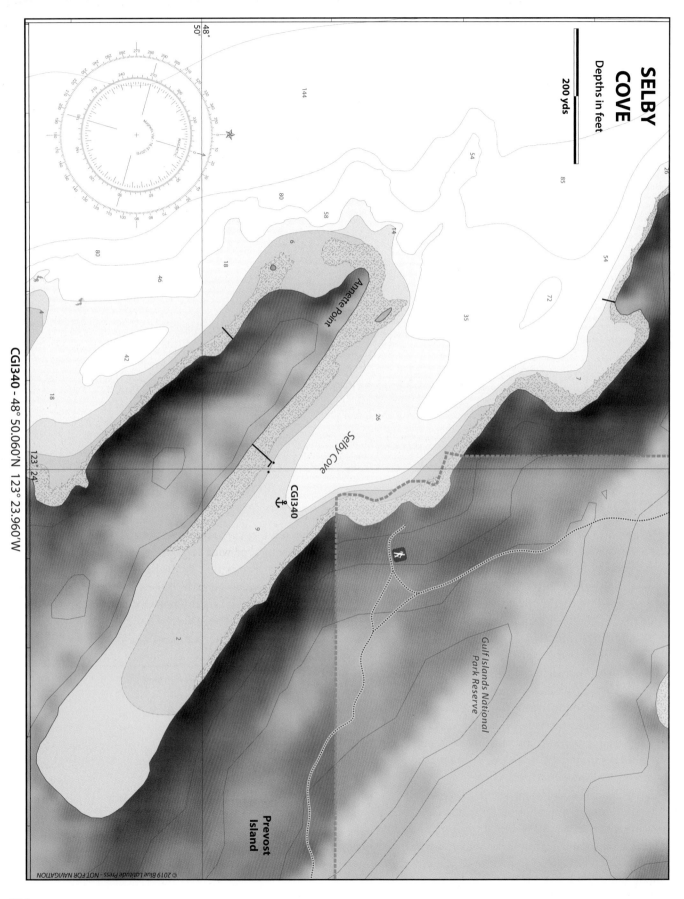

SELBY COVE

Depths in feet

200 yds

Annette Point

Selby Cove

CGI340 ⚓

Gulf Islands National Park Reserve

Prevost Island

CGI340 - 48° 50.060'N 123° 23.960'W

©Kevin Oke

Annette Inlet

Annette Inlet is a favorite among boaters for its calm and quiet waters with scenic shoreline views of rural Prevost Island. For paddlers, the inlet offers an excellent setting for afternoon excursions, exploring the rocky shore and shallow waters at the head of the bay. With ample room for a number of boats, the inlet also provides a serene escape from the hustle and bustle of nearby Ganges Harbour on Salt Spring Island.

Annette Inlet is located off Captain Passage on the west side of Prevost Island. The nearly 1.25 mile long inlet lies between the anchorages of Glenthorne Passage to the south and Selby Cove to the north. Entrance to the cove is taken south of Annette Pointe. Approaches to the inlet can be taken via Captain Passage which separates Salt Spring and Prevost Islands.

For boats approaching from the south, caution should be taken with a few hazards found in Captain Passage. Near mid-channel at the southern entrance to Captain Passage lies the Gulf Islands National Park Reserve, Channel Islands. These islands have a shoal spit extending 0.4 miles

southeast known as Deep Ridge. The southern portion of this spit is marked with a light buoy. Batt Rock, which lies 1.8 miles northwest of Channel Islands, has less than 6 feet of water over it. Batt Rock is marked by a navigation buoy. Horda Shoals lie 0.8 miles north-northeast of Batt Rock, and also has less than 6 feet of water of it. Horda

Annette Inlet to:		
	Ganges Harbour (*Salt Spring Island*)	5 nm
	Lyall Harbour (*Saturna Island*)	10 nm
	Montague Harbour (*Galiano Island*)	5 nm
	Nanaimo	30 nm
	Pirates Cove (*De Courcy Island*)	22 nm
	Princess Bay (*Portland Island*)	8 nm
	Roche Harbor (*USA*)	17 nm
	Sidney	12 nm
	Telegraph Harbour (*Thetis Island*)	17 nm
	Tod Inlet	21 nm
	Victoria	35 nm
	Wallace Island	10 nm

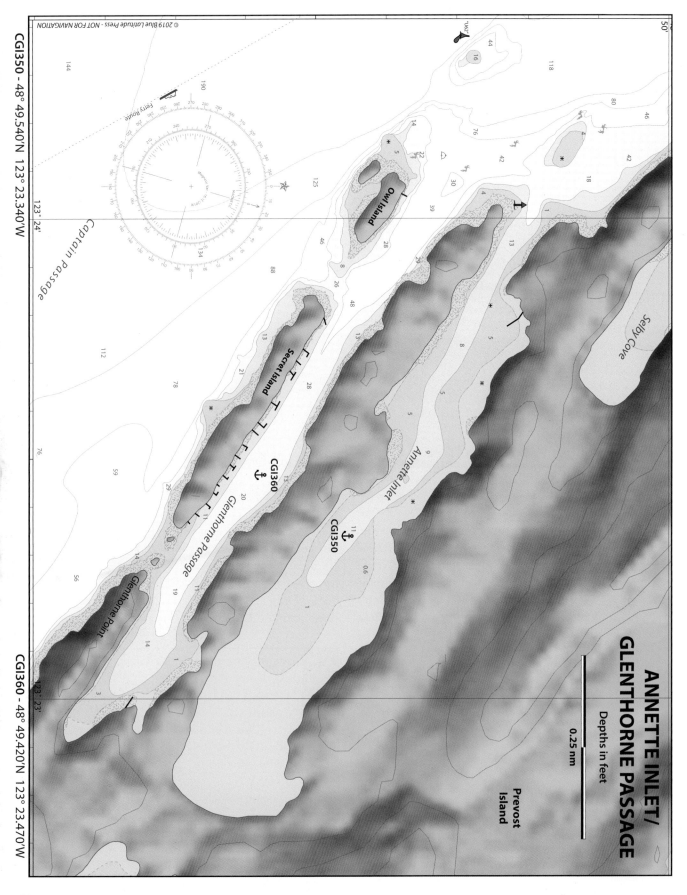

ANNETTE INLET/
GLENTHORNE PASSAGE

Depths in feet

0.25 nm

Prevost
Island

CGI350 - 48° 49.540'N 123° 23.340'W

CGI360 - 48° 49.420'N 123° 23.470'W

© 2019 Blue Latitude Press - NOT FOR NAVIGATION

Ferry Route

Captain Passage

Owl Island

Secret Island

Glenthorne Passage

Glenthorne Point

Annette Inlet

Selby Cove

CGI360

CGI350

The head of Annette Inlet

Shoals is marked with a lighted navigation buoy. Southeast of Horda Shoals is the Captain Passage light buoy "U62." Passage can be taken mid-channel between Horda Shoals and buoy "U62." Keep in mind that 2 to 4 knots of currents can ebb and flow through Captain Passage, with tide rips near Nose Point on Salt Spring Island.

Entrance to Annette Inlet should be taken with caution and careful attention to the chart as a rock hazard lies near mid-channel. Be sure to locate this unmarked rock on the chart prior to entering the inlet. Once inside, be aware of a second rock lying off the northern shore shortly after entering the inlet. Keep in mind Annette Inlet is shallow and may not be suitable for deeper draft boats. Anchorage can be taken throughout in 1 to 2 fathoms over a mud bottom. The head of the inlet is shoal. The inlet affords nearly all-round protection from wind and waves. While it is open to wind from the northwest, waves tend to dissipate within the inlet.

While Annette Inlet does not have any public access locations within the anchorage, a short dinghy or paddle north takes you to James Bay. The two beaches and trails at the head of James Bay are part of the national park and open to the public.

Annette Inlet is a perfect location for dinghy and kayak exploration. Families of Canada geese can be spotted resting shoreside, purple ochre starfish lie just under the water line, and curious bobbing heads of harbor seals are just a few of the wildlife sightings. The calm waters of Annette Inlet also make it a prime location for mooring very unique and intriguing houseboats.

Canada Geese

Looking northwest

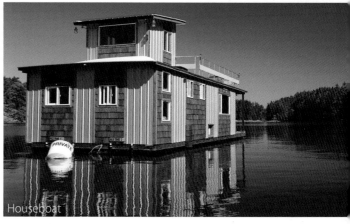
Houseboat

©Kevin Oke

Glenthorne Passage

One of the more narrow anchorages in the Gulf Islands, Glenthorne Passage offers boaters a true Gulf Islands experience. The remote island anchorage with passing traffic in the form of boats and seaplanes, rustic shoreside island cabins, and seabirds flying overhead complete the vision. With Ganges Harbour on nearby Salt Spring Island, for quick trips to town, Glenthorne Passage can be your island paradise to soak up the long days of summer.

The anchorage at Glenthorne Passage is found between Secret Island and Prevost Island's southwestern shore. Access to Glenthorne Passage is made via Captain Passage, which separates Salt Spring and Prevost Islands. Boaters should follow the chart and be aware of the hazards to navigation within Captain Passage. Keep in mind that 2 to 4 knots of currents can ebb and flow through Captain Passage, with tide rips near Nose Point on Salt Spring Island.

For boats approaching from the south, near mid-channel at the southern entrance to Captain Passage lies the Gulf Islands National Park Reserve, Channel Islands. These islands have a shoal spit extending 0.4 miles southeast known as Deep Ridge. The southern portion of this spit is marked with a light buoy. Approximately 0.6 miles northeast of Channel Islands and just off Prevost Islands southern tip are the Acland Islands. Passage between the southern Acland Island and Prevost Island is not recommended due to shallow water and rock hazards. Detached rocks also lie approximately 0.25 miles northwest of the northern most Acland Island and should be avoided. Batt

Glenthorne Passage to:		
Bedwell Harbour *(South Pender Island)*		10 nm
Ganges Harbour *(Salt Spring Island)*		5 nm
Ladysmith		23 nm
Montague Harbour *(Galiano Island)*		5 nm
Nanaimo		30 nm
Pirates Cove *(De Courcy Island)*		22 nm
Roche Harbor *(USA)*		17 nm
Russell Island		7 nm
Sidney		12 nm
Tod Inlet		21 nm
Victoria		35 nm
Wallace Island		10 nm

Rock, which lies 1.8 miles northwest of Channel Islands, has less than 6 feet of water over it. Batt Rock is marked by a navigation buoy. Horda Shoals lie 0.8 miles north-northeast of Batt Rock, and also has less than 6 feet of water over it.

Entrance to Glenthorne Passage for boats approaching from the south can be taken between Owl and Secret Islands. Passage can also be taken between the Captain Passage light buoy "U62" and Owl Island. Be aware that Owl Island has a reef extending off its western shore and to give it ample room when rounding.

For boats approaching from the north, be on the lookout for Horda Shoals which lie 0.8 miles north-northeast of Batt Rock. The shoals are marked with a lighted navigation buoy. When approaching the entrance to Glenthorne Passage from the north, be cautious of the unmarked rock lying near mid-channel at the entrance to Annette Inlet.

Anchorage can be taken within the narrow waterway in 2 to 3 fathoms over a mud bottom. A number of private moorings are scattered throughout the anchorage, however there is still room for a number of boats to anchor. Glenthorne Passage provides nearly all-round shelter from wind and waves with the exception of weather from the northwest.

While the only public access on Prevost Island is at the north and eastern ends within the Gulf Islands National Park Reserve, the unique deep inlets on the island are perfect for dinghy and kayak exploration. Secret Island is dotted with a number of summer cabins, each with its own dock securing a variety of boats and even a seaplane or two. From your dinghy or kayak in the clear shallow water, you can get a glimpse into the underwater world of flowery anemones, spiny urchins, and colorful seastars. To stretch your legs and enjoy a hike on the island, take the dinghy or kayak up to James Bay where trails lead from the campground out towards Peile Point.

Ellen Bay

While the majority of boats favor the deep inlets along Prevost Island's western shore, Ellen Bay and Diver Bay remain off the beaten path destinations on the southeast side of the island. The largest bay on the island, Ellen Bay has sweeping views of Swanson Channel and the distant snow-capped Olympic Mountain range.

Ellen Bay is located at the southeast end of Prevost Island. Approaches to the bay can be made via Swanson Channel from the north or south, or Captain Passage from the northwest. Keep in mind that the northern end of Swanson Channel near Enterprise Reef can experience stronger currents from 3 to 7 knots. If approaching via Captain Passage be aware of several hazards in the pass and pay close attention to the chart. See page 186 for detail information on Captain Passage.

Both entrance points to Ellen Bay have extending reefs and sufficient room should be given when rounding into the bay. Point Liddell, the southern most point on Prevost Island, has a reef that extends 0.2 miles and is marked by a daybeacon on the outermost rock. Red Islets, off the northern entrance point, also have surrounding reefs.

Much of Ellen Bay is fairly deep, however anchorage can be taken near the head of the bay in 5 to 10 fathoms over a mostly mud bottom. The anchorage is open to weather from the south and east, but provides shelter from north and west winds. It is also open to wake from the frequently passing BC Ferries in Swanson Channel. For this reason, many boaters choose the anchorages on the western side of Prevost Island.

Ellen Bay does not have any public access sites, however nearby Richardson Bay is part of the Gulf Islands National Park Reserve and is open to the public. A short trail at the head of the bay takes you out to the perfect picnic site at the picturesque Portlock Point light.

Looking south at Point Liddell daybeacon

Ellen Bay to:		
	Ganges Harbour *(Salt Spring Island)*	7 nm
	Ladysmith	26 nm
	Montague Harbour *(Galiano Island)*	7 nm
	Nanaimo	33 nm
	Princess Bay *(Portland Island)*	7 nm
	Roche Harbor *(USA)*	15 nm
	Sidney	11 nm
	Victoria	32 nm
	Wallace Island	13 nm
	Winter Cove *(Saturna Island)*	8 nm

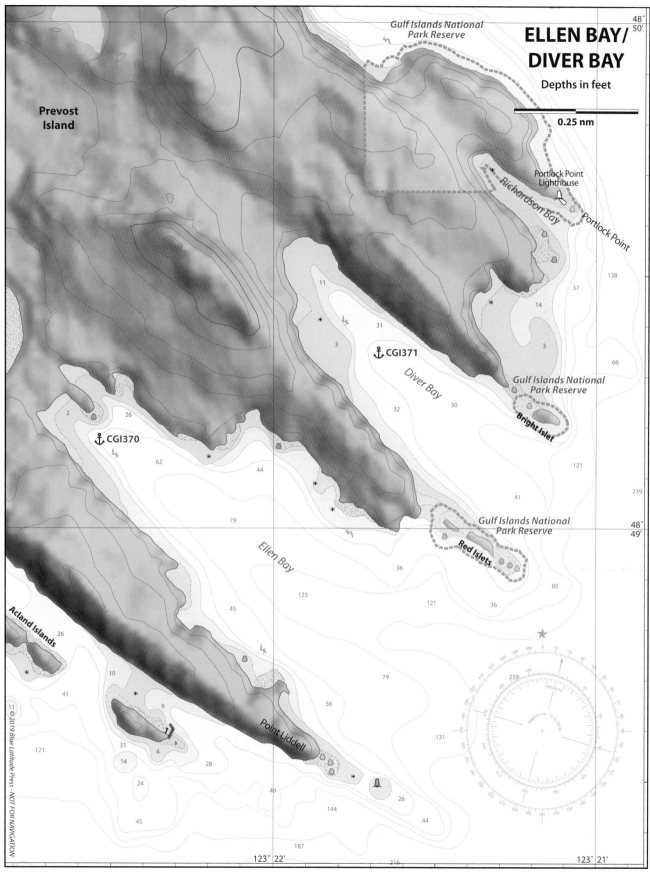

ELLEN BAY/
DIVER BAY

Depths in feet

0.25 nm

Gulf Islands National
Park Reserve

Prevost
Island

48°
50'

Portlock Point
Lighthouse

Richardson Bay

Portlock Point

138

⚓ CGI371

37

14

11

31

3

3

66

Diver Bay

50

32

Gulf Islands National
Park Reserve

Bright Islet

2

26

⚓ CGI370

62

44

79

121

239

48°
49'

41

Gulf Islands National
Park Reserve

Red Islets

Ellen Bay

36

85

125

121

36

Acland Islands

26

10

43

9

11

79

56

131

31

4

14

28

24

49

26

144

45

44

Point Liddell

187

216

123° 22'

123° 21'

MAGNETIC

259

CGI370 - 48° 49.170'N 123° 22.535'W   **CGI371** - 48° 49.350'N 123° 21.670'W

Diver Bay

Surrounded by thick forests of madrones, firs, and cedars, Diver Bay offers beautiful vistas of both land and water. Fronted by Swanson Channel, the bay has a perfect view of the variety of boats transiting the channel. Nearby Portlock Point light offers a scenic destination to stretch your legs and get off the boat.

Diver Bay is located on the east side of Prevost Island, and north of Ellen Bay. Approaches to the bay can be made via Swanson Channel from the north or south. Keep in mind that the northern end of Swanson Channel near Enterprise Reef can experience stronger currents from 3 to 7 knots. If approaching Swanson Channel via Captain Passage be aware of hazards in the pass. See page 186 for detail information on Captain Passage.

When approaching from the south, give ample room to Point Liddell. It is the southern most point on Prevost Island

with a reef extending 0.2 miles southeast. The outermost rock is marked by a daybeacon. Red Islets, off the southern entrance point to the bay, also have surrounding reefs. When approaching the entrance from the north, give Bright Islet ample room as well when rounding into the bay.

Anchorage can be taken within the bay in 4 to 5 fathoms over a mostly mud bottom. Be aware near the head of the bay on the western side is a rock and kelp forest that should be avoided. Diver Bay provides protection from north and west winds, but is open to the south and east. It is also open to wake from the frequently passing BC Ferries in Swanson Channel. For this reason, many boaters choose the anchorages on the western side of Prevost Island.

For trips to shore, nearby Richardson Bay offers a nice landing beach and is part of the Gulf Islands National Park Reserve. A short trail from the beach takes you out to the scenic Portlock Point light.

Portlock Point light

Diver Bay to:		
Ganges Harbour *(Salt Spring Island)*	7 nm
Montague Harbour *(Galiano Island)*	6 nm
Nanaimo	32 nm
Port Browning *(North Pender Island)*	8 nm
Princess Bay *(Portland Island)*	7 nm
Roche Harbor *(USA)*	15 nm
Sidney	11 nm
Telegraph Harbour *(Thetis Island)*	20 nm
Victoria	33 nm
Wallace Island	12 nm

Chapter 8

Galiano Island

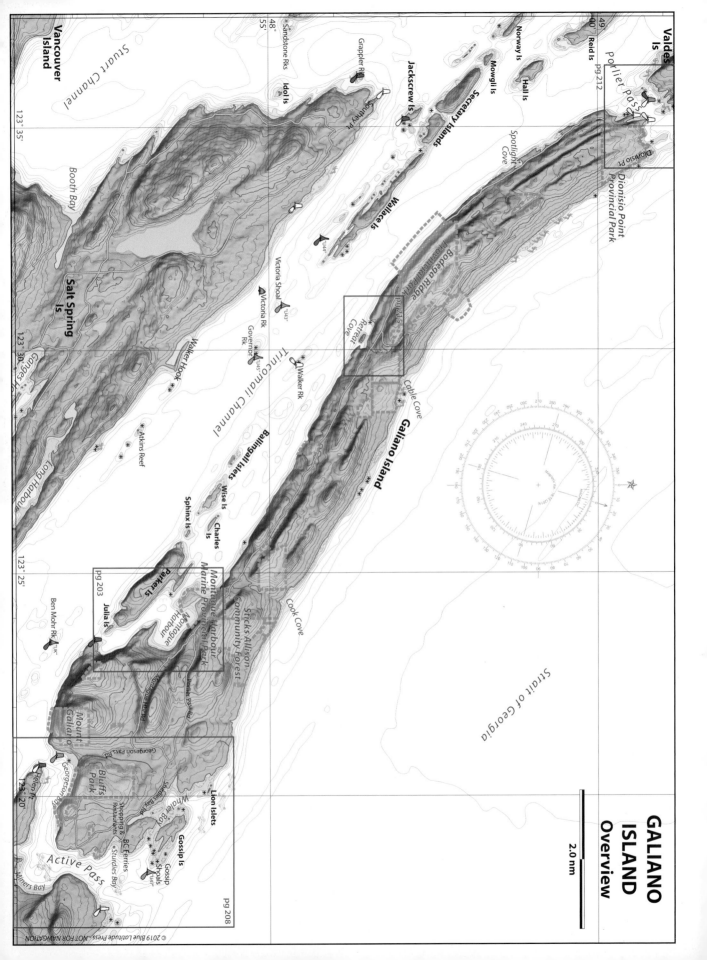

GALIANO ISLAND Overview

2.0 nm

49
00

Reid Is

Pollier Pass

Dionisio Pt

Dionisio Point Provincial Park

Norway Is

Mowgli Is

Halls Is

Spotlight Cove

Secretary Islands

Jackscrew Is

Courtney Pt

Wallace Is

Bodega Ridge Provincial Park

pg 215

Retreat Cove

Cable Cove

Galiano Island

Sandstone Rks

48
55'

Grappler Rk

Idol Is

Stuart Channel

Vancouver Island

Booth Bay

Salt Spring Is

Victoria Shoal

"U43"

Victoria Rk

Governor Rk

"U45"

Walker Rk

"U45"

Walker Hook

Trincomali Channel

Ballingall Islets

"U44"

Wise Is

Charles Is

Sphinx Is

Atkins Reef

Ganges Hbr

Long Harbour

123° 35'

123° 30'

123° 25'

Strait of Georgia

Cook Cove

Sticks Allison Community Forest

Montague Harbour Marine Provincial Park

pg 203

Parker Is

Julia Is

Ben Mohr Rk

"UK"

Montague Harbour

Mount Galiano

Bluffs Park

Georgeson Bay Rd

Georgeson Pass Rd

Helen Pt

Lion Islets

Whaler Bay

Gossip Is

Gossip Shoals

"U47"

Shopping & Restaurants

BC Ferries

Sturdies Bay

Active Pass

Miners Bay

123° 20'

pg 208

©Kevin Oke

Galiano Island

One of the longest islands in the Gulf archipelago chain at roughly 16 miles in length, Galiano Island is perfectly situated to enjoy all-round views of both the islands and the mountainous mainland landscape. The ferry serviced island has a population of just over 1,000 people, and boasts to have the driest climate and most days of sun in the area. Most boaters who visit Galiano Island stop at the nearly land-locked anchorage of Montague Harbour to enjoy the stunning provincial marine park located in the harbour's northern end.

Galiano's human history has been dated back to roughly 3,000 years ago using archaeological excavations around Montague Harbours' shell beaches. These midden beaches were once used by the indigenous Coast Salish who left behind thousands of years of castaway shells from harvested shellfish. Excavated arrows, spearheads and stone carvings, were also found and helped to date and learn about these previous cultures.

Galiano Island is named after the Spanish explorer, Captain Dionisio Alcalá Galiano. Galiano, who was trained by the renowned Spanish cartographer Vicente Tofiño de San Miguel, circumnavigated Vancouver Island in 1792. With tens of thousands coming to the area in 1848 for the Fraser River Gold Rush, pioneers slowly began to settle within the islands. Early settlers to Galiano Island took advantage of the fertile valleys for farm land and the surrounding bountiful waters for fishing.

Today, Galiano Island is home to an eclectic mix of longtime family residents, writers, craftsmen, artists, vactioners, and retirees. Visitors to the island can enjoy a host of galleries, studios, and bookstores showcasing the talent of the island. The Galiano Trails Society and the Galiano Island Parks and Recreation Commission have created miles of spectacular hiking trails across the island. For the best view and aerobic workout, be sure to check out Mount Galiano, standing at over 1,000 feet and offering unparalleled views.

Getting around Galiano Island's 23 square miles for boaters sans cars is best done by bike, moped rental (see page 205), or the island's new weekend shuttle service from April through September: activeislands.com/post/galianobus.

©Kevin Oke

Montague Harbour

Montague Harbour is a true gem and a top destination for nearly all boaters cruising the islands. The sizable all-weather harbor includes ample room for even the largest of yachts, as well as a small marina and park mooring buoys for alternatives to anchoring. At the head of the harbor lies the 250-acre Montague Harbour Provincial Marine Park which features a 240 foot dock, camping, walking trails, beautiful beaches, potable water, and even trash and recycle disposal. A small waterfront restaurant and general store at the marina provides an excellent afternoon away from the galley and a convenient provisioning stop.

Montague Harbour is located at the southwestern end of Galiano Island, which lies between the expansive Strait of Georgia to the east and Trincomali Channel to the west. The entrance to Montague Harbour is found off the southern end of Trincomali Channel and is fronted by Parker Island.

When approaching from the south, be aware of Enterprise Reef and Ben Mohr Rock, both located at the southern end of Trincomali Channel and both are marked by navigation lights. Entrance to the harbor can be taken between Phillimore Point on Gabriola Island and Julia Island, just southeast of Park Island. The entrance to the harbor is relatively deep and free of dangers. Overhead power cables are found between Galiano and Parker Islands. The cables are marked with red spheres and have a vertical clearance of 125 feet.

Approaching from the north, be on the lookout for Walker Rock, Governor Rock, Victoria Shoal, and Victoria Rock. These hazards lie near midway down the channel and are all marked by navigation buoys. Ballingall Islets lie roughly 1.3 miles northwest of Parker Island. These islets are low and have extending reefs off their northwest tip so be sure to give them ample room. Entrance to Montague

Montague Harbour to:		
	Ganges Harbour *(Salt Spring Island)*	7 nm
	Genoa Bay	20 nm
	Ladysmith	20 nm
	Nanaimo	28 nm
	Pirates Cove *(De Courcy Island)*	19 nm
	Princess Bay *(Portland Island)*	12 nm
	Port Browning *(North Pender Island)*	12 nm
	Roche Harbor *(USA)*	20 nm
	Sidney	16 nm
	Tod Inlet	23 nm
	Victoria	37 nm
	Wallace Island	7 nm

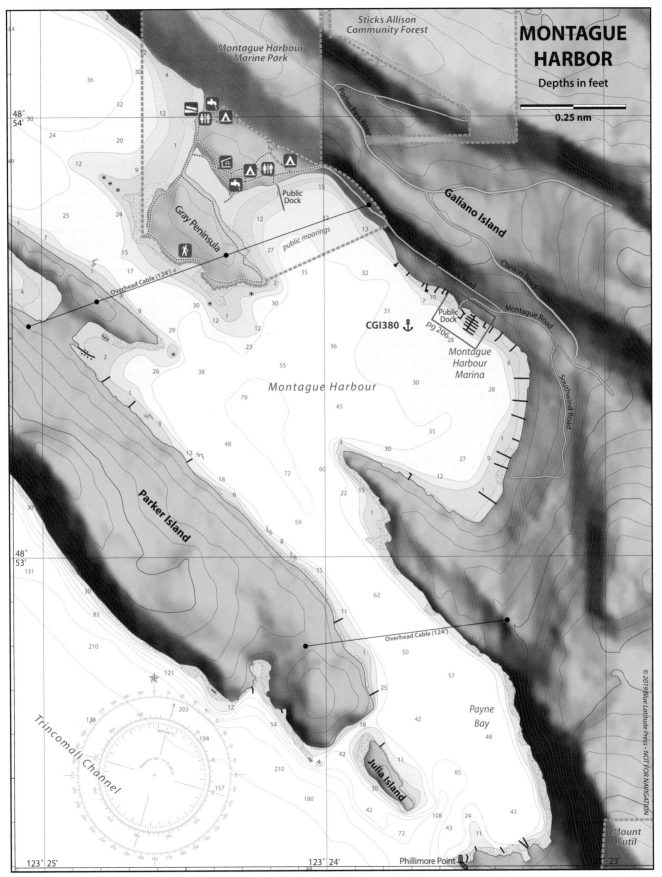

MONTAGUE HARBOR

Depths in feet

0.25 nm

Sticks Allison
Community Forest

Montague Harbour
Marine Park

Gray Peninsula

Public
Dock

public moorings

Galiano Island

Porlier Pass Road

Clanton Road

Montague Road

Southwind Road

Overhead Cable (124')

CGI380 ⚓

pg 206

Public
Dock

Montague
Harbour
Marina

Montague Harbour

Parker Island

Overhead Cable (124')

Payne
Bay

Julia Island

Trincomali Channel

Mount
Sutil

Phillimore Point

© 2019 Blue Latitude Press - NOT FOR NAVIGATION

CGI380 - 48° 53.535'N 123° 23.705'W

203

Montague Harbour Provincial Marine Park

Park campground

Harbour can be taken from the north between Parker and Galiano Islands. This north entrance is shallower than the southern entrance with a least depth mid-channel of 17 feet.

Anchorage can be taken within the harbor in 5 to 8 fathoms over a mostly mud bottom. During the peak summer months, this anchorage can become quite full. Additional anchorage is available in the bay north of Gray Peninsula. This area is usually less crowded and best suited for periods of calm or southerly weather. Montague Harbour provides good all-round protection with its nearly landlocked formation and protection by Parker Island.

Public park mooring buoys (35 buoys) are available for a nightly fee at the north end of the harbor near the park. The park also offers dock space for a nightly fee for boats 36 feet and under. Be sure to check the tide tables before heading to the park dock as this area is shallow, especially on a low tide.

Moorage may also be taken at the public CRD dock which is just north of the Montague Harbour Marina. This dock can be very congested with local boats especially during the summer season. A portion of the dock, marked in yellow, is reserved for emergency vessels and other service providers. For further information on CRD public wharfs check their website at: www.crd.bc.ca.

For trips to shore, a convenient dinghy dock is located at the park in the north portion of the harbor. The public

CRD dock is also available for dinghy tie-ups on the east side of the harbor, just north of the marina.

The best site to see in the harbor is by far the Montague Harbour Provincial Park. From the dinghy dock, the pier and staircase lead up to a kiosk with park information and a map. A pay station is here for those using park mooring buoys, overnighting on the dock, and/or camping (cash only). The park also offers a small recycling and garbage station here for boaters for a per bag fee. This is a great benefit as trash and recycling can be difficult to dispose of in the islands. Be sure to thank the parks department for this service by including full payment for your bags.

The park has over two miles of walking trails, including a trail circumnavigating Gray Peninsula. It is a good idea to try to visit the park during a low tide in order to have more access to the beaches. Historical First Nations shell middens can be found both within the harbor and along the north side of the park. Along the northwest shore of Gray Peninsula visitors can find a glacier carved reef with unusual striated patterns. A unique salt water marsh is also found linking Gray Peninsula to the park's campground.

For those camping or staying on the dock, be aware that raccoons at the park have been a problem. To prevent an unwelcome intruder, never feed the raccoons, close all hatches, store food and scented items in secure containers, do not leave food unattended, and dispose of garbage immediately. Raccoons are smart, bungee cords around coolers and plastic bins are no match for them!

For those looking for a night away from the galley, the Montague Harbour Marina is the place go. The Crane and Robin restaurant, which overlooks the marina, serves fresh and locally sourced ingredients in their delicious meals. The restaurant is open seasonally for lunch and dinner with beautiful outdoor waterfront dining tables and bars (www.craneandrobin.com). There is also the Hummingbird Pub which offers free bus service from the marina or campground to the pub located on Sturdies Bay Road. The eclectic bus operates throughout the summer, and the pub is open daily with a classic pub fare menu. For further information and the bus schedule check: hummingbirdpub.com.

To explore more of the interior of the island, check with Galiano Adventures for a moped rental. By the day or the hour, take a moped tour of Galiano Island, visiting shops and galleries or taking a hike at one of the island's many parks. Galiano Adventures is located at Montague Harbour Marina from May through September (www.galianoadventures.com). For those looking to explore by water, check with Galiano Kayaks located at the marina for kayak, canoe, and paddle board rentals or tours (seakayak.ca).

Park trails

North side of Gray Peninsula

General store and The Crane and Robin restaurant

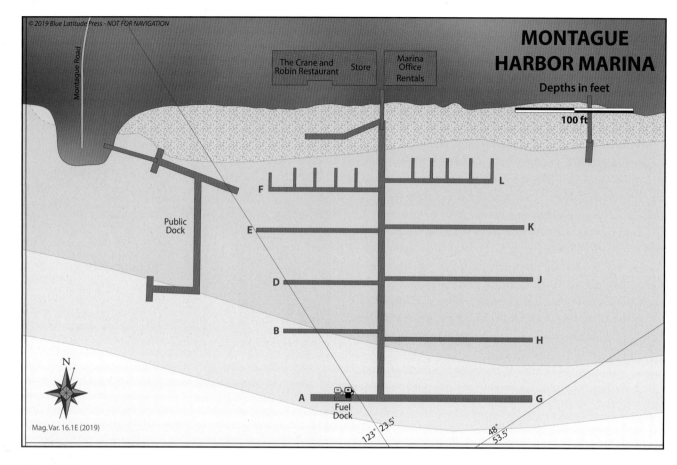

© 2019 Blue Latitude Press - NOT FOR NAVIGATION

Montague Road

The Crane and Robin Restaurant

Store

Marina Office Rentals

MONTAGUE HARBOR MARINA

Depths in feet

100 ft

F

L

Public Dock

E

K

D

J

B

H

N

A

G

Fuel Dock

123° 23.5'

48° 53.5'

Mag. Var. 16.1E (2019)

Montague Harbour Marina

Montague Harbour Marina offers both permanent and transient mooring options within the well protected Montague Harbour. The marina also has a fuel dock providing ethanol-free gas, diesel, and oils. Services at the marina include washrooms and a small general store that sells groceries, fishing and camping supplies, books, clothing, gift items and even ice cream cones. Due to saltwater intrusion in the well, water is not available on the docks. The marina is open for transient moorage seasonally from May through September.

Next to the general store is the amazing waterfront restaurant, The Crane and Robin. Also located at the marina is Gulf Island Kayaking which offers guided tours and rentals, and Galiano Adventures offering moped and boat rentals. See page 205 for detailed information.

Montague Harbour Marina
3451 Montague Road
Galiano Island, BC, V0N 1P0
(250) 539-5733
montagueharbourmarina@gmail.com
montagueharbour.com

The Crane and Robin

Active Pass

Active Pass connects the major waterway of the Strait of Georgia with the Gulf Island's Swanson and Trincomali Channels. It is located between Galiano and Mayne Islands. The deep horseshoe-shaped channel is well known for its strong currents and its regular use by commercial boats including BC Ferries. During the summer months it can be quite active with ferries, fishing boats, pleasure boats, tugs, and freighters.

For boats using Active Pass, caution should be taken due to its strong currents, which can attain rates of 8 knots, have heavy tide rips, and fast moving large ferries. Given the regularity of BC Ferries' schedule, it is possible to encounter up to three ferries within the pass, with some of the ferries on this route being over 500 feet in length. Due to the tortuous shape, visibility is also obscured within the pass. To help alert mariners, ferries, tugs in tow, and other large vessels will issue a sécurité warning on VHF channel 16 of their entrance into the pass.

For boats approaching the western entrance to Active Pass, be cautious of both Enterprise Reef and Ben Mohr Rock. Enterprise Reef is located approximately 0.7 miles southwest of Helen Point on Mayne Island. A navigation light located on the western rock of the reef and buoy "U51" marks the east end of the reef. Ben Mohr rock is located roughly 0.8 miles north-northeast of Peile Point on Prevost Island. The rock is marked with a lighted navigation buoy.

The western entrance to Active Pass is found between Collision Point on Galiano Island and Helen Point. According to the sailing directions, when approaching from the south, currents strengthen around Helen Point on a flood tide. A flood tide also has a strong set into Miners Bay along the north shore. On spring flood tides, extreme tide rips, which can be dangerous to smaller boats, are experienced between Laura Point and Mary Anne Point, and also around Fairway Bank. When leaving, the flood current of Active Pass meets with the current in the Strait of George, setting boats toward Gossip Shoals, which lie southeast of Gossip Island.

For boats approaching the northern entrance, be cautioned that heavy tide rips are found near Gossip Island, Lion Islets, Fairway Bank, and Salamanca Point, especially on a flood tide and an opposing northwest wind. Be aware of the navigation hazards at Georgina Shoals, Lion Islets, and Gossip Shoals. Entrance to Active Pass from the north lies between Georgina Point on Mayne Island and Rip Point on Galiano Island. On ebb tides, no extreme tide rips occur within Active Pass.

The currents and winding channel of Active Pass also create eddies. The largest eddy occurs in Miners Bay. On a flood tide, a clockwise eddy forms with currents off the wharf reaching 2.5 knots. On ebb tides, a counter-clockwise eddy forms with currents reaching 2 knots off the wharf. A second eddy can be found off Helen Point on ebb tides.

When planning a trip through Active Pass, be sure to check the current tables and plan for a transit near or at slack especially during periods of wind.

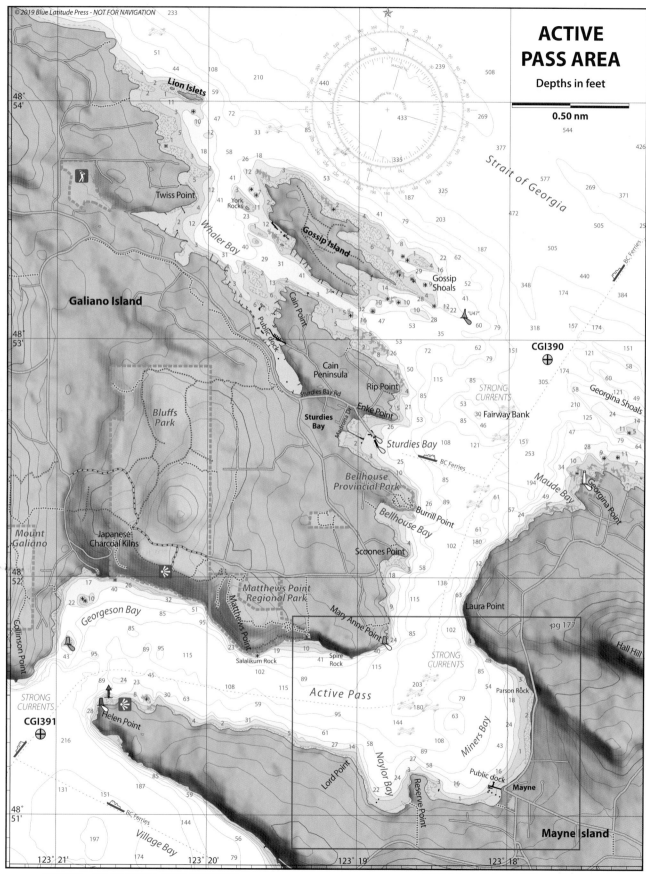

© 2019 Blue Latitude Press - NOT FOR NAVIGATION   233

ACTIVE PASS AREA

Depths in feet

0.50 nm

Strait of Georgia

Lion Islets

Twiss Point

Whaler Bay

York Rocks

Gossip Island

Gossip Shoals

"U47"

Galiano Island

Cain Point

Public dock

Cain Peninsula

Sturdies Bay Rd

Rip Point

CGI390

Enke Point

Sturdies Bay

Madrona Dr

Sturdies Bay

STRONG CURRENTS

Fairway Bank

BC Ferries

Bluffs Park

Bellhouse Provincial Park

Burrill Point

Georgina Shoals

Maude Bay

Georgina Point

Bellhouse Bay

Scoones Point

Mount Galiano

Japanese Charcoal Kilns

Matthews Point Regional Park

Laura Point

pg 177

Hall Hill

Matthews Point

Mary Anne Point

Georgeson Bay

Salalikum Rock

Spire Rock

STRONG CURRENTS

Parson Rock

Collinson Point

Active Pass

Miners Bay

STRONG CURRENTS

Helen Point

Lord Point

Naylor Bay

Public dock

CGI391

Reserve Point

Mayne

BC Ferries

Village Bay

Mayne Island

123° 21'   123° 20'   123° 19'   123° 18'

48° 54'
48° 53'
48° 52'
48° 51'

CGI390 - 48° 52.910'N 123° 17.760'W   **CGI391** - 48° 51.330'N 123° 21.130'W

©Kevin Oke

Sturdies Bay

Sturdies Bay, located within Active Pass, is home to the Galiano Island ferry terminal. Adjacent to the ferry pier is a small public dock. While this bay is best suited for day stops in settled weather, the public dock affords convenient moorage for quick stops to pick up friends arriving on the ferry or a bite to eat at one of the nearby restaurants.

Sturdies Bay is found on the southeast end of Galiano Island within Active Pass. Approaches to the bay can be taken from the west or north entrance to Active Pass. For detailed information on Active Pass, see page 207.

As Sturdies Bay is somewhat exposed to the wind and waves within the Strait of Georgia, along with strong current in Active Pass and wash from landing ferries, Sturdies Bay is best left for day stops in calm conditions. Anchorage can be taken within the bay, but keep in mind it is shallow at the head and to anchor outside of the ferry's docking area. Anchor in 2 to 4 fathoms.

Sturdies Bay also offers a public dock through the Capital Regional District (CRD). The dock is connected to the ferry pier on the west side and is approximately 80 feet in length. Roughly half of the dock is reserved for emergency vessels and essential service providers. Local island residents use the dock often. For those who do spend the night, wash from passing boats, including BC Ferries, tends to make this dock a bit rolly and uncomfortable. While there is no water or power on the dock, restrooms for the ferries is located at the head of the pier. For further information on CRD public wharfs check their website at: www.crd.bc.ca.

A number of businesses can be found near the ferry terminal including eateries and a small grocery. You can usually find a food truck within the ferry waiting lines, or across the street is the Sturdies Bay Bakery and Cafe. Also across from the ferry terminal is the all in one Galiano Garage. The store sells gas, diesel, and propane, as well as a full grocery and liquor store. For restaurants, try Scoops Ice Cream and Burger Bay located on Sturdies Bay Road, or the upscale Atrevida Restaurant & Orca Lounge at the Galiano Inn on Madrona Drive.

Whaler Bay

west wind. These tide rips can be dangerous to small boats when strong currents meet with opposing wind and waves.

Anchorage at Whaler Bay is quite limited due to shallow depths, lack of weather protection, reefs, and current. It is best suited as a temporary stop in settled weather.

A public dock is available, tucked into the narrow southern portion of Whaler Bay that provides protected moorage mostly for local island residents. During the summer months this dock is typically full with priority given to commercial fishing boats. The area near the dock is very shallow with a least depth of 1 foot recorded. The dock is maintained by the Whaler Bay Harbour Authority (250-539-2264).

Mount Galiano

Mount Galiano is the tallest peak on Galiano Island, standing at 1,020 feet. The Galiano Club, originally formed in 1924, holds the Mount Galiano Nature Perserve in trust with public access to the mountain's trails. From the top, the mountain offers sweeping views of the Gulf Islands and Vancouver Island.

A few trails lead to the top, one entirely within the nature preserve and some that cross private property. Be sure to stick to the trails for conservation as well as privacy for the land owners. The two most popular trails are the Galiano Club Trail with a trailhead at the end of Active Pass Drive, and the Lord Trail with a trailhead on Lord Road. Roundtrip, the hike is between 3 to 4 miles depending on the trail.

For a map of the trails, visit: www.galiander.ca. To reach the trailheads, bikes, moped rentals, or thumbing a ride from a local islander are the best options. Please note there are no bikes allowed on the trails, and there are no restroom facilities at the trailheads or the summit.

Whaler Bay

Whaler Bay is located across the narrow Cain Peninsula from Sturdies Bay on the southeast end of Galiano Island. The shallow and rocky bay provides shelter to a number of private docks and moorings as well as a small public dock controlled by Fisheries and Oceans Canada. Shallow draft boats occasionally use Whaler Bay as a staging location as they wait for slack tide in Active Pass.

Entrance to Whaler Bay can be taken from the southeast between Gossip Island and Cain Point, or from the north between Gossip Island and Twiss Point. Prior to approaching either entrance be sure to carefully study the chart and check the tide tables as this area is very shallow with numerous hazards in the form of unmarked rocks and underwater reefs. It is important to be aware of extreme tide rips that occur around Gossip Island, Lion Islets, and Salamanca Point, especially on a flood tide and opposing north-

©Kevin Oke

Porlier Pass

Porlier Pass separates the northern end of Galiano Island and the southern end of Valdes Island. The pass connects the waterways of the open Strait of Georgia to the more protected waters of Trincomali Channel. Currents in the pass can be quite strong, reaching velocities over 10 knots on large tides. The pass is relatively straight, however a number of hazards are found both mid-channel and along the shores of Valdes and Galiano Islands.

For boats using Porlier Pass, caution should be taken due to its strong currents and numerous rocks and reefs. Careful attention to the chart and current tables is recommended prior to entering the pass. Flood tides flow from Trincomali Channel into the Strait of Georgia, and the reverse direction for ebb tides.

From the west, Porlier Pass is entered between Alcala Point on Galiano Island and Cayetano Point on Valdes Island. Porlier Pass is entered from the east between Dionisio Point on Galiano Island and Vernaci Point on Valdes Island. Kelp covered underwater reefs extend northwest of Dionisio Point and should therefore be given ample room

when rounding into the pass. Underwater reefs and a rock also lie off Vernaci Point. For boats approaching from the northeast, be aware of rocks and shoal water lying between Vernaci Point and Shah Point 0.65 miles to the north. noe Islet, roughly 0.3 miles east of Shah Point has extending reefs nearly 0.2 miles in length.

There are three main reefs lying near mid-channel: Romulus Reef, Black Rock, and Virago Rock. Romulus Reef is roughly 0.25 miles southwest of Virago Point with 24 feet of water over the reef. Black Rock lies roughly 0.4 miles west-northwest of Virago Point and is marked with a daybeacon on its northwest end. Two additional covered rocks lie in close proximity to Black Rock on its southeast and northeast sides. Virago Rock is approximately 0.25 miles northwest of Virago Point and is marked by a navigation light. Virago Rock lies on a shoal with minimum depths of 6 feet.

When planning a trip through Porlier Pass, be sure to check the current tables and plan for a transit near or at slack especially during periods of strong winds and/or large tides.

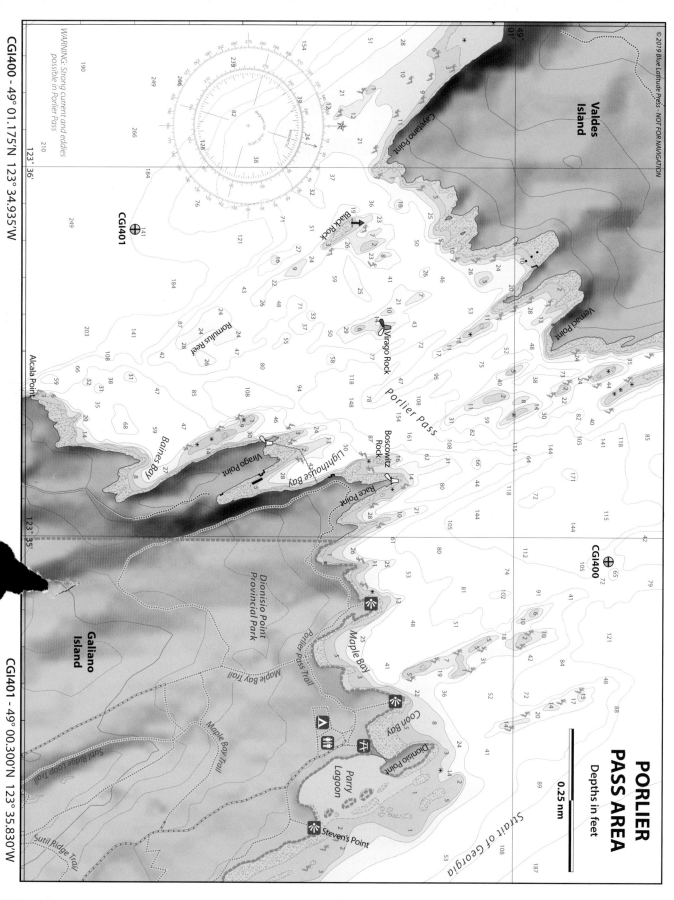

Valdes Island

Cayetano Point

Black Rock

Vernaci Point

Virago Rock

Porlier Pass

Romulus Reef

Boscowitz Rock

Baines Bay

Alcala Point

Virago Point

Lighthouse Bay

Race Point

CGI401

CGI400

Dionisio Point Provincial Park

Maple Bay Trail

Porlier Pass Trail

Maple Bay

Coon Bay

Dionisio Point

Galiano Island

Sutil Ridge Loop Trail

Maple Bay Trail

Sutil Ridge Trail

Parry Lagoon

Steven's Point

Strait of Georgia

PORLIER PASS AREA

Depths in feet

0.25 nm

CGI400 - 49° 01.175'N 123° 34.935'W

CGI401 - 49° 00.300'N 123° 35.830'W

WARNING: Strong current and eddies possible in Porlier Pass.

©Gordon Montgomery

Dionisio Point

Dionisio Point is located on the very northern tip of Galiano Island and is home to the Dionisio Point Provincial Park. Due to its location on Porlier Pass and lack of land access, this remote park has remained a fairly quiet destination. A beautiful sand beach, sweeping views of the Strait of Georgia and mountain-strewn mainland, along with camping make Dionisio Point a hidden gem on Galiano Island.

Dionisio Point is located on the northeastern tip of Galiano Island. Approaches to the point are made via Porlier Pass to the west and the Strait of Georgia to the east. For those approaching via Porlier Pass, keep in mind this pass has a number of hazards and strong current. For detailed information on transiting the pass, see page 211.

Maple Bay and Coon Bay are the most commonly used bays for boats accessing the park. When approaching these bays from either Porlier Pass or the Strait of Georgia, be aware of detached reefs and shallow water northwest, north, and east of the point. Anchorage can be taken in either bay, however both bays are open to northwest winds and waves in the Strait of Georgia, and current in Porlier Pass. These anchorages are best suited as temporary lunch stops in calm weather.

On shore, the park offers a number of excellent hiking trails, picnic tables, a well pump for water (boil first), and 30 campsites. As there is no public access by land to this park, visitors typically come by kayaks and small power-boats. The fine sand beach at Coon Bay provides an excellent location to soak up some warm sunshine and take advantage of an afternoon nap. The surrounding sandstone rocks provide excellent tide pool exploring at low tide.

Dionisio Point to:		
	Clam Bay (Thetis Island)	4 nm
	Ganges Harbour (Salt Spring Island)	17 nm
	Ladysmith	12 nm
	Montague Harbour (Galiano Island)	12 nm
	Nanaimo	18 nm
	Pirates Cove (De Courcy Island)	9 nm
	Princess Bay (Portland Island)	23 nm
	Port Browning (North Pender Island)	23 nm
	Sidney	27 nm
	Silva Bay (Gabriola Island)	11 nm
	Tod Inlet	30 nm
	Wallace Island	7 nm

©Peter Graham

Retreat Cove

Retreat Cove is an off the beaten path destination for most visitors traveling through the Gulf Islands. The small cove offers a well used public dock and a beautiful sandstone cave to explore.

Retreat Cove is found near the middle of Galiano Island on its western shore. Approaches to the cove are taken via Trincomali Channel. Retreat Island lies in the middle of the cove and is connected to Galiano Island by a drying flat. Scarrow Reef, along with a detached rock and pilings are found in the cove's northwestern end.

Due to reefs, private moorings, drying flats, and a submerged cable, there is not much opportunity for anchoring within Retreat Cove. However, moorage may be taken at the 80-foot public CRD wharf located in the southeast portion of the cove. During the summer months, the dock is used primarily by local island residents, and rafting may be required. No services or amenities are available at the dock including power and water. For further information on CRD public wharfs check their website at: www.crd. bc.ca, or call the wharfinger at (250) 539-5557.

Shore access is available at the public wharf. One of the highlights to visiting Retreat Cove is to explore the nearby sandstone cave. Through centuries of erosion, a cave has been carved out of the island's sandstone and created a very unique and artistic structure.

Retreat Cove to:		
	Bedwell Harbour (South Pender Island)	18 nm
	Chemainus	11 nm
	Clam Bay (Thetis Island)	7 nm
	Ganges Harbour (Salt Spring Island)	11 nm
	Montague Harbour (Galiano Island)	5 nm
	Nanaimo	23 nm
	Pirates Cove (De Courcy Island)	14 nm
	Princess Bay (Portland Island)	16 nm
	Sidney	20 nm
	Tod Inlet	27 nm
	Wallace Island	3 nm

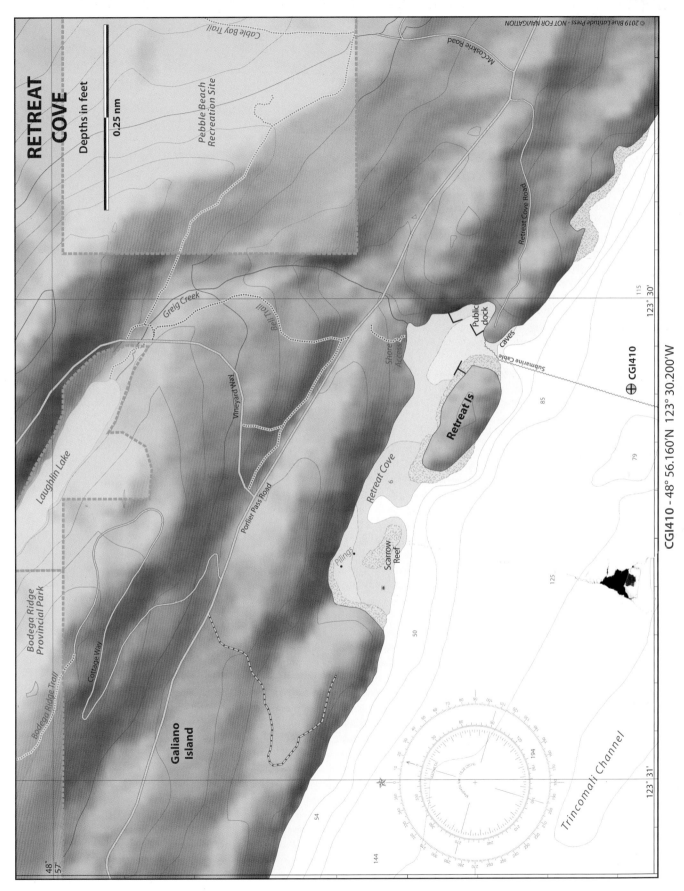

RETREAT COVE

Depths in feet

0.25 nm

Cable Bay Trail

Pebble Beach
Recreation Site

McCoskrie Road

Greig Creek

Bell Trail

Retreat Cove Road

Vineyard Way

Shore Access

Public dock

caves

Submarine Cable

Retreat Is

Laughlin Lake

Portlier Pass Road

Retreat Cove

6

Bodega Ridge
Provincial Park

Cottage Way

Pilings

Scarrow
Reef

Bodega Ridge Trail

Galiano
Island

115

85

79

125

50

54

144

194

Trincomali Channel

⊕ CGI410

CGI410 - 48° 56.160'N 123° 30.200'W

123° 30'

123° 31'

48°
57'

215

Chapter 8

Salt Spring Island

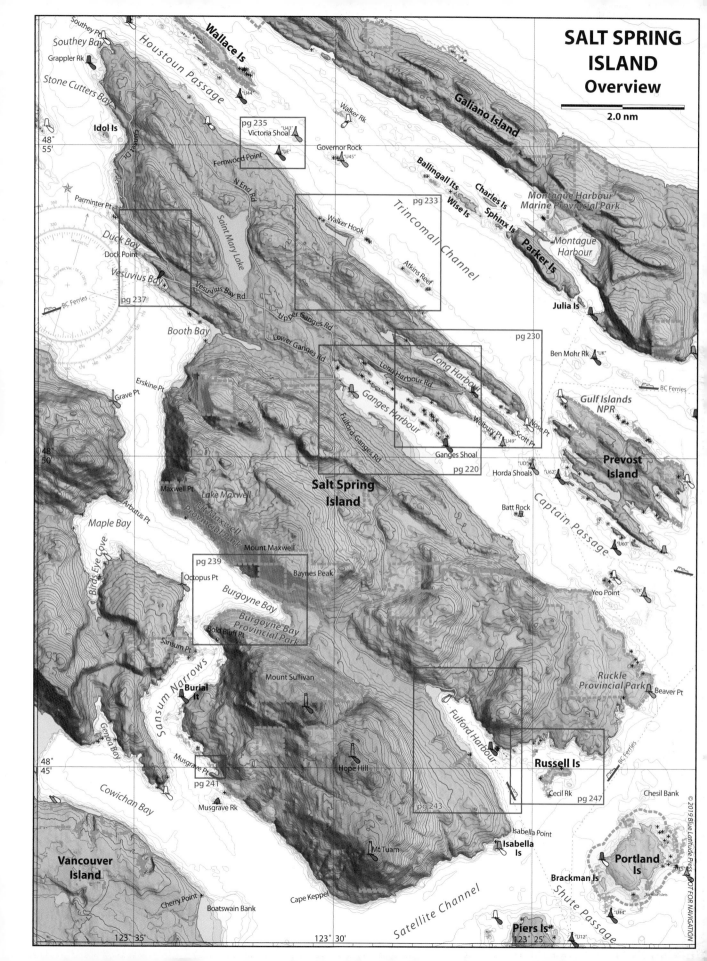

SALT SPRING
ISLAND
Overview

2.0 nm

Southey Pt
Southey Bay
Grappler Rk
Stone Cutters Bay
Idol Is
48°
55'
Houstoun Passage
Wallace Is
Walker Rk
pg 235
Victoria Shoal "U43"
"UE"
Fernwood Point
Governor Rock
"U45"
Galiano Island

Parminter Pt
Duck Bay
Dock Point
Vesuvius Bay
Booth Bay
N End Rd
Walker Hook
Saint Mary Lake
Ballingall Its
Charles Is
Wise Is
Sphinx Is
Parker Is
Montague Harbour
Marine Provincial Park
Montague
Harbour

pg 233
Trincomali Channel
Atkins Reef
Julia Is

BC Ferries
pg 237
Vesuvius Bay Rd
Upper Ganges Rd
Lower Ganges Rd
pg 230
Long Harbour Rd
Long Harbour
Ben Mohr Rk "UK"
BC Ferries

Grave Pt
Erskine Pt
Ganges Harbour
Fulford-Ganges Rd
Welbury Pt
Nose Pt
Scott Pt "U49"
Gulf Islands
NPR

48°
50'
Maxwell Pt
Salt Spring
Island
Ganges Shoal
pg 220
Horda Shoals
"UD"
"U62"
Prevost Island
Captain Passage

Arbutus Pt
Maple Bay
Birds Eye Cove
Lake Maxwell
Mt Maxwell
Provincial Park
Mount Maxwell
Baynes Peak
Batt Rock
"U60"
Yeo Point
"UD"

pg 239
Octopus Pt
Burgoyne Bay
Bold Bluff Pt
Burgoyne Bay
Provincial Park
Sansum Pt
Mount Sullivan
Ruckle
Provincial Park
Beaver Pt

Sansum Narrows
Burial
It
Fulford Harbour
Russell Is
BC Ferries

Genoa Bay
Musgrave Pt
pg 241
Hope Hill
Cecil Rk
pg 247
Chesil Bank
48°
45'
Cowichan Bay
Musgrave Rk
pg 243
Isabella Point
Isabella
Is
Portland
Is

Vancouver
Island
Mt Tuam
Brackman Is
Portland Islets

Cherry Point
Boatswain Bank
Cape Keppel
Satellite Channel
Piers Is
"U14"
Shute Passage
"U12"

123° 35'
123° 30'
123° 25'

© 2019 Blue Latitude Press • NOT FOR NAVIGATION

Fulford Valley and Mount Maxwell

Salt Spring Island

Salt Spring Island is the largest island within the Gulf Islands archipelago and also the most populated, with a residential community of over 10,000 people. Salt Spring lies in close proximity to Vancouver Island, making it an easily accessible destination for tourists and locals arriving by ferry. The island is celebrated for its farms with pastures of grazing sheep, fields of vegetables and hay, and orchard trees heavy with summer fruit.

Ganges is the island's main town with multiple marinas and plenty of options for shopping and dining. Ganges is also home to Salt Springs' renowned farmers market with bountiful displays of island grown produce and flowers, along with fresh baked breads, locally made cheese, crafts made by island artisans, and much more.

Salt Spring Island has a long history of habitation by the indigenous Coast Salish tribes. The Saanich, Cowichan, and Chemainus First Nations all have historical ties to the island dating back roughly 5,000 years ago. In the mid 1800's, many European and American immigrants began settlement of the rugged island. Dense forests and mountainous terrain proved difficult obstacles for the early pioneers. The island's abundant resources provided opportunities for fishermen, farmers and loggers.

Some of the original structures and families can still be found on the island including the Beaver Point Schoolhouse. Built in 1885, the school operated until 1951. The school was reopened in 1979, and is now a pre-school known as the Little Red School House. The oldest church on the island, St. Paul's Catholic Church, was also completed in 1885, and still stands today near the shores of Fulford Harbour. In 1872, Henry Ruckle landed at Salt Spring Island in search of farmland. By 1948, the Ruckle Heritage Farm had grown to 1196 acres. In the 1970's, 1000 acres of Ruckle family acreage was deeded to BC and is now the Ruckle Provincial Park. Today the 200 acre Ruckle Heritage Farm remains the oldest working farm still held by the original family in all of BC.

With a total of nearly 70 square miles, exploring Salt Spring Island can be cumbersome by foot. There are a number of good options for getting around the island including scheduled buses (www.bctransit.com/salt-spring-island), car and moped rentals, and catching rides with local islanders.

©Kevin Oke

Note photo taken before Salt Spring Marina renovations

Ganges Harbour

Ganges Harbour is an idyllic stop, showcasing the best of life in the Gulf Islands. The long harbor dotted with islands provides an endless stretch of anchoring options, as well as the perfect venue for kayak and dinghy exploration. The main town of Salt Spring Island is found at the head of the harbor, along with multiple marinas catering to visiting boats. Getting around town is easily done by foot with plenty of options for dining and shopping. One of the highlights to any visit to Ganges is the Saturday farmer's market. Over 140 farmers and artisans display their island grown, raised, or made items. Ganges is also centrally located for exploring the interior of Salt Spring Island by bike, bus, or car rentals.

Ganges Harbour is located on the east side of Salt Spring Island off Captain Passage. Approaches to the harbor can be made from the south via Swanson Channel or from the north via Trincomali Channel. If approaching from the south, be aware of a few hazards within Captain Passage. Channel Islands, which lie near the intersection of Swanson Channel and Captain Passage, are three islands that are part of the Gulf Islands National Park Reserve. Deep Ridge is

a shoal spit extending 0.4 miles southeast from the Channel Islands. The southern portion of this spit is marked with a light buoy. Batt Rock, which lies 1.8 miles northwest of Channel Islands, has less than 6 feet of water over it. Batt Rock is marked by a navigation buoy. Horda Shoals lie 0.8 miles north-northeast of Batt Rock, and also has less than 6 feet of water of it. Horda Shoals is marked with a lighted navigation buoy. Southeast of Horda Shoals is the Captain

Ganges Harbour to:		
	Bedwell Harbour *(South Pender Island)*	14 nm
	Clam Bay *(Thetis Island)*	17 nm
	Ladysmith	26 nm
	Montague Harbour *(Galiano Island)*	7 nm
	Nanaimo	33 nm
	Pirates Cove *(De Courcy Island)*	24 nm
	Princess Bay *(Portland Island)*	12 nm
	Roche Harbour *(USA)*	20 nm
	Sidney	16 nm
	Tod Inlet	23 nm
	Victoria	37 nm
	Wallace Island	12 nm

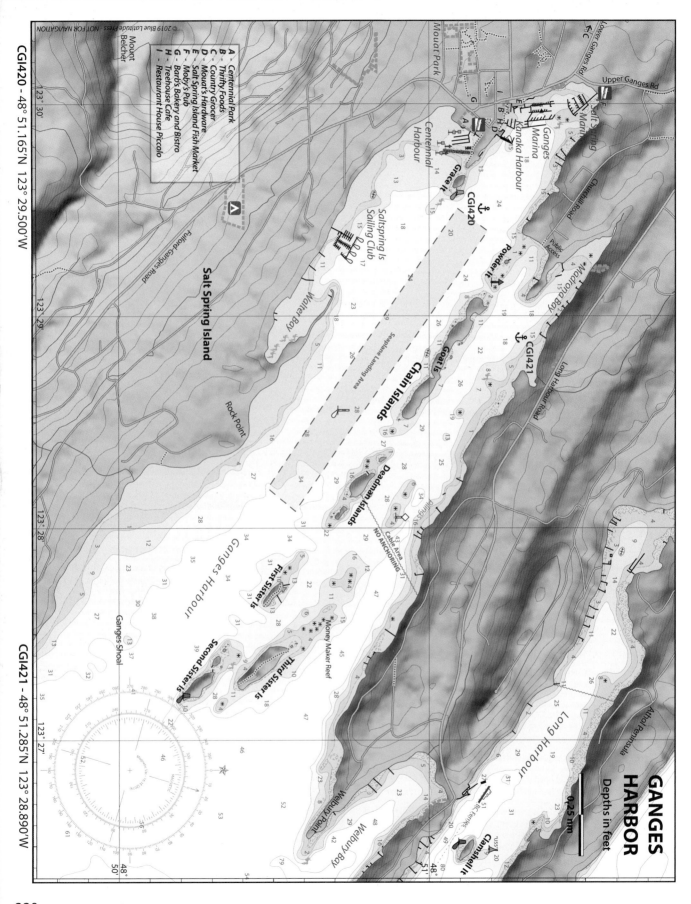

© 2019 Blue Latitude Press - NOT FOR NAVIGATION

A - Centennial Park
B - Thrifty Foods
C - Country Grocer
D - Mouat's Hardware
E - Salt Spring Island Fish Market
F - Moby's Pub
G - Barb's Bakery and Bistro
H - Treehouse Cafe
J - Restaurant House Piccolo

CGI420 - 48° 51.165'N 123° 29.500'W

CGI421 - 48° 51.285'N 123° 28.890'W

GANGES
HARBOR
Depths in feet

Mouat Belcher

Salt Spring Island

Fulford Ganges Road

Rock Point

Ganges Harbour

Ganges Shoal

Centennial Harbour

Saltspring Is Sailing Club

Walter Bay

Seaplane Landing Area

NO ANCHORING

Chain Islands

Goat Is

Deadman Islands

First Sister Is

Second Sister Is

Third Sister Is

Money Maker Reef

Cable Area

Grace It

Ganges Marina

Kanaka Harbour

Upper Ganges Rd

Lower Ganges Rd

Mouat Park

Churchill Road

Madrona Bay

Public Access

Powder It

Long Harbour Road

Long Harbour

Walbury Point

Walbury Bay

Athol Peninsula

Clamshell It

0.25 nm

CGI420

CGI421

Beach northwest of Powder Islet

Passage light buoy "U62." Passage can be taken mid-channel between Horda Shoals and buoy "U62." Keep in mind that 2 to 4 knots of currents can ebb and flow through Captain Passage, with tide rips near Nose Point on Salt Spring Island.

For boats approaching from the north, Trincomali Channel is mostly wide, deep and has few navigational hazards. Currents at the southern end of the channel can reach 1.5 knots. BC Ferries also transit this area, traveling through Active Pass to Long Harbour on Salt Spring Island and other various islands. At the southern end of the channel is Ben Mohr Rock which lies 0.8 miles northeast of Peile Point. Ben Mohr Rock has 13 feet of water over it and is marked by a lighted buoy.

When entering Ganges Harbour, be aware of Ganges Shoal and the Chain Islands. Ganges Shoal lies at the southern end of the entrance and has 13 feet of water covering it. The Chain Islands are a string of islands in the northeast portion of the harbor including First Sister, Second Sister, Third Sister, Deadman, and Goat Islands and Powder Islet. Most of these islands have surrounding reefs to watch out for, especially Third Sister Island and the aptly named Money Maker Reef. When staying south and west of the Chain Islands, the approach to Ganges Harbour is relatively free of dangers.

Anchorage can be taken throughout the harbor in 3 to 5 fathoms over a mostly mud bottom. Numerous private moorings buoys are found around the head of the harbor. Ganges Harbour provides good protection from most winds except wind and waves from the southeast.

A quiet alternative anchorage to the hustle and bustle of Ganges Harbour can be found to the northeast at Ma-

Seaplane

Harbor Seals

drona Bay. When approaching Madrona Bay and transiting the north and east side of the Chain Islands, be sure to study the chart carefully due to the numerous unmarked rocks and reefs. Anchorage can be taken in Madrona Bay in 3 to 5 fathoms over a mud bottom.

For trips to shore, dinghy docks are available at the Centennial Wharf, Kanaka Wharf, and the Rotary Marine Park. A nice beach with public access to Churchill Road is also found between Ganges Harbour and Madrona Bay, just northwest of Powder Islet. This beach is perfect for swimming and dog walks on the quiet residential roads.

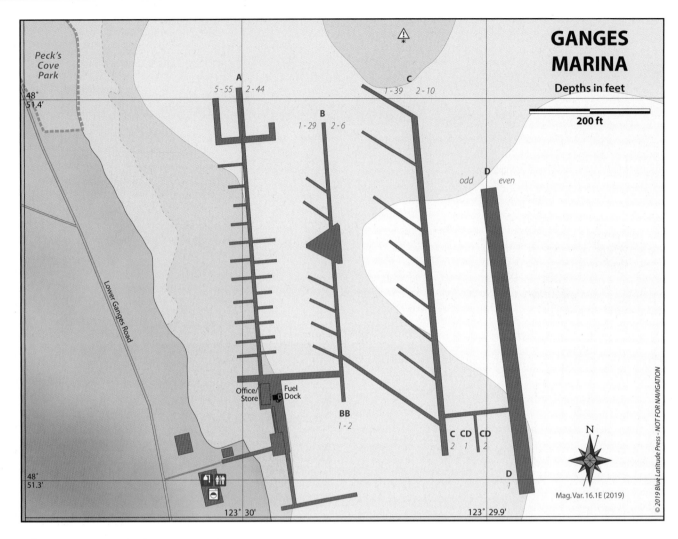

Ganges Marina

Ganges Marina is located in the heart of town within easy walking distance of all Ganges amenities. The marina can accommodate boats up to 400 feet in length. Each slip has access to power (15, 30 and 50 amps) and po-

table water hookups. During the summer months water is designated for filling tanks only. Services at the marina include a pump out station, restrooms, showers, garbage and recycling disposal, laundry facilities, and complimentary morning coffee and muffins (bring your own mug). The marina also provides a 100-foot fuel dock with a diesel and gasoline capacity of over 5,000 gallons for each. The marina store provides oils, lubricants, snack foods, cold drinks, ice, and other convenience items. When approaching the marina, be aware of the rock located just north of C dock.

Ganges Marina
Monitors VHF Channel 66A
161 Lower Ganges Road
Salt Spring Island, BC V8K 2T2
(250) 537-5242
gangesmarina@gmail.com
www.gangesmarina.com

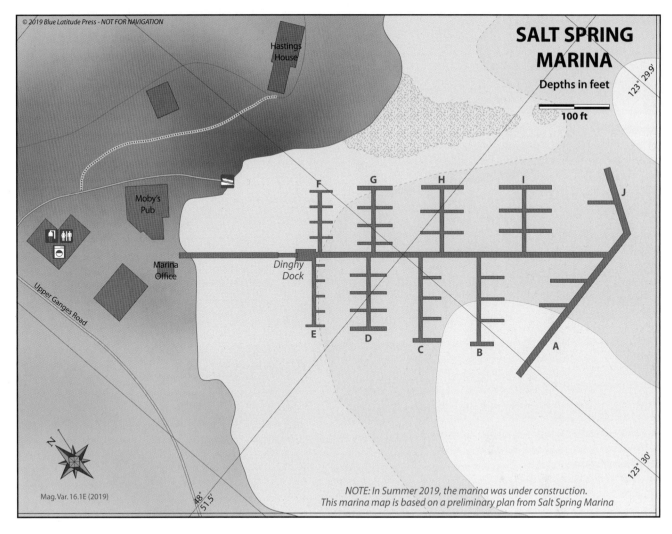

© 2019 Blue Latitude Press - NOT FOR NAVIGATION

SALT SPRING MARINA

Depths in feet

100 ft

123° 29.9'

Hastings House

Moby's Pub

Marina Office

Dinghy Dock

F G H I J

E D C B A

123° 30'

48° 51.5'

Mag. Var. 16.1E (2019)

NOTE: In Summer 2019, the marina was under construction. This marina map is based on a preliminary plan from Salt Spring Marina

Upper Ganges Road

N

Salt Spring Marina

Salt Spring Marina is undergoing a major overhaul with all new docks, dredging, and a new floating breakwater. The newly renovated marina is slated to reopen in 2019/2020. Due to the marina's proximity to the notorious Money Makers Rock, a new 10-foot wide main dock will cover the rock and eliminate the navigation hazard. Each slip will have access to power (30 and 50 amp) and potable water hookups. Services include a mobile pumpout station, boat ramp, restrooms, showers, laundry facilities, and wireless internet. The marina also offers complimentary shuttle service to and from the Uptown Centre for provisioning trips and to downtown Ganges during the summer months. For the current state of progress with the remodel of the marina contact the Salt Spring Marina harbormaster.

Salt Spring Marina
Monitors VHF channel 66A
124 Upper Ganges Road,
Salt Spring Island, V8K 2S2
(250) 537-5810
info@saltspringmarina.com
saltspringmarina.com

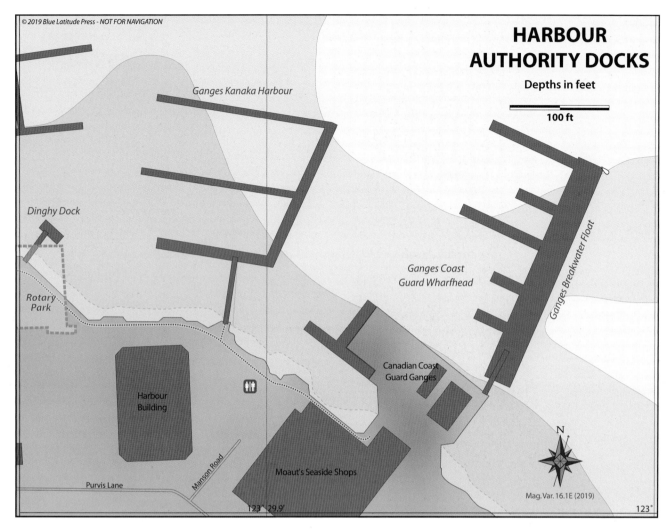

© 2019 Blue Latitude Press - NOT FOR NAVIGATION

HARBOUR AUTHORITY DOCKS

Depths in feet

100 ft

Ganges Kanaka Harbour

Dinghy Dock

Rotary Park

Ganges Breakwater Float

Ganges Coast Guard Wharfhead

Canadian Coast Guard Ganges

Harbour Building

Manson Road

Purvis Lane

Moaut's Seaside Shops

123° 29.9'

123°

N

Mag. Var. 16.1E (2019)

Harbour Authority of Salt Spring Island

The Harbour Authority of Salt Spring Island operates three facilities in Ganges Harbour: Ganges Centennial Wharf, Ganges Breakwater Float, and Ganges Kanaka Wharf. The Ganges Centennial Wharf is reserved for local commercial, fishing, and recreational vessels. The Centennial Wharf generally does not accommodate transient boats. The Ganges Breakwater Float is located off the Coast Guard Wharfhead. The main header float is used by commercial vessels for loading and off loading, as well as by larger transient vessels.

The Ganges Kanaka Wharf is located just west of the Ganges Breakwater Float and is used primarily for daily transient boats from May through September. Services at the Kanaka Wharf include potable water and 30 amp shore-power. Services also include access to the garbage disposal, waste oil disposal, showers, restrooms, and the boat launch ramp at Centennial Wharf.

Harbour Authority of Salt Spring Island
Monitors VHF Channel 9
127 Fulford-Ganges Road
Salt Spring Island, BC V8K 2T9
(250) 537-5711
harbour@hassi.ca
www.saltspringharbours.com

Kanaka Wharf

Centennial Park

Sights to See

The town of Ganges is perfectly situated around the harbor for beautiful waterfront views, scenic strolls, and a variety of shopping and dining options. Two waterfront parks and wooden boardwalks frame the downtown area of Ganges for pleasant walks and watching arriving boats and seaplanes. The northern park, Rotary Marine Park, is located up the ramp from the Rotary dinghy dock and is conveniently located next to Thrifty Foods for any provisioning needs. At the southern end is Centennial Park which overlooks the public Centennial Wharf. This park comes alive in the summer months when it hosts the Saturday and Tuesday Farmer's Market. Over 140 farmers and artisans gather every week at the park, displaying a variety of produce, flowers, art, textiles, food and more. See the sidebar on page 227 for further information.

To the west is the larger and local favorite, Mouat Park. This 57 acre wooded park boasts over 5 miles of well maintained trails. While not an off-leash park, pets are welcome to walk with you without a leash as long as they are in sight, under voice control, and leashed when approaching trailheads, other people, or wildlife. Mouat Park is also home to a wonderful 18-hole disc golf course. The course is open to all and is free of charge. Discs can be purchased at Mouat's Home Hardware. The park is also home to a newly constructed one acre family bike park. The dirt trail network with technical features was professionally designed to help build bike skills for children and youth from ages two and up. There are beginner and intermediate trails with table tops, berms, and roller coaster features. The bike park is open and free to the public.

While at Mouat Park, be sure to visit the historical Japanese charcoal pits. Two pits have been excavated within the park and are open to viewing with informative signs. In the early 1900's, Japanese immigrants brought an ancient method of making charcoal to the Gulf Islands. Large pit kilns similar to those in Mouat Park, are also found on Galiano and Mayne Islands. Using wood from the plentiful alder forests, the Japanese families would make charcoal to be used in the salmon canneries, for cooking, soap making, and in making explosives for clearing land.

Rotary dinghy dock

For those looking to experience the culture and arts of the islands, there is no greater place than Salt Spring Island. The island is full of studios and galleries featuring everything from island-made wines and cheeses to fine art paintings and sculptures. Salt Spring is home to weavers, painters, metal workers, potters, sculptors, chefs, wood workers, photographers, musicians, jewellers, glass makers, writers, and much more. Many of these artists come to the Saturday Farmer's Market, and many are featured at galleries and

Mouat Park disc golf course

Charcoal kilns

studios dotted around the island. For those with bikes or a rental car (see below for car and scooter rentals), a self guided studio tour is available with a free downloadable map at: saltspringstudiotour.com.

For those traveling with kayaks, Ganges Harbour provides an island studded paddling ground for taking in the sights and marine life. A chain of islands run the length of the harbor including Goat, Deadman, and the Sisters Islands. A number of these islands offer the perfect haulout locations for sunbathing harbor seals. For the more adventurous paddler, Long Harbour just to the north (see page 229) or nearby Prevost Island (see page 185) provide extended, day-trip paddle options.

Chandleries, Services, and Provisioning

BC Liquor Store
BC Liquor Stores offer a great selection of beers, wines and spirits. Located across from the Centennial Wharf on Fulford Ganges Road.

Country Grocer
Country Grocer is a local chain grocery selling fresh produce, dairy, meats, bakery items, and staples while supporting local farmers, growers, and producers whenever possible. Located in the shopping center roughly 0.75 miles from the Kanaka Wharf at 374 Lower Ganges Road.

Eagle Eye Marine
Eagle Eye Marine offers diving, towing, salvage services. They are also the Vessel Assist/Boat US contact for the Gulf Islands. (250) 883-7865, eagleeyemarine.ca

Harbour's End Marine
Harbour's End is a dealership and full service facility offering maintenance, repairs, and installs. They also offer emergency towing and mobile mechanic services. (250) 537-4202, www.harboursendmarine.com

Mouat's Home Hardware
Mouat's sells a little bit of everything including tools, hardware, paint, electrical and plumbing supplies, marine and fishing goods, toys, and more. Located in the shopping center across from the Ganges Breakwater Float on Fulford Ganges Road.

Pharmasave
Pharmasave is a chain pharmacy store providing prescription filling, over the counter medicines, and more. Located within the shopping center at 104 Lower Ganges Road. (250) 537-5534

Salt Spring Car Rentals
Salt Spring Car Rentals offers a variety of cars, vans and scooters for exploring the island. Located at the Salt

Ganges Breakwater Float

Salt Spring Market

Ganges is home to one of the most impressive farmers markets found throughout the Gulf Islands. The Saturday Salt Spring Market is host to over 140 farmers, artisans, and chefs who bring their produce, crafts, and food to the community of Salt Spring Island each week. Musicians and entertainers add a lively ambiance to the vendor-packed market which draws crowds from far and wide.

The market is held each Saturday from either the first weekend in April or Easter weekend (whichever comes first) through the last Saturday in October. The market opens at 9am, although some vendors may set up earlier during the long days of summer, and runs through the afternoon until 4pm. The market is held at the waterfront Centennial Park, where broad maple trees provide shaded relief during the warm summer months.

The guarantee of the market is, "make it, bake it, or grow it" and all products must be "vendor produced and sold." This simple philosophy provides customers an assured island-made product or experience from organic produce and local crafts to island tours and much more. The lengthy list of vendors include organic produce farmers, Salt Spring lamb farmers, fishermen, flower gardeners, cheese makers, bread and pastry bakers, potters, photographers, woodworkers, painters, clothing designers, soap and lotion makers, and the always tasty food vendors.

For those visiting Ganges not on a Saturday, you have a second chance to enjoy island grown and homemade food items on Tuesdays. Each Tuesday from June through October, the market hosts farmers, gardeners, and chefs (no crafts) from 2pm to 6pm. Enjoy organic produce, flower bouquets, meats, eggs, and homemade food, snacks, and drinks. The Tuesday market can be found at the same waterfront Centennial Park.

To shop the market and help reduce waste, consider bringing your own bags to transport your deliciously fresh food and beautiful crafts back to the boat. And for those traveling with pets, please note that dogs are not allowed within the market, so it is best to leave your pet on the boat. There is a volunteer SPCA organization on hand for one-on-one pet sitting, however services are limited to the number of volunteers on hand that day. For further information check the market website at: saltspringmarket.com.

Mouat's Home Hardware

Treehouse Cafe

Salt Spring Island Fish Market

Moby's Pub

Spring Marina next to Moby's Pub. (250) 537-3122, www.saltspringmarina.com

Salt Spring Island Fish Market

The Fish Market offers fresh, in season and frozen at sea fish and shellfish. The market also offers a deli with take out meals including fish and chips, seafood fried rice, Chinese style cooked crab, and more. Located near the Ganges Marina on Lower Ganges Road.

Thrifty Foods

Thrifty Foods is a chain grocery store selling fresh produce, meats, dairy, bakery items and all the staples. A liquor store is found on the west side of the building. Located across from the Kanaka Wharf on 114 Purvis Lane.

Windsor Plywood

Windsor Plywood is a chain lumber store offering building products and marine grade plywoods. Located at 166 Rainbow Road. (250) 537-5564, www.windsorplywood.com

Restaurants

Barb's Bakery and Bistro

A local favorite that began at the Ganges Saturday Farmer's Market. Barb's offers hand-made, fresh baked breads and pastries, along with soups, salads and sandwiches for breakfast and lunch. Open Tuesdays through Saturdays, 7am to 5pm. www.barbsbakeryandbistro.ca, (250) 537-4491

Moby's Pub

Located next to Salt Spring Marina, Moby's Pub offers indoor and patio seating with views of Ganges Harbour. Moby's also hosts live music and televised sporting events. Open for lunch and dinner, the menu offers tasty and traditional pub fare. mobyspub.ca, (250) 537-5559

Restaurant House Piccolo

Piccolo's is a fine dining restaurant set within an intimate and cozy heritage house. The menu specializes in perfectly cooked, locally sourced ingredients. Open for diner Wednesdays through Sundays. Located at 108 Hereford Avenue. housepiccolo.com, (250) 537-1844

Treehouse Cafe

The cafe is housed in a cottage built in the 1920's underneath a beautiful old plum tree. Indoor and outdoor dining is available with a menu of delicious made from scratch meals. During the summer months, the cafe offers 125 nights of live Music Under the Stars. Open everyday for breakfast, lunch, and dinner. Located at 106 Purvis Lane, up the ramp from the Kanaka Wharf. treehousecafe.ca, (250) 537-5379

Long Harbour

True to its name, Long Harbour is a rather lengthy inlet found along the eastern shore of Salt Spring Island. The harbor is home to one of three BC Ferry terminals found on the island, as well as outstation marinas for the Royal Vancouver and Victoria Yacht Clubs. The quiet shores of Long Harbour provide peaceful anchorage to visiting boats away from the hustle and bustle of nearby Ganges Harbour. The large lagoon at the head of the harbor offers a pleasant and protected paddling adventure.

Long Harbour is located near the intersection of Captain Passage and Trincomali Channel, across from Prevost Island. Entrance to the harbor is found between Nose Point to the northeast and Scott Point to the southwest on Salt Spring Island. The harbour stretches over 2 miles from the entrance points.

When approaching from the south, be aware of a few hazards within Captain Passage. Deep Ridge is a shoal spit extending 0.4 miles southeast from the Channel Islands. The southern portion of this spit is marked with a light buoy. Batt Rock, which lies 1.8 miles northwest of Channel Islands, has less than 6 feet of water over it. Batt Rock

is marked by a navigation buoy. Horda Shoals lie 0.8 miles north-northeast of Batt Rock, and also has less than 6 feet of water of it. Horda Shoals is marked with a lighted navigation buoy. Southeast of Horda Shoals is the Captain Passage light buoy "U62." Passage can be taken mid-channel between Horda Shoals and buoy "U62." A shoal lying 0.2 miles southwest of Scott Point is marked at the southern end by buoy "U49."

Long Harbour to:		
	Bedwell Harbour (South Pender Island)	13 nm
	Clam Bay (Thetis Island)	15 nm
	Ladysmith	23 nm
	Montague Harbour (Galiano Island)	5 nm
	Nanaimo	31 nm
	Pirates Cove (De Courcy Island)	22 nm
	Princess Bay (Portland Island)	11 nm
	Roche Harbor (USA)	19 nm
	Sidney	15 nm
	Tod Inlet	22 nm
	Victoria	36 nm
	Wallace Island	11 nm

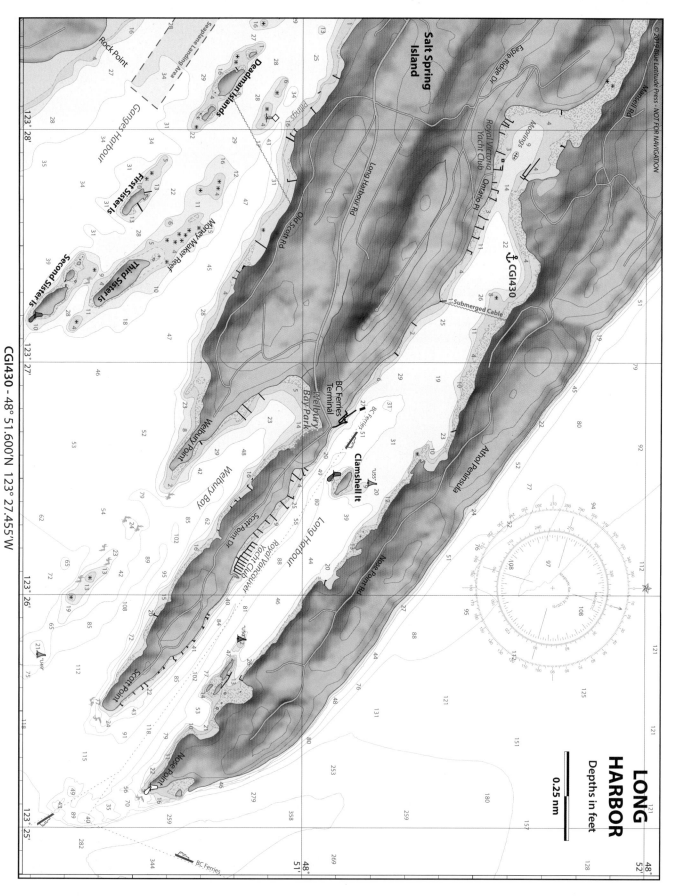

CGI430 - 48° 51.600'N 123° 27.455'W

LONG HARBOR

Depths in feet

0.25 nm

Head of Long Harbour

When approaching from the north or south, keep in mind that 2 to 4 knots of current can ebb and flow through Captain Passage, with tide rips found off Nose Point. Also, be on the lookout for BC Ferries that may be arriving or departing from Long Harbour. These large ferries have limited maneuverability, especially within the tight confines of Long Harbour.

Once inside Long Harbour, note buoy "U50," which marks a rock just northwest of a group of islets lying 0.4 miles northwest of Nose Point. Near the middle of the harbor lies Clamshell Islet. Just southwest of the islet, a rock is marked by a cylindrical tower, and north of the islet, foul ground is marked by buoy "U55."

Anchorage can be taken within the harbor in 3 to 5 fathoms over a mud bottom. Most anchored visiting boats are found closer to the head of the harbor, from Clamshell Islet and north. Be cautious of the underwater cable crossing the harbor near the northern end. At the far head of the harbor, numerous private mooring buoys and docks can be found. Much of the anchoring room in this shallower, more protected section of the harbor has been taken over by private mooring buoys. Long Harbour offers good wind and wave protection with the exception of weather from the southeast.

For trips to shore, public access is available at the end of Ontario Place, next to the Royal Victoria Yacht Club outstation. Ontario, and a few of the connecting roads, provide a nice way to stretch your legs along quiet country roads. Be sure to save time to explore the lagoon at the head of the harbor. As this area turns into a mud flat at low tide, it is better to wait for a high tide for the best paddle or dinghy experience.

Walker Hook

Walker Hook is an unexpected delight found on the northwestern side of Salt Spring Island. Fronted by an expansive crescent of sand beach, the anchorage provides a great stop for swimming or exploring the nearby lagoon by dinghy or kayak.

Walker Hook is located midway between Southey Point, the northern most extremity of Salt Spring Island, and Nose Point, at the entrance to Long Harbour. The hook is formed by a narrow, sandy isthmus connecting a small tree-covered peninsula. A shallow lagoon has formed on the north side of the isthmus which dries at low water.

Approaches to the anchorage are taken via Trincomali Channel. The channel is large and deep with relatively few hazards to navigation. Currents in the southeastern portion of the channel are somewhat light at 1.5 knots, but increase to 3 knots north of Wallace Island.

When approaching Walker Hook be sure to check the chart and be aware of the detached reefs paralleling the Salt Spring Island shore. Atkins Reef lies roughly 1 mile southeast off the east tip of the peninsula forming Walker Hook. Atkins Reef is marked by a daybeacon. A second reef is found approximately 0.2 miles east-southeast of the peninsula. This unmarked reef has less than 6 feet of water covering it.

Anchorage can be taken south of the sand beach in 3 to 4 fathoms over a sand bottom. While the anchorage does provide protection from west winds, it is best used as a calm weather or lunch stop anchorage due to its lack of protection.

Walker Hook does not have public access to trails or roads, so trips to shore must stay below the mean high water level on the beach. After soaking up the sun on the beach, be sure to paddle or dinghy around the peninsula to explore the lagoon at high water.

Walker Hook to:		
Bedwell Harbour (South Pender Island)		15 nm
Ganges Harbour (Salt Spring Island)		8 nm
Ladysmith		17 nm
Montague Harbour (Galiano Island)		5 nm
Nanaimo		25 nm
Pirates Cove (De Courcy Island)		16 nm
Princess Bay (Portland Island)		13 nm
Sidney		17 nm
Telegraph Harbour (Thetis Island)		12 nm
Tod Inlet		24 nm
Victoria		39 nm
Wallace Island		5 nm

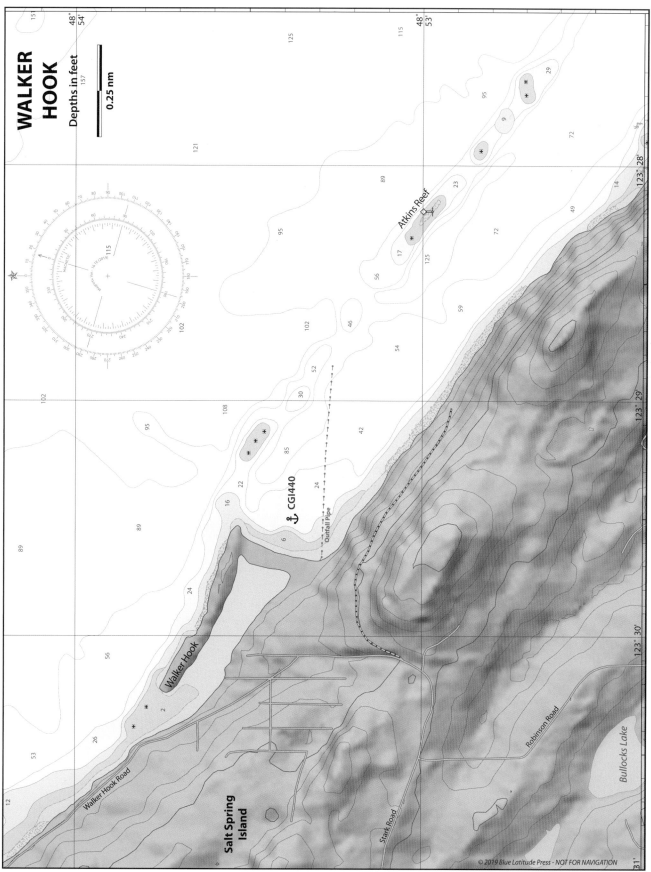

WALKER HOOK

Depths in feet

0.25 nm

CGI440 - 48° 53.360'N 123° 29.500'W

Atkins Reef

Walker Hook

Salt Spring Island

Outfall Pipe

CGI440

Walker Hook Road

Stark Road

Robinson Road

Bullocks Lake

©Kevin Oke

Fernwood Point

Fernwood Point is located on the northeast side of Salt Spring Island. A small public wharf extends into Houstoun Passage, used for short term stops by visiting boats and locals from nearby islands. On shore are two restaurants, making for a nice lunch stop in settled weather.

Fernwood Point is located roughly one mile southwest of Wallace Island. Large drying flats are found off the shore in this area requiring the public pier to extend 400 feet out into the eastern entrance to Houstoun Passage. The small public dock at the end of the pier is approximately 50 feet in length and is operated by the Capital Regional District (CRD). This dock is strictly a transient dock with a maximum stay of 24 hours. Use of this exposed dock is best during periods of settled weather.

At the end of the pier and along Fernwood Road are two eateries, Fernwood Road Cafe and Twig & Buoy. The Fernwood Road Cafe (www.fernwoodcafe.com) is open for breakfast and lunch daily during the summer months with reduced hours during the winter months. The cafe offers a tasty selection of baked treats, egg dishes, sandwiches and salads, and espresso beverages. Twig & Buoy (250-931-8944) offers locally sourced, elegant meals with a specialty of delicious wood fired pizzas. They are open for dinner with wine and beer menus.

Southey Bay

Lying at the northern extremity of Salt Spring Island is a small bay known locally as Southey Bay. Lined by homes, the small bay to the west of Southey Point provides protection from southeast winds.

Southey Bay is found at the northern end of Salt Spring Island, and roughly one mile west-southwest from Wallace Island. The eastern portion of the bay is protected by the narrow peninsula of Southey Point which is marked by a navigation light tower.

Approaches to Southey Bay can be made via Houstoun Passage. Approaching from the east, be sure to give Southey Point ample room due to drying rock ledges extending off the point. Approaching from the west, be aware of Grappler Rock lying roughly 0.4 miles southwest of Southey Point. There are three drying heads to this rock, with the southwestern edge marked by a navigation light tower. The western entrance point to the bay also has extending rock ledges and should be given ample room when rounding. Approaching from the north, passage can be taken between Norway Island and Mowgli Island, which connects Trincomali Channel with the north end of Houstoun Passage. A chain of islets and drying reefs lies southwest of Mowgli Island. A daybeacon with a starboard hand daymark is found on the north end of this rocky chain. A small islet lying just south of Norway Island is marked by a daybeacon with a port hand daymark. The passage between Norway and Mowgli Islands is 0.15 miles wide.

Anchorage can be taken within Southey Bay in 4 to 7 fathoms. The head of the bay holds drying flats preventing anchoring deep within the bay. Private docks and private mooring buoys can be found throughout the bay reducing the room for anchoring.

For trips to shore, access can be found at the end of Arbutus Road west of the bay. A short walk down the road is Fraser's Thimble Farms (www.thimblefarms.com), a small nursery specializing in rare, unusual and native plants including Hardy Orchids and Hardy Ferns.

Southey Bay to:		
Bedwell Harbour (South Pender Island)	21 nm
Clam Bay (Thetis Island)	4 nm
Ganges (Salt Spring Island)	14 nm
Ladysmith	11 nm
Montague Harbour (Galiano Island)	9 nm
Nanaimo	20 nm
Pirates Cove (De Courcy Island)	11 nm
Princess Bay (Portland Island)	19 nm
Sidney	23 nm
Wallace Island	2 nm

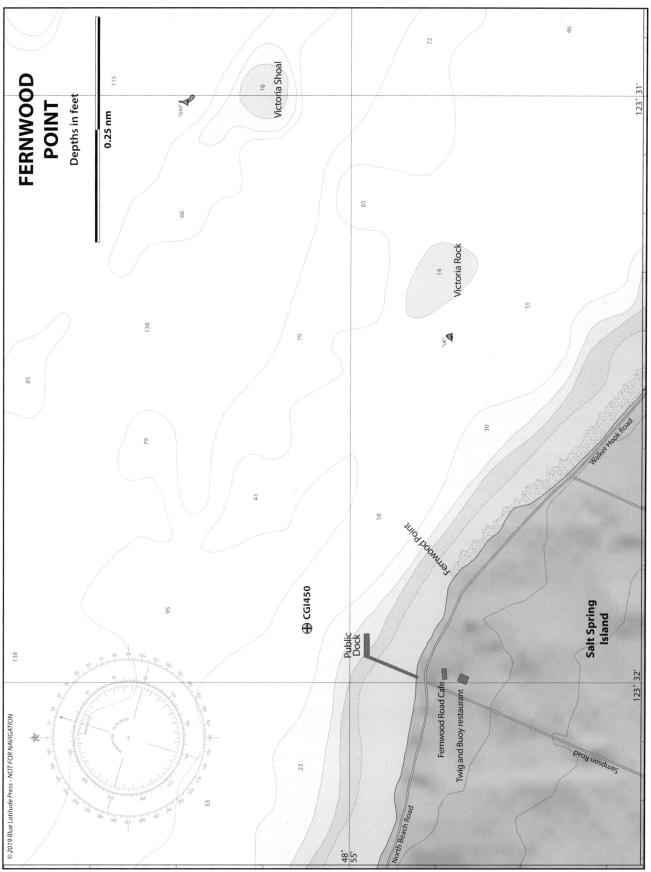

FERNWOOD POINT

Depths in feet

0.25 nm

Victoria Shoal
16

"U43"

115

72

46

66

138

85

65

Victoria Rock
14

"U5"

55

79

79

95

30

43

58

Fernwood Point

CGI450

Public
Dock

Walker Hook Road

Salt Spring
Island

Fernwood Road Cafe

Twig and Buoy restaurant

North Beach Road

Sampson Road

138

23

53

© 2019 Blue Latitude Press - NOT FOR NAVIGATION

48°
55'

123° 32'

123° 31'

CGI450 - 48° 55.050'N 123° 31.910'W

©Kevin Oke

Vesuvius and Duck Bays

Vesuvius Bay, and its neighbor to the north, Duck Bay, are located along the northwestern shore of Salt Spring Island. Vesuvius Bay is home to the BC Ferries terminal, linking Salt Spring Island with Vancouver Island via the town of Crofton. With a small public wharf, onshore dining options, and nearby walking trails, Vesuvius Bay makes for a nice lunch stop when transiting Sansum Narrows and Stuart Channel.

Vesuvius and Duck Bays are found on the northwestern end of Salt Spring Island along Stuart Channel. The two bays are separated by a narrow finger of land known as Dock Point. Approaches to the bays can be taken via Stuart Channel or Houstoun Passage from the north, or Sansum Narrows from the south. When approaching the bays, be cautious of the extending drying rock ledges found off both Dock Point and the southern entrance point to Vesuvius Bay. Be sure to give them ample room when rounding.

Anchorage can be taken within the bays over a mostly mud bottom, making sure to stay out of the ferry transit area. Numerous private moorings can be found in the bays. Vesuvius Bay offers a public wharf operated by the Harbour Authority of Salt Spring Island. The public wharf is located immediately north of the BC Ferry terminal. The roughly 50 foot dock is well used during the summer months. Keep in mind that wake from arriving and departing ferries can affect Vesuvius Bay.

For trips to shore, dinghies can be landed at the public wharf in Vesuvius Bay. While ashore, be sure to check out the walking trails at Duck Creek Park. The park is located less than a half mile walk from the ferry terminal. The 14 acre park is a mix of beautiful open meadow land and shaded forest. Loop trails cross the meadows and follow the creek through the forest. Dogs are welcome at the park with trash cans and bags available. Access to the park trails can be found off Sunset Drive or Broadwell Road.

Two eateries are found within Vesuvius Bay for a meal off the boat. Seaside Restaurant (www.seasiderestaurant-saltspring.com) is located next to the ferry terminal and is open daily for lunch and dinner. Indoor and outdoor deck seating is available for beautiful views of Stuart Channel. Menu options includes fresh local seafood, burgers, salads and more. Just down the road is the quaint Vesuvius Cafe (250-537-1515) that is open for breakfast and lunch. The cafe offers espresso beverages and homemade egg dishes, soups, sandwiches, rice bowls, and desserts.

Vesuvius Bay to:		
	Genoa Bay	11 nm
	Ladysmith	12 nm
	Montague Harbour *(Galiano Island)*	13 nm
	Nanaimo	24 nm
	Pirates Cove *(De Courcy Island)*	15 nm
	Russell Island	16 nm
	Sidney	19 nm
	Telegraph Harbour *(Thetis Island)*	7 nm
	Tod Inlet	21 nm
	Wallace Island	6 nm

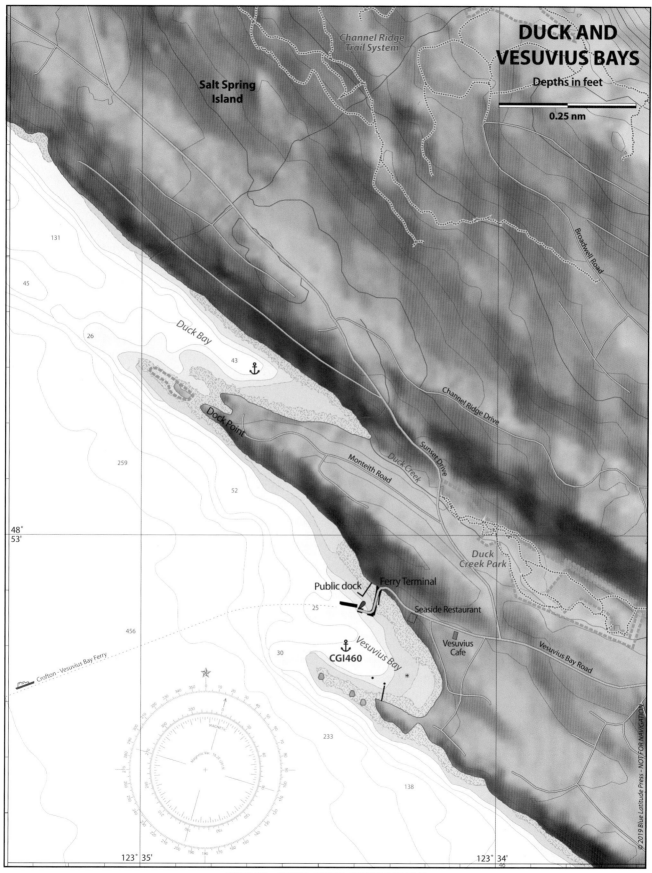

DUCK AND VESUVIUS BAYS

Depths in feet

0.25 nm

Salt Spring
Island

Channel Ridge
Trail System

Broadwell Road

131

45

Duck Bay

26

43 ⚓

Dock Point

Channel Ridge Drive

259

Duck Creek

Sunset Drive

Monteith Road

52

48°
53'

Duck
Creek Park

Public dock

Ferry Terminal

25

Seaside Restaurant

456

Vesuvius
Cafe

Vesuvius Bay Road

Crofton - Vesuvius Bay Ferry

30

⚓
CGI460

Vesuvius Bay

*

233

138

© 2019 Blue Latitude Press - NOT FOR NAVIGATION

123° 35'

123° 34'

CGI460 - 48° 52.800'N 123° 34.435'W

Burgoyne Bay

Situated at the base of Mount Maxwell Provincial Park, Burgoyne Bay is a true hikers paradise. Baynes Peak, at nearly 2,000 feet, offers unparalleled views of the islands along with heart-pumping trails from sea to sky. The large bay holds an eclectic mix of fishing boats, pleasure boats, and even a few float homes. A public dock at the head of the bay provides easy access to shore and the miles of trails crisscrossing the provincial park.

Burgoyne Bay is located along the western shore of Salt Spring Island near the northern entrance to Sansum Narrows. Approaches to the bay can be made via Stuart Channel and Houstoun Passage to the north and Sansum Narrows to the south. Approaches from the north are relatively free of hazards in the southern end of Stuart Channel. Currents in this portion of the channel are minimal, attaining velocities around 1 knot.

Approaching from the south, passage is taken via Sansum Narrows where current in the narrowest sections can attain velocities up to 3 knots. Occasional whirlpools and tide rips can be found around Burial Islet and between Sansum

Point and Bold Bluff Point. Burial Islet is found approximately 0.65 miles south-southwest of Sansum Point and is marked by a navigation light tower. Pass west of Burial Islet.

Burgoyne Bay is a large, deep bay with drying mud flats found at the head. Private mooring buoys and floats can be found throughout the bay. Anchorage can be taken

Burgoyne Bay to:	Bedwell Harbour (South Pender Island)	19 nm
	Ganges Harbour (Salt Spring Island)	22 nm
	Genoa Bay	6 nm
	Ladysmith	17 nm
	Montague Harbour (Galiano Island)	19 nm
	Nanaimo	30 nm
	Pirates Cove (De Courcy Island)	21 nm
	Russell Island	12 nm
	Sidney	14 nm
	Telegraph Harbour (Thetis Island)	13 nm
	Tod Inlet	16 nm
	Victoria	37 nm

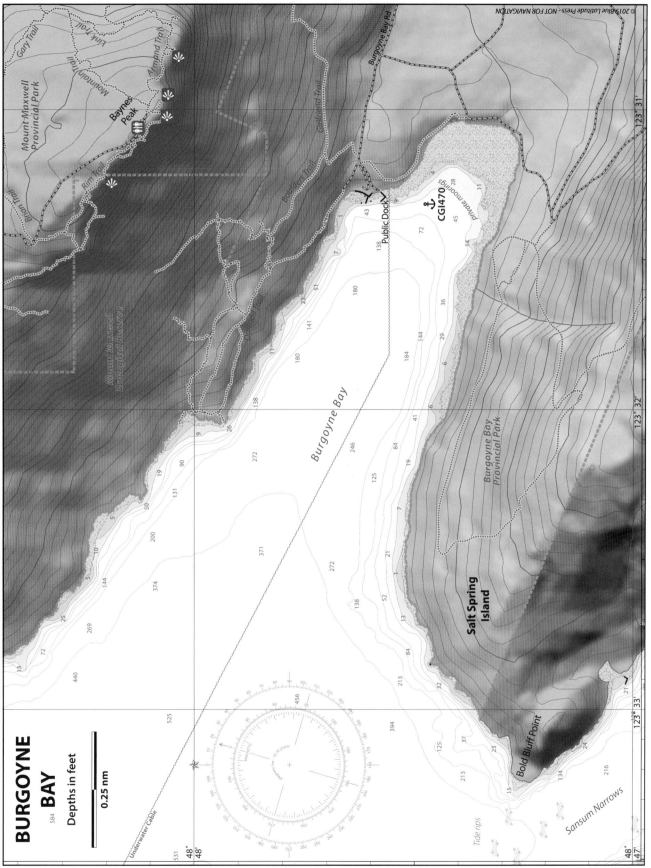

BURGOYNE
BAY

584 Depths in feet

0.25 nm

Underwater Cable

© 2019 Blue Latitude Press – NOT FOR NAVIGATION

CGI470 – 48° 47.440'N 123° 31.325'W

Mount Maxwell
Provincial Park

Baynes
Peak

Gary Trail

Link Trail

Mountain Trail

Armand Trail

Rim Trail

Bvan Trail

Mount Maxwell
Ecological Reserve

Boulder Trail

Gibliland Trail

Dufferin Trail

Burgoyne Bay Rd

Public Dock

CGI470

private moorings

Burgoyne Bay

Burgoyne Bay
Provincial Park

Salt Spring
Island

Bold Bluff Point

Sansum Narrows

Tide rips

239

Public wharf

over a mud bottom in 5 to 9 fathoms. Be sure to avoid the underwater cables stretching from the public wharf to Vancouver Island when anchoring. Northerly winds can funnel down Stuart Channel and into the anchorage. Southeast winds can also funnel across the Fulford Valley and into Burgoyne Bay, however the bay will provide protection from southeast waves.

A public wharf is also located within the bay and is operated by the Harbour Authority of Salt Spring Island. The roughly 60 foot dock is available for transient use for a maximum of 48 hours. The northeast side of the dock (tie up rail is painted yellow) is reserved for Burgoyne Bay Residents Association boats only.

For trips to shore dinghies can be conveniently moored to the south end of the public dock. Trailheads and Mount Maxwell Provincial Park information signs can be found a short walk north of the public wharf on Burgoyne Bay Road. For those looking for a shorter, less strenuous walk, head northwest from the parking lot on the Daffodil Trail which leads to a lookout at Daffodil Point. For those looking for a challenge with rewarding, breathtaking views at the top of Baynes Peak, head northeast from the parking lot on the Girlfriend Trail. Close to the top, the Girlfriend Trail intersects with the Armand Trail to the peak. This trail is steep and challenging, climbing 2,000 feet over roughly 2 miles. Be sure to bring a map, phone, plenty of water, and snacks for the adventure.

After a long day hiking the park trails, reward yourself at one of island's breweries or wineries. Salt Spring Island Ales (www.saltspringislandales.com) is a roughly 2 mile walk from the public wharf along Burgoyne Bay Road with a turn to the south on Furness Road (#270). Enjoy a tasting flight and fill your growler at their quaint loft tasting room. Garry Oaks Estate Winery (garryoakswinery.com) is a roughly 1.5 mile walk along Burgoyne Bay Road with a turn to the north on Fulford-Ganges Road (#1880). From their wine store, sample a tasting of their wines while overlooking the vineyards. A short walk further down Fulford-Ganges Road to Lee Road (#151) takes you to the beautiful and lush grounds of Salt Spring Vineyards. Enjoy a tasting and a picnic around the pond while listening to live music on Fridays and Saturdays during the summer.

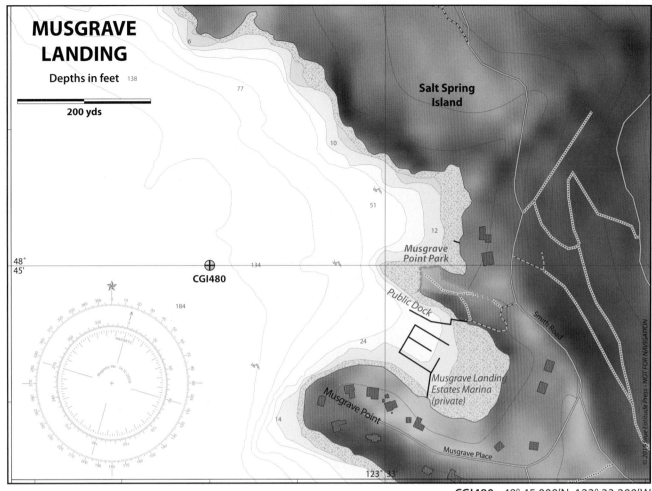

MUSGRAVE LANDING

Depths in feet 138

200 yds

Salt Spring Island

CGI480

Musgrave Point Park

Public Dock

Smith Road

Musgrave Landing Estates Marina (private)

Musgrave Point

Musgrave Place

123° 33'

© 2019 Fine Latitude Press - NOT FOR NAVIGATION

CGI480 - 48° 45.000'N 123° 33.200'W

Musgrave Landing

The highlight to Musgrave Landing is a small public wharf tucked into the north shore of this pocket-sized cove. Situated at the south end of Sansum Narrows, the dock has a prime view of the boating traffic transiting the channel. Island homes dot the shoreline and surrounding quiet country roads provide nice walking paths.

Musgrave Landing is found at the southwest end of Salt Spring Island, across from Separation Point on Vancouver Island. Approaches from the north can be taken via Sansum Narrows and from the south via Satellite Channel. Currents in Sansum Narrows in the narrowest sections can attain velocities up to 3 knots. Occasional whirlpools and tide rips can be found around Burial Islet and between Sansum Point and Bold Bluff Point. Burial Islet is found approximately 0.65 miles south-southwest of Sansum Point and is marked by a navigation light tower. Pass west of Burial Islet. Approaching from the south, be aware of Musgrave Rock which lies roughly 0.5 miles south-southeast of Musgrave Point. Musgrave Rock is covered by 7 feet of water and is marked by starboard hand buoy "U26."

Moorage can be taken at the public wharf for a nightly fee. The 120 foot dock is operated by the Harbour Authority of Salt Spring Island. During the summer months, this transient dock can become quite popular.

Public wharf

241

©Kevin Oke

Fulford Harbour

For those looking for a quieter experience to majestic Salt Spring Island, Fulford Harbour is a welcome alternative to the hustle and bustle of Ganges Harbour. With the exception of an occasional visit by BC Ferries, Fulford Harbour offers visitors a peaceful anchorage, a public wharf, and shoreside amenities including a well stocked mercantile and dining options. The oldest church on the island, dating back to 1880, provides a glimpse to the early settlers' history of the area.

Fulford Harbour is located on the southeast end of Salt Spring Island, across from Portland Island's Princess Margaret Marine Park. Entrance to the harbor is taken between Isabella Point and Eleanor Point, rounding either side of nearby Russell Island.

Approaches to the harbor are taken via Satellite Channel from the east or west, and Shute Passage from the south. When approaching from the west, be aware of Isabella Island lying off Isabella Point. The island and nearby small islet are connected to Salt Spring Island by a drying shoal. The island is marked by a navigation light on its southeast side.

Approaching from the east and between Russell and Salt Spring Islands, be cautious of Louisa Rock, Jackson Rock, and other reefs lying off the shore of Salt Spring Island.

The western shore, as well as the head of Fulford Harbour, has drying flats extending into the bay. Private mooring buoys can be found throughout the harbor. Anchorage can be taken near the head, avoiding the route of

Fulford Harbour to:		
	Bedwell Harbour *(South Pender Island)*	10 nm
	Burgoyne Bay *(Salt Spring Island)*	13 nm
	Ganges Harbour *(Salt Spring Island)*	12 nm
	Ladysmith	28 nm
	Montague Harbour *(Galiano Island)*	13 nm
	Nanaimo	41 nm
	Pirates Cove *(De Courcy Island)*	33 nm
	Roche Harbor *(USA)*	15 nm
	Russell Island	2 nm
	Sidney	8 nm
	Tod Inlet	14 nm
	Victoria	30 nm

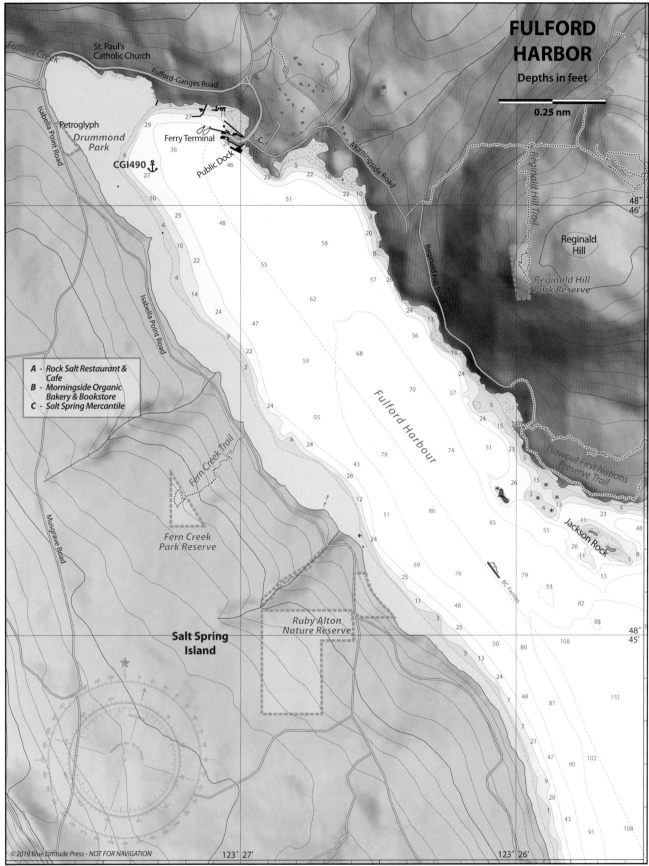

FULFORD HARBOR

Depths in feet

0.25 nm

St. Paul's
Catholic Church

Fulford Creek

Fulford-Ganges Road

Isabella Point Road

Petroglyph

Drummond Park

Ferry Terminal

CGI490

Public Dock

A
C
B

Morningside Road

Reginald Hill Trail

48°
46'

Reginald
Hill

Reginald Hill
Park Reserve

Reginald Hill Road

A - *Rock Salt Restaurant & Cafe*
B - *Morningside Organic Bakery & Bookstore*
C - *Salt Spring Mercantile*

Fern Creek Trail

Isabella Point Road

Musgrave Road

Fulford Harbour

Tsawout First Nations
Preserve Trail

Jackson Rock

**Fern Creek
Park Reserve**

BC Ferries

**Ruby Alton
Nature Reserve**

**Salt Spring
Island**

48°
45'

123° 27'

123° 26'

48°

© 2019 Blue Latitude Press - NOT FOR NAVIGATION

CGI490 - 48° 46.070'N 123° 27.330'W

243

Rock Salt Cafe

Drummond Park

Public Wharf

BC Ferries, in 4 to 6 fathoms over a mud bottom. Fulford Harbour offers protection from most directions except from southerly wind and waves.

A public wharf, operated by the Harbour Authority of Salt Spring Island, is also available for transient boats to use for a nightly fee. This roughly 70 foot dock is located just south of the BC Ferry terminal and is known as the Fulford Outer Harbour wharf. A second public wharf, known as the Fulford Inner Harbour wharf, is located just north of the ferry terminal, however it is reserved for long term leases and commercial fishing vessels.

Access to shore is made convenient through the use of the public wharf which is situated in the heart of the Fulford village. On shore, there are dining and shopping options, as well as quiet roads for strolling and a historical point of interest. Located a short walk northwest on Fulford-Ganges Road is Saint Paul's Church, the oldest church on Salt Spring Island (see below). The church and surrounding cemetery are a well-maintained piece of island history.

Nearby eateries in the village include the Rock Salt Restaurant & Cafe and the Morningside Organic Bakery Cafe & Bookstore. The Rock Salt (rocksaltrestaurant.com) is open daily for breakfast, lunch and dinner with a wide ranging menu and beautiful bakery items. The Morningside Bakery (morningsideorganic.com) is a unique collection of bakery items, beverages, soups, sandwiches and books. Next to the bakery is the Salt Spring Mercantile (saltspringmercantile.com). The Mercantile offers grocery items as well as an in-house bakery and deli selection.

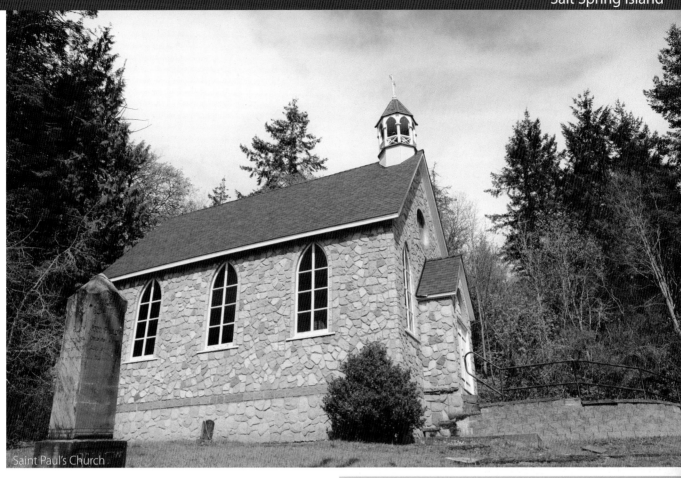
Saint Paul's Church

Across from the harbor from the ferry terminal is Drummond Park. Dinghies can be landed on the beach for easy access. The park offers a children's playground, picnic tables, a covered picnic area with barbecue, restrooms, and beautiful beach area. The highlight to the park is a preserved petroglyph by the T'sawout First Nations who inhabited the Fulford Harbour area. The native rock carving of a seal was originally found on the shores of Fulford Harbour.

Saint Paul's Church

Saint Paul's Church was founded in 1878 by Father Gustave Donckele, the first Roman Catholic missionary to the Gulf Islands. Father Donckele, who rowed to the island from the mission at Cowichan Bay, began construction of the church in 1880 with the help of local settlers including the Hawaiian Catholic community. The original doors to the church, as well as the bell and a stained glass window, were ferried to the island from Cowichan Bay to Burgoyne Bay by canoe. They were then transported across the valley via a stone-boat sled pulled by oxen. Construction of the church was completed in the spring of 1885.

©Kevin Oke

Russell Island

Russell Island is a true gem within the islands for both its natural beauty and preserved history. Now part of the Gulf Islands National Park Reserve, the island is open for the enjoyment of all, providing walking trails and an interesting history of First Nations and Hawaiian inhabitants. A park dinghy dock and striking beaches on the north side of the island provide easy access to the island for boaters and kayakers alike.

Russell Island is located near the mouth of Fulford Harbour on Salt Spring Island. Approaches to the island can be made via Satellite Channel from the east and west, or Shute Passage from the south. When approaching from the west, be aware of Isabella Island lying off Isabella Point. The island and nearby small islet are connected to Salt Spring Island by a drying shoal. The island is marked by a navigation light on its southeast side. Approaching from the east and between Russell and Salt Spring Islands, be cautious of Louisa Rock, Jackson Rock, and other reefs lying off the shore of Salt Spring Island. Upon approach to Russell Island from the south, be aware of Cecil Rock which lies 0.2 miles south off the southwestern end of the island and has

less than 6 feet of water covering it. The western side of the island also has a detached rock and shoal water lying close off the shore. Approaching from the south off the eastern side of the island, be aware of a detached shoal lying 0.2 miles south. This shoal is covered by 14 feet of water.

Anchorage can be taken off the northwest side of island in 3 to 8 fathoms over a mostly mud bottom. During the summer months, this anchorage can become quite

Russell Island to:		
	Bedwell Harbour (South Pender Island)	8 nm
	Cabbage Island	20 nm
	Ganges Harbour (Salt Spring Island)	10 nm
	Ladysmith	27 nm
	Montague Harbour (Galiano Island)	11 nm
	Nanaimo	36 nm
	Pirates Cove (De Courcy Island)	27 nm
	Princess Bay (Portland Island)	4 nm
	Roche Harbor (USA)	14 nm
	Sidney	7 nm
	Tod Inlet	13 nm
	Victoria	28 nm

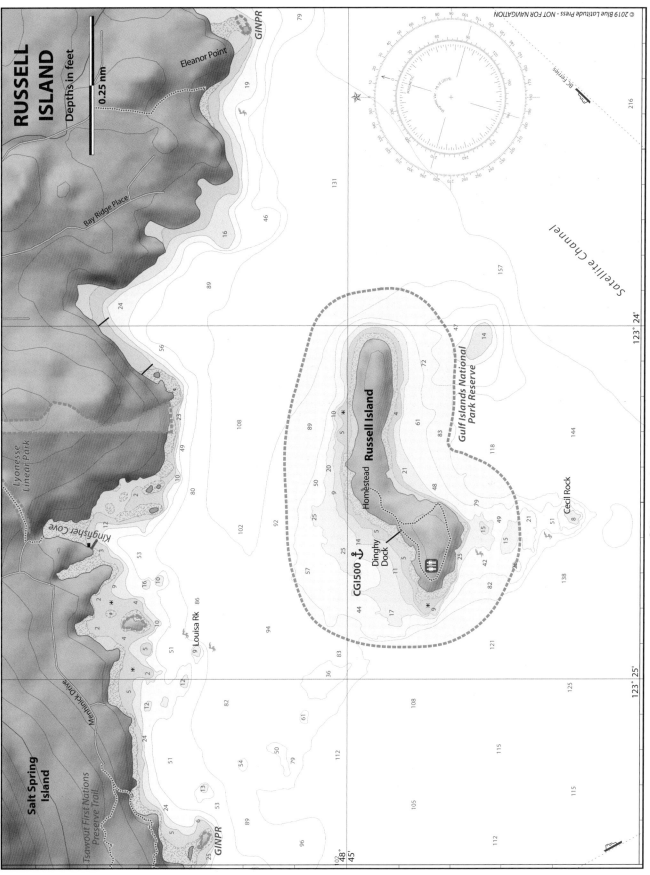

CGI500 - 48° 44.975'N 123° 24.640'W

Hawaiians

As trade routes developed between Asia and North America in the 1700 and 1800's, Hawaii became a natural reprovisioning stop for ships. A number of Hawaiians joined the passing ships as crewmen or laborers in the fur trade. After working aboard the ships or with the Hudson's Bay Company on Vancouver Island, many settled in the area, including Fulford Harbour, Russell Island, and Portland Island.

William Haumea, a Hawaiian settler at nearby Eleanor Point, was granted Russell Island in 1886 by the Crown. Haumea cleared areas of the island for pasture, and planted fruit orchards and strawberry fields. In 1901, Hawaiian Maria Mahoi inherited the island upon Haumea's death. She and her second husband, George Fisher, moved to the island and built their home, which was completed in 1907. Mahoi, who had seven children from her first marriage, expanded her family with Fisher with six additional children. Together, they continued to work the land.

In 1959, the Mahoi family sold Russell Island to the Rohrer family, who held the island until it was sold to the Pacific Marine Heritage Legacy in 1997. Today, descendants of the Mahoi family return each summer as volunteer hosts, residing in the Mahoi home and sharing family stories about life on Russell Island.

popular. The island offers south wind and wave protection. For trips to shore, a park dinghy dock is provided on the northwestern side of the island.

Russell Island provides a number of activities including walking trails, beautiful swimming beaches, and a glimpse into the history of the early inhabitants of the island. Most notably are the beautiful white shell middens found along the north side of the island. Coast Salish were the first inhabitants, leaving behind mounds of clam and oyster shells. Through excavation studies, Russell Island is believed to have been a site of clam gardens, where natural clam beds were enhanced to increase the production of these bivalves. Gardens were selected and built between areas of rock in order to prevent seaweed and predators from invading the beds. The gardens were tended by tilling the sand in order to provide more oxygen to the area and remove any debris or predators. These special food gardens are believed to be roughly 1,000 years old.

From the top of the dinghy dock ramp, a trail and boardwalk leading east takes visitors to the historical site of the Mahoi family homestead (see sidebar). During July and August, descendants from the family stay in the Mahoi home and are park volunteers, providing insightful memories and wonderful stories of early life on Russell Island. Fruit trees, landscaping, and pasture surround the beautiful waterfront homestead.

Chapter 9

Cowichan Bay to Ladysmith

COWICHAN BAY
to LADYSMITH
Overview

2.0 nm

Yellow Pt

Miami It

Deer Pt

Woodley Range

Kulleet Bay

Ragged Its

North Cove

Pilkey Pt

Valdes Is

Ladysmith Harbour

Fraser Pt

Theris Is

Rose Its

Reid Is

Dionisio Pt

Porlier Pass

Galiano Island

Ladysmith

Crescent Pt

Leech Is

Clam Bay

Hall Is

Norway Is

Secretary Is

Trincomali Channel

Hunter Pt

Coffin Pt

Coffin Is

Holland Bank

Sharpe Pt

Stuart Channel

False Reef

Preedy Harbour

Foster Pt

Penelakut Is

Mowgli Is

Wallace Is

Houstoun Passage

Panther Pt

Scott Is

Dayman Is

Telegraph Harbour

Jackscrew Is

Boulder Pt

Hudson Is

Alarm Rock

Active Pt

Escape Reef

Josling Pt

Grappler Rock

Southey Pt

Victoria Shoal

pg 272

Chemainus Bay

Tent Is

North Reef

Fernwood Pt

Hospital Pt

Bare Pt

Chemainus

Saint Mary Lake

Mount Brenton

Fuller Lake

Shoal Islands

Willy Is

Parminter Pt

Dock Pt

Vesuvius

Chemainus River

Indian Reef

Booth Bay

Ganges

Big Sicker Mountain

Crofton

Osborn Bay

pg 269

Sherard Pt

Mount Richards

Crofton Lake

Grave Pt

Erskine Pt

pg 263

Quamichan Lake

Maple Bay

Birds Eye Cove

Arbutus Pt

Maxwell Pt

Salt Spring Island

Octopus Pt

Burgoyne Bay

Sansum Narrows

Bold Bluff Pt

Vancouver Island

Sansum Pt

Mt Tzouhalem

pg 258

Cowichan River

Koksilah River

Separation Pt

Musgrave Pt

Cowichan Bay

Genoa Bay

Cowichan Bay

Musgrave Rock

pg 253

Cherry Pt

Boatswain Bank

49° 00'

48° 55'

48° 50'

48° 45'

©Kevin Oke

Cowichan Bay

Cowichan Bay is a true seaside village. A patchwork of docks, floating homes, and boats of all shapes and sizes adorn the waterfront of this laid back village. Charming shops and eateries straddle the waterfront, with one foot on land and one in the water. The beautiful surrounding scenery and eclectic character have made this coastal town a popular stop for visitors touring Vancouver Island.

Cowichan Bay is located on Vancouver Island and accessed via Satellite Channel. The village at Cowichan Bay is found on the southwestern shore of the bay. The head of the bay is an estuary with extensive mud flats. A mill, log booms, and a commercial shipping terminal are also located at the head of the bay. Occasionally large ships may anchor in the bay. When entering the bay, be aware that there may be numerous crab floats during the season.

For boats approaching from the south via Saanich Inlet, be aware of Patey Rock which lies at the north end of the inlet, near mid channel. Patey Rock is marked with a tower navigation light. Roughly 1.4 miles northwest of

Patey Rock is Boatswain Bank. This bank lies between Hatch and Cherry Points on Vancouver Island, with drying flats and shallow water extending east. Be sure to give Boatswain Bank ample room when passing.

For boats approaching from the north via Sansum Narrows be aware that whirlpools and tide rips can be

Cowichan Bay to:		
	Chemainus	17 nm
	Ganges Harbour (Salt Spring Island)	20 nm
	Ladysmith	28 nm
	Montague Harbour (Galiano Island)	20 nm
	Nanaimo	34 nm
	Pirates Cove (De Courcy Island)	26 nm
	Port Browning (North Pender Island)	23 nm
	Princess Bay (Portland Island)	11 nm
	Roche Harbor (USA)	20 nm
	Sidney	12 nm
	Tod Inlet	13 nm
	Victoria	34 nm

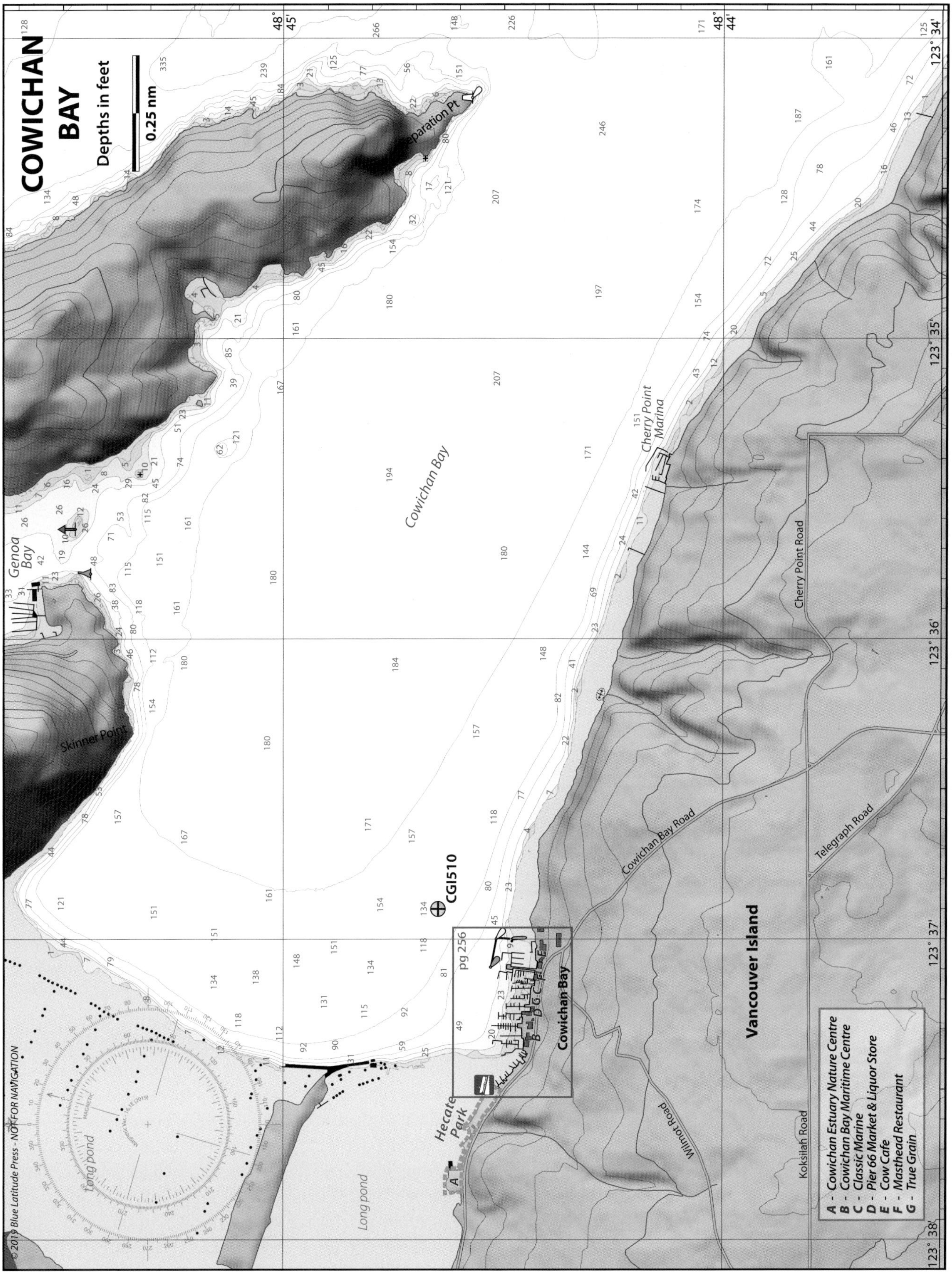

COWICHAN BAY

Depths in feet

0.25 nm

Genoa Bay

Separation Pt

Cowichan Bay

Skinner Point

Cherry Point Marina

Long pond

Hecate Park

Long pond

Cowichan Bay

Vancouver Island

Cowichan Bay Road

Cherry Point Road

Telegraph Road

Wilmot Road

Koksilah Road

pg 256

CGI510

A - Cowichan Estuary Nature Centre
B - Cowichan Bay Maritime Centre
C - Classic Marine
D - Pier 66 Market & Liquor Store
E - Cow Cafe
F - Masthead Restaurant
G - True Grain

© 2019 Blue Latitude Press - NOT FOR NAVIGATION

CGI510 - 48° 44.650'N 123° 36.900'W

48° 45'

48° 44'

123° 34'

123° 35'

123° 36'

123° 37'

123° 38'

Rental buoys

Classic Marine Chandlery

found around Burial Islet and between Sansum and Bold Bluff Points. Current flowing through Sansum Narrows is roughly 1 to 2 knots in the wider sections, and can reach up to 3 knots in the narrow section. Wind can funnel through the narrows and down the valleys of the bordering islands.

Anchorage is possible off the village in 8 to 13 fathoms over a mostly mud bottom, although not highly recommended. A number of boats have sank in the bay over the years, and their wrecks tend to snag the anchors and chains of unsuspecting visiting boats. Better moorage options when visiting Cowichan Bay are renting a mooring buoy or staying at a marina. Transient mooring buoys can be rented from Classic Marine, a marine chandlery shop located in the village. Classic Marine buoys are well marked and offer contact information via VHF radio channel 66A and phone (250) 746-1093.

Sights to See

Walking the waterfront village at Cowichan Bay is a true treat for boat lovers. The eclectic wharf area is a mix of new and old, commercial and recreational. There is always something to watch and interesting boats to see for the avid dock walker. Various shops and eateries easily tempt anyone passing by.

The Cowichan Bay Maritime Centre, operated by the Cowichan Wooden Boat Society, is a wonderful stop when touring the village. The center offers a museum and exhibits including models, historical photos, a marine library, a small fleet of traditional small craft, and more. The Society also operates a historic marine ways for the hauling and cleaning of boats. For further information, including current hours, please visit their website at: www.classicboats.org.

While out walking the village, be sure to visit the waterfront Hecate Park and the Cowichan Estuary Nature Centre. The park sits on the shore of the Cowichan Estuary, and is less than a half mile walk west of the main village. Along with sweeping views of the bay and estuary, the park provides picnic tables and a new dock for kayak launching. Within the park is the interpretive center offering interactive opportunities for visitors to learn about the vital importance of the Cowichan Estuary and watershed. At the Cowichan Estuary Nature Centre, visitors can see and touch marine life in the aquarium and touch tank, use microscopes and telescopes, and watch the local marine wildlife along the interpretive trail and from a viewing tower. For further information on hours, programs, and events, check the center's website at: www.cowichanestuary.ca.

Cowichan Estuary Nature Center

Marine Chandleries and Services

Classic Marine

Classic Marine is a marine chandlery selling marine parts and supplies, including fishing gear and nautical gifts. Classic Marine also provides rental mooring buoys in the bay. Classic Marine monitors VHF radio channel 66A. (250) 746-1093, classicmarine.ca

Provisioning

Pier 66 Market & Liquor Store

Pier 66 Market & Liquor Store offers beverages, snacks and convenience items. The market also offers a fully stocked liquor store with beer, wine, and spirits.

Restaurants

Cow Cafe

Located in the heart of the village, the Cow Cafe offers indoor and patio view seating. Open for breakfast, lunch, and dinner, the cafe serves a wide ranging menu including breakfast favorites, grilled meats, fresh seafood, burgers, salads, and more. cowcafe.ca

Masthead Restaurant

The waterfront Masthead Restaurant is located in the former Columbia Hotel built in 1863. The fine dining restaurant is open daily for dinner offering elegant meals and wine pairings. themastheadrestaurant.com

True Grain

True Grain is an exceptional bakery using old world techniques using 100% BC organic, stone milled flour. Pastries, cookies, and breads are made fresh daily and are not to be missed! Open daily near the center of the village. www.truegrain.ca

Maritime Center

Maritime Center

True Grain Bakery

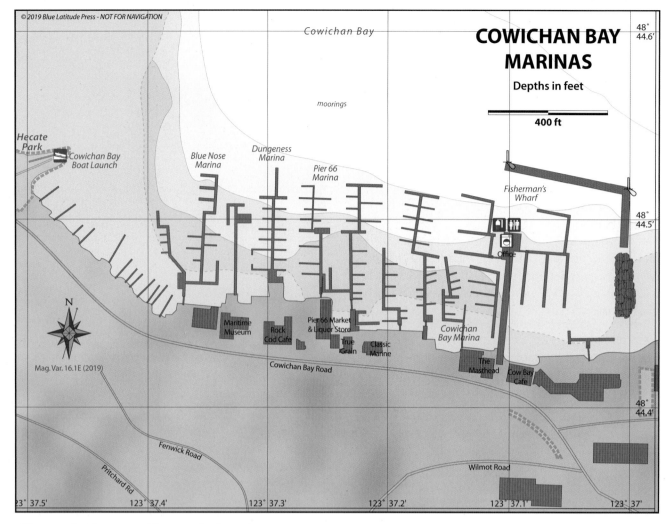

© 2019 Blue Latitude Press - NOT FOR NAVIGATION

Cowichan Bay Marinas

Wwhile there are a number of small marinas within Cowichan Bay, most are reserved for long term leases. It may be possible that a guest slip is available at one of the private marinas or docks including Bluenose Marina (www.thebluenosemarina.com, (250)748-2222), Pier 66 Marina (pier66marina.com, (250) 510-7711), or Dungeness Marina (250-748-6789).

The most popular and available to transient boats is the Cowichan Bay Fisherman's Wharf Association. This marina, located on the east side of the village, offers ample linear dock space on its floating breakwater. Services include clean restrooms, showers, garbage drop off, oil disposal, and laundry facilities. Commercial fishing boats do have priority, however there is typically room for transient boats. Day moorage is available up until 2pm. After 2pm overnight moorage rates are charged.

Cowichan Bay Fisherman's Wharf Association
Monitors VHF Channel 66A
1699 Cowichan Bay Road
Cowichan Bay, BC
(250) 746-5911

©Kevin Oke

Genoa Bay

Reef at entrance to bay

Whether staying with the friendly, family run Genoa Bay Marina, or anchoring out in the calm waters of the bay, Genoa Bay is quick to win your heart as a favorite stop on your journey through the Gulf Islands. Located within Cowichan Bay, Genoa Bay is the perfect mix of natural beauty, comfortable amenities, and tranquil surroundings. Highlights of the area include the fantastic hike up Mount Tzouhalem and day trips to the nearby coastal village of Cowichan Bay.

Genoa Bay is located on Vancouver Island within Cowichan Bay on its north shore. The entrance to Cowichan Bay is found at the intersection of the west end of Satellite Channel and the south end of Sansum Narrows. For boats approaching from the south via Saanich Inlet, be aware of Patey Rock which lies at the north end of the inlet, near mid channel. Patey Rock is marked with a tower navigation light. Roughly 1.4 miles northwest of Patey Rock is Boatswain Bank. This bank lies between Hatch and Cherry Points on Vancouver Island, with drying flats and shallow water extending east. Be sure to give Boatswain Bank ample room when passing.

Genoa Bay to:		
	Bedwell Harbour *(South Pender Island)*	17 nm
	Ganges Harbour *(Salt Spring Island)*	20 nm
	Ladysmith	28 nm
	Montague Harbour *(Galiano Island)*	20 nm
	Nanaimo	34 nm
	Pirates Cove *(De Courcy Island)*	26 nm
	Roche Harbor *(USA)*	20 nm
	Russell Island	10 nm
	Sidney	12 nm
	Tod Inlet	13 nm
	Victoria	34 nm
	Wallace Island	16 nm

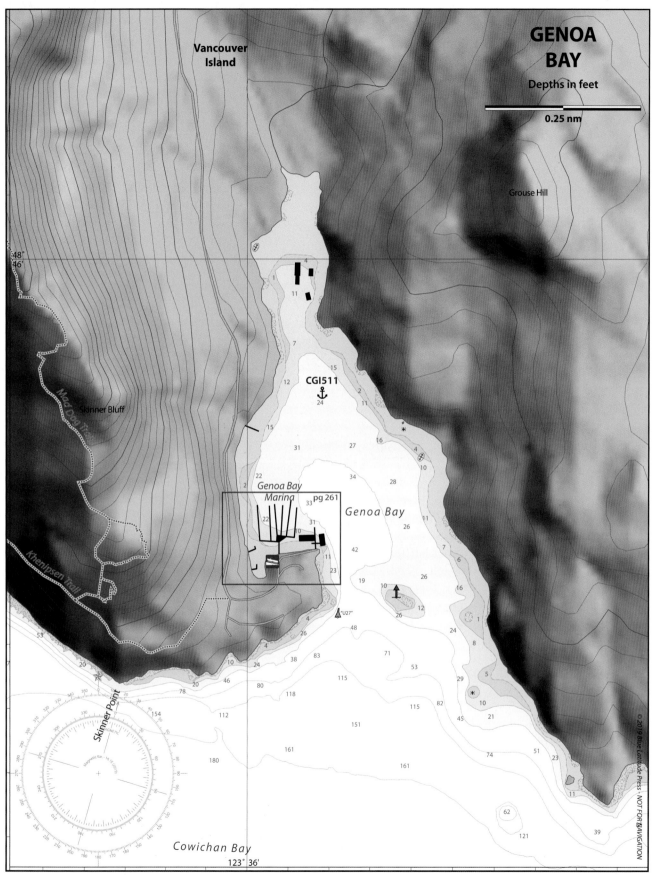

GENOA BAY

Depths in feet

0.25 nm

Grouse Hill

Vancouver
Island

Skinner Bluff

Mad Dog Trail

Khenipsen Trail

CGI511

Genoa Bay
Marina   pg 261

Genoa Bay

"U27"

Skinner Point

Cowichan Bay
123° 36'

© 2019 Blue Latitude Press · NOT FOR NAVIGATION

CGI511 - 48° 45.780'N 123° 35.820'W

Genoa Bay Marina

For boats approaching from the north via Sansum Narrows be aware that whirlpools and tide rips can be found around Burial Islet and between Sansum and Bold Bluff Points. Current flowing through Sansum Narrows is roughly 1 to 2 knots in the wider sections, and can reach up to 3 knots in the narrow section. Wind can funnel through the narrows and down the valleys of the bordering islands.

Entrance to Genoa bay is found on the north side of Cowichan Bay. A drying reef is located near mid channel at the entrance to the bay. The reef is marked by a day-beacon. On the west side of the entrance to the bay, buoy "U27" marks a drying rock. Entrance to the bay can be taken between the mid channel reef and buoy "U27."

Anchorage can be taken within Genoa Bay in 4 to 6 fathoms over a mud bottom. Private moorings can be found north of the marina as well as in the far north and east sides of the bay. Genoa Bay provides good, nearly all round protection.

At the southwest end of the bay, visitors can find the welcoming Genoa Bay Marina. The marina not only houses boats, but also floating homes, boat houses, a gallery, and a store. The store at the marina supplies a nice mix of gifts, reading materials, marine chandlery and fishing items, ice, snacks, and beverages. At the head of the ramp is the Genoa Bay Cafe. The covered outdoor deck of the restaurant affords beautiful waterfront views of the marina

Floating homes

Genoa Bay Cafe

Mad Dog Trail

Mad Dog Trail

Marina bathroom building

and bay. Open for lunch and dinner (reduced hours during the winter), the cafe's menu highlights the foods of Vancouver Island and the Pacific Northwest, including fresh, local seafoods. For menus and reservations check their website at: www.genoabaycafe.com or call (250) 746-7621.

Sights to See

Two of the best activities at Genoa Bay include touring the quaint village at Cowichan Bay (see page 252) and hiking the area's spectacular terrain. The community at Cowichan Bay is located roughly 1.5 miles by water from Genoa Bay. The village has become a charming mix of working waterfront and tourist shops. Boats and floating homes of all shapes and sizes line the docks with vintage wood piers and buildings connecting the waterfront. Restaurants able to take advantage of the local fishing industry and farming community of the Cowichan Valley, offer delicious menus showcasing the area's local bounty. Artisan galleries and gift shops provide unique art and souvenirs to take back home.

For those interested in hitting the trails at Genoa Bay, the nearby Mad Dog Trail offers exceptional views and a heart pumping hike. The 2.5 mile trail to the summit follows the ridgeline of Mount Tzouhalem which stands at an impressive 1,650 feet. Along the way, there are a handful of beautiful lookout points making for perfect stops to catch your breath, enjoy the view, and snap a few photos. The hike travels through beautiful forests of native Garry oaks, madrones, and firs. If you're lucky enough to visit in the spring, the grass meadows along the ridgeline bloom with native camas and shooting star wildflowers.

The trailhead is found on Genoa Bay Road, just west of the marina where the road takes a 90 degree turn to the north. The trail begins following a fence line marking private property on the other side. Roughly a third of a mile in, the trail splits. To the right, is a steeper short cut trail that reconnects with the main Mad Dog Trail. To the left, the trail eventually connects with the Khenipsen Trail. At the intersection of the Khenipsen and Mad Dog Trails, take a right (north) to stay on the Mad Dog Trail. From here, the trail heads up Mount Tzouhalem, following the ridgeline. During the summer months, hiking this trail in the morning, before the day heats up, can be quite helpful. Be sure to pack plenty of water and snacks to help keep you refreshed while trekking up and back down the mountain. Near the top of the mountain, a number of side trails can be found which can be confusing. Be sure to bring a map and/or smart phone with GPS tracking ability. This trail is also widely used by mountain bikers so keep an eye out especially on blind corners.

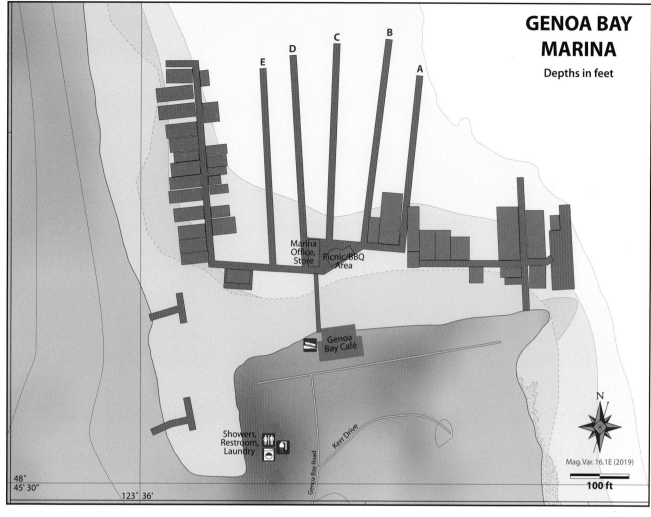

GENOA BAY MARINA

Depths in feet

Mag. Var. 16.1E (2019)

100 ft

Genoa Bay Marina

The Genoa Bay Marina is tucked into quiet and protected Genoa Bay. This friendly marina offers over 1,200 feet of dock space for both transient and permanent moorage. New wooden docks provide water and power (15, 30 and 50 amp) hookups. The marina can accommodate boats from 12 to 120 feet in length. Services include a beautiful restroom and shower building, laundry facilities, a launch ramp, wifi access, covered picnic and barbecue area, car and dvd rentals. The marina office and store stocks a nice mix of local products, marine chandlery items, books, sundry items, snacks, beverages, and ice cream. The Genoa Bay Cafe is located at the head of the dock for a delicious meal off the boat.

Genoa Bay Marina
Monitors VHF channel 66A
5000 Genoa Bay Road, Unit #1
Duncan, BC V9L 5Y8
(250) 746-7621
info@genoabaymarina.com
www.genoabaymarina.com

©Kevin Ok

Maple Bay

Maple Bay is a small seaside village tucked into the southern end of Stuart Channel. The main community is found at the northern end of the bay while much of the marine facilities are located at the southern end in Birds Eye Cove. A public wharf is found at the northern end of the bay.

Maple Bay is located on Vancouver Island near the northern entrance to Sansum Narrows. The bay is entered between Arbutus Point to the north and Paddy Mile Stone to the south. Approaches to the bay can be taken via Stuart Channel to the north or Sansum Narrows to the south.

For boats approaching from the south via Sansum Narrows be aware that whirlpools and tide rips can be found around Burial Islet and between Sansum and Bold Bluff Points. Current flowing through Sansum Narrows is roughly 1 to 2 knots in the wider sections, and can reach up to 3 knots in the narrow section. Wind can funnel through the narrows and down the valleys of the bordering islands. Be aware of a boulder lying close off Paddy Mile Stone when rounding into the bay.

Much of the northern portion of Maple Bay is deep with steep shorelines. A small patch of shallow water can be found just south of the public wharf. Within this shal-low area lies a submerged rock with less than 6 feet of water covering it. A number of private moorings are found in the area south of the public wharf.

The Municipality of North Cowichan operates the public wharf in Maple Bay. The U-shaped wharf offers over 300 feet of dock space. During the summer months this dock can be quite popular.

A short walk north of the public wharf is the Lion Rampant Scottish Pub (www.lionrampant.ca). The restaurant is open for lunch and dinner serving classic pub fare.

Maple Bay to:		
Bedwell Harbour *(South Pender Island)*	21 nm
Chemainus	10 nm
Ganges Harbour *(Salt Spring Island)*	22 nm
Ladysmith	15 nm
Montague Harbour *(Galiano Island)*	18 nm
Nanaimo	28 nm
Pirates Cove *(De Courcy Island)*	20 nm
Princess Bay *(Portland Island)*	14 nm
Roche Harbor *(USA)*	24 nm
Sidney	16 nm
Tod Inlet	17 nm
Victoria	38 nm

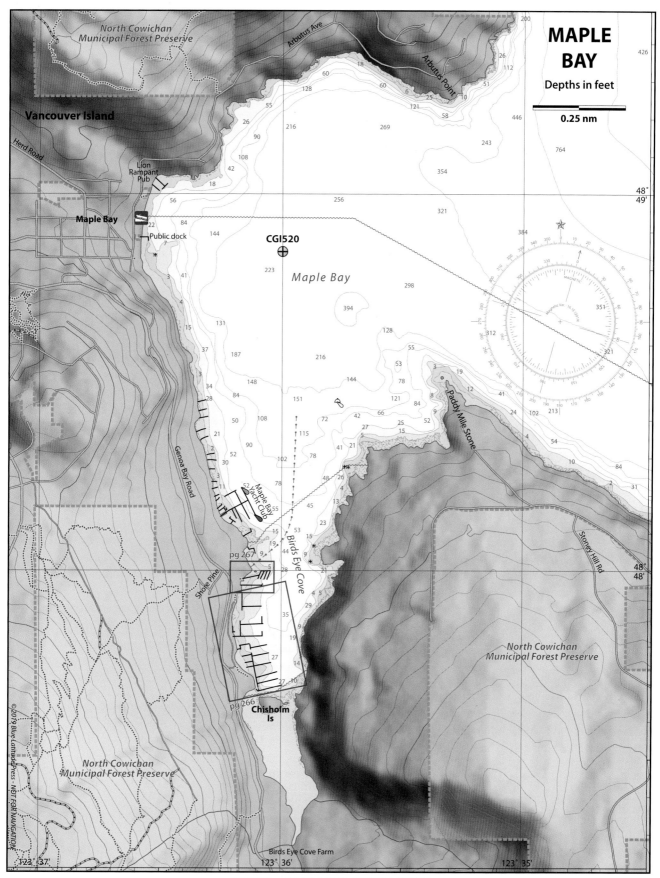

MAPLE BAY

Depths in feet

0.25 nm

North Cowichan Municipal Forest Preserve

Vancouver Island

Herd Road

Arbutus Ave

Arbutus Point

Lion Rampant Pub

Maple Bay

Public dock

CGI520

Maple Bay

Genoa Bay Road

Maple Bay Yacht Club

Paddy Mile Stone

Birds Eye Cove

Shole Pine

pg 267

pg 266

Stoney Hill Rd

North Cowichan Municipal Forest Preserve

Chisholm Is

North Cowichan Municipal Forest Preserve

Birds Eye Cove Farm

© 2019 Blue Latitude Press - NOT FOR NAVIGATION

123° 37'   123° 36'   123° 35'

CGI520 - 48° 48.840'N 123° 36.000'W

Birds Eye Cove

The well protected Birds Eye Cove is found in the far southern reaches of Maple Bay. Marinas, covered boat houses, and even a handful of floating homes are tucked into the shelter of Birds Eye Cove. Haulout yards, chandleries, and ample dock space make this a popular boating haven. The protected waters of the cove, along with the larger expanse of Maple Bay, offer miles of shoreline for afternoon kayak adventures.

Birds Eye Cove is located on Vancouver Island in the southern end of Maple Bay. Entrance to the cove is taken via Maple Bay which is entered between Arbutus Point to the north and Paddy Mile Stone to the south. Approaches to the bay are taken through Stuart Channel to the north or Sansum Narrows to the south.

For boats approaching from the south via Sansum Narrows be aware that whirlpools and tide rips can be found around Burial Islet and between Sansum and Bold Bluff Points. Current flowing through Sansum Narrows is roughly 1 to 2 knots in the wider sections, and can reach up to 3 knots in the narrow section. Wind can funnel through the narrows and down the valleys of the bordering islands. When rounding into the bay, be sure to give Paddy Mile Stone ample room to avoid a detached rock lying north of the point.

At the entrance to Birds Eye Cove, a buoy marks the speed limit at a maximum of 4 knots within the cove. Seaplanes also frequent the area with a seaplane dock located

Birds Eye Cove to:		
	Bedwell Harbour (South Pender Island)	21 nm
	Ganges Harbour (Salt Spring Island)	22 nm
	Montague Harbour (Galiano Island)	18 nm
	Nanaimo	28 nm
	Pirates Cove (De Courcy Island)	20 nm
	Roche Harbor (USA)	24 nm
	Russell Island	13 nm
	Sidney	16 nm
	Telegraph Harbour (Thetis Island)	12 nm
	Tod Inlet	17 nm
	Victoria	37 nm
	Wallace Island	11 nm

at Maple Bay Marina. A "No Anchoring" channel is found between the eastern edge of the marinas and the western edge of the anchorage/mooring buoy area for seaplane and vessel traffic. Anchorage can be taken along the eastern side of the cove in 4 to 9 fathoms. Due to a large number of private mooring buoys found within the cove, room for anchoring is unfortunately extremely limited. Be sure to check the chart and note local signs which denote underwater cable crossing areas, pipelines, and dock anchor lines.

A number of marinas and the Maple Bay Yacht Club are found within the bay. The Maple Bay Marina is the largest and offers a convenient 75 foot fuel dock with new pump out station. For a meal off the boat, the Shipyard Restaurant & Pub (www.shipyardrestaurant.com) is located at the marina with ample patio and indoor seating. The restaurant is open daily for lunch and dinner serving traditional pub fare and cold beverages.

For those visiting during the summer season, be sure to take the short walk (0.7 miles) south to Birds Eye Cove Farm (birdseyecovefarm.com). At the entrance to the farm on Genoa Bay Road, is the Gypsy Wagon. Open daily, the wagon sells farm produce, free range eggs, Highland beef, Berkshire pork, preserves, meat pies and freshly prepared meals such as Shepard's pie and lasagne to take home and bake. On Mondays and Wednesdays the farm opens their doors for Pizza Night. Visitors can enjoy delicious wood fired pizzas while sitting at picnic tables within the beautiful farm setting.

Cove Yachts

Lindstrom Marine

265

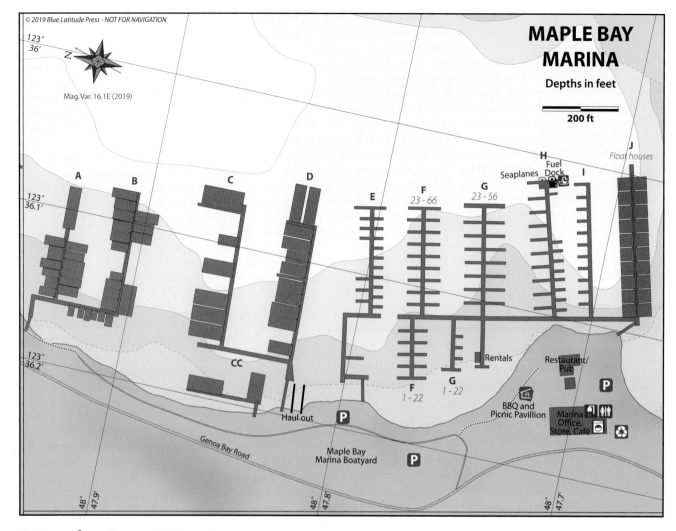

© 2019 Blue Latitude Press - NOT FOR NAVIGATION

123° 36'

N

Mag. Var. 16.1E (2019)

123° 36.1'

123° 36.2'

MAPLE BAY MARINA

Depths in feet

200 ft

A B C D

CC

Haul out

Genoa Bay Road

Maple Bay
Marina Boatyard

E F 23-66 G 23-56

F 1-22 G 1-22

H J
Fuel Dock Float houses
Seaplanes I

Rentals

Restaurant/ Pub

BBQ and
Picnic Pavillion

Marina
Office,
Store, Café

48° 47.9' 48° 47.8' 48° 47.7'

Maple Bay Marina

The expansive Maple Bay Marina is located within the protection of Birds Eye Cove. The marina offers both transient and permanent moorage options. Services include bathrooms, showers, a laundry facility, free wifi, covered patio and barbecue area, and garbage and recycling disposal. Additional services include a small market, restaurant, car rentals, and kayak rentals. A fuel dock and new pump out station is located on H dock offering gas, diesel, propane, oil and lubricants as well as snacks, water and ice.

The marina also offers a repair/maintenance haulout yard through Lindstrom Marine (www.lindstrommarine. com). The Travelift is able to haul vessels up to 50 tons. Lindstrom Marine also operates the chandlery, Marine Supply Store, found next to the marina office. The chandlery has an assortment of boating supplies such as antifouling and topside paints, epoxies and fillers, zinc anodes, plumbing supplies and more. If items are not in stock, most can be ordered and shipped by the following business day.

Maple Bay Marina
Monitors VHF channel 66A
6145 Genoa Bay Road
Maple Bay, BC V9L 5T7
(250) 746-8482
info@maplebaymarina.com
www.maplebaymarina.com

Fuel dock

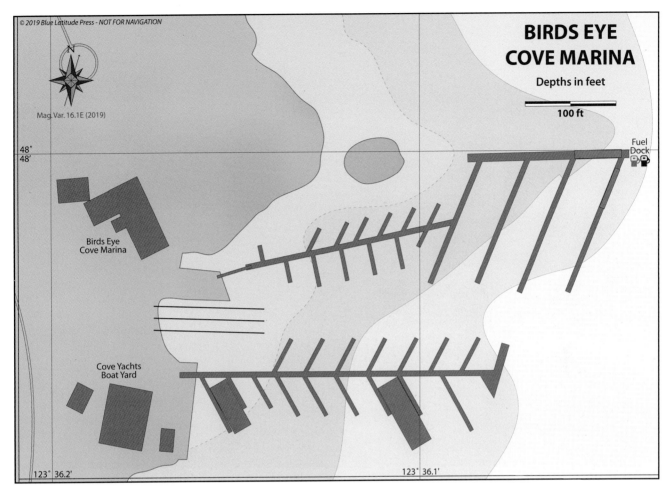

Cove Yachts

Cove Yachts is a full-service boatyard with a small marina for repairs and maintenance. They operate a 100 ton marine railway that can accommodate vessels up to 90 feet in length and up to 24 feet in beam. The yard also operates a 25 ton Travel Lift that can haul boats up to 50 feet in length and up to 13 feet 9 inches in beam. A 5 ton crane is on hand for stepping masts, lifting engines and other heavy equipment. Additional services include a 70 foot enclosed boathouse for in-water repairs/maintenance, a well stocked marine chandlery, well-equipped workshops and marina space for boats up to 90 feet in length. Cove Yachts specializes in wooden boat repairs and maintenance.

Cove Yachts
6261 Genoa Bay Road
Duncan, BC V9L 5Y4
(250) 748-8136
coveyachts@gmail.com
coveyachtrepairs.com

Birds Eye Cove Marina

This small, family-owned marina has been in operation for more than 40 years. Although the marina has limited overnight moorage, they do offer a diesel fuel dock (no gasoline) and small store for snacks and fishing gear.

Birds Eye Cove Marina
6271 Genoa Bay Road
Duncan, BC V9L 5Y4
(250) 746-5686
birdseyecovemarina2014@gmail.com
www.birdseyecoveduncan.ca

©Kevin Oke

Crofton

Crofton is a small seaside town located roughly 13 miles southeast of Ladysmith on Vancouver Island. Crofton is home to a large pulp and paper mill as well as a BC Ferries terminal with service to nearby Salt Spring Island. The town offers a small store for provisioning along with dining options for a night away from the galley.

Crofton is located within Osborne Bay on Vancouver Island. The bay is entered between Sherard Point to the south and the southern end of the Shoal Islands to the north. Approaches to Crofton are taken via Stuart Channel or Houstoun Passage from the north, or Sansum Narrows from the south. When approaching from the south, be aware that current in the narrows can reach 3 knots with whirlpools and tide rips possible around Burial Islet and Sansum Point. When rounding Sherard Point into Osborne Bay, be cautious of mud and sand drying banks extending 0.1 miles offshore from the point to the public wharf.

When approaching from the north, be aware of both North Reef and Shoal Islands. North Reef is a narrow rocky islet lying roughly 0.4 miles southwest of Tent Island. The reef is marked by a navigation light. Shoal Islands are found

between Crofton and Chemainus, near the Vancouver Island shoreline. The Shoal Islands is made up of numerous islands, islets, rocks, and an extensive mud and sand drying flat reaching a mile offshore. When rounding into Osborne Bay, be sure to give Shoal Islands along with adjacent Indian Reef (marked by a daybeacon) ample room. The Crofton navigation light is found near the southeast end of Shoal Is-

Crofton to:		
	Ganges Harbour *(Salt Spring Island)*	19 nm
	Ladysmith	12 nm
	Montague Harbour *(Galiano Island)*	14 nm
	Nanaimo	24 nm
	Pirates Cove *(De Courcy Island)*	16 nm
	Princess Bay *(Portland Island)*	18 nm
	Sidney	19 nm
	Silva Bay *(Gabriola Island)*	20 nm
	Telegraph Harbour *(Thetis Island)*	7 nm
	Tod Inlet	21 nm
	Victoria	41 nm
	Wallace Island	7 nm

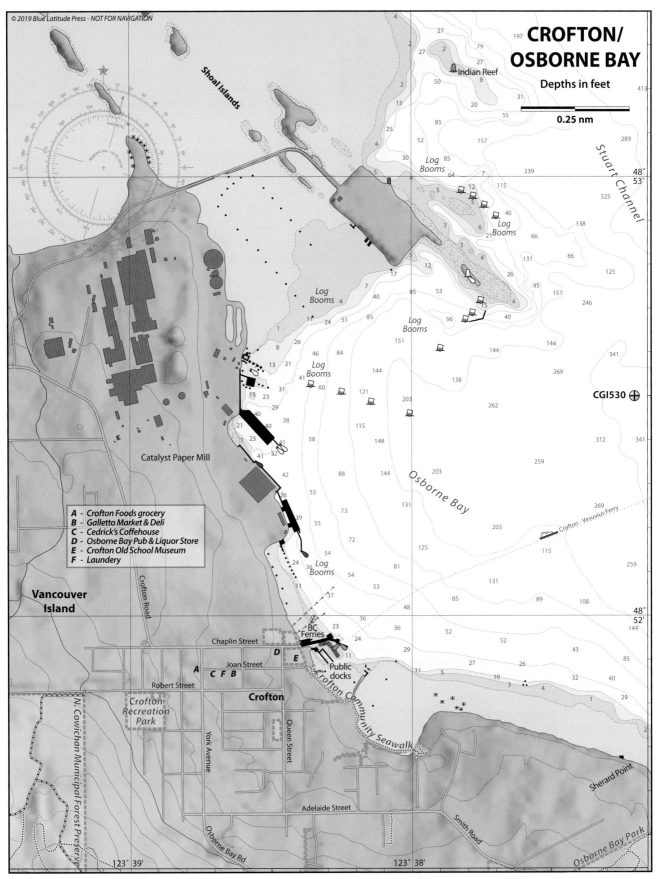

© 2019 Blue Latitude Press - NOT FOR NAVIGATION

CROFTON/ OSBORNE BAY

Depths in feet

0.25 nm

Shoal Islands

Indian Reef

Log Booms

Stuart Channel

48° 53'

CGI530

Catalyst Paper Mill

A - Crofton Foods grocery
B - Galletto Market & Deli
C - Cedrick's Coffeehouse
D - Osborne Bay Pub & Liquor Store
E - Crofton Old School Museum
F - Laundery

Osborne Bay

Crofton - Vesuvius Ferry

48° 52'

Vancouver Island

Crofton Road

BC Ferries

Chaplin Street

Joan Street

D
E

Public docks

A
C F B

Robert Street

Crofton

York Avenue

Queen Street

Crofton Community Seawalk

N. Cowichan Municipal Forest Preserve

Crofton Recreation Park

Adelaide Street

Sherard Point

Osborne Bay Rd

Smith Road

Osborne Bay Park

123° 39'

123° 38'

CGI530 - 48° 52.500'N 123° 37.200'W

Crofton Old School Museum

Public Wharf

Osborne Bay Pub

lands. Booming grounds and anchored barges can be found at the south end of Shoal Islands and within Osborne Bay near the pulp and paper mill.

Osborne Bay is a working port with numerous commercial vessels found entering, departing, and anchored within the bay. Tugs, barges, tankers, cargo ships, fishing vessels and ferries use the bay. Keep a careful watch when entering this area. While anchoring is possible in the bay, wake from passing boats and hourly ferries, along with a fairly open anchorage make this a marginal spot to drop the anchor.

The Department of Fisheries and Oceans owns the public wharf in Crofton which is operated by the Municipality of North Cowichan. The U-shaped small craft dock provides nearly 1,000 feet of moorage protected by a rock breakwater. While the majority of moorage here is for commercial vessels and local boats, some transient moorage may be available when the fishing fleet is out for the summer months. Water and power (20 and 30 amp) hookups are available along with restrooms and showers. Keys for the shower are available from the BC Ferries ticket booth at the information center.

Provisioning and Restaurants

Crofton Foods
Crofton Foods is a small local grocery with in-store deli and takeout options. Located at the intersection of York and Joan Avenues.

Galletto Market and Deli
Galletto Market is a small convenience store and deli. Located on Joan Avenue near Cedrick's Coffeehouse.

Cedrick's Coffeehouse
With proceeds helping to fund the charitable organization Kids International Development Society (K.I.D.S), Cedrick's is a local favorite. Open for breakfast and lunch. Located on Joan Avenue across from Crofton Foods. cedricksteacoffee.ca

Osborne Bay Pub, Cafe, and Liquor Store
Osborne Bay Pub offers sea to table, fresh and local meals. The pub overlooks the waterfront serving pub favorites and specializing in seafood. Open for lunch and dinner daily with live music on Fridays and Saturdays. A new liquor store is also open next to the pub. Located near the public wharf at the corner of Joan Avenue and Queen Street. osbornebaypub.com

©Kevin Oke

Chemainus

Made famous for its city-wide outdoor murals and sculptures, the quaint town of Chemainus revitalized itself in the wake of declining natural resource based industries. Today, the seaside town of Chemainus is a very popular tourist stop for its unique murals depicting early life in the area, charming shops and eateries, and its waterfront views backed by mountains. Chemainus is also home to a BC Ferry terminal with ferry service to and from Thetis and Penelakut Islands.

Chemainus is located roughly 7 miles southeast of Ladysmith on Vancouver Island. The port town is found within Chemainus Bay which is entered between the narrow peninsula of land holding Bare Point to the east and Hospital Point to the west. At the head of the bay lies a mill with extensive booming grounds south-southwest of Bare Point within the bay.

Approaching from the northwest be cautious of the shallow and rocky area lying approximately 0.5 miles northwest of Hospital Point. Approaching the entrance to Chemainus Bay, be aware of Hospital and Bird Rocks. Hospital Rock is located roughly 0.1 miles northeast of Hospital Point with 10 feet of water covering it. Hospital Rock is marked by the lighted buoy "U30." Bird Rock

lies approximately 0.2 miles north of Hospital Point and is connected to shore by drying flats. Bird Rock is marked by a daybeacon.

The extensive booming areas at the head of Chemainus Bay prevent anchoring within the bay. An exposed anchorage is available near Kinsmen Beach Park and public boat launch. Most who visit Chemainus use the public docks found immediately south of the BC Ferry terminal.

The Municipality of North Cowichan operates the public wharf in Chemainus. The newer remodel of the

Chemainus to:		
Bedwell Harbour (South Pender Island)	29 nm
Clam Bay (Thetis Island)	9 nm
Ladysmith	6 nm
Montague Harbour (Galiano Island)	15 nm
Nanaimo	19 nm
Pirates Cove (De Courcy Island)	11 nm
Princess Bay (Portland Island)	23 nm
Roche Harbor (USA)	33 nm
Sidney	24 nm
Tod Inlet	26 nm
Victoria	46 nm
Wallace Island	8 nm

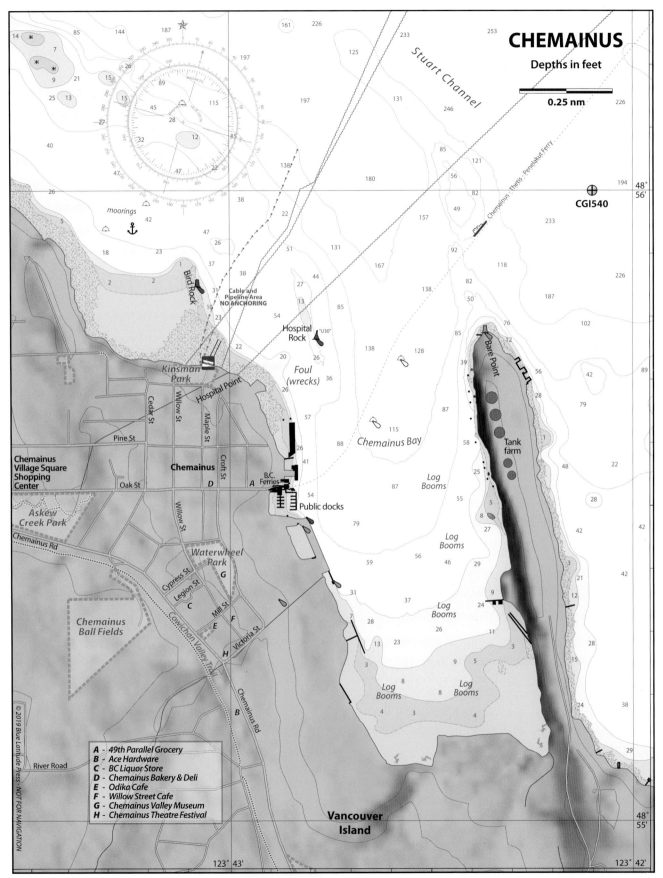

CHEMAINUS

Depths in feet

0.25 nm

Stuart Channel

Chemainus - Thetis - Penelakut Ferry

CGI540

Bird Rock

Cable and Pipeline Area
NO ANCHORING

moorings

Hospital Rock

"U30"

Kinsman Park

Hospital Point

Foul (wrecks)

Cedar St

Willow St

Maple St

Pine St

Chemainus
Village Square
Shopping
Center

Oak St

Croft St

Chemainus

D

A

B.C. Ferries

Public docks

Chemainus Bay

Bare Point

Tank farm

Log Booms

Log Booms

Log Booms

Askew Creek Park

Chemainus Rd

Willow St

Waterwheel Park

G

Cypress St

Legion St

C

Mill St

F

E

Chemainus Ball Fields

Cowichan Valley Trail

H

Victoria St

Chemainus Rd

B

River Road

A - 49th Parallel Grocery
B - Ace Hardware
C - BC Liquor Store
D - Chemainus Bakery & Deli
E - Odika Cafe
F - Willow Street Cafe
G - Chemainus Valley Museum
H - Chemainus Theatre Festival

Log Booms

Log Booms

Vancouver Island

48° 56'

48° 55'

© 2019 Blue Latitude Press - NOT FOR NAVIGATION

123° 43'

123° 42'

CGI540 - 48° 56.000'N 123° 42.100'W

docks provides both individual slips as well as a 170 foot side tie dock able to accommodate larger vessels. Each slip provides access to water and power (30 and 50 amp) hookups. Restrooms and showers are also available. The wharf does accept reservations, which are recommended during the summer months. Contact the harbormaster via VHF channel 66A, by phone (250) 246-4655, or email harmen.chemainus.munimarina@gmail.com.

Sights to See

In town, Chemainus is a delight to tour, taking in the artistry of the charming port town. In the early 1980's, the struggling town began a downtown revitalization project in hopes of driving tourism to Chemainus. Part of that project included the Chemainus Festival of Murals which began with just four outdoor murals painted on the sides of buildings. Today, the town now boasts 44 historical murals, 11 sculptures, five community mural projects, and an Emily Carr series dedicated to the legendary Canadian artist. To tour these wonderful works of art, the Chemainus Festival of Murals Society has put together walking guides as well as descriptions of all the murals and sculptures. Visit their website at: muraltown.com, for the guides and further information.

While walking around town, be sure to stop by the Chemainus Valley Museum to venture back in time and learn the history of Chemainus. The museum is located in the beautiful Water Wheel Park at the corner of Alder and Croft Streets. At the park visitors will find a replica water wheel, similar to those once used to power lumber mills. Water Wheel Park is also home to a stage which hosts outdoor music concerts throughout July and August each Tuesday evening.

For those who enjoy the theater, there is no better place to catch an amazing performance than at the stately Chemainus Theatre Festival. The Festival attracts talented actors, directors, musicians and designers from across North America to put on year-round, professional performances. The beautiful building is located at the corner of Victoria Street and Chemainus Road, within easy walking distance of the public wharf. For a current listing of their upcoming performances, check their website at: chemainustheatrefestival.ca.

Provisioning

49th Parallel Grocery

A local island chain grocery offering produce, dairy, meats, bakery items, and all the staples. In store deli and cafe as well. Open daily on Oak Street near the public wharf, and a new larger store in the Chemainus Village Square shopping center on Oak Street.

Kin Beach Park

Public Wharf

Ace Hardware

An international chain hardware store with a variety products including hardware, plumbing, electrical, and automotive. Located at 9630 Chemainus Road. www.ace-canada.ca

BC Liquor Store

BC Liquor Stores offer a great selection of beers, wines and spirits. Located on Legion Street next to the library.

Restaurants

Chemainus Bakery & Deli

For lovers of small town bakeries, this is your spot. The bakery offers a nice selection of fresh baked delights including sweet and savory pastries, breads, and cookies. Located at 2871 Oak Street.

Odika Cafe

The Odika Cafe is a local favorite using local ingredients in its eclectic and globally inspired menu. Open for dinner Tuesday through Saturday. Located at 2976 Mill Street. www.odikacafe.com

Sawmill Taphouse and Grill

The Sawmill Taphouse specializes in Pacific Northwest craft beers and wood fired pizzas. Open daily for lunch and dinner. Located at 3055 Oak Street, a half mile walk from the marina in the shopping center. www.sawmilltaphouse.com

Willow Street Cafe

Known for their freshly baked scones and beautiful salads. Open for breakfast and lunch with indoor and patio seating. Located at 9749 Willow Street. www.willowstreetcafe.com

©Kevin Oke

Ladysmith

Wonderful and welcoming Ladysmith is definitely a stop not to miss. Set within a deep inlet and surrounded by thick, forested mountains, Ladysmith not only offers beauty, but a wealth of fun activities. Enjoy live music and walks on the beach at the amazing Transfer Beach Park, dine at one of the many inviting restaurants in town, and soak up the area's history at the Heritage Centre and Ladysmith Museum. Along with ample activities and small town charm, Ladysmith also offers full service marinas, protected anchoring options, provisioning shops and easy access to Vancouver Island's main highway, Highway 1.

The town of Ladysmith lies on the southwestern shore of Ladysmith Harbour on Vancouver Island. By land, Ladysmith is roughly 13 miles south of Nanaimo and 6 miles north of Chemainus. The harbor is entered between Boulder Point to the south and Sharpe Point to the north.

When approaching Ladysmith Harbour from the south, be aware that Boulder Point has a large covered rock lying east of the point. Davis Lagoon lies 0.8 miles northwest of Boulder Point and has shallow waters extending out from the lagoon. 1.3 miles northwest of Davis Lagoon is

Halland Bank. This bank has forms a large drying mud flat and should be given ample room when passing.

Approaching from the north, be sure to give Coffin Island a wide berth to avoid the detached rock, Nares Rock, lying off its eastern side. Coffin Island is marked by a navigation light from a tower on the island. If entering Evening Cove, be aware of Collins Shoal lying near the middle of cove.

Ladysmith to:		
Bedwell Harbour *(South Pender Island)*		34 nm
Ganges Harbour *(Salt Spring Island)*		25 nm
Montague Harbour *(Galiano Island)*		20 nm
Nanaimo		18 nm
Pirates Cove *(De Courcy Island)*		10 nm
Princess Bay *(Portland Island)*		28 nm
Roche Harbor *(USA)*		38 nm
Sidney		30 nm
Silva Bay *(Gabriola Island)*		15 nm
Telegraph Harbour *(Thetis Island)*		8 nm
Tod Inlet		31 nm
Victoria		51 nm

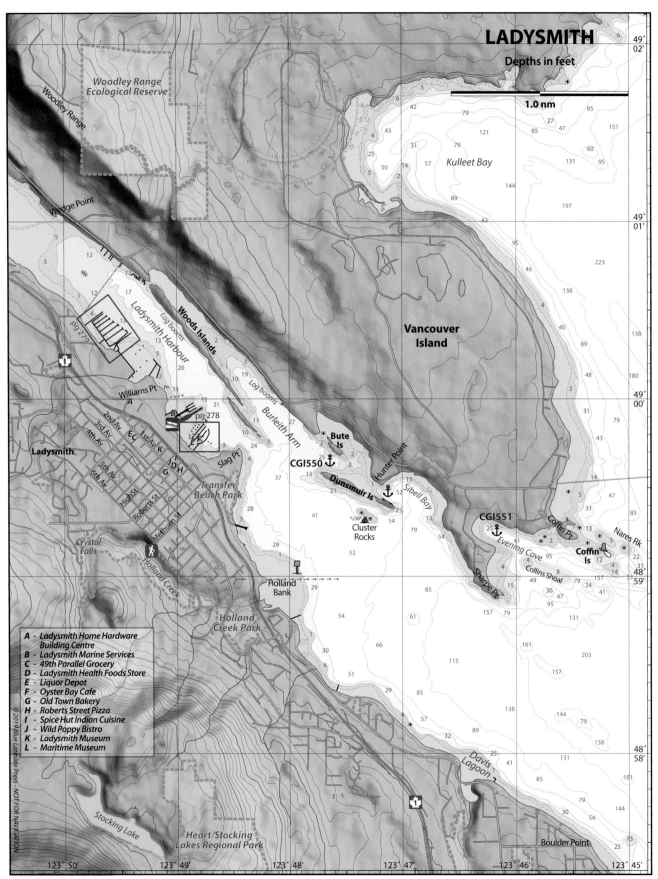

LADYSMITH

Depths in feet

1.0 nm

Woodley Range
Ecological Reserve

Woodley Range

Wedge Point

Kulleet Bay

Ladysmith Harbour

Woods Islands

Williams Pt

Log booms

Burleith Arm

**Vancouver
Island**

Hunter Point

**Bute
Is**

CGI550

Dunsmuir Is

Sibell Bay

"U36"

**Cluster
Rocks**

CGI551

Coffin Pt

Nares Rk

**Coffin
Is**

2nd Av

3rd Av

EC

4th Av

Ladysmith

1st Av

K

5th Av

6th Av

High St

D H

G

Roberts St

Methuen St

**Transfer
Beach Park**

Slag Pt

Sharpe Pa

Evening Cove

Collins Shoal

**Crystal
Falls**

Holland Creek

Holland
Bank

**Holland
Creek Park**

Davis
Lagoon

A - Ladysmith Home Hardware
    Building Centre
B - Ladysmith Marine Services
C - 49th Parallel Grocery
D - Ladysmith Health Foods Store
E - Liquor Depot
F - Oyster Bay Cafe
G - Old Town Bakery
H - Roberts Street Pizza
I - Spice Hut Indian Cuisine
J - Wild Poppy Bistro
K - Ladysmith Museum
L - Maritime Museum

Stocking Lake

**Heart/Stocking
Lakes Regional Park**

Boulder Point

123° 50'   123° 49'   123° 48'   123° 47'   123° 46'   123° 45'

49°
02'

49°
01'

49°
00'

48°
59'

48°
58'

CGI550 - 48° 59.655'N 123° 47.655'W   **CGI551 - 48° 59.260'N 123° 46.185'W**

Anchorage off Dunsmuir Islands

Keep in mind that Ladysmith Harbour is also a working port with log booms under tow and stationary within the harbor. Booming grounds can be found in Burleith Arm, along the west side of Woods Islands, and north and south of Williams Point. Be sure to give tugs under tow ample berth as they are severely limited in their maneuverability.

Anchorage can be taken within the harbor at Evening Cove, Sibell Bay, and off the northeast tip of Dunsmuir Islands. If anchoring off Dunsmuir Islands, be cautious of the shallow water and drying flats lying between the islands and Hunter Point, as well as the area southeast and north of Bute Island. Anchor in 4 fathoms over a mud bottom off Dunsmuir Islands. Both Evening Cove and Sibell Bay afford protection from northerly winds, however they are open to the south. The anchorage off Dunsmuir Islands provides nearly all round protection.

For those continuing on to the marinas, pass between Slag Point to the south and the southern tip of Woods Islands. The Ladysmith Community Marina is located on the western shore just northwest of Slag Point. The Ladysmith public wharf is next to the Community Marina, separated by a rock breakwater. Further northwest, past the Western Forest Products plant is the Ladysmith Marina

Ladysmith Community Marina

Log boom

Transfer Beach Park

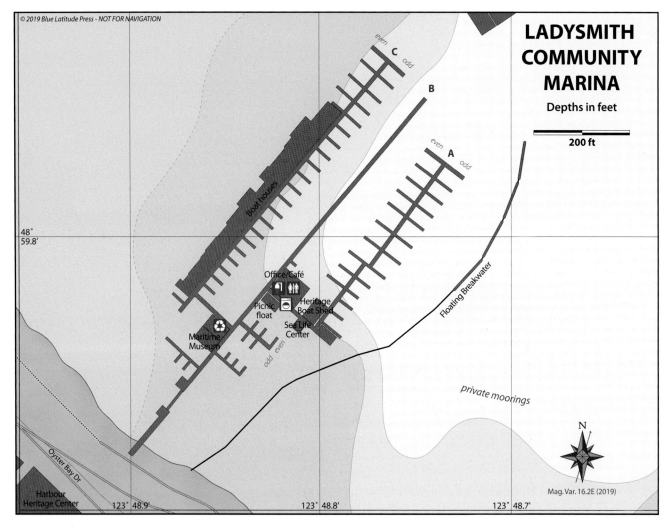

© 2019 Blue Latitude Press - NOT FOR NAVIGATION

LADYSMITH COMMUNITY MARINA

Depths in feet

200 ft

Mag. Var. 16.2E (2019)

Ladysmith Community Marina

The Ladysmith Community Marina is a favorite for its friendly staff and going the extra mile to make sure your stay is as pleasant and comfortable as possible. The marina is located near the heart of downtown and next to the impressive Transfer Beach Park. The marina offers over 1,100 feet of visitor moorage as well as additional overflow space with water and 30 amp power hookups. The newer floating Welcome Centre houses the marina office, bathrooms, showers, laundry facilities, free wifi, meeting room (available for rent), the Oyster Bay Cafe, and even a fireside lounge with large TV. A large float with picnic tables, awnings and a barbecue are perfect for meeting fellow boaters or hosting a rendezvous. While at the marina, be sure to explore the Maritime Museum, Harbour Heritage Centre, and the restored heritage vessels. For kids, view the underwater world at the Sea Life Centre.

Ladysmith Community Marina
Monitors VHF channel 66A
610 Oyster Bay Drive
Ladysmith, BC
(250) 245-1146
info@lmsmarina.ca
www.lmsmarina.ca

Welcome Centre and Cafe

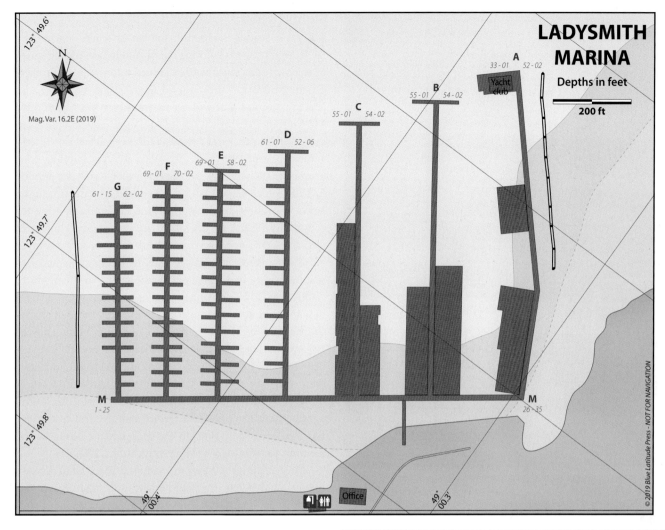

LADYSMITH MARINA

Depths in feet

200 ft

Mag. Var. 16.2E (2019)

© 2019 Blue Latitude Press - NOT FOR NAVIGATION

Ladysmith Marina

Ladysmith Marina is part of the Oak Bay Marine Group, which also operates North Saanich Marina, Oak Bay Marina and Pedder Bay Marina. Ladysmith Marina can accommodate boats over 100 feet in length. Marina services include bathrooms, showers, parking, and wifi at the marina office. Power (30 and 50 amp) and water hookups are available for each slip.

Ladysmith Marina
Monitors VHF channel 66A
901 Gladden Road
Ladysmith , BC, V9G 1K4
(250) 245-4521
ladysmithmarina@obmg.com
ladysmithmarina.com

©Kevin Oke

Ladysmith Community Marina

Heritage Centre

Old Town Bakery

Sights to See

When visiting Ladysmith for the first time, one of the highlights to exploring the town is to take the self-guided walking tour. The town has created informative pamphlets detailing historical sites around town. Walk through Ladysmith's preserved past with items on display like Locomotive #11 built in 1923 which hauled logs from Nanaimo Lakes to Ladysmith's mills, or the scales used to weigh rail cars loaded with coal during the town's early days as a coal shipping port. View heritage buildings like the Anglican Church dating back to 1900 which sits on land donated by Ladysmith's founder James Dunsmuir, or the Agricultural Hall built in 1922 for community social events where singers Buddy Holly and Jerry Lee Lewis once headlined. Each stop provides a glimpse into Ladysmith's early years of mining, forestry, rail, and marine industries. Download the pamphlets at: www.ladysmith.ca/discover-ladysmith/history-heritage.

To complete the historical journey through Ladysmith's past, be sure to visit the Ladysmith Museum (721 1st Avenue) and the Ladysmith Maritime Society's, Maritime Museum (Ladysmith Community Marina) and Harbour Heritage Center. The Ladysmith Museum features artifacts from 1900 to the present, illustrating Ladysmith's development through industry, agriculture, and education. For further information on the museum including hours, see their website at: www.ladysmithhistoricalsociety.ca.

At the Maritime Museum, visitors are treated to displays of local maritime history, shipwright tools, marine communication, a "Captain's Cabin" display, and a restored skiff from the Royal Navy base in Esquimalt dating back to 1898. Nearby is the Bill Adair Heritage Boathouse that is home to *Saravan*, a local 1938 restored tug boat, and *C.A. Kirkegaard,* a restored crew boat later turned ferry. A short walk up from the marina is the Harbour Heritage Centre housed in the restored 1943 Comox Logging and Railway Company's Machine Shop. The Centre provides a unique waterfront experience through displays, legends, stories, slideshows and activities depicting the area's fishing, logging, coal, and oyster history. For further information regarding the Ladysmith Maritime Society's displays, see their website at: www.lms-marina.ca/welcome/museums-heritage-boats.

After a day of history, be sure to treat yourself to one of the nicest waterfront parks of the area. The Transfer Beach Park is the perfect place for families and pets to enjoy the long, warm days of summer at a picturesque beachside park. During the first half of the 1900's, the Transfer Wharf dominated this area where fully loaded rail cars could be loaded and off loaded from a railway car barge. Today, sand and gravel beaches, fields of green grass, and tall shade trees have replaced the old industrial wharf. For children, the park offers an amazing playground and splash water park. For pet owners an off leash area is provided to let your furry pal stretch their legs. The park also offers food truck concessions, a basketball court, a sand volleyball court, horseshoe pits, a picnic shelter and kayak rentals. During the summer months, the park is also home to the "Concerts in the Park" series at its waterside amphitheater. Each week from July through August, listen to live music with the incredible views of Stuart Channel and the Gulf Islands (donations are greatly appreciated).

Roberts Street Pizza

Purple Martins

Purple Martins are the largest swallow in North America and get their name from the dark purple color of the mature males. Historically, the birds chose nest sites in the cavities of trees or old wood-pecker holes. They feed primarily on flying insects with dragonflies a preferred meal while nesting. Each year the Martins make the long trek to the warm weather of South America, with large popula-tions found around the Amazon Basin in Brazil.

Over the recent decades, populations of Purple Mar-tins, especially in the west, has been declining. By the mid 1900's, the birds had disappeared from BC's lower mainland and by 1985 only 5 breeding pairs remained on Vancouver Island's southeast coast. Reasons for this decline are not well known, but believed to result from competition of nesting sites. To combat the decline, in 1985 a volunteer program was launched to install nesting boxes on pilings at Cowichan Bay. By the end of the 2016 season, the BC Purple Martin Stewardship and Recovery Pro-gram reported 1200 breeding pairs had successfully raised 2900 young along the Strait of Georgia, the Fraser River Valley, and southern Vancouver Island. Ladysmith is home to the largest recovery colony of the Purple Martins in BC. During the summer months be sure to watch and listen for these beauti-ful and acrobatic birds.

Grocery

Waterfront Art Gallery and Harbour Heritage Centre

Old rail tracks

Ore hand cart

For those looking for a little exercise and to stretch your boat-bound legs, take a hike through the forest on the well-groomed Holland Creek Trail. The 4 mile loop trail can be picked up at the end of Methuen Street (0.9 miles from the Ladysmith Community Marina), and follows both sides of the creek. Along the way the trail takes you past Crystal Falls and the Colliery Dams. During the fall months spawning salmon can be spotted in the creek. The Holland Creek Trail allows well-behaved, off leash dogs on the trail. For further information on trails visit: www.ladysmith.ca/parks-recreation-culture/trails.

Marine Chandleries and Services

Ladysmith Home Hardware Building Centre
Offering a selection of tools, hardware, plumbing, electrical and lumber supplies. Located at 1010 Ludlow Road, northeast of Fisherman's Wharf. (250) 245-3441

Ladysmith Marine Services
Located at Fisherman's Wharf and next to Ladysmith Community Marina, Ladysmith Marine Services is a full service marine repair, maintenance and haulout yard. ladysmith-marineservices.com, (250) 714-6206

Provisioning

49th Parallel Grocery
A large local chain style grocery offering fresh produce, meats, bakery items, dairy and all the staples. Located on the corner of 1st Avenue and Symonds Street.

Ladysmith Health Foods Store
Offers a wide range of products, including vegan and gluten free foods, supplements, a bulk food section and herbal teas. Located 1st Avenue near High Street.

Liquor Barn
Located next to 49th Parallel Grocery. Selling beer, wine and spirits.

Restaurants

Oyster Bay Cafe
Located within the Welcome Centre float at Ladysmith Community Marina, the cafe serves homemade breakfast and lunch meals overlooking the marina. Open daily in the summer months.

Old Town Bakery
A popular local haunt famous for their fresh baked cinnamon buns. Other bakery items include breads, cakes, pies, pastries, sausage rolls and Cornish pasties. Located on 1st Avenue near Gatacre Street.

Roberts Street Pizza
If you're in the mood for pizza Roberts Street Pizza is the local favorite. It's bright yellow exterior is easy to spot on Roberts Street.

Spice Hut Indian Cuisine
Popular East Indian food restaurant with delicious curries, along with vegetarian, vegan and gluten-free options. Located across Highway 1 from the Ladysmith Community Marina.

Wild Poppy Bistro
Open for breakfast and lunch, this bistro and bakery serves healthy, gluten-free, homemade meals. Menu items change daily. Located on the corner of 1st Avenue and High Street.

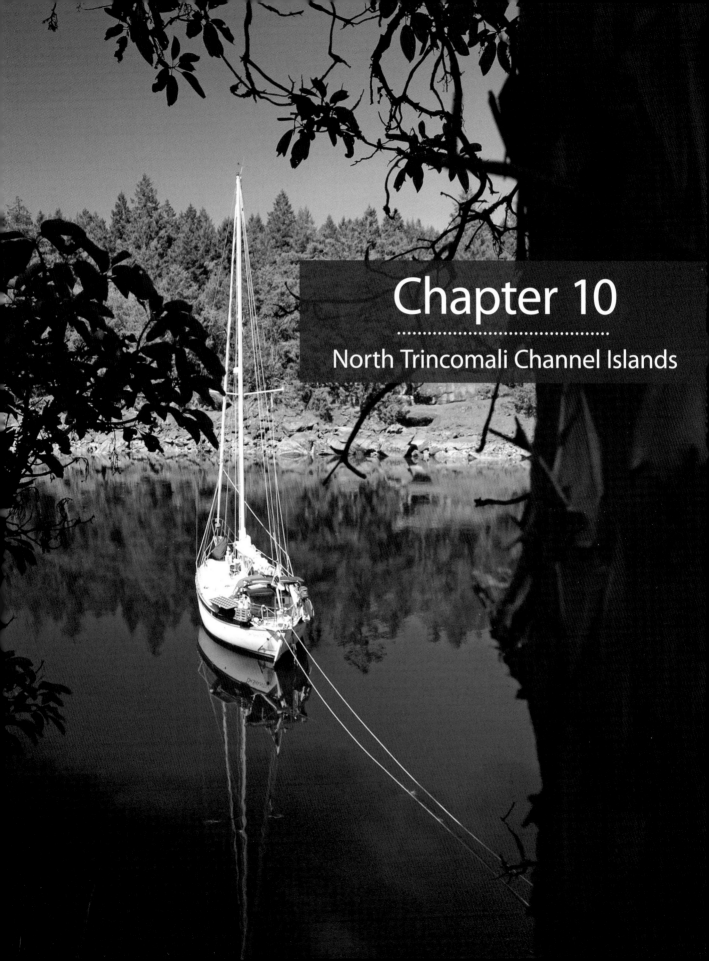

Chapter 10

North Trincomali Channel Islands

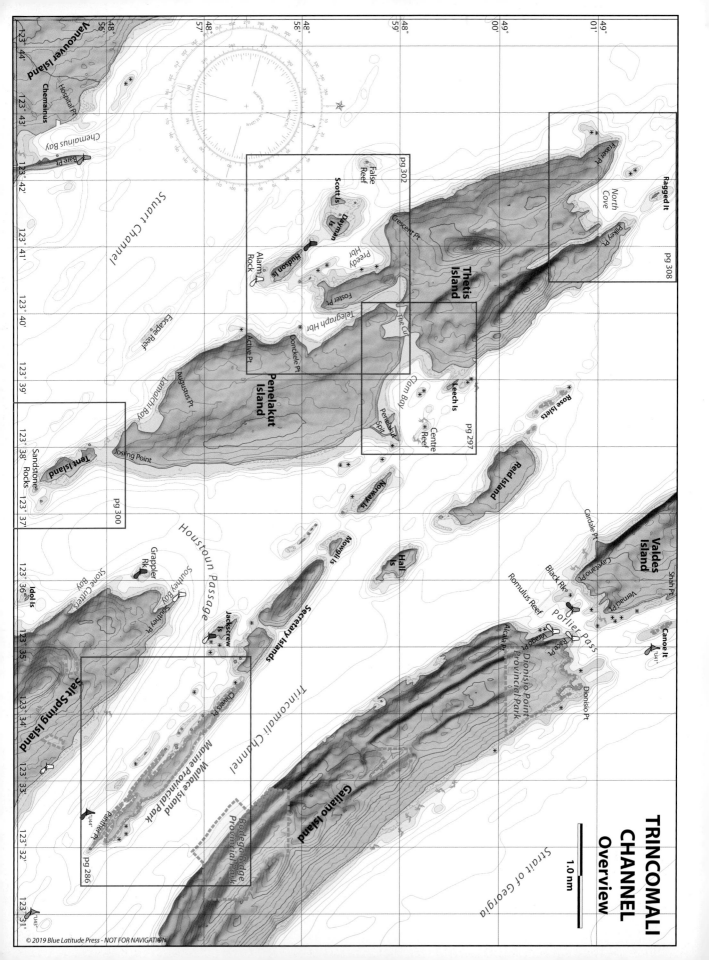

TRINCOMALI CHANNEL Overview

1.0 nm

Strait of Georgia

Vancouver Island

Chemainus

Hospital Pt

Chemainus Bay

Bare Pt

Stuart Channel

Escape Reef

Lamalchi Bay

Augustus Pt

Penelakut Island

Active Pt

Pondelele Pt

Scott Is

Dayman Is

False Reef

Hudson Is

Alarm Rock

Preedy Hbr

Foster Pt

Telegraph Hbr

pg 302

Crescent Pt

Thetis Island

The Cut

Clam Bay

Leech Is

Penelakut Spit

Centre Reef

pg 297

Ragged It

North Cove

Fraser Pt

Pilkey Pt

pg 308

Rose Islets

Reid Island

Josling Point

Sandstone Rocks

Tent Island

pg 300

Houstoun Passage

Grappler Rk

Southey Bay

Southey Pt

Stone Cutters Bay

Idol Is

Jackscrew Is

Secretary Islands

Norway Is

Mowgli Is

Hall Is

Trincomali Channel

Chivers Pt

Panther Pt

pg 286

Salt Spring Island

Wallace Island Marine Provincial Park

Bodega Ridge Provincial Park

Galiano Island

Cardale Pt

Black Rk

Romulus Reef

Porlier Pass

Cayetano Pt

Virago Rk

Race Pt

Alcala Pt

Dionisio Point Provincial Park

Dionisio Pt

Valdes Island

Shah Pt

Vernaci Pt

Canoe It

041°

044°

045°

©Kevin Oke

Wallace Island

Wallace Island Marine Provincial Park includes over 200 beautiful acres of forest land, beaches, and unique anchorages. This enticing island has become a popular stop on most itineraries through the islands, offering visitors an abundance of activities including hiking, kayaking, swimming, camping, and wildlife viewing. Two protected coves are notched into the island, providing intimate anchorages as well as convenient dock space.

This wonderful marine park was established in 1990, and includes nearly the entire island. Only two properties remain on the island in private ownership. Anchorages at both Princess Bay and Conover Cove offer secure stern tie rings and dinghy docks, with Conover Cove also providing dock space for boats under 36 feet in length. Nearly 3.5 miles of trails allow visitors to explore the full length and each of the beaches on the island. Park amenities also include campsites, picnic tables, pit toilets, and an eclectic covered shelter (campfires are not permitted).

Wallace Island takes its name after Rear-Admiral Wallace Houstoun, captain of the *HMS Trincomalee* from 1852 to 1857. In 1889, Scotsman and prospector Jeremiah Chivers was granted 145 acres of land on Wallace Island from the Crown. Over the years he built two houses (one burned down in a fire) and planted a small fruit orchard which remains today. Chivers lived on the island until his death in 1927. He is buried at Saint Mark's Anglican Church cemetery on Salt Spring Island.

In 1936, the island was purchased by a California boy's school and was turned into a summer camp, where David Conover worked as a camp counselor. Conover was in the Army during World War II, and in 1945 was sent by Ronald Reagan to take publicity shots of women working at the Radioplane munitions factory. One of the women he photographed was Norma Jean Dougherty, known today as Marilyn Monroe, and jump started her career into modeling and eventually her iconic movie roles.

After the war, Conover and his wife Jeanne purchased Wallace Island and left Los Angeles. Originally living in Chiver's cabin, the Conovers' transformed the island into a resort destination, building rental cabins, a recreation hall, and a small store. A few of these buildings still stand and are historical sights around Conover Cove. Conover was also an author and wrote a handful of books including *Once Upon an Island* and *One Man's Island*, which details his time on Wallace Island.

In 1960, the majority of the island was sold to a group from Seattle. This group owned the island until it was purchased by the provincial government in 1990.

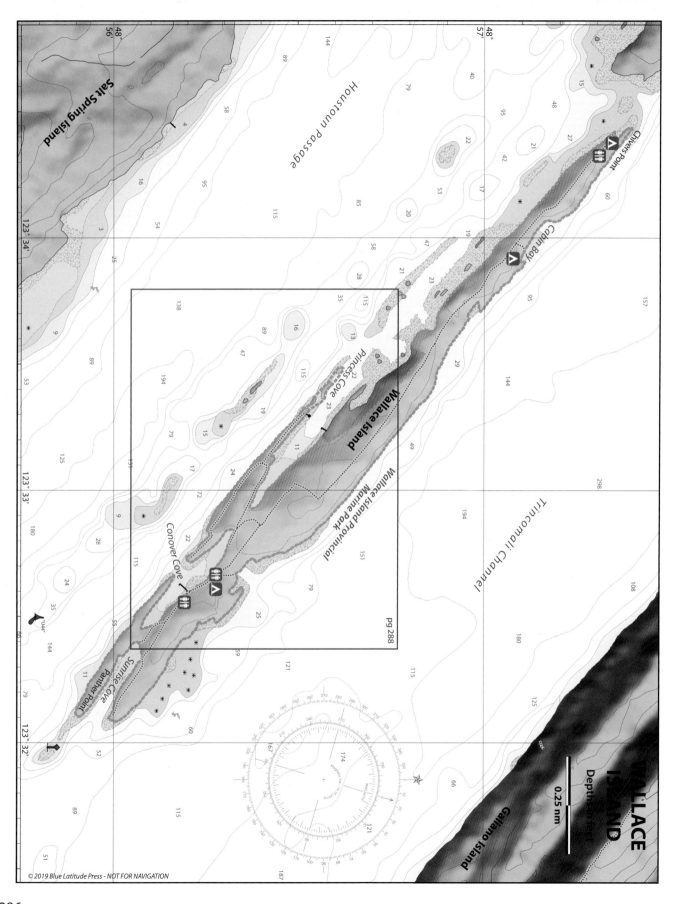

Salt Spring Island

Houstoun Passage

Chivers Point

Cabin Bay

Wallace Island

Wallace Island Provincial
Marine Park

Princess Cove

Conover Cove

Sunrise Cove

Panther Point

"1044"

Trincomali Channel

pg 288

Galliano Island

WALLACE ISLAND

Depth in feet

0.25 nm

©Kevin Oke

Conover Cove

Conover Cove is a small bight found near the south end of Wallace Island. This popular, yet shallow cove offers room for anchoring with stern lines to shore, as well as a small park dock for moorage of boats under 36 feet in length. The cove takes its name from a family who ran a successful summer resort on the island. Buildings and clearings still remain around the cove from the time of the resort and provide an interesting look at the island's history.

Conover Cove is located on Wallace Island which lies between the north end of Salt Spring Island and Galiano Island. The east side of Wallace Island lies along Trincomali Channel, while the west side lies along Houstoun Passage. Conover Cove is located on the southwest end of Wallace Island with entrance to the cove taken via Houstoun Passage.

Approaching from the south, be aware of rock hazards in Trincomali Channel including Governor Rock, Victoria Shoal and Victoria Rock, and Walker Rock. These rocks are marked by lighted buoys and lie between 1 to 2 miles southeast of Panther Point on Wallace Island. Approaching the entrance to the cove in Houstoun Passage, a chain of reefs and islets are found off the southwestern shore of

Wallace Island. The southern end of this chain is marked by lighted buoy "U44." Passage can be taken between this chain of reefs and Wallace Island.

From the north, the channel between Mowgli Island and Norway Island connects Trincomali Channel to Houstoun Passage. When approaching from the north, be cautious of a string of reefs and islets lying 0.2 miles south of Mowgli Island. The northern end of the reefs and islets

Conover Cove to:		
	Bedwell Harbour (South Pender Island)	18 nm
	Clam Bay (Thetis Island)	6 nm
	Ganges Harbour (Salt Spring Island)	11 nm
	Ladysmith	14 nm
	Montague Harbour (Galiano Island)	7 nm
	Nanaimo	22 nm
	Pirates Cove (De Courcy Island)	13 nm
	Princess Bay (Portland Island)	16 nm
	Roche Harbor (USA)	25 nm
	Sidney	21 nm
	Tod Inlet	27 nm
	Victoria	42 nm

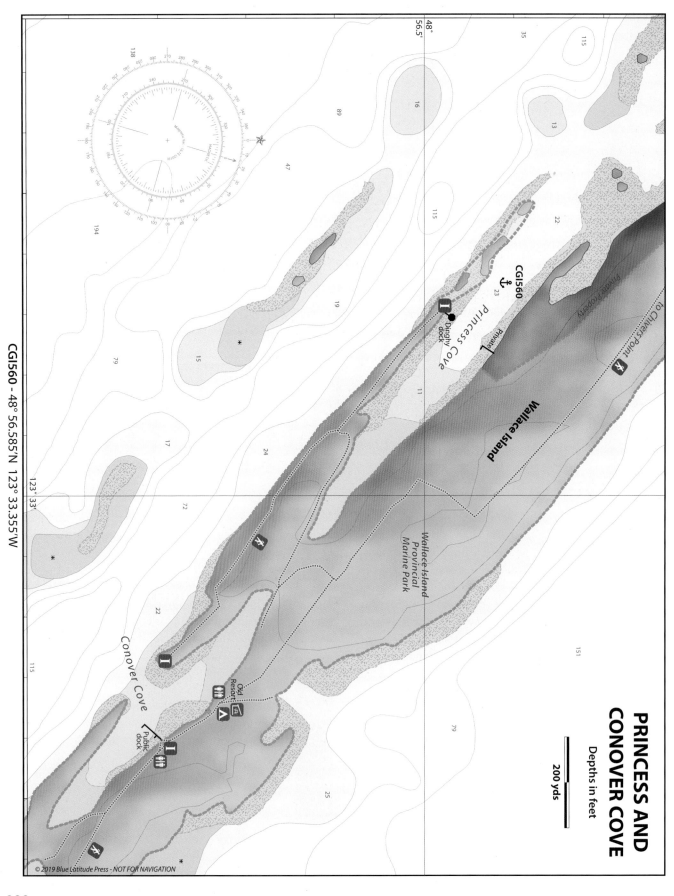

PRINCESS AND CONOVER COVE

Depths in feet

200 yds

CGI560 - 48° 56.585'N 123° 33.355'W

CGI560

Princess Cove

Dinghy dock

Private

Wallace Island

Wallace Island Provincial Marine Park

to Chivers Point

Private Property

Conover Cove

Old Resort

Public dock

© 2019 Blue Latitude Press - NOT FOR NAVIGATION

is marked by a daybeacon and the southern end is marked by cardinal buoy "UV." Due to detached rocks and shallow water off the east side of Jackscrew Island, it is recommended to pass west and south of the island.

Approaching the western shore of Wallace Island, careful attention should be paid to the chart. A number of reefs are found at and around the entrance to Conover Cove so be sure to keep a steady watch and approach cautiously.

The entrance to Conover cove is narrow and shallow with extending reefs off the north and south entrance points. This cove is best suited for shallower draft boats. At zero tide, the navigable portion of the cove is roughly 1 fathom with the north and south ends of the cove drying mud flats. Be sure to check the tide tables prior to entering to make sure you have ample depth once tied to the dock or anchored throughout your stay.

During the busier summer months, most anchored boats will take a stern line to shore and tie to one of the park's rings or a nearby tree. This enables many boats to use an otherwise tight anchorage. As the cove can be crowded, it is best to have your stern line and dinghy prepared ahead of time to enable you to quickly get a line to shore, and prevent your boat from swinging into your neighbor once anchored. Conover Cove affords good protection from most weather.

For trips to shore, dinghies can be landed at the park dock. Various park signs are found around the cove including a trail map and signs relating the history of the resort. One of the most interesting of the buildings is the old store/lounge. Today the building showcases the creative artwork of years of visitors to the island both inside and out. From every surface, planks and bits of driftwood lovingly inscribed with names and dates drape the walls and ceiling.

For a bit of exercise, the island provides over 3 miles of well maintained and well marked walking paths. These trails lead to nearly every point on the island as well as the various campsites found at Conover Cove, Chivers Point, and Cabin Bay. The now gnarled fruit trees from Jeremiah Chivers' orchard can be seen on the trail around Cabin Bay. An old rusting truck from the days of the resort can be found along the grassy isthmus trail between Princess Cove and Conover Cove. Along your travels, be sure to keep an eye out for various island residents including black-tailed deer, river otters, mink, bald eagles, and harbour seals. Various points around the island also offer a look at the unique folded rock formations and lace-like rock erosion along the beaches.

Princess Cove

During the calm and warm months of summer, this surprisingly small, sliver of a cove becomes one of the more popular anchorages in the Gulf Islands. Thanks to convenient anchored chains hanging down the hillside, numerous boats are able to easily stern tie to shore. Princess Cove, along with its neighboring anchorage of Conover Cove, are part of the Wallace Island Marine Provincial Park. This 220 acre park provides sheltered anchorage for boats, campsites, and miles of well-maintained walking trails.

Princess Cove is located on Wallace Island, which lies between the northern ends of Salt Spring and Galiano Islands. The cove is found on the western side of Wallace Island, along Houstoun Passage. Approaching from the south, be aware of a few rock hazards within Trincomali Channel including Governor Rock, Victoria Shoal and Victoria Rock, and Walker Rock. These rocks are marked by lighted buoys and lie between 1 to 2 miles southeast of Panther Point on Wallace Island. Approaching the southern entrance to the cove within Houstoun Passage, a chain

of reefs and islets are found off the southwestern shore of Wallace Island. The southern end of this chain is marked by lighted buoy "U44." Passage can be taken between this chain of reefs and Wallace Island.

From the north, the channel between Mowgli Island and Norway Island connects Trincomali Channel to

Princess Cove to:		
	Bedwell Harbour *(South Pender Island)*	18 nm
	Ganges Harbour *(Salt Spring Harbour)*	12 nm
	Ladysmith	14 nm
	Montague Harbour *(Galiano Island)*	8 nm
	Nanaimo	22 nm
	Pirates Cove *(De Courcy Island)*	13 nm
	Princess Bay *(Portland Island)*	14 nm
	Roche Harbor *(USA)*	26 nm
	Sidney	22 nm
	Telegraph Harbour *(Thetis Island)*	8 nm
	Tod Inlet	28 nm
	Victoria	43 nm

Houstoun Passage. When approaching from the north, be cautious of a string of reefs and islets lying 0.2 miles south of Mowgli Island. The northern end of the reefs and islets is marked by a daybeacon and the southern end is marked by cardinal buoy "UV." Due to detached rocks and shallow water off the east side of Jackscrew Island, it is recommended to pass west and south of the island.

Approaching the entrance to Princess Cove, careful attention should be paid to the chart. A number of reefs are found at and around the entrance so be sure to keep a steady watch and approach cautiously.

Once inside the cove, anchorage can be taken in 3 to 4 fathoms over a mud bottom. During the busier summer months, most anchored boats will take a stern line to the western shore and tie to one of the many anchored chains along the hillside. This enables many boats to use an otherwise tight anchorage. As the cove can be crowded, it is best to have your stern line and dinghy prepared ahead of time to enable you to quickly get a line to shore, and prevent your boat from swinging into your neighbor once anchored.

Princess Cove affords good protection from most weather except for wind and waves from the northwest. If you are stern tied and possibly on shorter scope due to the confines of the anchorage, your boat will be beam on to the area's predominate northwesterly or southeasterly winds. In stronger winds, it can be possible for stern tied boats that are beam on to the wind to drag anchor. This can create a domino effect through the anchorage as one boat drags into the next downwind neighboring boat. For this reason, Princess Cove is best suited for settled weather when the anchorage is crowded and boats are stern tied to shore.

For trips to shore, there is a convenient dinghy dock available on the western shore. To the east, across from the dinghy dock, is a private dock and a small parcel of privately held land that is not part of the park. For smaller boats and kayakers, the provincial park offers 18 campsites on the island, along with picnic tables and pit toilets. Potable water is not available on the island and campfires are not permitted.

The main activities at the island include hiking, paddling, swimming, and relaxing. Up the ramp from the dinghy dock is a trailhead and park kiosk sign with a map and information on Wallace Island. The trail heads southeast to the isthmus separating Princess Cove and Conover Cove. At the isthmus, the trail splits, with paths leading northwest to Chivers Point at the northern tip of the island, or southeast to Conover Cove and beyond towards Panther Point at the southern end of the island. The trails are well-groomed and well marked at the intersection points. Along with beautiful forests and beaches, sights on the trails include old fruit orchards, a vintage truck, and the old resort complex.

For paddlers, Wallace Island is a dream to circumnavigate. Reefs and islets lie off the shoreline, offering sunny rest stops for harbor seals and plenty of marine birds. A handful of protected little coves are found along the way, providing good opportunities to view the underwater world in clear water. Campsites are located at Chivers Point, Cabin Bay, and Conover Cove.

For those looking to leave their mark on the island, be sure to bring your carving tools or paint brushes. A remnant building from the resort located near Conover Cove has become something of a boater's shrine. Names and dates are scrawled on bits of flotsam and jetsam, lining every inch of the old building (see page 290).

Panther Point

Anchored chains for stern lines

©Kevin Oke

Thetis, Penelakut, and Tent Islands

Lying roughly midway between Vancouver Island and the barrier islands of Galiano and Valdes is the island group of Thetis, Penelakut, and Tent Islands. Ferry service from Chemainus to both Thetis and Penelakut Islands connects the communities to Vancouver Island. Good anchorages and full service marinas offer visitors a welcome stop on a tour through the Gulf Islands.

Thetis and Penelakut Islands are narrowly separated by a dredged channel known locally as The Cut. For use by dinghies and shoal draft boats, The Cut connects Clam Bay with the community and the two marinas found in Telegraph Harbour on Thetis Island. Services in the harbor include marinas, fuel docks, restaurants, small stores for grocery items, and a liquor store. For exercise off the boat, Thetis Island has a number of quiet country roads for strolling and stretching your legs.

Penelakut and Tent Islands belong to the Penelakut First Nation. Generally, Penelakut Island is not open to public visitation without prior invitation by the Penelakut Band Council. Tent Island, lying off the southern tip of Penelakut Island is a popular anchorage for local boaters during the calm months of summer. Day use of the beach and/or overnight use of the campsites on Tent Island require permission by the Penelakut First Nation and a per person/campsite fee (see page 299).

Thetis and the formerly named Kuper (Penelakut) Islands were named after Augustus Leopold Kuper who was captain of the *HMS Thetis*. In April 1863, the "Battle of Lamalcha" began at Penelakut Island when the Royal Navy's gunboat *HM Forward,* fired upon the island's village. Colonial officials believed men harbored in the village to be suspects in the murders of two European settlers. The villagers returned fire, causing the *Forward* to retreat, marking a short lived victory. Following the defeat, colonial government officials fearing an uprising, mounted one of the largest naval operations against First Nation's people in BC's history. Naval ships and hundreds of men spread across the Gulf Islands and Vancouver Island. In the end, many First Nations' possessions and property were destroyed or taken. Several people were arrested and forced to face unjust trials in Victoria, and ultimately were hung.

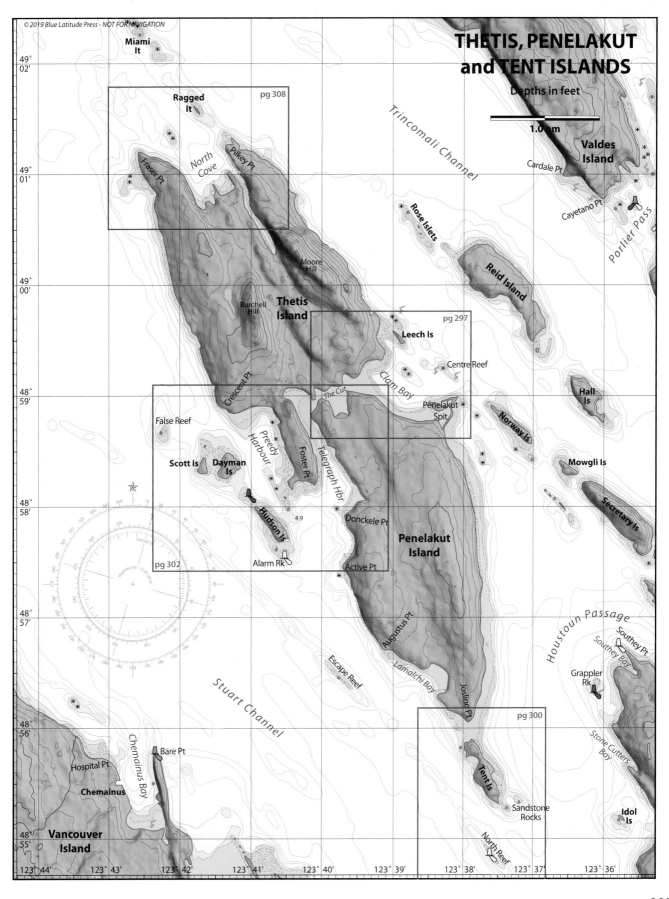

© 2019 Blue Latitude Press - NOT FOR NAVIGATION

**THETIS, PENELAKUT
and TENT ISLANDS**

Depths in feet

1.0 nm

Miami
It

Ragged
It   pg 308

Fraser Pt   North
Cove   Pilkey Pt

Trincomali Channel

Valdes
Island

Cardale Pt

Cayetano Pt

Porlier Pass

Rose Islets

Moore
Hill

Reid Island

Burchell
Hill   Thetis
Island

Leech Is   pg 297

Centre Reef

Crescent Pt   The Cut   Clam Bay

False Reef   Preedy
Harbour   Foster Pt

Penelakut
Spit

Hall
Is

Norway Is

48°
59'

Scott Is   Dayman
Is

Telegraph Hbr

Mowgli Is

Hudson Is   4.9

Donckele Pt

Penelakut
Island

Secretary Is

Alarm Rk   Active Pt

pg 302

Augustus Pt

Houstoun Passage

Southey Pt

Southey Bay

Escape Reef   Lamalchi Bay   Grappler
Rk

Stuart Channel   Josling Pt   pg 300

Stone Cutters
Bay

Chemainus Bay   Bare Pt

Hospital Pt   Tent Is

Chemainus   Sandstone
Rocks

Idol
Is

Vancouver
Island   North Reef

123° 44'   123° 43'   123° 42'   123° 41'   123° 40'   123° 39'   123° 38'   123° 37'   123° 36'

©Kevin Oke

Clam Bay

Clam Bay affords a beautiful anchorage able to accommodate numerous boats of all sizes, while offering protection from the area's predominate northwesterly and southeasterly winds. The anchorage is also an easy and prime location to wait for slack tides at Dodd Narrows and Porlier Pass. At the west end of the bay, a dredged channel for small boats between Thetis and Penelakut Islands allows easy access to the shoreside amenities at Telegraph Harbour.

Clam Bay lies between the eastern shores of Thetis and Penelakut Islands along the northern stretch of Trincomali Channel. The southern portion of the bay is formed by the low, sandy point known as Penelakut Spit on Penelakut Island. The northern portion of the bay is formed by Leech Island and reefs extending between Leech and Thetis Islands.

Approaches to Clam Bay can be made via Trincomali Channel or Houstoun Passage. A large number of islands,

©Kevin Oke

Clam Bay to:		
	Bedwell Harbour *(South Pender Island)*	24 nm
	Ganges Harbour *(Salt Spring Island)*	17 nm
	Ladysmith	10 nm
	Montague Harbour *(Galiano Island)*	12 nm
	Nanaimo	17 nm
	Pirates Cove *(De Courcy Island)*	8 nm
	Princess Bay *(Portland Island)*	22 nm
	Roche Harbor *(USA)*	30 nm
	Sidney	26 nm
	Victoria	47 nm
	Wallace Island	5 nm

©Kevin Oke

Telegraph Harbour

Charming Telegraph Harbour offers visitors two full service marinas in a unique, nearly landlocked setting. Formed by the shores of both Thetis and Penelakut Islands, Telegraph Harbour's main entrance lies off Stuart Channel. A second shoal-draft boat entrance is found off Trincomali Channel through the dredged waterway known as The Cut. Thetis Island provides a quiet setting to enjoy a waterfront meal at the Thetis Island Marina, a morning paddle through The Cut to Clam Bay, or a peaceful walk along the country roads of Thetis Island.

Telegraph Harbour is found at the northwest end of Penelakut Island and the southern end of Thetis Island. Entrance to the harbor is between Active Point to the east and Alarm Rock to the west with approaches made via Stuart Channel. Approaching from the south, be aware of North Reef lying roughly 0.45 miles southwest of Tent Island, and Escape Reef lying roughly 2 miles northwest of North Reef. Both reefs are long and narrow. North Reef is marked by a navigation light and Escape Reef is marked by a daybeacon. Give both Active Point and Donckele Point on Penelakut Island ample room when rounding to avoid shallow water and detached rocks lying off the points.

Approaching from the north, passage can be taken either west of Dayman and Hudson Islands, or east of the islands through Preedy Harbour. Passing west of False Reef and Dayman and Hudson Islands provides a more hazard-free approach. False Reef is marked by a daybeacon, and Alarm Rock off the south end of Hudson Island is marked by a navigation light. If approaching by passing through Preedy Harbour, be sure to pay close attention to the chart and keep a careful watch as a number of reefs lie in this area.

Telegraph Harbour to:		
	Bedwell Harbour (South Pender Island)	30 nm
	Ganges Harbour (Salt Spring Island)	20 nm
	Ladysmith	7 nm
	Montague Harbour (Galiano Island)	15 nm
	Nanaimo	18 nm
	Pirates Cove (De Courcy Island)	10 nm
	Princess Bay (Portland Island)	24 nm
	Roche Harbor (USA)	33 nm
	Sidney	25 nm
	Tod Inlet	27 nm
	Victoria	47 nm
	Wallace Island	8 nm

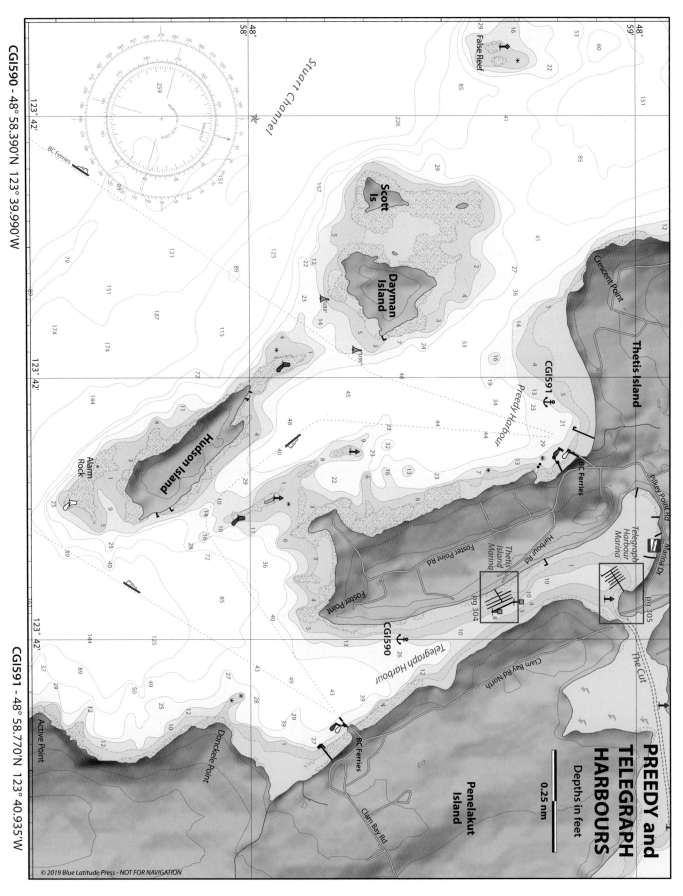

CGI590 - 48° 58.390'N 123° 39.990'W

CGI591 - 48° 58.770'N 123° 40.935'W

PREEDY and TELEGRAPH HARBOURS

Depths in feet

0.25 nm

Stuart Channel

BC Ferries

Scott Is

Dayman Island

False Reef

Thetis Island

Crescent Point

CGI591

Preedy Harbour

BC Ferries

Pilkey Point Rd

Telegraph Harbour Marina

Marina Dr

Hudson Island

Alarm Rock

Foster Point Rd

Harbour Rd

Thetis Island Marina

pg 304

pg 305

Foster Point

The Cut

CGI590

Telegraph Harbour

Clam Bay Rd North

Active Point

Donckele Point

BC Ferries

Penelakut Island

Clam Bay Rd

Looking northwest into the harbor

Enter mid-channel between Crescent Point on Thetis Island and Dayman Channel. A chain of drying reefs lie northeast of Hudson Island. Daybeacons mark the north and middle sections of this reef with a navigation light marking the south end. Stay mid-channel between these reefs and Hudson Island. This is the route used by BC Ferries. Do not pass between the chain of drying reefs and Thetis Island.

Anchorage can be taken within the harbor in 2 to 7 fathoms over a mostly mud bottom. Keep in mind a channel runs along the eastern side of the inner harbor for boat and seaplane traffic. Anchorage is not permitted in the channel. Many private moorings are found north and south of the Thetis Island Marina reducing room for anchoring. More room for anchoring can be found northeast of Foster Point.

Thetis Island Marina covered barbecue area

Ashore, enjoy pleasant walks on the quiet roads of Thetis Island. A short walk from either marina takes visitors over to Preedy Harbour where there is a public wharf, ferry terminal, and beautiful beach to stroll. The Thetis Island Marina provides a small print out of island sites and a map which is handy for taking walks around the island. For an extra adventure, jump on the ferry at Preedy Harbour and head over to the charming tourist town of Chemainus. Enjoy a day of shopping and touring their renowned outdoor murals (see page 271). The Thetis Island Marina also hosts a Saturday market during the summer where local residents sell produce, baked and canned goods, and art including carvings from the Penelakut First Nations.

Penelakut Island ferry terminal

For dining ashore, there is no better place to watch boats come and go than the outdoor patio at the Thetis Island Marina restaurant. The restaurant is open daily and offers a traditional pub menu along with cold beverages. Be sure to visit Pot of Gold Coffee Roasting Company at the north end of the harbor to take home some freshly roasted beans. This small family run business has been roasting for over 30 years and provides mail order shipments as well.

Thetis Island Marina restaurant

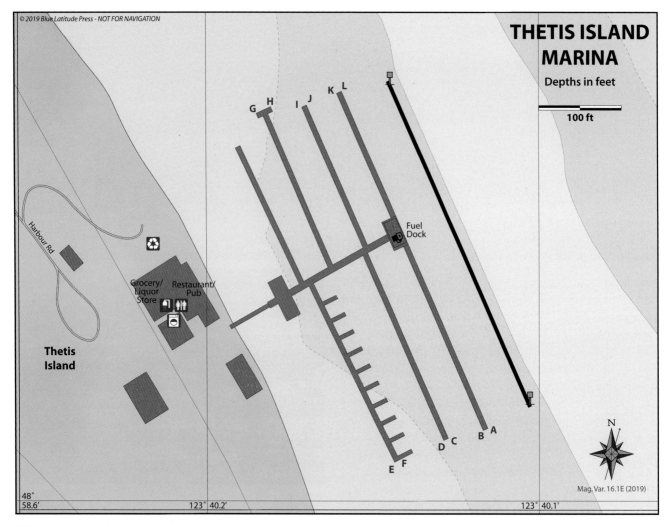

THETIS ISLAND MARINA

Depths in feet

100 ft

G H I J K L

Fuel Dock

Harbour Rd

Grocery/Liquor Store   Restaurant/Pub

Thetis Island

D C   B A

E F

N

Mag. Var. 16.1E (2019)

48° 58.6'   123° 40.2'   123° 40.1'

Thetis Island Marina

Thetis Island Marina is located on the western shore of Telegraph Harbour. The marina offers newly updated docks, power (15 and 30 amp) hookups, water from a reverse osmosis desalinator, remodeled restrooms and showers, laundry facilities, free wifi, garbage drop off, and propane tanks fills. A convenient fuel dock provides gasoline and diesel fuel with a newly updated dispensing system. Overlooking the marina is a restaurant with indoor and beautiful outdoor patio seating. A small grocery and liquor store are attached to the restaurant. The marina also offers a barbecue area with covered picnic tables, horseshoe pits, and an open lawn area.

Thetis Island Marina
Monitors VHF Channel 66A
46 Harbour Road
Thetis Island BC
(250) 246-1443 (May - August)
(250) 246-3464 (off season)
marina@thetisisland.com
www.thetisisland.com

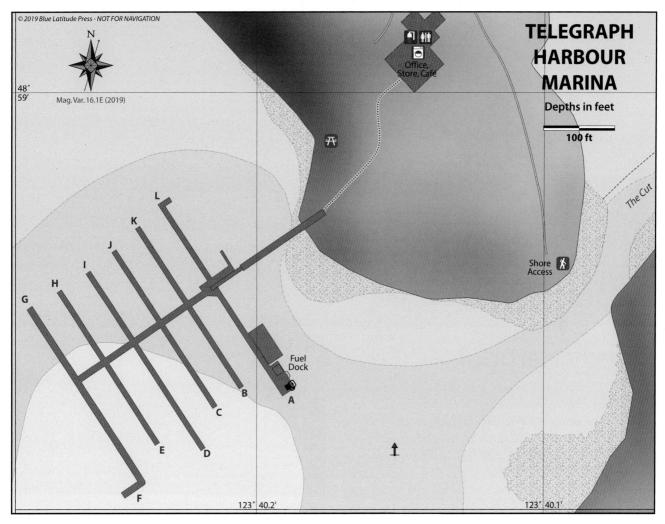

TELEGRAPH HARBOUR MARINA

Depths in feet

100 ft

Telegraph Harbour Marina

Telegraph Harbour Marina is located in the far north end of the harbor. Each slip has access to power (15 or 30 amp) and limited water hook ups. Services at the marina include restrooms, showers, laundry facilities, garbage drop off, and free wifi. The marina fuel dock provides gasoline and diesel, as well as lubricants and alcohol and kerosene for stove fuel. The marina offers a dinghy dock which is located on the east side of the fuel dock and requires a daily tie up fee. The marina store offers groceries, fresh vegetables, gifts, and books. The marina grounds offer a park-like setting with walking paths, dog area, swings, a horseshoe pit, shuffleboard, and more. The marina, store, and fuel dock are open from May through September.

Telegraph Harbour Marina
Monitors VHF channel 66A
76 Marina Drive
Thetis Island, BC V0R 2Y0,
(250) 246-9511
www.telegraphharbour.com

©Kevin Oke

Preedy Harbour

Preedy Harbor is a lovely spot with its beautiful beach and pastoral views. Along with a BC Ferries terminal, Preedy Harbour also offers a public dock for convenient shoreside access. An easy walk to Telegraph Harbour gives visitors access to the restaurant and store at Thetis Island Marina.

Preedy Harbour is located on the west side of Thetis Island, across the channel from Ladysmith Harbour. Approaches from the north and south can be taken via Stuart Channel. Be aware that the area around Preedy Harbour has number of reefs and rocky islands requiring close attention to the chart and a careful watch.

Approaching from the north, mid-channel passage can be taken between Dayman Island and Crescent Point on Thetis Island. Be aware of False Reef which lies roughly 0.5 miles northwest of Dayman Island and is marked by a daybeacon. The northwest portion of Preedy Harbour has an extensive area of shoal and shallow water and should be given ample room when rounding into the harbour.

Approaching from the south, passage can be taken either between Dayman and Hudson Islands, or between Hudson Island and a narrow chain of rocky reefs and islets lying off Thetis Island. Both routes are taken by BC Ferry boats. When passing between Dayman and Hudson Islands, be cautious of the large reef extending off the northern tip of Hudson Island. When passing between Hudson Island and the narrow chain of reefs and islets off Thetis Island, stay mid-channel. This narrow chain of drying reefs and islets are marked by daybeacons mark on the north and middle sections of the reef with a navigation

Ferry terminal and public dock

light marking the south end. Do not attempt pass between this chain of reefs and Thetis Island.

Anchorage can be taken in Preedy Harbour in 2 to 5 fathoms over a mostly mud bottom. Be sure to anchor well clear of the ferry's path. An octagon-shaped day use public dock is located just south of the ferry terminal.

On shore, a beautiful crescent of sand and pebble beach is found at the head of the harbor and is perfect for strolling. Just above the beach is the impressive and well-landscaped Capernwray Harbour Bible Centre. This area above the high tide line is privately owned by the centre. For public access to the island and for walks on the quiet country roads, please use the public dock south of the ferry terminal.

©Kevin Oke

North Cove

Aptly named North Cove is located at the northern end of Thetis Island. This large cove offers ample room for anchoring and a unique inlet for dinghy and kayak exploration. A youth summer camp is found at the western head of the cove.

North Cove is lies between Fraser Point to the west and Pilkey Point to the east on the north shore of Thetis Island. Approaches to the cove can be taken via Stuart or Trincomali Channels. Approaching from the north, be aware of Danger Reefs and Miami Islet. Danger Reefs is an area of underwater reefs, drying reefs, and shallow water found approximately 1 mile southwest of Pylades Island. Danger Reefs are marked by a navigation light. Miami Islet lies 1 mile south-southeast of Danger Reefs. Underwater reefs and shallow water extend off both the northwest and southeast shores of the islet. The northwest end of the reef at Miami Islet is marked by hand buoy "U40."

Near the entrance to North Cove and 0.3 miles northwest of Pilkey Point is Ragged Islets. The northern most islet is marked by a daybeacon. The water between Ragged Islets and Pilkey Point is mostly shallow with reefs extending off Pilkey Point. Lying roughly 0.3 miles east-northeast of Fraser Point is an area of shallow water and underwater rocks. This area is not marked and careful attention should be paid to the chart when entering or leaving North Cove.

Anchorage can be taken within the cove in 5 to 7 fathoms over a mud bottom. North Cove provides protection from most directions except northerly winds. Better north wind protection can be found at nearby Telegraph Harbour or Ladysmith. A number of private moorings and a few docks are found within the cove.

While anchored at North Cove, be sure to take a dinghy or kayak adventure to explore the rocky shorelines of the cove as well as the extensive Cufra Inlet. As much of Cufra Inlet dries, plan your trip around a higher tide.

North Cove to:		
	Bedwell Harbour *(South Pender Island)*	27 nm
	Chemainus	7 nm
	Ganges Harbour *(Salt Spring Island)*	20 nm
	Montague Harbour *(Galiano Island)*	15 nm
	Nanaimo	14 nm
	Pirates Cove *(De Courcy Island)*	6 nm
	Princess Bay *(Portland Island)*	25 nm
	Sidney	29 nm
	Silva Bay *(Gabriola Island)*	10 nm
	Tod Inlet	31 nm
	Victoria	50 nm
	Wallace Island	8 nm

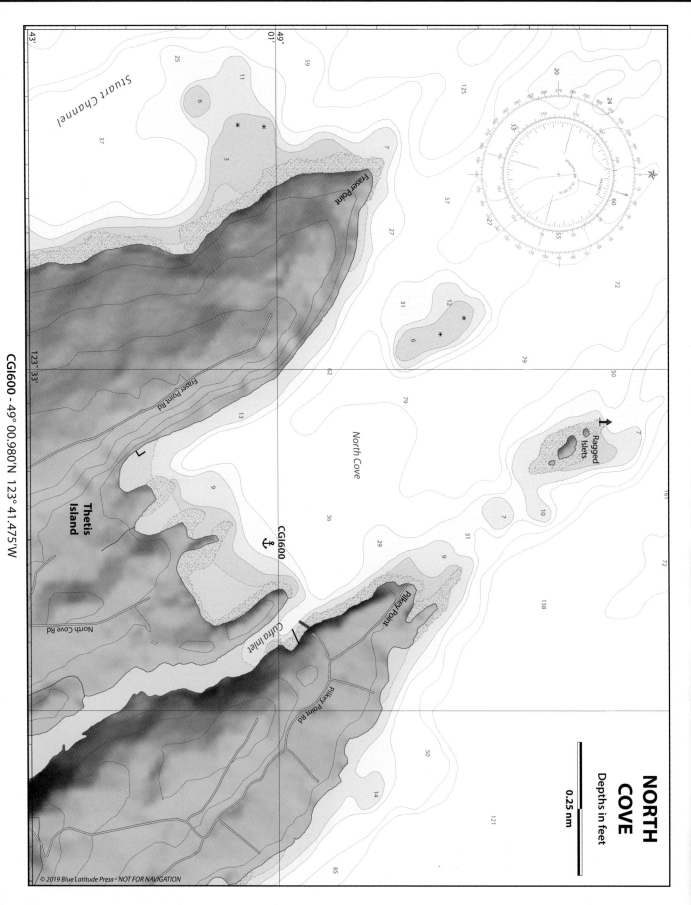

Stuart Channel

Fraser Point

Fraser Point Rd

Thetis Island

North Cove Rd

North Cove

CGI600

Cufra Inlet

Pilkey Point

Pilkey Point Rd

Ragged Islets

NORTH COVE

Depths in feet

0.25 nm

CGI600 - 49° 00.980'N 123° 41.475'W

© 2019 Blue Latitude Press - NOT FOR NAVIGATION

Chapter 11

Valdes and Gabriola Islands Area

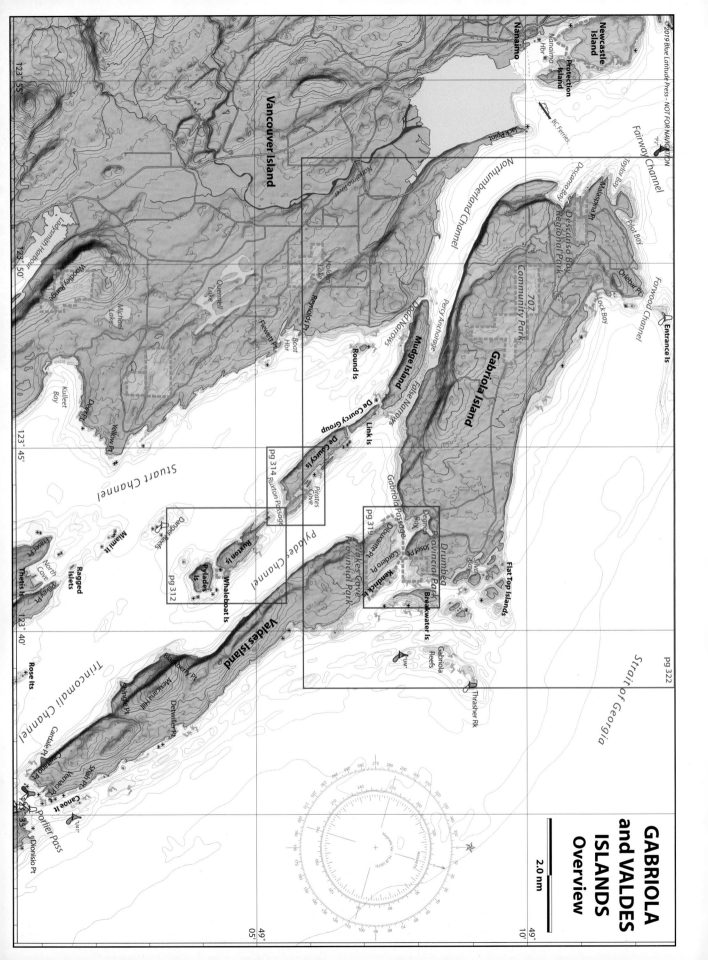

© 2019 Blue Latitude Press - NOT FOR NAVIGATION

GABRIOLA
and VALDES
ISLANDS
Overview

2.0 nm

Nanaimo

Newcastle Island

Protection Island

Nanaimo Hbr

BC Ferries

Jack Point

Fairway Channel

Forwood Channel

Northumberland Channel

Descanso Bay

Malaspina Pt

Pilot Bay

Orlebar Pt

Lock Bay

Entrance Is

707 Community Park

Descanso Bay Regional Park

Gabriola Island

Vancouver Island

Nanaimo River

Dodd Narrows

Percy Anchorage

Mudge Island

False Narrows

Holden Lake

Reynolds Pt

Round Is

De Courcy Group

Link Is

De Courcy Is

Gabriola Passage

Degnen Bay

Josef Pt

Drumbeg Provincial Park

Flat Top Islands

Ladysmith Harbour

Woodley Range

Michael Lake

Quennell Lake

Flewett Pt

Boat Hbr

pg 314

Ruxton Passage

Pirates Cove

pg 319

Dixon Pt

Gracie Pt

Wakes Cove Provincial Park

Kendrick Is

Breakwater Is

Gabriola Reefs

Killeet Bay

Dogan R

Yellow Pt

Stuart Channel

Danger Reefs

Pylades Channel

Ruxton Is

pg 312

Pylades Is

Whaleboat Is

Valdes Island

"UW"

Thrasher Rk

Miami Is

Fraser Pt

North Cove

Pilkey Pt

Ragged Islets

Thetis Is

Trincomali Channel

Blackberry Pt

Shingle Pt

Mexicana Hill

Detwiller Pt

pg 322

Strait of Georgia

49° 10'

49° 05'

Rose Its

Cardale Pt

Cleveland Pt

Shah Pt

Vernaci Pt

Canoe It

"UW"

Dionisio Pt

Porlier Pass

123° 55'

123° 50'

123° 45'

123° 40'

123° 35'

Herring Bay

Ruxton Island

Ruxton Island is part of the De Courcy Group of islands which separates the northen end of Stuart and Pylades Channels. The island is private with a number of homes lining the shores. The main anchorage for visiting boats is found on the north end of the island at Herring Bay. Herring Bay provides easy access across Ruxton Passage to Pirates Cove Marine Provincial Park.

Herring Bay is located on the north end of Ruxton Island. Approaches to the bay can be taken via Ruxton Passage or Stuart Channel. The west side of Herring Bay is protected by a long, narrow drying reef marked at its north end by a daybeacon. Due to this reef, it is important to pay careful attention to the chart and keep watch when entering. At high tide the reef is underwater making it difficult to spot.

Entrance to the bay can be taken from the north via Ruxton Passage, passing between the northern tip of Ruxton Island and the daybeacon. Entrance can also be taken south of the reef approaching via Stuart Channel. This west entrance is more challenging due to an unmarked dangerous rock lying off the southeast end of the reef and unmarked drying reefs extending off the northwestern tip of Ruxton Island.

Anchorage can be taken within Herring Bay in 2 to 4 fathoms over a mostly mud bottom. When anchoring, be aware of the unmarked rock south of the reef and to check the tide tables. Herring Bay is best suited for calm conditions.

Although the island does not have any public access, the reef and surrounding shell beach is the perfect spot for a picnic at low tide. Nearby Pirates Cove Marine Provincial Park is also a short dinghy ride away.

Whaleboat Island

Whaleboat Island was once known as Eagle Island before becoming an undeveloped marine provincial park in 1981. Accessing the island's interior is extremely difficult due to the island's steep rocky banks and lack of any developed trails. The island, including the remainder of the De Courcy Group islands, are however a pleasant paddling destination.

Whaleboat Island is located off the southeastern end of Ruxton Island and along Whaleboat Passage. Due to the depth of Whaleboat Passage, it is best left to dinghies, kayaks, and other shoal-draft boats. A small anchorage for one or possibly two small boats is found off Whaleboat Island's southwestern end. Keep in mind a dangerous rock within the anchorage is found roughly midway between the southern most ends of Whaleboat and Ruxton Islands. A number of private mooring buoys can be found along the southern shore of Ruxton Island.

Ruxton Island to:		
Bedwell Harbour (South Pender Island)	30 nm
Clam Bay (Thetis Island)	8 nm
Ganges Harbour (Salt Spring Island)	23 nm
Ladysmith	10 nm
Montague Harbour (Galiano Island)	18 nm
Nanaimo	10 nm
Princess Bay (Portland Island)	28 nm
Sidney	32 nm
Silva Bay (Gabriola Island)	6 nm
Victoria	54 nm
Wallace Island	12 nm

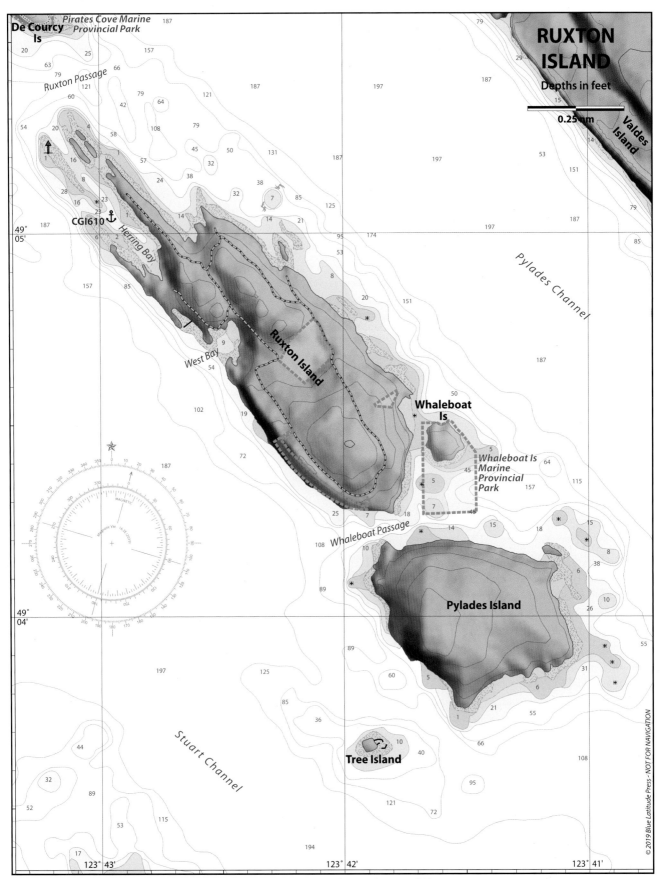

De Courcy Is

Pirates Cove Marine Provincial Park

RUXTON ISLAND

Depths in feet

0.25 nm

Valdes Island

Ruxton Passage

CGI610

Herring Bay

West Bay

Ruxton Island

Pylades Channel

Whaleboat Is

Whaleboat Is Marine Provincial Park

Whaleboat Passage

Pylades Island

MAGNETIC

Stuart Channel

Tree Island

© 2019 Blue Latitude Press - NOT FOR NAVIGATION

49° 05'

49° 04'

123° 43'

123° 42'

123° 41'

CGI610 - 49° 05.040'N 123° 42.940'W

De Courcy Island

De Courcy Island is part of the De Courcy Group which includes Mudge, Link, Whaleboat, Ruxton, and Pylades Islands. During the summer months, boaters flock to De Courcy Island to enjoy the magical Pirates Cove Marine Provincial Park. The 75 acre park offers two beautiful anchorages, dinghy docks, camping, trails, and even potable water.

De Courcy Island is found mid-way between the north end of Valdes Island and Vancouver Island. The west side of the island lies along the northern portion of Stuart Channel, the east side along Pylades Channel, and the southern end along Ruxton Passage. The north end of the island is partially connected to Link Island by drying rock ledges.

A number of shell middens on the island, dating back more than 3,000 years, are telling of the island's great history with its original inhabitants. A large midden is found under the park's present day campground. The island was named after Michael de Courcy who was captain of the *HMS Pylades* from 1859 to 1861 during its tour at the Royal Navy's Pacific Station.

An interesting part of De Courcy Island's more recent past involves Edward Arthur Wilson, also known as Brother XII. Born in England in 1878, Wilson trained with the Royal Navy, becoming a navigator and sea captain. During his worldly travels he believed he heard the voice of an Egyptian deity from an occult known as the Great White Lodge. The voice instructed him to prepare for armagedon and lead a new civilization that would survive the destruction. After writing a successful manifesto, Brother XII moved to Vancouver Island in 1927 to establish the headquarters of the Aquarian Foundation at Cedar-by-the-Sea. The headquarters was based seven miles south of Nanaimo and additional properties were purchased in the islands including De Courcy. The farm at De Courcy Island eventually become his home, along with a select group of followers.

Brother XII was an inspiring and charasmatic man, winning the spiritual hearts of many, including a number of wealthy and prominant people. Large contributions from these followers were made to the foundation. Over the years Brother XII became erratic and paranoid, fortifying the farm at De Courcy Island and arming his followers. Allegations of mistreatment and misappropriation of foundation funds surfaced. With criminal proceedings emminant, Brother XII fled the area along with the foundation's money. No one is certain of what became of Brother XII, some believe he was found dead only a few years later in Switzerland, while other sightings found him in San Francisco. The most intriguing rumors are those of hidden gold on the island left behind after his quick departure.

©Kevin Oke

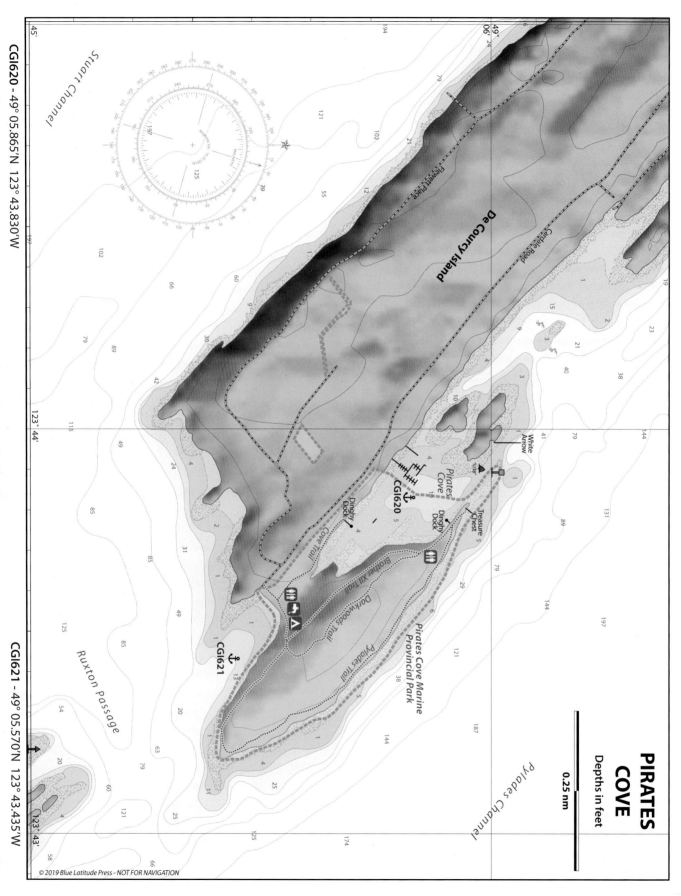

CGI620 - 49° 05.865'N 123° 43.830'W

Stuart Channel

De Courcy Island

Flewett Place

Cardale Road

Pirates Cove

White Arrow

Dinghy Dock

CGI620

Dinghy Dock

Treasure Chest

Cove Trail

Brother XII Trail

Darkwoods Trail

Pirates Trail

Pirates Cove Marine Provincial Park

CGI621

Ruxton Passage

Pylades Channel

CGI621 - 49° 05.570'N 123° 43.435'W

PIRATES COVE

Depths in feet

0.25 nm

©Kevin Oke

Pirates Cove

Pirates Cove is a favorite stop for any boater's cruise through the Gulf Islands, especially during the warm, calm months of summer. Protected anchorage, hiking trails, camping, and a beautiful landscape make Pirates Cove one of the most enchanting destinations. In 1966, with the help of the Council of British Columbia Yacht Clubs, 76 acres on De Courcy Island was purchased to be designated as a provincial marine park. Today Pirates Cove Provincial Marine Park is host to countless boaters and kayakers enjoying the beauty of this special place.

Pirates Cove is located at the southeast end of De Courcy Island. Approaches to the cove are taken via Pylades Channel, which lies between Valdes Island to the east and the De Courcy Group to the west. The channel can attain up to 2 knots of current. For boats transiting along the Vancouver Island shoreline, Ruxton Passage connects Stuart and Pylades Channels.

The entrance to Pirates Cove is narrow, shallow, and fringed by reefs requiring careful attention to the chart and tide tables. The eastern entrance point is a narrow peninsula of land and extending reefs. This point is marked by a port hand daybeacon, however it does not mark the extreme end of the reef. Starboard hand buoy "U38" is west of the daybeacon forming a channel into the cove.

Pirates Cove to:		
	Bedwell Harbour (South Pender Island)	31 nm
	Clam Bay (Thetis Island)	8 nm
	Dodd Narrows	6 nm
	Ganges Harbour (Salt Spring Island)	24 nm
	Ladysmith	10 nm
	Montague Harbour (Galiano Island)	19 nm
	Nanaimo	11 nm
	Princess Bay (Portland Island)	29 nm
	Sidney	33 nm
	Tod Inlet	35 nm
	Victoria	55 nm
	Wallace Island	12 nm

©Kevin Oke

Anchorage along Ruxton Passage

©Kevin Oke

White arrow

Pirates Cove entrance

In order to help boats avoid the extensive underwater reefs off the eastern entrance point, a form of range markers have been placed on the small island forming the western entrance point. A white arrow has been painted on a rock ledge along the shoreline (see photo to the left), and a white cross is found in a tree above it. Lining up the arrow and the cross helps boaters to clear the north end of the reef before making the turn to enter the marked channel. Before entering the shallow channel, be sure to check the tide table to ensure adequate depth for your draft.

Anchorage can be taken within the cove in 1 to 2 fathoms over a mud bottom. Be aware that the holding in Pirates Cove is only fair. In stronger winds boats are known to drag anchor, which can cause a domino effect when the cove is crowded. During the busier summer months, most anchored boats will take a stern line to shore and tie to one of the many anchored stern tie chains installed by the park department. This enables many boats to use an otherwise tight anchorage. As the cove can be crowded, it is best to have your stern line and dinghy prepared ahead of time to enable you to quickly get a line to shore, and prevent your boat from swinging into your neighbor once anchored. A float near the southern portion of the cove is reserved for the volunteer park host. The private marina in the cove is for the use of the residents of De Courcy Island.

Alternative anchorage can be found southeast of Pirates Cove along Ruxton Passage. This too can be a popular spot, especially during the summer months. The head of the bay is part of the park and quite shallow, but it is an easy place to land dinghies and kayaks. Anchorage can be taken in 3 to 9 fathoms with protection from north winds.

Two dinghy docks within Pirates Cove make shore access easy and convenient. Park kiosk signs are located near the top of the ramps with park information and trail maps. For those who are camping, the campground, pit toilet (another located near the east dinghy dock), and water pump are located at the south end of the park near Ruxton Passage.

For those in search of the pirates' booty, a stop at the Pirates Cove treasure chest is a must. Over the season, fellow boaters stock the sizable chest with various trinkets and toys making a true treasure trove. An inscription on the chest reads:

> *If it be treasure you're after...then you've come to the right place...Please feel free to take a bit...and, leave a bit.*

Pirates Cove offers nearly 3 miles of well groomed trails traversing the park. These trails travel through beautiful forests of firs, madrones, and Garry oaks. Along the way, you may spot a few plants more often found in the drier areas of the mainland including Rocky Mountain Juniper, satin flower, and even poison oak. Due to the islands' dry summers, these plants can survive and grow. To avoid coming in contact with any poison oak, as well as to protect the native vegetation of the park, it is best to remain on the trails.

While exploring the park, be sure to check out the sandstone rock formations along the shoreline. Intricate, lacy webs of rock have been formed over the years as waves have eroded the soft sandstone. Large ledges of sandstone along the eastern shore of the park provide perfect spots for sunbathing and watching boats pass by. A number of these areas have patches of brilliant white crushed shells, telling of the island's history and aboriginal inhabitants.

Common wildlife sightings on the island include black-tailed deer, harbor seals, river otters, mink and raccoons. Keep your eyes out for a few visitors to the island including oystercatchers, bald eagles, great blue herons, and porpoise.

For those looking for a kayak or dinghy adventure, the De Courcy Group provides a wonderful chain of islands to explore. A short paddle to the south are the islands of Ruxton, Whaleboat, and Pylades. Ruxton Island has a number of beautiful reefs to watch the underwater world of the intertidal zone. Further south is Whaleboat Island Provincial Marine Park. To the north, the east side of De Courcy and Link Islands offer a number of rocky nooks, small coves, and reefs to tour.

Gabriola Passage (looking east)

©Kevin Oke

Valdes Island

While Valdes Island is one of the largest islands in the Gulf Islands archipelago, the majority of the island has remained untouched by development as seen on many of the other islands. There is no BC Ferry service to the island, nor are there any public roads or utilities. A small population resides and spends seasonal time on Valdes Island, many using old logging roads to access various areas of the island.

Valdes Island is one of the traditional and sacred lands of the Lyackson First Nation. Roughly one third of the island is managed by the Lyackson. According to archaelogical surveys, Lyackson ancestors have been using the island for more than 5,000 years. When visiting the island please respect Lyackson property and the protected archeological sites and burial grounds on the island.

One of the most impressive features of Valdes Island are the immense sandstone cliffs found on the island's northwestern shore. These sandstone cliffs are the result of uplifted sedimentary layers and are quite a sight to see.

The northeast end of the island was the former site of Brother XII's Aquarian Foundation settlement of Mandieah. Brother XII (see page 313) was a British cult leader in the 1920's and 1930's who formed settlements in various areas of the islands including Vancouver, De Courcy, and Valdes Islands. Most of the settlement was dismantled with only a few scattered bricks remaining today.

Gabriola Passage

Gabriola Passage is a narrow pass lying between the north end of Valdes Island and the southeast end of Gabriola Island. Due to the number of reefs in the area, especially at the east entrance, careful attention should be paid to the chart. Currents in the pass can attain velocities up to 9 knots with the highest velocities found between Josef and Cordero Points.

Dibuxante Point on Valdes Island marks the west entrance point to the passage. A long reef extends north off the point and is marked by a navigation light. Breakwater Island lies at the east entrance to the pass. The island's east and southeast shores have extensive reefs and detached rocks. Detached reefs also lie east of Kendrick Island. The middle reef is marked by a navigation light. Rogers Reef lies roughly 0.2 miles west of Breakwater Island and is marked by a navigation light.

©Kevin Oke

Valdes Island sandstone cliffs

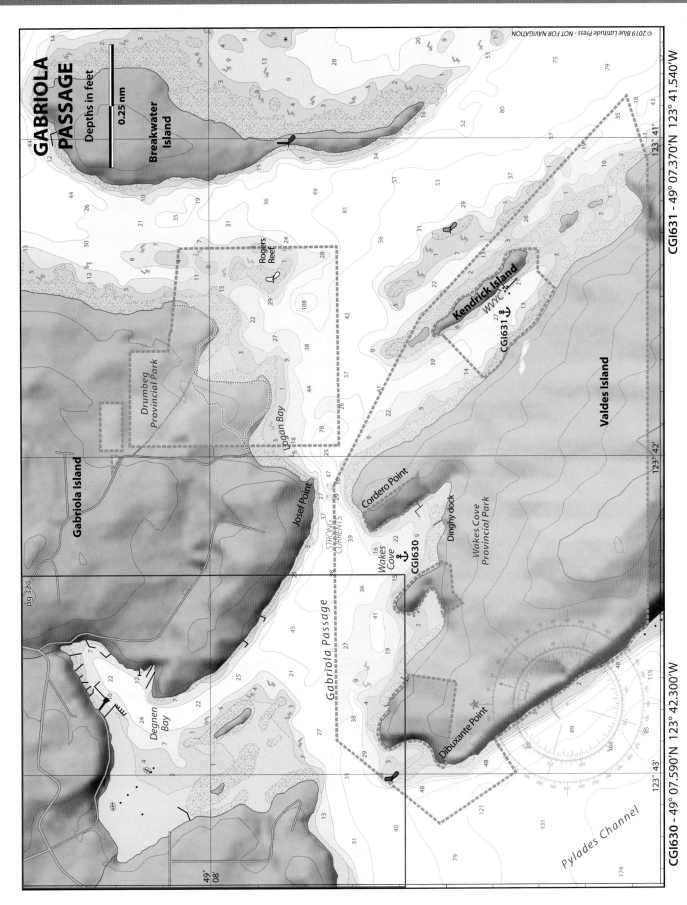

GABRIOLA
PASSAGE

Depths in feet

0.25 nm

Breakwater
Island

© 2019 Blue Latitude Press - NOT FOR NAVIGATION

Rogers
Reef

Drumbeg
Provincial Park

Logan Bay

Kendrick Island

WYC

CGI631

Valdes Island

Josef Point

Cordero Point

Wakes Cove
Provincial Park

Dinghy dock

STRONG
CURRENTS

Wakes
Cove

CGI630

Gabriola Island

pg 324

Degnen
Bay

Gabriola Passage

Dibuxante Point

Pylades Channel

CGI631 - 49° 07.370'N 123° 41.540'W

CGI630 - 49° 07.590'N 123° 42.300'W

49°
08'

123° 41'

123° 42'

123° 43'

©Kevin Oke

Wakes Cove (right) and Dogfish Bay (left)

Wakes Cove

Wakes Cove and the Wakes Cove Provincial Park, established in 2002, are located at the far northern tip of Valdes Island. The cove has long been a popular spot for boats waiting for slack tide in Gabriola Passage. The 500 acre provincial park provides wonderful hiking trails through new and old growth forests of fir, cedar, madrones, maples, and a scattering of Garry oaks. The wide trails are primarily old logging roads traversing the park from beach to forest.

Wakes Cove is located on the north end of Valdes Island along Gabriola Passage. Approaching from the west, be aware of the reef extending off Dibuxante Point. The end of the reef is marked by a navigation light. Approaching from the east, pay careful attention to the chart and current tables. Hazardous reefs and current that can attain velocities up to 9 knots are found within Gabriola Passage (see page 318).

Anchorage can be taken within the cove in 2 to 3 fathoms over a mixed bottom of mud and kelp. The Canadian Sailing Directions report the holding to be marginal with debris from previous logging efforts found on the bottom. Alternative anchorage can be found at nearby Dogfish or Degnen Bays. The large dock and mooring buoys on the east side of the cove are private.

For trips to shore a convenient park dinghy dock is available at the head of the cove. At the top of the ramp a trail heads east, passing through an old homestead site to the sandstone beaches at Dogfish Bay. The trail south or to the west is a loop trail taking visitors through a beautiful forest setting. Please respect the park and private property boundaries. The boundary lines are well marked with signs.

Dogfish Bay

Dogfish Bay, similar to its neighboring anchorage at Wakes Cove, is typically an off the beaten path destination for the majority of boats traveling through the Gulf Islands. This quiet anchorage is home to the West Vancouver Yacht Club outstation on Kendrick Island. A few boats, including commercial tugs, may use the bay to wait for favorable weather or slack tide in Gabriola Passage. The bay also provides easy access to the beautiful Drumbeg Provinical Park located just across the pass on Gabriola Island.

Dogfish Bay is formed by the narrow and rocky Kendrick Island, lying just east of Valdes Island. Approaches to the bay are taken via Gabriola Passage. Due to extensive reefs and current that can reach 9 knots in the pass, pay careful attention to the chart and current tables.

Approaching from the west, be aware of the reef extending off Dibuxante Point. The end of the reef is marked by a navigation light. Approaching from the east, be cautious of Breakwater Island's reefs and detached rocks off its east and southeast shore. Detached reefs also lie east of Kendrick Island. The middle reef is marked by a navigation light. Rogers Reef, which lies 0.2 miles west of Breakwater Island on the north side of the east entrance to Gabriola Passage, is marked by a navigation light. When rounding into the bay from the east, be sure to give ample room to the north end of Kendrick Island to avoid the extending reef.

Anchorage can be taken within the bay in 4 to 7 fathoms over a mostly mud bottom. Mooring buoys and the dock on Kendrick Island are part of the yacht club outstation and are private.

Silva Bay looking west

Gabriola Island

Set along the western edge of the Strait of Georgia, Gabriola Island offers incredible ocean views set against the impressive backdrop of the mainland's Coast Mountains range. The island is known for its unique sandstone formations carved and eroded by centuries of waves. The sandstone also provides an important link to the island's human history through sacred petroglyphs left behind by the ancestors of the Snuneymuxw First Nation.

Gabriola Island lies at the very north end of the southern Gulf Islands chain. The western end of the island lies less than 2.5 miles from the major city of Nanaimo on Vancouver Island. Ferry service from Nanaimo supports a rapidly growing resident and seasonal population on Gabriola Island, making it the third most populated in the Gulf Islands. Prior to 1950, Gabriola Island's population did not exceed 300 people. Today, the island is home to just over 4,000 residents.

The history of Gabriola Island begins with the Snuneymuxw First Nation, who are the aboriginal inhabitants of the island. Their largest village on the island was found near the protected waters of False Narrows. Sandstone petroglyphs carved by the Snuneymuxw are found throughout the island and mark sacred natural places. While the soft sandstone is difficult to date, these petroglyphs are approximated to be between 100 to 3,000 years old.

In the late 1700's, Spanish and English explorers arrived including José María Narváez, Dionisio Alcalá Galiano, and Cayetano Valdés, who are credited with mapping the Strait of Georgia. By the mid 1800's, Gabriola Island began to see its first European settlers with the discovery of coal in Nanaimo. The end of the century brought the arrival of Gabriola Brickyard. The shale quarry and brickyard were found along False Narrows and were a vital industry to the island up until their closure in the 1950's. Withey's Shipyard in Silva Bay began after World War II. The shipyard produced hundreds of boats and was the island's largest employer. Upon Les Withey's retirement, the yard was sold in 1974, and continues operation today as Silva Bay Shipyard.

Silva Bay on the island's eastern end is the main boating center with a protected harbor and two marinas for visiting boats. Degnen Bay on the island's southeast shore is a popular boating hub for island residents with a protected harbor and public wharf. The island's main shopping village for groceries and supplies is found at the western end near the ferry terminal in Descanso Bay.

To access the various areas of Galiano Island there is a very convenient public bus system known as GERTIE (Gabriola Environmentally Responsible Trans-Island Express). GERTIE operates on a "flag down" method where riders stand by the side of the road in a safe location and wave to the driver. The buses have regular routes around the entire island and offer daily unlimited ride passes. Well behaved dogs and bikes (racks on all buses) are welcome. For more information on schedules and routes visit: gertie.ca.

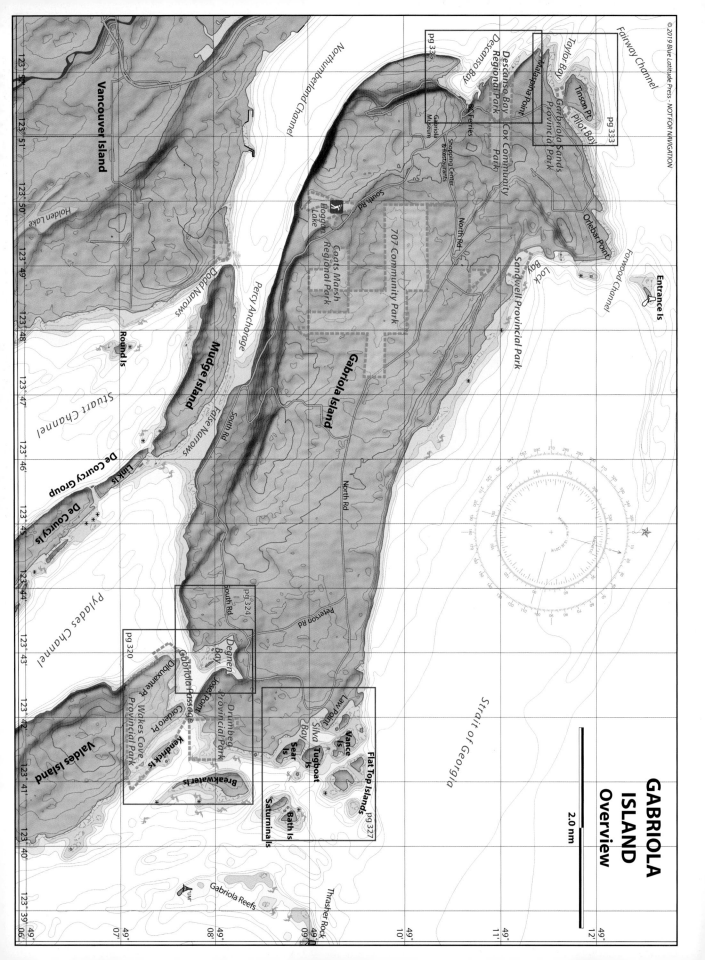

GABRIOLA ISLAND Overview

2.0 nm

Vancouver Island

Holden Lake

Northumberland Channel

Fairway Channel

Taylor Bay

pg 333

Malaspina Point

Descanso Bay Regional Park

Descanso Bay

Gabriola Sands Provincial Park

Tinson Pt

Pilot Bay

Forwood Channel

Lock Bay

Orlebar Point

Sandwell Provincial Park

Entrance Is

Gabriola Museum

Shopping Center & Restaurants

South Rd

North Rd

Hoggan Lake

Coats Marsh Regional Park

707 Community Park

Gabriola Island

Dodd Narrows

Percy Anchorage

Mudge Island

False Narrows

South Rd

Round Is

Stuart Channel

De Courcy Group

Link Is

De Courcy Is

North Rd

Peterson Rd

Pylades Channel

pg 324

Degnen Bay

South Rd

pg 320

Gabriola Passage

Dibuxante Pt

Cordero Pt

Josef Point

Drumbeg Provincial Park

Valdes Island

Wakes Cove Provincial Park

Kendrick Is

Breakwater Is

Lamb Point

Silva Bay

Vance Is

Sear Is

Tugboat Is

Flat Top Islands

pg 327

Bath Is

Saturnina Is

Strait of Georgia

Gabriola Reefs

Thrasher Rock

pg 335

Cox Community Park

BC Ferries

123° 52'

123° 51'

123° 50'

123° 49'

123° 48'

123° 47'

123° 46'

123° 45'

123° 44'

123° 43'

123° 42'

123° 41'

123° 40'

123° 39'

49° 12'

49° 11'

49° 10'

49° 09'

49° 08'

49° 07'

49° 06'

©Kevin Oke

Degnen Bay

Degnen Bay derives its name from one of the original few European settlers to arrive at Gabriola Island back in the mid 1800's. Irish immigrant, Thomas Degnen, and his Cowichan First Nation wife, Jane, farmed land around the northeastern portion of the bay. Towards the end of the 1800's, a public wharf was installed at or very near its current location to help with the transportation of people and supplies between Nanaimo and Gabriola Island. Today Degnen Bay remains a popular port offering good protection for local island residents' pleasure crafts, commercial fishing boats, and visitors.

Degnen Bay is located on the southeastern side of Gabriola Island. Approaches to the bay are made via Gabriola Passage. Be aware that a number of hazardous reefs are found in the area, especially at the east end of the pass, requiring careful attention to the chart. Currents in Gabriola Pass can attain velocities up to 9 knots with the highest velocities found between Josef and Cordero Points. Transiting the pass should be planned for slack tides.

Approaching from the west, Dibuxante Point on Valdes Island marks the west entrance point to Gabriola Passage. A long reef extends north off the point and is marked by a navigation light. Approaching from the east, Breakwater Island lies in front of the east approach to the pass. Be cautious of the extensive reefs and detached rocks lying off the

Degnen Bay to:		
Bedwell Harbour (South Pender Island)	32 nm
Clam Bay (Thetis Island)	10 nm
Ganges Harbour (Salt Spring Island)	25 nm
Ladysmith	12 nm
Montague Harbour (Galiano Island)	20 nm
Nanaimo (through Dodd Narrows)	13 nm
Pirates Cove (De Courcy Island)	3 nm
Princess Bay (Portland Island)	30 nm
Sidney	35 nm
Vancouver (Burrard Inlet)	25 nm
Victoria	56 nm
Wallace Island	14 nm

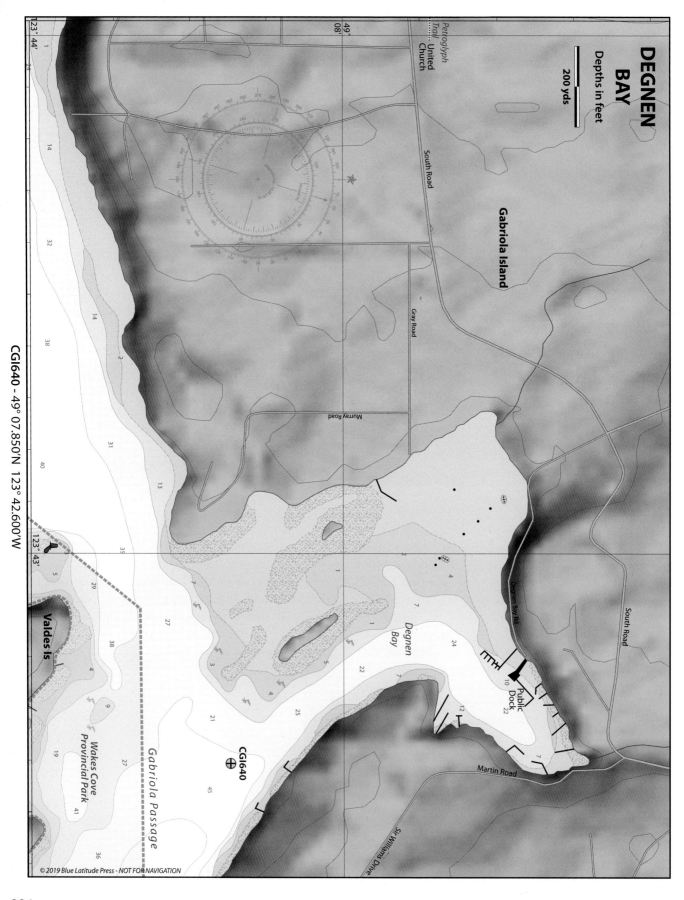

DEGNEN
BAY

Depths in feet

200 yds

Gabriola Island

Pettoglyph
Trail
United
Church

South Road

Gray Road

Murray Road

49°
08'

49°
08'

Degnen Bay Rd

South Road

Public Dock

Degnen
Bay

Martin Road

Valdes Is

Wakes Cove
Provincial Park

Gabriola Passage

CGI640

Sir Williams Drive

CGI640 - 49° 07.850'N 123° 42.600'W

123°
44'

123°
43'

© 2019 Blue Latitude Press - NOT FOR NAVIGATION

east shore and southeast end of the island. A chain of reefs also lie east of Kendrick Island with the middle reef marked by a navigation light. On the north side of the east entrance to the pass lies Rogers Reef. Rogers Reef lies 0.2 miles west of Breakwater Island and is marked by a navigation light.

When rounding into Degnen Bay, be aware that nearly the entire west side of the bay is shoal. Do not enter the bay west of the islet lying near the middle of the bay. Favor the east side of the entrance, and enter between the east side of the islet and Gabriola Island.

Anchorage can be taken within the bay in 4 fathoms over a mostly mud bottom, however anchors fouled by debris has been reported by the Canadian Sailing Directions. Much of Degnen Bay is filled by private moorings resulting in very limited room for anchoring.

On the north shore of the bay is the public wharf operated by the Degnen Bay Harbour Authority (red railings on the pier). The large L-shaped dock is quite popular and finding space can be difficult especially during the busy summer months. Priority is given to fishing vessels and rafting is common. Power hookups are available as well as garbage disposal for dock guests. No water is available at the dock.

For trips to shore the public dock provides convenient tie ups for dinghies. The nearest services are found at Silva Bay, a roughly 1.5 mile walk north on South Road. One of the highlights to Degnen Bay is visiting the nearby Drumbeg Provincial Park located on Gabriola Passage. A roughly one mile walk by road or one mile dinghy trip by water takes you to the 50 acre park. The park offers a beautiful sand and pebble beach setting and roughly one mile of trails. Be aware that the park does contain the giant hogweed plant.

Sap from the plant iritates and blisters skin when exposed to sunlight. To avoid coming into contact with the plant, be sure to stay on the trails.

Another highlight to visiting Degnen Bay is a walk through a sacred area of First Nations petroglyphs. A roughly one mile walk from the public wharf leads visitors to the trailhead of this magical area. This walk begins near the United Church at the corner of South and Price Roads with signs marking the trailhead on the north side of South Road. Along the trail, faint carvings of the petroglyphs can be seen in the flat mossy area around the trail. Visitors are asked to avoid walking on the rock to avoid further erosion of the petroglyphs. At the west end of the petroglyphs, the trail continues north to Petroglyph Way. Follow the signs and flagging to stay on the trail and avoid the private property bordering the walk. Please remember, this is a sacred and historical area, and to treat this special place with respect.

Gabriola Land & Trails Trust

Gabriola Island offers a wonderful system of trails and hikes for exploring the island. The Gabriola Land & Trails Trust (GaLTT) was developed in 2004 "…to secure, develop and sustain a network of parkland and trails on Gabriola Island for the benefit of the public, and to preserve sites of environmental, historical, and social importance." Keep in mind that trails not on their maps or signposted are most likely on private land. For a full listing of maps and island hikes available, visit their website at: www.galtt.ca.

©Kevin Oke

Silva Bay

Surrounded by a patchwork of forest-capped islands and sandstone islets, Silva Bay is a welcome haven for boats crossing the Strait of Georgia or those cruising the Gulf Islands. The picturesque bay offers a bounty of services including marinas, fuel docks, and the historic shipyard. A convenient public transit system allows visitors to explore the beauty and history of Gabriola Island while leaving their boats in a secure harbor.

Silva Bay is located on the northeast end of Gabriola Island and is accessed via the Strait of Georgia. The entrance to Silva Bay is protected by the Flat Top Islands which include Saturnina, Bath, Acorn, Gaviola, Carlos, Lily, Vance, Tugboat, and Sear Islands. Acorn Island has two detached drying reefs lying off its shores. Brant Reef lies 0.1 miles northeast of Acorn Island, and a second lying 0.05 southeast of the island. Due to the number of islands, islets, and rocky reefs surrounding the entrance to Silva Bay, careful attention to the chart and tide tables is necessary.

There are three main passages into Silva Bay from the north, east and south. The deeper and more commonly used passage is from the east between Vance and Tugboat Islands, accessed via Commodore Passage. The south pas-sage, between Sear and Gabriola Islands, is shallow with a least depth of 3 feet. The south entrance to this passage has extensive unmarked reefs, and is best suited for shallow draft boats with local knowledge. The north passage, between Lily and Vance Islands, is also shallow with a least depth of approximately 11 feet. This too is best suited for shallower draft boats with local knowledge.

For boats approaching from the east and southeast within the Strait of Georgia, be aware of the extensive Ga-

Silva Bay to:		
	Bedwell Harbour *(South Pender Island)*	35 nm
	Clam Bay *(Thetis Island)*	12 nm
	Ganges Harbour *(Salt Spring Island)*	28 nm
	Ladysmith	15 nm
	Montague Harbour *(Galiano Island)*	23 nm
	Nanaimo	12 nm
	Pirates Cove *(De Courcy Island)*	5 nm
	Princess Bay *(Portland Island)*	33 nm
	Sidney	37 nm
	Tod Inlet	40 nm
	Vancouver *(Burrard Inlet)*	23 nm
	Victoria	58 nm

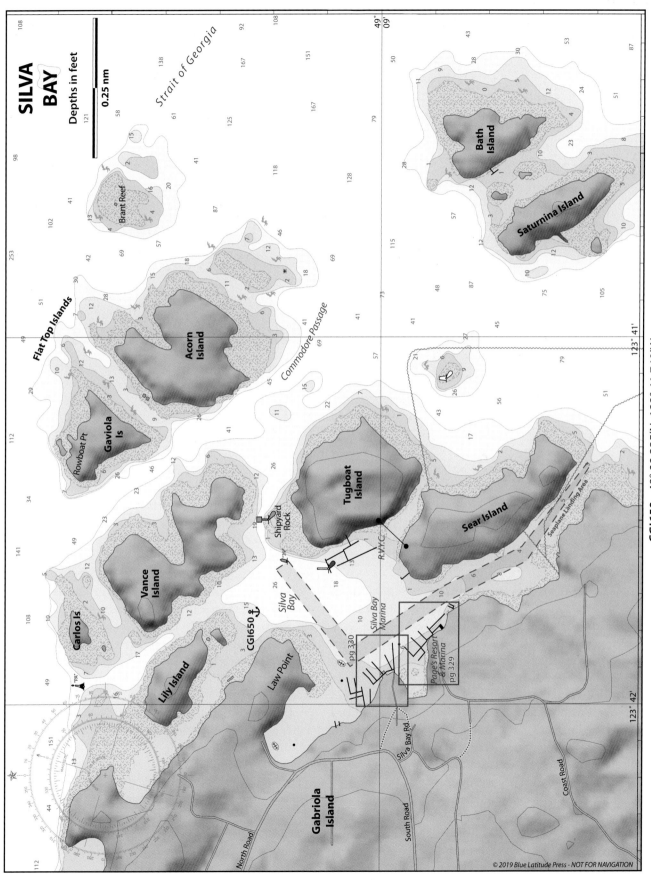

SILVA BAY

Depths in feet

0.25 nm

Strait of Georgia

Flat Top Islands

Brant Reef

Acorn Island

Gaviola Is

Rowboat Pt

Vance Island

Carlos Is

Lily Island

Law Point

Shipyard Rock

Silva Bay

CGl650 ⚓

pg 330

Tugboat Island

R.Y.Y.C.

Silva Bay Marina

Commodore Passage

Sear Island

Seaplane Landing Area

Page's Resort & Marina
pg 329

Silva Bay Rd.

Gabriola Island

South Road

North Road

Coast Road

Bath Island

Saturnina Island

49° 09'

49° 09.235'N 123° 41.740'W

123° 41'

123° 42'

CGl650 - 49° 09.235'N 123° 41.740'W

© 2019 Blue Latitude Press - NOT FOR NAVIGATION

Shipyard Rock daymark

briola Reefs. These reefs stretch nearly 1.5 miles in length and are a mix of drying reefs and underwater rocks. The north end of the reef complex begins at Thrasher Rock which is marked by a navigation light. The south end of the reefs are marked by light buoy "UM."

Approaching Commodore Passage from the south, be aware of a drying reef located 0.15 miles east-southeast of the southern tip of Tugboat Island. This reef is marked by a navigation light and passage can be taken either side of the reef. Approaching Commodore Passage from the west or north, be cautious of the extending reef off Carlos Island.

From Commodore Passage, entrance to Silva Bay can be taken between Vance and Tugboat Islands. Be aware this passage is very narrow and encumbered by reefs especially off the northwest end of Tugboat Island, which includes Shipyard Rock. As the name suggests, boats have run aground here so pay very close attention to the charts

and keep a careful watch. Shipyard Rock is marked by a port hand daymark. This channel between Vance and Tugboat Islands, north of Shipyard Rock, has a least depth of 19 feet. Port hand buoy "U39" marks the northwest extrimity of the reef off Tugboat Island.

Once inside Silva Bay, a number of mooring buoys, docks, and marinas can be found. Official seaplane lanes are found from the "U39" buoy to the seaplane dock on the western shore, and from the seaplane dock southeast, through the southern passage. As of early 2019, these lanes are not marked with buoys, however the chart on page 327 illustrates their location. These lanes are designated "No Anchor Zones."

Over the years many private mooring buoys have been added within the bay to the extent that there is little room left for visiting boats to anchor. Occasionally, old moorings and derelict vessels are removed which may open the anchorage once again in the future. Anchorage can sometimes be found north of the seaplane lane and northeast of Law Point in 2 to 3 fathoms. Keep in mind that Silva Bay is along the Strait of Georgia. Northwest and southeast winds will usually be stronger in the open strait than in the protected inner islands.

For visiting boats, there are two marinas on the west side of the bay that offer transient moorage slips. During the summer months, it is recommended to reserve a slip ahead of time as the marinas can get quite busy and anchorage opportunities are very limited. On the west side of Tugboat Island, the Royal Vancouver Yacht Club has an outstation and large dock complex.

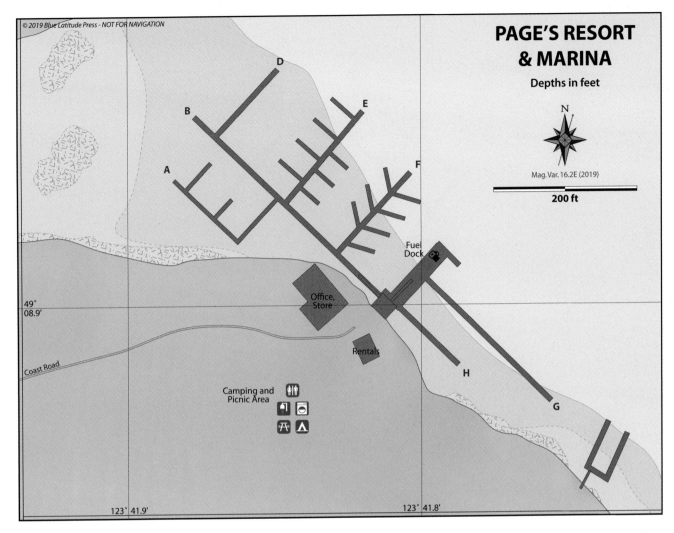

© 2019 Blue Latitude Press - NOT FOR NAVIGATION

PAGE'S RESORT & MARINA

Depths in feet

N

Mag. Var. 16.2E (2019)

200 ft

D

E

B

A

F

Fuel Dock

49° 08.9'

Office, Store

Coast Road

Rentals

H

G

Camping and Picnic Area

123° 41.9'

123° 41.8'

Page's Resort & Marina

Page's Resort & Marina is located at the southwestern end of Silva bay. The marina can accommodate boats up to 70 feet with power (15 and 30 amp) hookups available. Services at the marina include a fuel dock, restrooms, showers, laundry facilities, free wifi, and picnic grounds with tables and a propane barbeque. The store at the resort has a beautiful selection of books and charts, coffee, bakery items, produce, ice cream, ice, and a freezer filled with amazing pre-made meals from the Woodfire Restaurant near Descanso Bay. The resort provides a large campground, cottage rentals, kayak rentals, and mountain bike rentals for exploring the island. Pages Resort & Marina is also home to the Silva Bay Yacht Club reciprocal dock.

Page's newest acquisition is the Page's Inn & Marina located just north of the seaplane and fuel dock. The marina here is reserved for guests staying at the Inn and for permanent moorage customers. For further information on

rooms at the Inn, check their website at: www.pagesinn. com, or call (250) 247-9351.

Page's Resort & Marina
Monitors VHF channel 66A
3350 Coast Road
Gabriola Island, BC V0R 1X7
(250) 247-9351
info@pagesresort.com
www.pagesresort.com

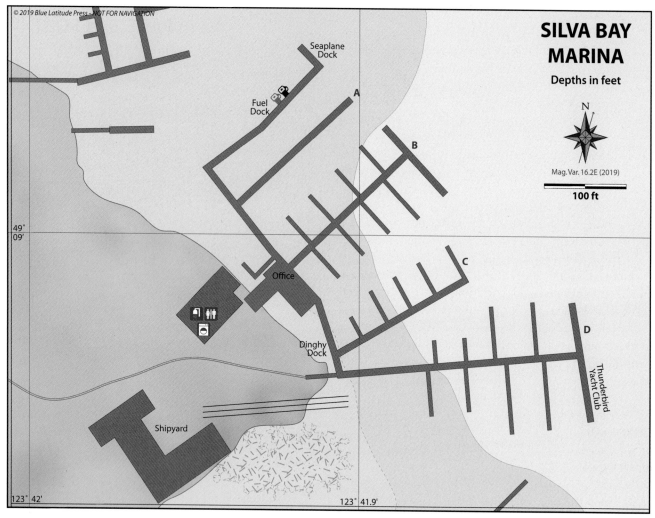

© 2019 Blue Latitude Press – NOT FOR NAVIGATION

SILVA BAY MARINA

Depths in feet

Mag. Var. 16.2E (2019)

100 ft

Seaplane Dock

Fuel Dock

A

B

C

D

Office

Dinghy Dock

Shipyard

Thunderbird Yacht Club

49° 09'

123° 42'

123° 41.9'

Silva Bay Marine Resort

Silva Bay Marine Resort is located on the west side of Silva Bay. The marina offers transient moorage on A and B docks with accommodation of boats up to 165 feet in length. Each slip has access to power (30, 50 and 100 amp) hookups with potable water available at the fuel dock. Services at the marina include a fuel dock, restrooms, showers, laundry facilities, and garbage disposal.

In the fall of 2017, the restaurant and liquor store at the marina suffered a total loss by fire. As of early 2019, the new owners of the marina and resort are working to rebuild the restaurant with an opening date hopeful for 2019/2020.

The Silva Bay Shipyard is also found at the resort. The yard operates an 8 ton Travelift as well as a 70 ton marine railway for hauling boats. A small chandlery at the yard provides many needed marine supplies, and can order other supplies not in stock. For maintenance and repairs, Silva Bay Marina Repairs is a marine and small engine repair shop found at the yard. For further information, check their website at: www.silvabayshipyard.com or by phone at: (250) 247-9800.

Silva Bay Marine Resort
Monitors VHF channel 66A
383 South Road
Gabriola, BC V0R 1X7
(250) 247-8662
info@silvabay.com
silvabay.com

Sights to See

One of the highlights to staying in the protected waters of Silva Bay is taking advantage of the public bus system (see page 321) on the island and heading out for a day of adventure. The first stop on the island tour is the Gabriola Museum and Petroglyph Park. The museum is the perfect first stop to appreciate Gabriola Island's natural and cultural history through both indoor and outdoor exhibits. Surrounding the museum is Petroglyph Park. Elders of the Snuneymuxw First Nation granted permission to create replicas of a number of the island's eroding petroglyphs, many of which reside on private land. The park allows visitors the chance to experience these replicated carvings and learn about the island's aboriginal inhabitants. The museum and park are located near the west side of the island at 505 South Road. For further information on the museum and park including hours of operation, check their website at: gabriolamuseum.org.

While venturing on the west side of the island, be sure to check out the shopping, provisioning and dining options on North Road near Descanso Bay. Groceries, hardware, and restaurants can all be found within the village (see page 336).

A short walk or bike ride away from Silva Bay is Drumbeg Provincial Park. The 50-acre park is situated on Gabriola Passage and provides a wonderful picnic spot overlooking the pass. Roughly one mile of trails cross the park, which also offers a a beautiful sand and pebble beach, as well as forest and open grasslands. Be aware that the park does contain the giant hogweed plant. Sap from the plant iritates and blisters skin when exposed to sunlight. To avoid coming into contact with the plant, be sure to stay on the trails.

The protected waters of Silva Bay and surrounding maze of islands and rocky reefs make the bay a perfect area for exploring by kayak. Clear water and an amazing scene of underwater wildlife make for a magical paddle adventure. For those without kayaks, rentals are available at Page's Resort & Marina.

Page's Resort store

Silva Bay Shipyard

Silva Bay Marina fuel dock

Page's bike rentals

©Kevin Oke

Pilot and Taylor Bays

Pilot and Taylor Bays are found at the northwestern end of Gabriola Island. The bays are narrowly separated by a tombolo formation with beautiful sand beaches on either side. Gabriola Sands Provincial Park includes these beaches, which are popular with picnickers especially on warm summer days. Nearby Twin Beaches Mall offers a variety of convenience items, including ice cream and cold beverages.

Pilot Bay lies east of Taylor Bay, and are both found on the northwest end of Gabriola Island. Approaches to the bays are made via Fairway and Forwood Channels, located within the Strait of Georgia. Approaching from the east, passage can be taken either north of Entrance Island or south through Forwood Channel. Detached rocks lie west and southwest of Entrance Island with the southern most rock marked by hand buoy "PO" and the northern most by cardinal buoy "PE." Approaching from the west, passage via Fairway Channel, which lies between Snake and Gabriola Islands, can be taken. A shoal area lies southeast of Snake Island. The southern extrimity of the shoal is marked by lighted bell buoy "P2."

When entering either bay, be sure to check the chart and tide tables as drying reefs and shallow areas are found surrounding both bays and entrances. For Taylor Bay, both entrance points have large extending reefs and shallow areas so be sure to give them ample room when rounding into the bay. The same is true for Pilot Bay with drying reefs and shallow water off Tinson Point.

Anchorage can be taken within either bay in 2 to 4 fathoms over a mostly sand and mud bottom. This is a popular swimming area so keep a careful watch on your approach for swimmers. Many private moorings are found in the bays which may limit room for anchoring. Due to their proximity to the open Strait of Georgia, these bays can be exposed to northwest winds in the strait and waves wrapping around the points.

For trips to shore, the Gabriola Sands Provincial Park at the head of both bays provides a beautiful beach landing. These beaches change greatly with the tides so be prepared when securing your dinghy or kayak. The park provides picnic tables, a large grass area, and pit toilets. A short walk down Ricardo Road leads to the Twin Beaches Mall for convenience items and ice cream. Be sure to check out the Malaspina Galleries off Malaspina Point near Taylor Bay. These galleries showcase striking sandstone formations carved by centuries of erosion and wave action.

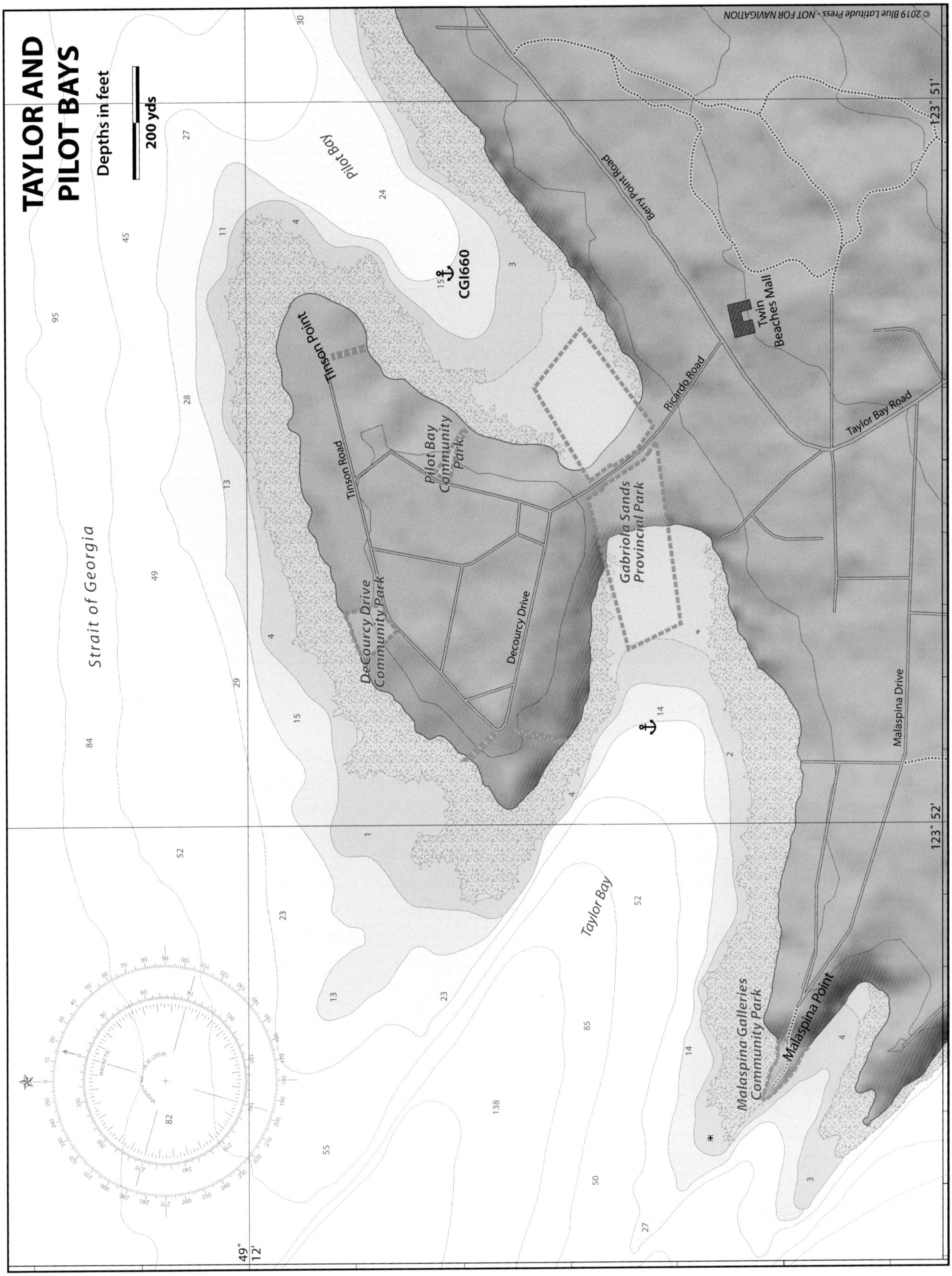

TAYLOR AND PILOT BAYS

Depths in feet

200 yds

© 2019 Blue Latitude Press - NOT FOR NAVIGATION

30

Pilot Bay

27

45

24

95

11

4

15 ⚓ CGI660

3

28

Tinson Point

Tinson Road

13

Pilot Bay Community Park

Berry Point Road

Twin Beaches Mall

Ricardo Road

Taylor Bay Road

Strait of Georgia

49

29

4

DeCourcy Drive Community Park

Decourcy Drive

Gabriola Sands Provincial Park

⚓ 14

2

Malaspina Drive

84

15

4

1

52

23

13

23

Taylor Bay

52

⚓ 85

138

55

14

Malaspina Galleries Community Park

Malaspina Point

4

82

50

3

27

49° 12'

49°
12'

123° 52'

123° 51'

CGI660 - 49° 11.800'N 123° 51.230'W

©Chris Hill

Descanso Bay

Descanso Bay, on Gabriola Island's western shore, is a short hop from downtown Nanaimo. The bay is home to the BC Ferries terminal, connecting the island with the city of Nanaimo. A short walk from the bay takes visitors to the village servicing Gabriola Island including shops, provisioning, restaurants, and the island's impressive historical museum.

Descanso Bay is found on the west end of Gabriola Island, less than 3 miles from Nanaimo's waterfront harbor. Approaches to the bay are taken via Fairway Channel from the north, or Northumberland Channel from the south and west. Approaching the bay from the north, be cautious of the extending reefs found off Malaspina Point lying roughly 0.8 miles north-northwest of the bay. Be sure to give the long and narrow drying rock ledges found between Malaspina Point and Descanso Bay ample room.

Approaching from Northumberland Channel or Nanaimo, be aware this is a heavily trafficed area. Seaplanes, pleasure boats, tugs in tow, large commercial ships including ferries, and log booms frequent this area. For boats crossing from Nanaimo, currents off Jack Point, which is just north of the Duke Point terminal, can be strong.

Anchorage can be taken in the southern portion of Descanso Bay in 4 to 8 fathoms. As Descanso Bay is open to the northwest and the open Strait of Georgia, this anchorage is best suited for periods of calm or southerly weather. During the summer months, northwest winds are common and make this anchorage unfavorable.

For trips to shore, dinghies can be landed at the head of the drying beach at the south end of the bay. From the

Descanso Bay to:		
	Bedwell Harbour *(South Pender Island)*	39 nm
	Clam Bay *(Thetis Island)*	16 nm
	Ganges Harbour *(Salt Spring Island)*	32 nm
	Ladysmith	17 nm
	Montague Harbour *(Galiano Island)*	26 nm
	Nanaimo	3 nm
	Pirates Cove *(De Courcy Island)*	10 nm
	Princess Bay *(Portland Island)*	39 nm
	Vancouver *(Burrard Inlet)*	30 nm
	Sidney	40 nm
	Tod Inlet	42 nm
	Victoria	63 nm

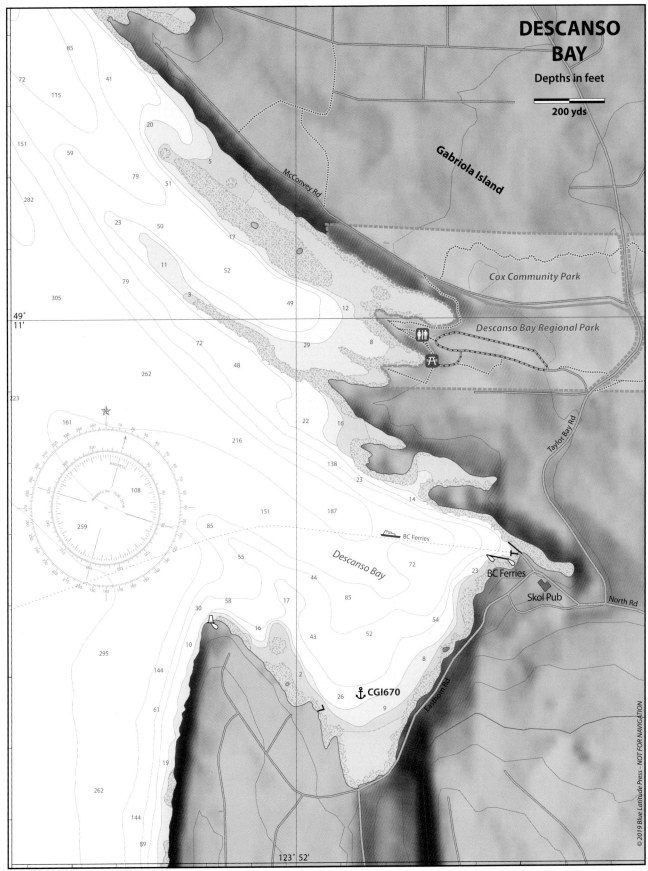

DESCANSO BAY

Depths in feet

200 yds

Gabriola Island

McConvey Rd

Cox Community Park

Descanso Bay Regional Park

Taylor Bay Rd

49°
11'

BC Ferries

Descanso Bay

BC Ferries

Skol Pub

North Rd

Easthom Rd

CGI670

© 2019 Blue Latitude Press - NOT FOR NAVIGATION

123° 52'

CGI670 - 49° 10.485'N 123° 51.845'W

beach, it is roughly a one mile walk on Easthom and North Roads to the village.

To get a true feel for the history and culture of Gabriola Island, a visit to Petroglyph Park and Gabriola Museum is a must. Gabriola is home to more than 70 known petroglyphs scattered around the island. These sacred and historical records were carved into sandstone bedrock or boulders roughly between 100 to possibly 3,000 years ago. As most of these petroglyphs reside on private land, along with the ever present threat of erosion, permission to create replicas of the petroglyphs was provided in 1996 by the elders of the Snuneymuxw First Nation. Over 30 reproductions can be found at Petroglyph Park with interpretive signs describing the history and details.

At the center of the park is the Gabriola Museum. The museum showcases the natural and cultural history of Gabriola Island through both indoor and outdoor exhibits. The Gabriola Museum is open May through October with the outdoor exhibits and native plant garden open year round. For current hours and further information contact the museum at (250) 247-9987 or check their website at: www.gabriolamuseum.org.

If you're lucky enough to visit the island on a weekend, be sure to check out the Gabriola Growers and Makers Market held at the Agi Hall. From May through October (10am -2pm), farmers and artisans from Gabriola and Mudge Islands bring their produce, crafts, bakery items, and more to the market each Saturday. Agi Hall is located near the intersection of South and North Roads, across from the post office. For further information, visit: agihall.com.

Provisioning

Arbutus Home Building Centre
Offering a selection of tools, hardware, plumbing, electrical and lumber supplies. Located on the corner of Ross Way and North Road. Open daily. (250) 247-8157

BC Liquor Store
A chain liquor store selling a nice selection of beer, wine and spirits. Located next to the gas station on North Road. Open daily. (250) 247-0271

Island Home and Garden
A newer store reminiscent of the old general mercantiles carrying a little bit of everything for the home and garden, including sporting goods. Located next to Arbutus Home Building Centre. Open daily. (250) 247-8800

Island Meat and Deli
Island Meat offers housemade sausages, meats, fresh and frozen seafood, along with deli items like sausage rolls and meat pies. Located across the street from Village Food Market. Open daily in the summer. (250) 247-8828

Village Food Market & Liquor Store
A full-service grocery store located on North Road in the Folklife Village. Village Food Market offers all the grocery staples including fresh meat and produce, in-house baked goods, dairy selections, a deli, purified water and more. Open daily 8am - 7pm (Sundays 10am - 7pm). (250) 247 8755

Restaurants

The Kitchen
A delightful bistro open for lunch and dinner serving homemade meals and latenight pizzas. Patio seating available. Located on North Road, next to Village Food Market. www.thekitchengabriola.com, (250) 325-5505

Robert's Place
A local haunt open for breakfast, lunch and dinner. Save room for the dessert selections including mile high cakes and fruit pies. Located on North Road, across from Village Food Market. www.robertsplacegabriola.com, (250) 247-2010

Skol Pub
Located across from the ferry terminal, the Skol Pub offers classic pub fare and ice cold beverages. The pub provides indoor and outdoor patio seating, a pool table, and karaoke nights. Open daily for lunch and dinner. (250) 247-9988

Woodfire Restaurant
Using local ingredients, Woodfire serves a menu of gourmet woodfire pizzas, Italian pastas and items from the grill. Open daily for dinner. Located within the Madrona Marketplace on North Road. www.woodfirerestaurant.ca, (250) 247-0095

Morning slack at Dodd Narrows heading south

Dodd Narrows

Dodd Narrows is a small pass connecting Stuart and Northumberland Channels. The pass is widely used by pleasure boats and tugs in tow heading to or from Nanaimo. Currents in the narrows can be strong with sizable tide rips. For boats that enter at slack tide, Dodd Narrows is not a challenge and relatively straightforward.

Dodd Narrows is formed by Purvis Point on Mudge Island to the east and Joan Point on Vancouver Island to the west. The narrowest portion spans roughly 200 feet with current velocities attaining rates up to nearly 10 knots. Tide rips form off the north entrance during the flood, and around the overhead cable on the ebb. The overhead cable at the south entrance has a vertical clearance of 120 feet.

Due to the strong currents and tide rips, transit Dodd Narrows at slack tide. Prior to slack, boats will linger around the entrances. Once slack is reached, boats begin their transit. During the summer months, when boating traffic is at its peak, many boats can be found heading north and southbound. Due to the narrow confines of the pass, it is best to allow boats from one direction to pass through before heading in the opposite direction. Do not get in the way of any tugs in tow transiting the narrows.

To avoid encountering a boat mid-channel, some boaters will issue a call on VHF channel 16 (**low power**) prior to entering. For example, "Sécurité, Sécurité, Sécurité. This is sailing vessel *Om Shanti* entering Dodd Narrows northbound. *Om Shanti* standing by on channel 16." For boats that are within a line transiting the narrows, only the first boat is necessary to issue a call to avoid clogging up channel 16.

Due to the volume of traffic through the narrows, be patient and courteous to fellow boaters by keeping your speed and boat wake to a minimum, do not pass slower boats in the narrows, and keep a careful watch.

Percy Anchorage, found west of False Narrows, is a convenient anchorage to wait for slack tide for boats transiting southbound through Dodd Narrows. Northumberland Channel is known for its numerous log booms and working tugs servicing the nearby mill. Northumberland Channel is also different in that it has a continuous set to the east with a maximum current of 1 to 2 knots.

False Narrows

False Narrows is formed by Mudge Island to the southwest and Gabriola Island to the north, connecting Pylades and Northumberland Channels. False Narrows is only advisable for shallow draft boats with local knowledge.

Surrounded by large drying ledges as well as a mid-channel narrow ledge, transiting the narrows can be difficult. Shallow water and thick kelp beds are found throughout. Range markers at the east and west entrances help to guide boats to the channel north of the long drying ledge. Currents in False Narrows are less than those in Dodd Narrows.

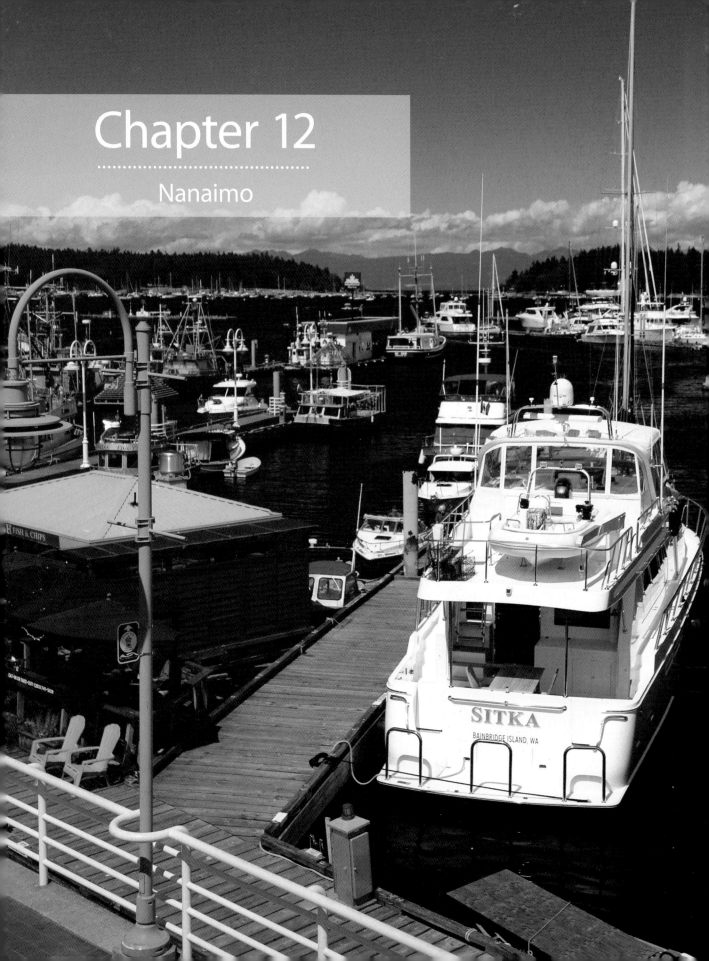

Chapter 12

Nanaimo

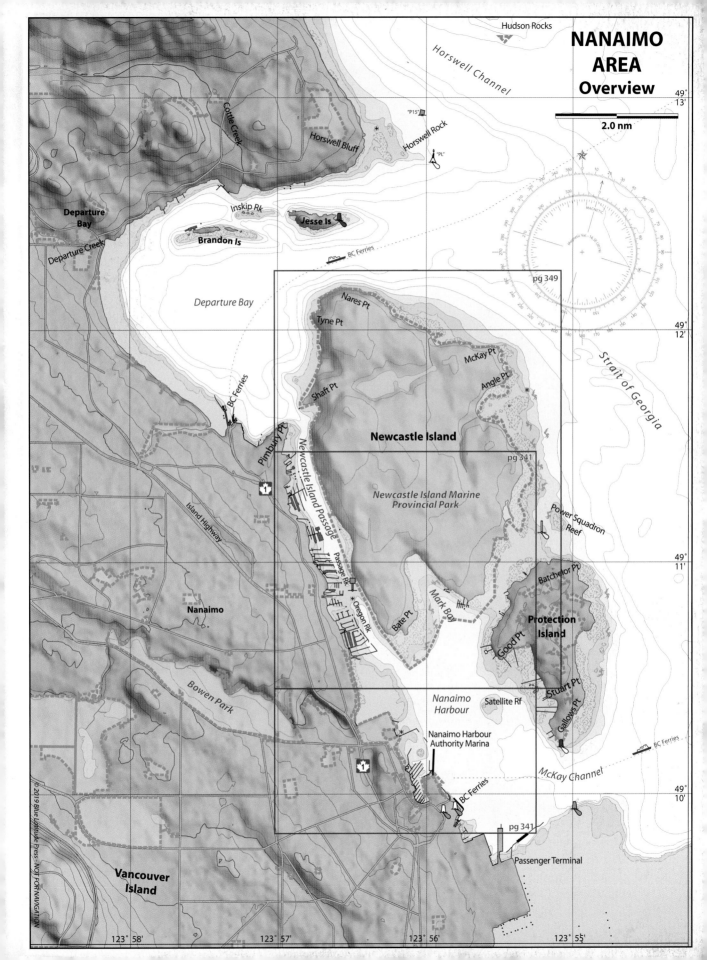

Hudson Rocks

Horswell Channel

2.0 nm

49° 13'

"P15"

Horswell Rock

"PL"

Horswell Bluff

Cottle Creek

Departure Bay

Inskip Rk

Jesse Is

Brandon Is

Departure Creek

Departure Bay

pg 349

Nares Pt

Tyne Pt

49° 12'

Strait of Georgia

McKay Pt

Angle Pt

Shaft Pt

BC Ferries

BC Ferries

Pimbury Pt

Newcastle Island

Newcastle Island Passage

pg 341

Island Highway

Newcastle Island Marine
Provincial Park

Power Squadron
Reef

49° 11'

Nanaimo

Passage Rk

Batchelor Pt

Mark Bay

**Protection
Island**

Bate Pt

Oregon Rk

Good Pt

Bowen Park

Stuart Pt

Nanaimo
Harbour

Satellite Rf

Gallows Pt

Nanaimo Harbour
Authority Marina

BC Ferries

BC Ferries

McKay Channel

49° 10'

pg 341

Passenger Terminal

**Vancouver
Island**

123° 58'   123° 57'   123° 56'   123° 55'

©Kevin Oke

Nanaimo

Nanaimo is a vibrant city that radiates out from its historic waterfront. The large municipal marina puts visitors in the heart of town with convenient access to shopping, restaurants, and activities. Nearby Newcastle Island Provincial Park not only offers an expansive and well-protected anchorage, but endless opportunities for adventure on the 900-acre island. For those continuing north to Desolation Sound, Nanaimo makes for a great provisioning and fuel stop.

Nanaimo lies at the northern end of the Gulf Islands, and west of the mountain-studded city of Vancouver. Approaches to Nanaimo can be taken via the Strait of Georgia, or via Dodd Narrows and Northumberland Channel. Newcastle and Protection Islands lie within the harbor, providing additional shelter and anchorage for visiting boats.

For those approaching via Northumberland Channel and Dodd Narrows, keep in mind that due to boats waiting for slack tide, a stream of boats will often be heading to Nanaimo. With the varying speeds of different boats, most will spread out in Northumberland Channel once through the narrows. Be patient and courteous through the initial bottleneck, and watch your wake when passing other boats.

Northumberland Channel is known for its numerous log booms and working tugs servicing the nearby mill.

Northumberland Channel is also different in that it has a continuous set to the east with a maximum current of 1 to 2 knots. During periods of wind opposing current, the channel can be a bit choppy. When rounding Jack Point into Nanaimo's harbor, be aware that currents be can strong off the point.

For boats approaching from the Strait of Georgia, there are three main channels leading into Nanaimo: Horswell, Rainbow, and Fairway Channels. Horswell Channel is a north approach, and lies between Hudson Rocks and

Nanaimo to:		
Clam Bay (Thetis Island)	17 nm
Ganges Harbour (Salt Spring Island)	33 nm
Ladysmith	18 nm
Montague Harbour (Galiano Island)	28 nm
Pirates Cove (De Courcy Island)	11 nm
Princess Bay (Portland Island)	40 nm
Port Browning (North Pender Island)	39 nm
Roche Harbor (USA)	46 nm
Sidney	42 nm
Tod Inlet	43 nm
Vancouver (Burrard Inlet)	33 nm
Victoria	63 nm
Wallace Island	21 nm

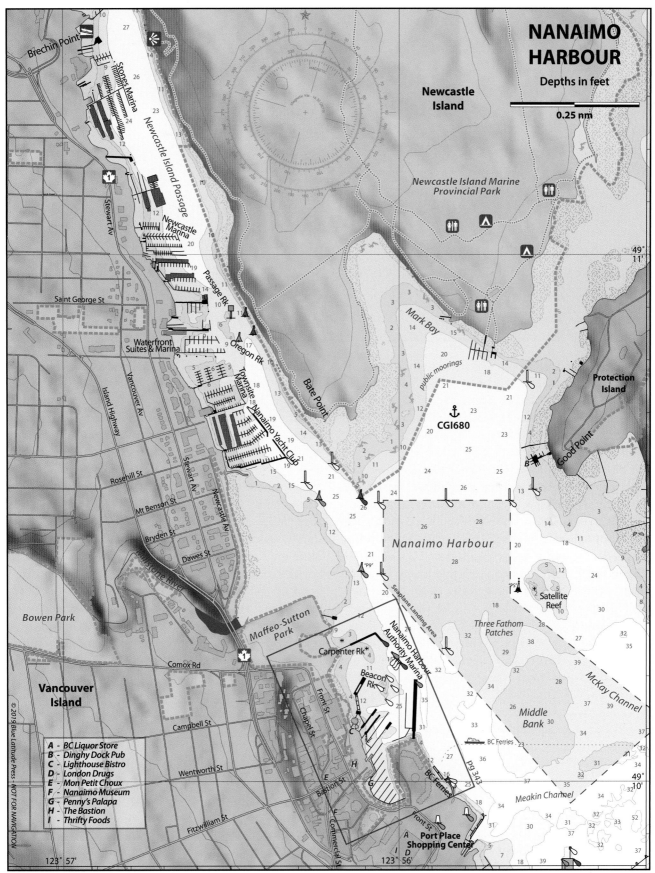

NANAIMO HARBOUR

Depths in feet

0.25 nm

Newcastle
Island

Newcastle Island Marine
Provincial Park

Mark Bay

public moorings

Protection
Island

Good Point

⚓ CGI680

Nanaimo Harbour

Satellite
Reef

Three Fathom
Patches

McKay Channel

Middle
Bank

BC Ferries

Meakin Channel

Brechin Point

Stones Marina

Newcastle Island Passage

Stewart Av

Newcastle
Marina

Passage Rk

Saint George St

Island Highway

Vancouver Av

Waterfront
Suites & Marina

Oregon Rk

Bate Point

Townsite
Marina

Nanaimo Yacht Club

Rosehill St

Stewart Av

Newcastle Av

Mt Benson St

Bryden St

Dawes St

Millstone River

Bowen Park

Comox Rd

Maffeo-Sutton
Park

Vancouver
Island

Carpenter Rk

Beacon
Rk

Nanaimo Harbour
Authority Marina

Seaplane Landing Area

Chapel St

Front St

Campbell St

Wentworth St

Bastion St

Fitzwilliam St

Front St

BC Ferries

Pg 343

Port Place
Shopping Center

A - BC Liquor Store
B - Dinghy Dock Pub
C - Lighthouse Bistro
D - London Drugs
E - Mon Petit Choux
F - Nanaimo Museum
G - Penny's Palapa
H - The Bastion
I - Thrifty Foods

© 2019 Blue Latitude Press · NOT FOR NAVIGATION

49°
11'

49°
10'

123° 57'

123° 56'

CGI680 - 49° 10.700'N 123° 55.810'W

©Kevin Oke

Vancouver Island. Rainbow Channel is also a north approach, and lies between Five Finger and Snake Islands. Fairway Channel is an east approach, and lies between Snake and Gabriola Islands. Both Rainbow and Fairway Channels are used by BC Ferries.

Boats approaching from the north can enter Departure Bay and transit Newcastle Island Passage. This passage is narrow and shallow with rock hazards. Oregon Rock, marked by port hand buoy "P13," and Passage Rock, marked by a port hand daymark, lie near the south end of the channel. When transiting Newcastle Island Passage, stay east of Oregon Rock. Due to drying shoals, passage should not be taken between Newcastle and Protection Islands except for dinghies and shoal draft boats at higher tides.

Nanaimo's harbour is busy with frequent traffic from ferries, seaplanes, pleasure boats, fishing boats, tugs in tow, and large commercial ships. Three ferry terminals are located within the harbor at Departure Bay, downtown Nanaimo, and Duke Point. Two commercial seaplane docks are found in Departure Bay and downtown Nanaimo. Cargo, lumber, and pulp transport ships as well as log booms also frequent the area with docks and boom grounds found south of downtown, along Duke Point, and within Northumberland Channel. When entering and leaving the Nanaimo area, be sure to keep a careful watch and to stay out of the way of these vessels and planes. A speed limit of 5 knots is mandated by the Nanaimo Port Authority for Nanaimo Harbour, excluding Dodd Narrows.

Two water aerodromes have been created within Nanaimo's harbor for seaplane landings and take offs. "Sea-plane Landing Area A" is located between Newcastle and Protection Islands and Nanaimo's downtown waterfront. "Seaplane Landing Area B" is located at the south end of Departure Bay. There is no anchoring allowed within the boundaries of these landing zones. An aeronautical strobe light, located on the middle breakwater near the seaplane dock, is activated by the plane to alert boaters of an aircraft landing or taking off in landing area "A". A strobe light for landing area "B" is located on Shaft Point on Newcastle Island at the north entrance to Newcastle Island Passage.

The anchorage for Nanaimo is found between Newcastle and Protection Islands. Mooring buoys and docks are available through the provincial park at Newcastle Island (see page 348). Anchorage can be taken north of "Landing Area A," and south of Mark Bay on Newcastle Island. The northern boundary of "Landing Area A" is marked by buoys. Due to ocean floor restoration efforts, anchoring is not permitted in Mark Bay. During busy summer weekends, this anchorage, along with the park mooring buoys and dock, can become quite congested with visiting boats.

There are a number of marinas in the Nanaimo area with the most popular for transient boats being the centrally located Nanaimo Port Authority marina. There are a number of private marinas along Newcastle Island Passage, many of which only offer permanent or seasonal moorage. Some do provide transient moorage when they have space available. These may include Stones Marina & Boatyard (250) 753-4232, Newcastle Marina (250) 753-1431, Waterfront Suites & Marina (250) 753-7111, and the Nanaimo Yacht Club for reciprocal moorage (250) 754-7011.

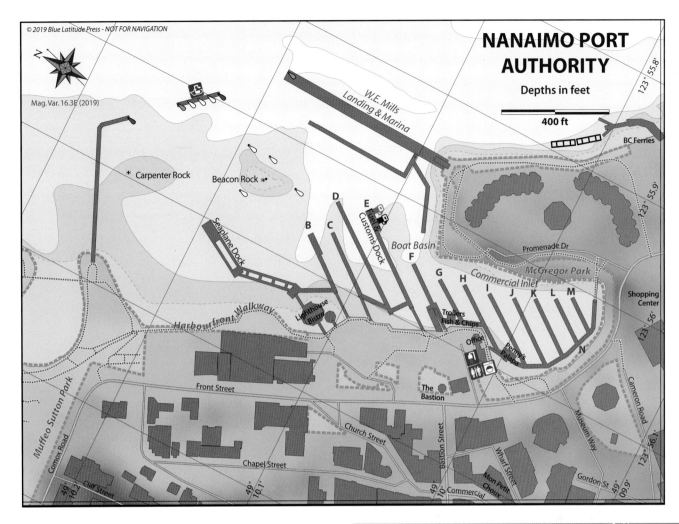

Nanaimo Port Authority

Nanaimo Port Authority operates two neighboring marinas with over 7,000 feet of moorage for transient and permanent vessels. The well protected Inner Boat Basin provides space for small to medium sized boats. The W.E. Mills Landing & Marina, formerly known as the Cameron Island Marina, was originally designed to attract small cruise ships and other vessels too large to use other docking facilities in the harbour. The W.E. Mills Landing & Marina is able to accommodate large vessels with 600 feet of pier space. Each slip has access to water and power (20/30, 50 and 100 amp) hookups. Services at the marina include a customs dock, floating pump out station, restrooms, showers, laundry facilities, used oil recycling, garbage and recycling drops, and staff to assist with dock lines. The docks are secured at night with locked gates from 11pm to 7am. The marina provides a 90 foot fuel dock with diesel, gasoline, oil lubricants, 20 pound propane canister exchanges, ice, snacks, and beverages.

Nanaimo Port Authority is also home to a Canadian Border Services Agency (CBSA) customs dock for boats

needing to clear into Canada. Customs is located on E-Dock next to the fuel barge.

Nanaimo Port Authority
Monitors VHF Channel 67
10 Wharf Street
Nanaimo, BC V9R 2X3
Phone: 250-754-5053
marina@npa.ca
www.npa.ca

343

History of Nanaimo

For thousands of years the protected waters and abundant resources of the Nanaimo area has been part of the Snuneymuxw First Nation. Snuneymuxw territory spans from the middle region of Vancouver Island to the Gulf Islands and across the Strait of Georgia to the Fraser Valley. Many sacred petroglyphs carved by the ancestors of the Snuneymuxw can be found in the area.

Europeans arrived in the late 1700's, with Spanish and English ships exploring and mapping the area. It wasn't until the development of Fort Victoria in 1843 by the Hudson's Bay Company (HBC), that Europeans first began to settle Vancouver Island.

In 1851, an HBC employee learned of coal deposits in the Nanaimo area. The following year, HBC readied the new company town at Nanaimo, building employee houses and the historic Bastion. The first load of coal from the Nanaimo mines was sent to Fort Victoria in September of 1852. To help supplement the newly growing town, twenty four families totaling 75 people from Staffordshire, England arrived in Nanaimo in 1854. For the next several years the town slowly grew around the mine, lumber mill, and shipping industries.

Ten years after mining the first load of coal, HBC sold their mining interests in Nanaimo to the British owned

Vancouver Coal Mining and Land Company in 1862. The company expanded mining operations, auctioned off city lots, and offered miners five acre farms on a lease-to-own basis. The coal mining and transport via railroads and ships was a booming business in Nanaimo. The growing city was incorporated in 1874, making it the 6th oldest municipality in BC.

In the evening hours of May 3, 1887, tragedy hit when two explosions in the No. 1 Esplanade Mine, which ran under the harbor towards Protection Island, killed 150 miners. Many of the miners were sealed off in side shafts waiting for rescue until their oxygen ultimately ran out. Only seven miners survived the explosion. It is marked as the worst mining accident in BC history and second in all of Canada.

By the 1920's, Nanaimo's coal industry began to decline as oil became the favored fuel, and the remaining coal deposits were increasing deeper and more costly to extract. Nanaimo began to shift gears from mining to forestry.

In 1947, successful timber exporter, Harvey R. MacMillan built the Harmac Pulp Mill just south of Nanaimo's Duke Point. The mill became a top producer of northern bleached softwood kraft pulp (NBSK), and still operates today. In 2008, the employees and local investors rescued the mill after the current owners filed for bankruptcy. Today, the mill, Harmac Pacific, continues to be owned and operated by its employees.

Nanaimo today is home to over 90,000 residents, making it Vancouver Island's second largest city next to Victoria. The city is also an important transportation hub with three ferry terminals linking it with two mainland destinations and Gabriola Island.

Sights to See

To learn first hand about the area's history, there is no better place to visit than the Nanaimo Museum. The museum is located a block from the marina in the Vancouver Island Conference Centre. A few of the permanent exhibits include the early history of Nanaimo's coal mining and logging industries, the arrival of the Hudson's Bay Company in 1852, and the early traditions and daily life of the Snuneymuxw First Nation. The First Nations collection is held in trust for the Snuneymuxw First Nation with whom the museum works closely to interpret their story. Along with permanent exhibits, the museum also has an interesting mix of rotating featured exhibits and a new sports hall of fame. For further information regarding the museum visit: nanaimomuseum.ca.

To further your history tour, be sure to check out The Bastion, an original structure built by the Hudson's Bay Company and completed in 1853. The three storied bastion

Bathtub Race fireworks

is available for dinghies. For further information regarding the island, visit: newcastleisland.ca.

While visiting Newcastle Island, be sure to dinghy over to the unique Dinghy Dock Pub on Protection Island. After enjoying a nice meal and cold beverage overlooking the harbor, be sure to check out Protection Island. The ramp from the pub allows visitors to walk the island, explore the beaches, relax at the parks, or visit the local museum. With a population of roughly 350 people, the island has remained quiet with mostly golf carts used as local transport.

For a bit of exercise and to explore the waterfront, the city of Nanaimo offers the Maffeo Sutton Park and Harbourfront Walkway. Over a mile in length, visitors can walk the waterfront from the W.E. Mills Landing & Marina up to the Nanaimo Yacht Club. Along the way, the Harbourfront Walkway passes through the Maffeo Sutton Park located just north of the seaplane dock. The park occasionally hosts community events and includes a playground, Swy-a-Lana lagoon and swimming beach, Lions Pavilion covered stage, ferry access to Newcastle Island, and restrooms.

If you happen to visit during the weekend, be sure to drop by the Nanaimo Downtown Farmer's Market for a taste of the island. Every Saturday from May through September (9am to 2pm), farmers, artisans, and food vendors gather on Front Street near The Bastion to sell their beautiful island grown, raised, and made products.

Each July since 1967, Nanaimo has hosted one of the town's largest events, the Great World Championship Bathtub Race. The weekend-long festivities include a street fair, concerts, parade, children's carnival, fireworks show, and the headlining event, the bathtub race. From 1967 to 1996, motorized bathtubs raced across the open Strait of Georgia from Nanaimo to Vancouver. Today the race begins and ends in downtown Nanaimo, rounding Entrance and Maud Islands, covering 36 total miles. For further information and schedules, visit: www.bathtubbing.com.

Marine Chandleries and Services
Brechin Boat Ramp
Brechin Boat Ramp is a public access boat ramp located next to the BC Ferries terminal. The ramp has been recently upgraded with three lanes, docks, and trailer parking. Located at 1890 Zorkin Road. www.nanaimo.ca

Harbour Chandler
Harbour Chandler is one of the largest marine chandleries on Vancouver Island. The store offers good selections on fishing gear, electronics, plumping items, cleaners, paints, sailing gear, fasteners, and more. Located at 52 Esplanade, behind the shopping center next to the marina. www.harbourchandler.ca, (250) 753-2425

is a landmark for Nanaimo's waterfront and is located near the Nanaimo Port Authority's marina office. While the timbers of the Bastion are original, the interior has been remodeled to represent what the early structure might have looked like during the post's early mining period from 1852 to 1862. During the summer months, The Bastion is open every day for tours, and at noon, a cannon firing ceremony takes place. The Bastion is part of the Nanaimo Museum and further information can be found on the museum's website.

One of the highlights to visiting Nanaimo is a trip out to Newcastle Island Marine Provincial Park. The island has roughly 14 miles of trails to keep you active all day long. Along with trails, the island offers beautiful beaches, camping, and open grass fields for lounging or tossing the frisbee. For a snack on the island, the Saysutshun Bistro provides casual fare including cold drinks, and ice cream. Access to the island is via boat. Foot ferries serve the island and a dock

Sunrise off Nanaimo's waterfront

Newcastle Marina and Haulout Yard

The Newcastle Marina offers a 60 ton Marine Travelift and haulout facilities. They provide marine services including hauls, shaft and propeller repair, boat engine maintenance, boat parts and more. Scaffolding and ladders are available free of charge. Located at 1300 Stewart Avenue. newcastlemarina.ca, (250) 753-1431

Stones Marina & Boatyard and The Marine Store

Stones Boatyard provides haulouts with an 83 ton Marine Travelift as well as marine services and repairs. On-site equipment rentals are offered including scaffolding, ladders, tarps, power tools, and more. The Marine store is a fully stocked marine chandlery including paints, cleaners, zincs, fasteners, and electrical supplies. Located at 104-1840 Stewart Avenue. www.nanaimoboatyard.ca, (250) 716-9065

Provisioning

BC Liquor Store

BC Liquor Stores offer a great selection of local, national and international beers, wines and spirits. Located next to Thrifty Foods on Front Street in the shopping center.

London Drugs

A chain pharmacy store located next to Thrifty Foods in the shopping center on Front Street.

Thrifty Foods

Conveniently located in a shopping center near the Nanaimo Port Authority marina on Front Street. A large chain grocery store open 24/7 supplying fresh produce, meats, dairy, bakery items and all the staples.

Restaurants

Dinghy Dock Pub

The famous Dinghy Dock Pub is a must stop when visiting Nanaimo. The floating pub, which is located off Protection Island, offers indoor and outdoor seating with sweeping views of the harbor. The pub offers traditional pub fare and local beers. Scheduled ferry service to the pub is available from Nanaimo and Newcastle Island. Open daily for lunch and dinner. dinghydockpub.com

Lighthouse Bistro & Pub

The Lighthouse is built over the water and next to the seaplane dock, offering perfect views of the harbor and arriving seaplanes. The Bistro and Pub provide indoor and outdoor patio seating. Their menu offers casual fare as well as seafood classics. Open daily for lunch and dinner. www.lighthousebistro.ca

Mon Petit Choux

Serving authentically baked French pastries and breads as well as delicious espresso drinks for dipping and savoring. Don't forget to try the region's famous Nanaimo bars as well. Open daily. Located at 101 - 120 Commercial Street. www.monpetitchoux.ca

Penny's Palapa

Penny's Palapa is a floating restaurant serving Mexican dishes and fresh squeezed margaritas with a west coast flair. An outdoor patio, complete with heaters and blankets for cooler days, allows diners to enjoy the views of the marina. Located on H dock, near the Nanaimo Port Authority's office. Open for lunch and dinner daily. www.pennyspalapa.com

©Kevin Oke

Newcastle Island

Newcastle Island is one of the top highlights to any visit to Nanaimo. The 900-acre island is a marine provincial park offering miles of hiking trails, camping, beautiful sandstone beaches, and ample protected moorage. Newcastle Island, or Saysutshun, is part of the Snuneymuxw First Nation territory. It has long been a source of traditional natural medicines and a place associated with physical and spiritual healing for the Snuneymuxw.

Newcastle Island is located within Nanaimo's harbor. The main anchorage is found on the island's south end near Protection Island and overlooking the city of Nanaimo. Approaches to the island can be taken via Newcastle Island Passage along the island's western shore, or via McKay Channel, south of Protection Island. There is no passage between Protection and Newcastle Islands except for shoal-draft dinghies as the pass is very shallow and dries at low water.

The Newcastle Island Marine Provincial Park offers mooring buoys and dock space for visiting boats for a nightly fee. Over 40 new buoys have been installed within

and southeast of Mark Bay. There are two types of mooring buoys available: those for boats 30 feet (LOA) or less, and those for boats 40 feet (LOA) or less. Anchoring within Mark Bay is not permitted due to recovery efforts for the ocean floor and marine life in the bay. The dock area can accommodate a number of boats with ample space for dinghies to tie up.

Newcastle Island to:		
Clam Bay (Thetis Island)	17 nm
Ganges Harbour (Salt Spring Island)	33 nm
Maple Bay	28 nm
Ladysmith	18 nm
Pirates Cove (De Courcy Island)	11 nm
Port Browning (North Pender Island)	39 nm
Roche Harbor (USA)	46 nm
Russell Island	37 nm
Sidney	42 nm
Tod Inlet	43 nm
Vancouver (Burrard Inlet)	33 nm
Victoria	63 nm

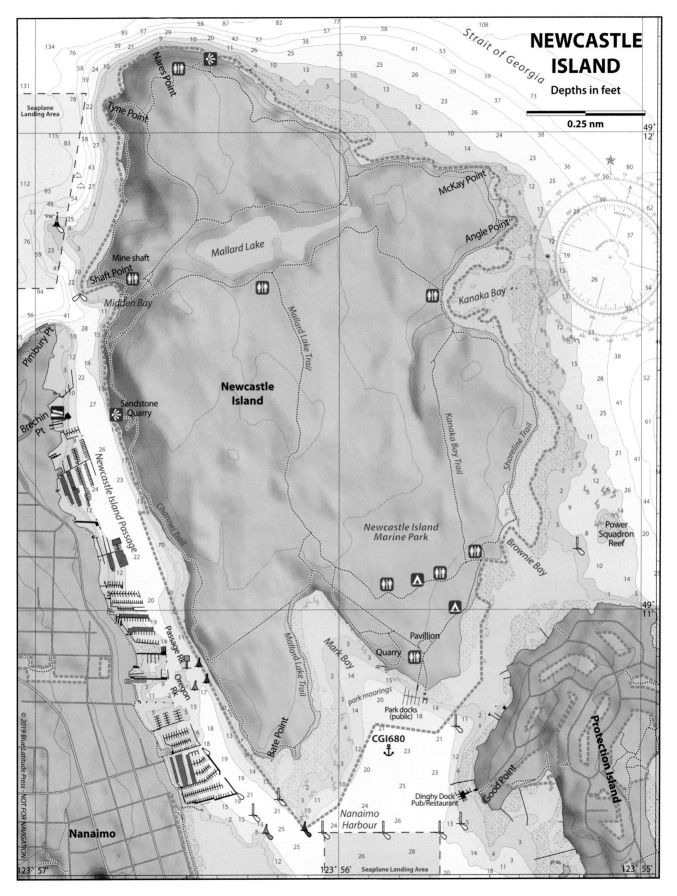

NEWCASTLE ISLAND

Depths in feet

0.25 nm

Strait of Georgia

Nares Point

Tyne Point

"PW"

Mine shaft

Shaft Point

Midden Bay

Mallard Lake

McKay Point

Angle Point

Kanaka Bay

Pimbury Pt

Brechin Pt

Sandstone Quarry

Newcastle Island

Mallard Lake Trail

Kanaka Bay Trail

Shoreline Trail

Power Squadron Reef

Newcastle Island Passage

Channel Trail

Newcastle Island Marine Park

Brownie Bay

Passage Rk

Oregon Rk

Mallard Lake Trail

Mark Bay

Pavillion

Quarry

Bate Point

park moorings

Park docks (public) 18

CGI680

Nanaimo Harbour

Dinghy Dock Pub/Restaurant

Good Point

Protection Island

Nanaimo

123° 57'

123° 56'

123° 55'

49° 12'

49° 11'

For boats looking to anchor, there is space available south of the park moorings and north of "Seaplane Landing Area A." The northern boundaries of this area is marked by buoys. Keep in mind there is no anchoring allowed within the boundaries of this landing zone. During the busier summer months, the park mooring buoys, dock, and anchorage can become quite crowded. Anchor in 3 to 5 fathoms over a mud bottom. The anchorage provides good protection from the summer's typical northwest winds.

The history of Newcastle Island begins with the ancestors of the Snuneymuxw First Nation who once had thriving villages on the island around present day Mark and Midden Bays. The island was later used as a sacred burial site. The discovery of coal brought English miners to Newcastle in the mid 1800's, who named the island after their home mining town in England. The island's thick deposits of sandstone also supported a long standing quarry. Japanese immigrants, who originally came to the area during the coal mining years, developed fish canneries, salteries, and a shipyard on the island. With the start of World War II, the Japanese citizens were removed to internment camps to the interior of BC. In the 1930's, the Canadian Pacific Railway bought the island and used it as a grand scale resort. After World War II the island was sold to the city of Nanaimo and later to the BC government to be used as a public park.

Today visitors to the island can enjoy a variety of trails crisscrossing the island, totaling over 14 miles. The trails take visitors past historical areas like old mine shafts and quarries, as well as scenic points of interest like Mallard Lake and Giovando Lookout. The trails are well groomed with a few open to bicycles. Dogs are welcome on the island, however in 2018 a cougar was spotted on the island. If there are recent cougar sightings, many trails may be closed to pets.

The island is also home to a thriving raccoon population, including a rare and elusive blond raccoon. Caused by a recessive gene, blond raccoons seem to be more prevalent on Newcastle Island. For campers and boaters at the dock, be sure to properly store food, garbage and scented items to prevent nighttime raids.

Most of the park's development is centered to the east of Mark Bay. Amenities at the park include a large campground, restroom buildings, showers, potable water (seasonal), picnic shelters, a soccer field, playground, and a pavilion housing a visitor center and bistro.

For a meal off the boat, there are two nearby dining options. At the park, the Saysutshun Bistro is open seasonally and offers a wide menu including beverages, ice cream, soups, salads, and burgers. Just across from the park at Protection Island is the famous Dinghy Dock Pub. Enjoy a seat outside at the floating restaurant and take in the view of the harbor and the cityscape of Nanaimo.

Dinghy Dock Pub

Waypoints

Name	Description	Waypoint	
Chapter 1: Victoria Area			
CGI001	Victoria Harbour Entrance	48° 24.850'N	123° 23.930'W
CGI010	Oak Bay Anchorage	48° 25.640'N	123° 18.090'W
CGI020	Cadboro Bay Anchorage	48° 27.310'N	123° 17.590'W
CGI030	Cordova Bay Anchorage	48° 29.805'N	123° 19.086'W
Chapter 2: Sidney Area			
CGI040	Saanichton Bay Anchorage	48° 35.690'N	123° 22.860'W
CGI050	Sidney Spit Anchorage	48° 38.570'N	123° 20.600'W
CGI060	Sidney Approach	48° 38.960'N	123° 23.080'W
CGI070	Roberts Bay Anchorage	48° 39.875'N	123° 23.820'W
CGI080	Tsehum Harbour Approach	48° 40.190'N	123° 23.700'W
CGI090	Canoe Cove Marina Entrance	48° 40.980'N	123° 24.000'W
CGI100	Princess Bay Anchorage	48° 43.050'N	123° 22.160'W
CGI110	Royal Cove Anchorage	48° 44.090'N	123° 22.285'W
Chapter 3: Saanich Inlet			
CGI120	Deep Cove Anchorage	48° 40.900'N	123° 28.700'W
CGI130	Mill Bay Anchorage	48° 38.890'N	123° 32.890'W
CGI140	Coles Bay Anchorage	48° 37.670'N	123° 28.080'W
CGI150	Brentwood Bay Approach	48° 34.650'N	123° 28.050'W
CGI160	Tod Inlet Anchorage	48° 33.600'N	123° 28.220'W
Chapter 4: Pender Islands			
CGI170	Camp Bay Anchorage	48° 44.630'N	123° 11.000'W
CGI180	Bedwell Harbour Approach	48° 43.850'N	123° 13.400'W

Name	Description	Waypoint	
Chapter 4: Pender Islands			
CGI181	Bedwell Harbour Anchorage	48° 44.980'N	123° 13.890'W
CGI182	Medicine Beach Anchorage	48° 45.560'N	123° 15.875'W
CGI190	Port Browning Anchorage	48° 46.470'N	123° 16.260'W
CGI200	Hope Bay Approach	48° 48.200'N	123° 15.950'W
CGI210	Grimmer Bay Anchorage	48° 48.725'N	123° 19.275'W
CGI220	Otter Bay Anchorage	48° 47.815'N	123° 18.430'W
Chapter 5: Saturna Island Area			
CGI230	Winter Cove Anchorage	48° 48.565'N	123° 11.665'W
CGI240	Lyall Harbour Anchorage	48° 47.900'N	123° 11.840'W
CGI241	Boot Cove Anchorage	48° 47.490'N	123° 11.925'W
CGI250	Narvaez Bay Anchorage	48° 46.535'N	123° 06.265'W
CGI260	Cabbage Island Anchorage	48° 47.840'N	123° 05.580'W
CGI270	Irish Bay Anchorage	48° 49.085'N	123° 12.415'W
CGI280	Horton Bay Anchorage	48° 49.640'N	123° 14.730'W
CGI290	Bennett Bay Anchorage	48° 50.695'N	123° 14.730'W
CGI300	Campbell Bay Anchorage	48° 51.545'N	123° 16.230'W
CGI310	Miners Bay Approach	48° 51.270'N	123° 18.270'W
CGI320	Village Bay Anchorage	48° 50.570'N	123° 19.615'W
Chapter 6: Prevost Island			
CGI330	James Bay Anchorage	48° 50.475'N	123° 23.870'W
CGI340	Selby Cove Anchorage	48° 50.060'N	123° 23.960'W
CGI350	Annette Bay Anchorage	48° 50.475'N	123° 23.870'W
CGI360	Glenthorne Passage Anchorage	48° 49.420'N	123° 23.470'W

Name	Description	Waypoint	
Chapter 6: Prevost Island			
CGI370	Ellen Bay Anchorage	48° 49.170'N	123° 22.535'W
CGI371	Diver Bay Anchorage	48° 49.350'N	123° 21.670'W
Chapter 7: Galiano Island			
CGI380	Montague Harbour Anchorage	48° 53.535'N	123° 23.705'W
CGI390	Active Pass Northeast Approach	48° 52.910'N	123° 17.760'W
CGI391	Active Pass Southwest Approach	48° 51.330'N	123° 21.130'W
CGI400	Porlier Pass Northeast Approach	49° 01.175'N	123° 34.935'W
CGI401	Porlier Pass Southwest Approach	49° 00.300'N	123° 35.830'W
CGI410	Retreat Cove Approach	48° 56.160'N	123° 30.200'W
Chapter 8: Salt Spring Island			
CGI420	Ganges Harbour Anchorage	48° 51.165'N	123° 29.500'W
CGI421	Madrona Bay Anchorage	48° 51.285'N	123° 28.890'W
CGI430	Long Harbour Anchorage	48° 51.600'N	123° 27.455'W
CGI440	Walker Hook Anchorage	48° 53.360'N	123° 29.500'W
CGI450	Fernwood Point Approach	48° 55.050'N	123° 31.910'W
CGI460	Vesuvius Bay Anchorage	48° 52.800'N	123° 34.435'W
CGI470	Burgoyne Bay Anchorage	48° 47.440'N	123° 31.325'W
CGI480	Musgrave Landing Approach	48° 45.000'N	123° 33.200'W
CGI490	Fulford Harbour Anchorage	48° 46.070'N	123° 27.330'W
CGI500	Russell Island Anchorage	48° 44.975'N	123° 24.640'W
Chapter 9: Cowichan Bay to Ladysmith			
CGI510	Cowichan Bay Approach	48° 44.650'N	123° 36.900'W
CGI511	Genoa Bay Anchorage	48° 45.780	123° 35.820'W
CGI520	Maple Bay Approach	48° 48.840'N	123° 36.000'W
CGI530	Crofton Approach	48° 52.500'N	123° 37.200'W
CGI540	Chemainus Approach	48° 56.000'N	123° 42.100'W

Name	Description	Waypoint	
Chapter 9: Cowichan Bay to Ladysmith			
CGI550	Ladysmith Anchorage	48° 59.655'N	123° 47.655'W
CGI551	Evening Cove Anchorage	48° 59.260'N	123° 46.185'W
Chapter 10: North Trincomali Channel Islands			
CGI560	Princess Cove Anchorage	48° 56.585'N	123° 33.355'W
CGI570	Clam Bay Anchorage	48° 59.050'N	123° 39.110'W
CGI580	Tent Island Approach	48° 55.650'N	123° 38.090'W
CGI590	Telegraph Harbour Anchorage	48° 58.390'N	123° 39.990'W
CGI591	Preedy Harbour Anchorage	48° 58.770'N	123° 40.935'W
CGI600	North Cove Anchorage	49° 00.980'N	123° 41.475'W
Chapter 11: Valdes and Gabriola Islands			
CGI610	Herring Bay Anchorage	49° 05.040'N	123° 42.940'W
CGI620	Pirates Cove Anchorage	49° 05.865'N	123° 43.830'W
CGI621	Pirates Cove South Anchorage	49° 05.570'N	123° 43.435'W
CGI630	Wakes Cove Anchorage	49° 07.590'N	123° 42.300'W
CGI631	Kendrick Island Anchorage	49° 07.370'N	123° 41.540'W
CGI640	Degnen Bay Entrance	49° 07.850'N	123° 42.600'W
CGI650	Silva Bay Anchorage	49° 09.235'N	123° 41.740'W
CGI660	Pilot Bay Anchorage	49° 11.800'N	123° 51.230'W
CGI670	Descanso Bay Anchorage	49° 10.485'N	123° 51.845'W
Chapter 12: Nanaimo			
CGI680	Nanaimo/Newcastle Island Anchorage	49° 10.700'N	123° 55.810'W

Charts

The following charts are available from the Canadian Hydrographic Service (CHS). The complete catalog of CHS charts is available at **www.charts.gc.ca**.

Chart #	Title
3313	Gulf Islands and Adjacent Waterways Atlas
3462	Juan de Fuca Strait to Strait of Georgia
3463	Strait of Georgia, Southern Part
3440	Race Rocks to D'Arcy Island
3441	Haro Strait, Boundary Pass, Satellite Channel
3442	North Pender Island to Thetis Island
3443	Thetis Island to Nanaimo
3412	Victoria Harbor (w/ Portage Inlet)
3424	Approaches to Oak Bay
3479	Approaches to Sidney (Tsehum Harbour, Sidney, Iroquois & John Passes)
3478	Plans Salt Spring Island
3477	Plans Gulf Islands (Bedwell, Telegraph, Preedy, Pender Canal)
3473	Active Pass, Porlier Pass, Montague Harbour
3475	Plans Stuart Channel (Chemainus, Ladysmith, Dodd Narrows)
3458	Approaches to Nanaimo
3447	Nanaimo Harbor and Departure Bay

The following charts are available from the US Government offices of NIMA/NOAA. The complete catalog of NIMA/NOAA charts is available at **www.charts.noaa.gov**

Chart #	Title
18400	Strait of Georgia and Strait of Juan de Fuca
18421	Strait of Juan de Fuca to Strait of Georgia; Drayton Harbor
18432	Boundary Pass
18433	Haro-Strait-Middle Bank to Stuart Island
18465	Strait of Juan de Fuca-eastern part

Suggested Reading

Books

Alden, Peter and Dennis Paulson. *National Audubon Society Field Guide to the Pacific Northwest*. New York City, NY: Random House Books, 2002.

Arnett, Chris. *The Terror of the Coast*. Vancouver, BC: Talonbooks, 1999.

Cannings, Richard, Tom Aversa, Hal Opperman. *Birds of British Columbia and the Pacific Northwest: A Complete Guide*. Victoria, BC: Heritage House Publishing, 2015.

Conover, David. *Once Upon an Island*. Kenmore, WA: San Juan Publishing, 2003.

Canadian Hydrographic Service. *Canadian Tide and Current Tables, Volume 5*. Ottawa, ON: Fisheries and Oceans Canada, 2018.

Canadian Hydrographic Service. *Current Atlas: Juan de Fuca Strait to Strait of Georgia*. Ottawa, ON: Fisheries and Oceans Canada, 2018.

Canadian Hydrographic Service. *Sailing Directions, PAC 201*. Ottawa, ON: Fisheries and Oceans Canada, 2018.

Kahn, Charles. *Hiking the Gulf Islands of British Columbia*. Vancouver, BC: Harbour Publishing, 2018.

Pojar, Jim and Andy MacKinnon. *Plants of the Pacific Northwest Coast*. Vancouver, BC: Lone Pine, 2004.

Romano, Craig. *Day Hiking the San Juan and Gulf Islands*. Seattle, WA: Mountaineers Books, 2014.

Websites

a.atmos.washington.edu/data/marine_report.html   Coastal waters forecast for the inland waters of western Washington and the northern and central Washington coastal waters including the Olympic Coast National Marine Sanctuary.

www.crd.bc.ca   The Capital Regional District (CRD) is the regional government for 13 municipalities and three electoral areas on southern Vancouver Island and the Gulf Islands.

www.env.gov.bc.ca/bcparks/   BC Provincial Parks website with maps and park information.

www.nauticalcharts.noaa.gov   The Office of Coast Survey is responsible for producing the suite of nautical charts, coast pilots, sailing directions, tides and currents, and other publications that cover the coastal waters of the U.S. and its territories.

www.ngdc.noaa.gov   The National Geophysical Data Center (NGDC), is a part of the US Department of Commerce (USDOC), National Oceanic & Atmospheric Administration (NOAA), National Environmental Satellite, Data and Information Service (NESDIS).

www.passageweather.com   Wind, wave and weather reports covering the world.

www.thecanadianencyclopedia.ca   A national encyclopedia about Canada.

weather.gc.ca/marine/   Marine forecasts and warnings for Canada.

Index

A

Acland Island 194
Acorn Island 326
Active Pass 207
Active Point 301
Aitken Point 171
Alarm Rock 301
Alcala Point 211
All Bay 78
Anglers Anchorage Marina 110
Annette Inlet 191
Anniversary Island 173, 174
Arbutus Point 262
Armstrong Point 76
Artificial Reef Society of British Columbia 91
Atkins Reef 232
Auchterlonie Point 139

B

Ballingall Islets 202
Bare Point 271
Batt Rock 186, 219
Baynes Channel 43, 48
BC Ferries 13
Beacon Hill Park 38
Beaumont Marine Park 125, 127
Bedwell Harbour 123
Belle Chain Islets 173, 174
Ben Mohr Rock 188, 202, 207
Bennett Bay 173
Berens Island 29
Bird Rock 271
Birds Eye Cove 264
Black Rock 211
Blue Heron Basin 78
Blunden Islet 121
Boat Isle 142
Boat Passage 153
Boatswain Bank 252, 257
Boiling Reef 166
Bold Bluff Point 254, 259
Boot Cove 161
Boulder Point 275
Boundary Pass 123
Brant Reef 326
Breakwater Island 318, 320, 323
Brentwood Bay 106
Bright Islet 198
British Columbia Provincial Parks 17
Brooks Point Regional Park 121
Brotchie Ledge 28

Brother XII 313, 318
Burgoyne Bay 238
Burial Islet 238, 254, 259
Butchart Cove 114
Butchart Gardens 113
Bute Island 277

C

Cabbage Island 164
Cabin Bay 290, 293
Cadboro Bay 48
Cadboro-Gyro Park 50
Cadboro Point 50
Cain Peninsula 210
Cain Point 210
Camp Bay 121
Campbell Bay 174
Campbell Point 173, 174
Canada Day Lamb Barbecue 156
Canadian Border Services Agency
    Bedwell Harbour 125
    Canoe Cove 84
    Nanaimo 343
    Oak Bay 45
    Sidney 69
    Tsehum Harbour 80
    Victoria 29
Canoe Bay 84
Canoe Cove 84
Canoe Rock 92
Captain Passage 186, 196, 219, 229
Carlos Island 328
Carney Point 78
Car Stops
    Mayne Island 169
    Pender Islands 120
Cattle Point 46
Cayetano Point 211
CBP ROAM app 13
Cecil Rock 246
Center for Whale Research 18
Center Reef 298
Chads Island 94
Chain Islands 221
Chain Islets 43, 48
Channel Islands 219
Chart Legend 8
Charts 10, 356
Chatham Island 51
Chemainus 271
Chemainus Bay 271
Cherry Point 252, 257
Chinatown - Victoria 39

Chivers Point 290, 293
Clam Bay 296
clam gardens 249
Clamshell Islet 231
Clover Point 28
Coal Island 78
Coal Point 98
Coffin Island 275
Coles Bay 104
Coles Bay Regional Park 104
Collins Shoal 275
Collision Point 207
Commodore Passage 326
Commodore Point 48
Conconi Reef 153, 157
Conover Cove 287
Coon Bay 213
Cooper Reef 88
Cordova Bay 53
Cordova Channel 60
Cordova Spit 53, 60
Cormorant Point 53
Cowichan Bay
    Genoa Bay 257
Crane Point 180
Crescent Point 303, 306
Crispin Rock 157
Crofton 268
Cufra Inlet 307
Curlew Island 169
Currency. See Money
Currents and Tides 11
Curteis Point 76
Customs
    Bedwell Harbour 125
    Canoe Cove 84
    Nanaimo 343
    Oak Bay 45
    Sidney 69
    Tsehum Harbour 80
    Victoria 29

D

Danger Reefs 307
Daphne Islet 106, 114
D'Arcy Island 58
D'Arcy Shoals 58
Davis Lagoon 275
Dayman Channel 303
Dayman Island 301, 306
Deadheads 14
Deadman Island 221
De Courcy Group 311, 313
De Courcy Island 313
    Pirates Cove 315
Deep Cove 98

Deep Ridge 186, 219
Degnen Bay 323
Departure Bay 342
Descanso Bay 334
Dibuxante Point 318, 323
Dinner Bay 180
Dinner Bay Community Park 182
Dionisio Point 211, 213
Discovery Island 28, 51
Discovery Island Marine Provincial Park 51
Diver Bay 198
Dock Island 65
Dock Point 236
Dodd Narrows 337
Dogfish Bay 320
Donckele Point 301
Drew Rock 130
Drumbeg Provincial Park 320, 325, 331
Duck Bay 236
Duke Point 334
Dunsmuir Islands 277
Dyer Rocks 104

E

Eagle Island (Whaleboat Island) 311
East Point 162, 166
East Point Park 152
Echo Bay 162
Edith Point 173, 174
Eleanor Point 242
Ellen Bay 196
Emergency Contacts 13
Emily Islet 45
Enchanted Forest Park 128
Enterprise Channel 28
Enterprise Reef 180, 202, 207
Escape Reef 299
Evening Cove 275

F

Fairway Bank 207
Fairway Channel 332, 340
False Narrows 337
False Reef 301, 306
Fane Island 139
Farmer's Markets
    Gabriola Growers and Makers Market 336
    Mayne Island Farmer's Market 178
    Nanaimo Downtown Farmer's Market 346

North Pender Island Market 137
Oak Bay Village Market 46
Port Browning Marina 137
Salt Spring Market 227
Sidney Street Market 72
Thetis Island Saturday Market 303
Fernie Island 84
Fernwood Point 234
Ferries 13
Fiddle Reef 45, 48
Finnerty Cove 53
First Sister Island 221
Fishing Licenses 14
Five Finger Island 342
Flat Top Islands 326
Forwood Channel 332
Fraser Point 307
Fuel
  Birds Eye Cove Marina 267
  Canoe Cove Marina 87
  Gabriola Island
    Page's Resort & Marina 329
    Silva Bay Marine Resort 330
  Galiano Island
    Montague Harbour Marina 206
  Maple Bay Marina 266
  Mill Bay Marina 103
  Nanaimo Port Authority 343
  Salt Spring Island
    Ganges Marina 222
  South Pender Island
    Poets Cove Resort 126
  Thetis Island
    Telegraph Harbour Marina 305
    Thetis Island Marina 304
  Tsehum Harbour
    North Saanich Marina 81
    Van Isle Marina 80
  Vancouver Island
    Birds Eye Cove Marina 267
    Maple Bay Marina 266
    Nanaimo Port Authority 343
  Victoria
    Victoria Marine Fuels 29
Fulford Harbour 242
Fulford Reef 48

G

Gabriola Environmentally Responsible Trans-Island Express (GERTIE) 321
Gabriola Land & Trails Trust 325
Gabriola Passage 318
Gabriola Reefs 326
Gabriola Sands Provincial Park 332
Galiano Island Parks and Recreation Commission 201
Galiano Island shuttle service 201
Galiano Trails Society 201
Galloping Goose Regional Trail 39
GaLTT 325
Ganges Centennial Wharf 224
Ganges Harbour 219
Ganges Shoal 221
G.B. Church 91
Genoa Bay 257
George Hill Community Park 144
Georgeson Island 173, 174
Georgeson Passage 157, 167, 169, 173
Georgina Point 207
Georgina Point Lighthouse 178
Georgina Shoals 207
GERTIE 321
Glenthorne Passage 194
Goat Island 221
Golf Island Disc Park 137
Gordon Head 53
Gordon Rock 53
Gossip Island 210
Gossip Shoals 207
Goudge Island 76, 84
Governor Rock 202, 287, 291
Gowlland Point Regional Park 121
Gowlland Tod Provincial Park 114
Graham Rock 74, 76
Grappler Rock 234
Gray Peninsula 204
Great Chain Island 43, 48
Greater Victoria Harbour Authority 26
Greenburn Lake 127
Grimmer Bay 142
Gulf Islands National Park Reserve 17

H

Halibut Island 65
Halland Bank 275
Harbour Heritage Centre 280
Haro Strait 65, 123
Harris Island 43, 48

Hatch Point 98, 252, 257
Haul Out 10
Haulout Yards
  Canoe Cove Marina 87
  Philbrooks Boatyard 82
  Silva Bay Shipyard 330
  Vancouver Island
    Cove Yachts 267
    Maple Bay Marina 266
    Newcastle Marina and Haulout Yard 347
    Stones Marina & Boatyard 347
  Van Isle Marina 80
  Westport Marina 82
Hawaiians 91, 248
Hay Point 125
Helen Point 207
Henderson Point 106
Herring Bay 311
Hood Island 93
Hope Bay 139
Horda Shoals 186, 219
Horswell Channel 340
Horton Bay 171
Hospital Point 271
Hospital Rock 271
Hospitals 13
Houstoun Passage 234, 287, 291
Hudson Island 301, 306
Hudson Rocks 340
Hudson's Bay Company 34, 345
Hunter Point 277
Hyashi Cove 145

I

Immigration 12
Indian Reef 268
Irish Bay 167
Iroquois Passage 76, 84
Isabella Island 242
Isabella Point 242
Islands Trust Conservancy 132
Island View Beach Regional Park 62
Isle-de-Lis 88
Itineraries 20

J

Jack Point 334, 340
Jackscrew Island 292
Jackson Rock 242
James Bay 186
James Island 60, 62
Japanese charcoal pits 225
Joan Point 337

John Passage 76
Johnstone Reef 53
Josling Point 299
Julia Island 202

K

Kanakas 91
Kelp Reefs 58
Kendrick Island 320
Killer Whales 18
Kingfisher Point 78
King Islets 157
Kinsmen Beach Park 271
Kolb Island 84

L

Ladysmith 275
Lamb Barbecue 156
Laura Point 207
Laurel Point 29
Leech Island 296
Leechtown 39
Lee Rock 43
Leper Colony 58
Lewis Reef 45, 48
Lily Island 326
Link Island 313
Lion Islets 207
Little Group 65, 76
Little Zero Rock 53, 60
Lizard Island 169
Lochside Regional Trail 39, 72
Long Harbour 229
Loon Bay Park 50
Louisa Rock 242
Lyall Harbour 157

M

Macaulay Point 26
Mad Dog Trail 260
Madrona Bay 221
Magic Lake 132
Malaspina Point 334
Mandarte Island 65
Maple Bay 262
  Birds Eye Cove 264
Maple Bay (Galiano Island) 213
Marinas
  Brentwood Bay
    Anglers Anchorage Marina 110
    Brentwood Bay Resort & Spa Marina 109
    Portside Marina 109
  Canoe Cove
    Canoe Cove Marina 87
  Deep Cove Marina 98

Gabriola Island
  Degnen Bay Harbour Authority 325
  Page's Inn & Marina 329
  Page's Resort & Marina 329
  Silva Bay Marine Resort 330
Galiano Island
  Montague Harbour CRD Wharf 204
  Montague Harbour Marina 206
  Retreat Cove CRD Wharf 214
  Sturdies Bay CRD Wharf 209
  Whaler Bay Fisheries and Oceans Canada dock 210
Mayne Island
  Horton Bay CRD Wharf 171
  Miners Bay CRD Wharf 178
Mill Bay Marina 103
North Pender Island
  Grimmer Bay CRD Wharf 142
  Hope Bay CRD Wharf 139
  Otter Bay Marina 149
  Port Browning CRD Wharf 135
  Port Browning Marina 136
Oak Bay Marina 47
Poets Cove Resort & Spa 126
Port Sidney Marina 70
Salt Spring Island
  Burgoyne Bay Public Wharf 240
  Fernwood Point CRD Wharf 234
  Fulford Harbour Public Wharf 244
  Ganges Breakwater Float 224
  Ganges Centennial Wharf 224
  Ganges Kanaka Wharf 224
  Ganges Marina 222
  Musgrave Landing Public Wharf 241
  Salt Spring Marina 223
Saturna Island
  Lyall Harbour CRD Wharf 159
Thetis Island
  Telegraph Harbour Marina 305

Thetis Island Marina 304
Tsehum Harbour
  North Saanich Marina 81
  Van Isle Marina 80
Vancouver Island
  Birds Eye Cove Marina 267
  Causeway Marina 30
  Chemainus Municipal Wharf 271
  Cove Yachts 267
  Crofton Municipal Wharf 270
  Genoa Bay Marina 261
  Ladysmith Community Marina 278
  Ladysmith Marina 279
  Maple Bay Marina 266
  Maple Bay Public Wharf 262
  Nanaimo Port Authority 343
  Ship Point Marina 30
Victoria
  Causeway Floats 26
  Ship Point Wharf 26
  Victoria International Marina 32
  Wharf Street Marina 26
Marine Chandleries and Services
  Brentwood Bay 111
  Cowichan Bay 255
  Ladysmith 282
  Salt Spring Island
    Ganges Harbour 226
  Sidney 73
  Tsehum Harbour 82
  Vancouver Island
    Nanaimo 346
  Victoria 40
marine weather forecasts 18
Mark Bay 342, 348
Mary Anne Point 207
Mary Tod Island 45
Mayne Island 169
Mayor Channel 43, 48
McKay Channel 348
McKenzie Bight 117
Medicine Beach 130
Medicine Beach Nature Sanctuary 130
Miami Islet 307
Mikuni Point 153
Military Exercise Area WC 53
Mill Bay 100
Miners Bay 176
Miners Channel 65
Minx Reef 155, 167
Monarch Head 162

Money 17
Money Maker Reef 221
Montague Harbour 202
Montague Harbour Provincial Marine Park 202
Moresby Island 92
Moresby Passag 94
Moresby Passage 92
Mortimer Spit 128
Moses Point 98
Mouat Reef 28
Mount Douglas Park 53
Mount Galiano 210
Mount Maxwell 238
Mount Norman 127
Mount Tzouhalem 260
Mowgli Island 234, 287, 291
Mudge Island 337
murals 271
Musclow Islet 84
Musgrave Landing 241

N

Nanaimo 340
Nares Rock 275
Narvaez Bay 162
Navy Channel 139, 153, 157
Newcastle Island 348
Newcastle Island Passage 342, 348
NEXUS 13
North Cove 307
North Pender Island 120
North Reef 268, 299
Northumberland Channel 334, 337, 340
Norway Island 234, 287, 291
Nose Point 186, 221, 229
Nymph Point 79

O

Oak Bay 43
Ogden Point 26
Om Shanti 7
orcas 18
Oregon Rock 342
Osborn Bay 268
Otter Bay 145
Owl Island 195

P

Pacific Flyway 66
Paddon Point 171
Paddy Mile Stone 262
Page Passage 84
Panther Point 287, 291
Parker Island 202
Parks 17
  Beacon Hill Park 38

Beaumont Marine Park 127
Beaumont Marine Park (GINPR) 125
Bennett Bay (GINPR) 173
Brooks Point Regional Park 121
Cabbage Island (GINPR) 164
Cadboro-Gyro Park 50
Coles Bay Regional Park 104
D'Arcy Island (GINPR) 58
Dinner Bay Community Park 182
Dionisio Point Provincial Park 213
Discovery Island Marine Provincial Park 51
Drumbeg Provincial Park 325, 331
Drumbeg Provinical Park 320
Drummond Park 245
Duck Creek Park 236
East Point Park (GINPR) 152
Enchanted Forest Park 128
Gabriola Sands Provincial Park 332
George Hill Community Park 144
Georgina Point (GINPR) 178
Gowlland Point Regional Park 121
Gowlland Tod Provincial Park 114
Greenburn Lake (GINPR) 127
Island View Beach Regional Park 62
Isle-de-Lis (GINPR) 88
Loon Bay Park 50
Magic Lake 132
Medicine Beach Nature Sanctuary 130
Montague Harbour Provincial Marine Park 202
Mouat Park 225
Mount Douglas Park 53
Mount Maxwell Provincial Park 238
Narvaez Bay (GINPR) 162
Newcastle Island Marine Provincial Park 348
Petroglyph Park 331
Pirates Cove Provincial Marine Park 315
Prevost Island (GINPR) 185
Princess Margaret Marine Park (GINPR) 89

Queens Park 45
Roesland (GINPR) 147
Rotary Marine Park 225
Russell Island (GINPR) 246
Sidney Spit (GINPR) 63
Swimming Hole park 132
Transfer Beach Park 280
Tumbo Island (GINPR) 164
Uplands Park 46
Wakes Cove Provincial Park 320
Wallace Island Marine Provincial Park 285
Willows Beach Park 46
Winter Cove (GINPR) 153
Passage Rock 342
Patey Rock 98, 252, 257
Payne Point 157
Peile Point 186
Pellow Islets 92, 94
Pelly Island 29
Pender Canal 129
Pender Islands 120
Penelakut Island 294
Penelakut Spit 296
Percy Anchorage 337
Petroglyph Park 331
Phillimore Point 202
Pilkey Point 307
Pilot Bay 332
Pirates Cove 315
Plumper Passage 43, 48
Plumper Sound 133, 139, 153, 157, 161
Point Liddell 196, 198
Porlier Pass 211
Port Browning 133
Portland Island 89
Portlock Point 196
Port Washington 142
Powder Islet 221
Preedy Harbour 306
Prevost Island 185
Princess Bay 92
Princess Cove 291
Princess Margaret Marine Park 89
Protection Island 342, 348
Provisioning
    Cowichan Bay 255
Pumpout Station
    Anglers Anchorage Marina 110
    Mill Bay Marina 103
    Port Sidney Marina 70
    Salt Spring Island
        Ganges Marina 222
        Salt Spring Marina 223
    Vancouver Island

Nanaimo Port Authority 343
W.E. Mills Landing & Marina 343
Victoria
    Fisherman's Wharf 29
Purple Martins 117, 281
Purvis Point 337
Pylades Channel 315, 337

R

Race Rocks 26
Ragged Islets 307
Rainbow Channel 340
Ralph Grey Point 153
Raymur Point 29
Razor Point 133
Reef Harbour 164
Retreat Cove 214
Retreat Island 214
Richardson Bay 196, 198
Rip Point 207
ROAM app 13
Roberts Bay 74
Robson Channel 169
Robson Reef 45
Rocket Shoal 298
Roe Islet 145
Roe Lake 145
Roesland 145
Rogers Reef 318, 325
Romulus Reef 211
Royal Cove 94
Rudlin Bay 51
Rum Island 88
Russell Island 246
Ruxton Island 311
Ruxton Passage 311

S

Saanich Peninsula 67, 98
Saanichton Bay 60
Salamanca Point 207
Salt Spring Island 218
Samuel Island 167
Sandstone Rocks 299
sand verbena moth 62
Sansum Narrows 238, 257, 262
Sansum Point 238
Satellite Channel 94, 242, 246
Saturna Island 152
Saturna Point 157, 161
Scarrow Reef 214
Scott Point 229
Sear Island 326
Second Sister Island 221
Secret Island 194
Selby Cove 189
Selby Point 186, 189

Senanus Island 106, 114
Shah Point 211
Shark Cove 129
Sharpe Point 275
Sherard Point 268
Shingle Bay 145
Shipyard Rock 328
Shoal Harbour 76
Shoal Islands 268
Shoal Point 29
Sibell Bay 277
Sidney 67
Sidney Channel 65
Sidney Island
    Sidney Spit 63
Sidney Spit 63
Silva Bay 326
Silva Bay Shipyard 330
Slag Point 277
Sluggett Point 106
Snake Island 332, 342
Southey Bay 234
South Pender Island 120
Staqeya 51
Stern Lines 10
Strait of Georgia 164, 207, 211, 321, 326, 332, 340
Strait of Juan de Fuca 26
Stuart Channel 236, 262, 268, 301, 337
Sturdies Bay 209
Swanson Channel 142, 145, 196
Swartz Bay 88
Swartz Head 84
Swimming Hole park 132

T

Taylor Bay 332
Teece Point 121
Telegraph Harbour 301
Tent Island 294, 299
Tent Island Reef 299
The Cut 294, 298
Thetis Island 294
Third Sister Island 221
Thrasher Rock 328
Thumb Point 78
Tides, Currents and 11
Tilikum 40
Tilly Point 123
Tinson Point 332
Tod Inlet 114
Tom Point 88
Tortoise Islets 92
Transfer Beach Park 280
Transportation
    Tsehum Harbour 83
Trevor Islet 161
Trial Islands 28
Trincomali Channel 186, 202,

229, 287, 291
Tsehum Harbour 76
Tsehum Harbour North 78
Tugboat Island 326
Tumbo Channel 164
Tumbo Island 164
Turkey Head 45
Turnbull Reef 94
Turn Point 125
Twiss Point 210

U

Unit Rocks 58
Uplands Park 46

V

Valdes Island 318
Vance Island 326
Vernaci Point 211
Vesuvius Bay 236
Victoria 26
Victoria International Airport 67
Victoria Rock 202, 287, 291
Victoria Shoal 202, 287, 291
Village Bay 180
Virago Rock 211
Virtue Rock 48
Voss, Captain John 40

W

Wain Rock 98
Wakes Cove 320
Walker Hook 232
Walker Rock 202, 287, 291
Wallace Island 285
Wallace Point 123
Water Wheel Park 273
Waypoints 352
Weather 17
Whaleboat Island 311
Whaleboat Passage 311
Whaler Bay 210
Whales 18
Wharf Street Marina 26, 31
Whisky Point 100
Willis Point 106
Willows Beach Park 46
Winter Cove 153
Winter Point 153
Woods Islands 277

Y

Yarrow Point 104
Yellow Sand Verbena 62

Z

Zero Rock 53, 60

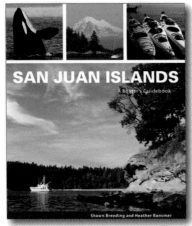
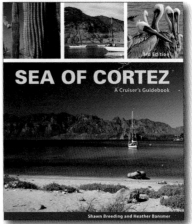
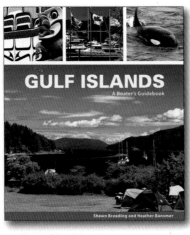